D1430047

Section 1: Questions

(page intentionally left blank)

Horizontal Curves #1

__Find:__ R [ft] — the radius of the curve

__Given:__

L = 50 [ft]
the length of the curve

C = 45 [ft]
the long chord of the curve

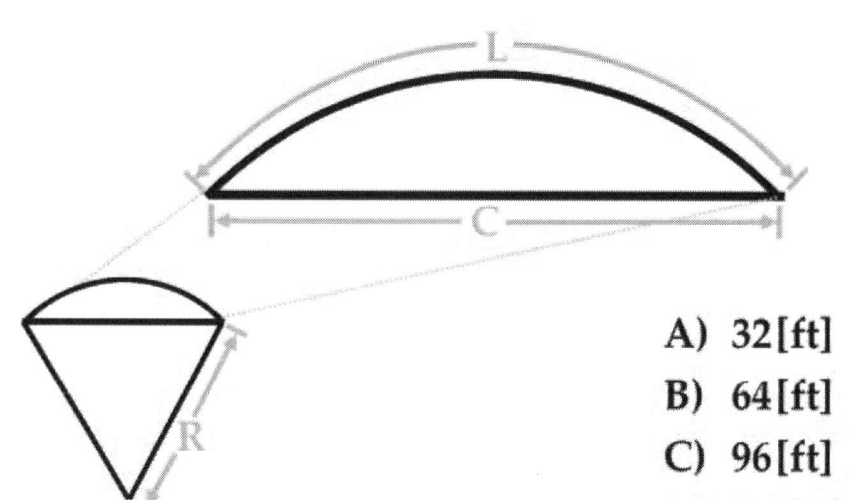

A) 32 [ft]
B) 64 [ft]
C) 96 [ft]
D) 128 [ft]

Horizontal Curves #2

__Find:__ M — middle ordinate, also called the "horizontal sightline offset" (HSO)

__Given:__

R = 120 [m] — the radius of the curve

T = 40 [m] — the tangent distance

Points A and B represent the beginning and end of the curve.

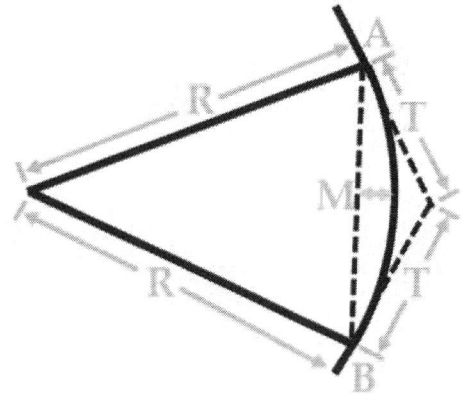

A) 2 [m]
B) 4 [m]
C) 6 [m]
D) 8 [m]

Horizontal Curves #3

__Find:__ L_{AB} [ft] — the length along the horizontal curve from point A to point B

__Given:__

Area = 20,000 [ft²] — the area swept out by the curve (the shaded area)

R = 200 [ft] — the radius of the curve

points A and B represent the beginning and end of the curve

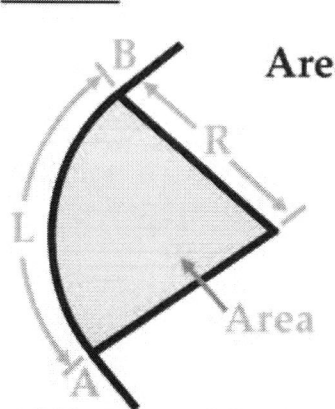

A) 100 [ft]
B) 150 [ft]
C) 178 [ft]
D) 200 [ft]

Surveying Practice Problems

Horizontal Curves #4

<u>Find:</u> STA$_B$ ← the stationing at point B

<u>Given:</u>

STA$_A$=42+51 ← the stationing at point A

I=15°24'00" ← interior angle

T=85[ft] ← tangent distance

points A and B represent the beginning and end of the curve

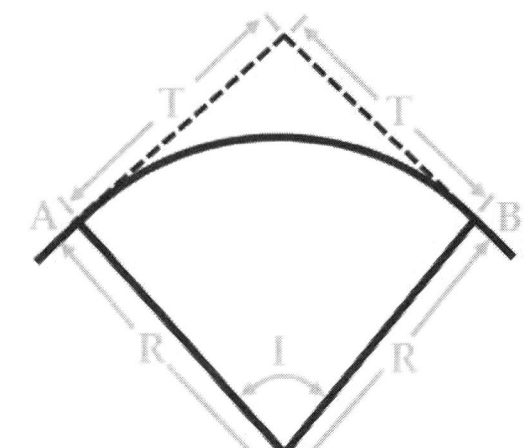

A) 43+36

B) 44+20

C) 44+36

D) 48+80

Horizontal Curves #5

<u>Find:</u> C$_m$ (for L=100[ft]) ← find the minor chord length, for a segment of the curve 100[ft] long

"m" for "minor" chord

<u>Given:</u>

T=800[ft]

the tangent distance (for the entire curve)

C=500[ft]

the long chord (for the entire curve)

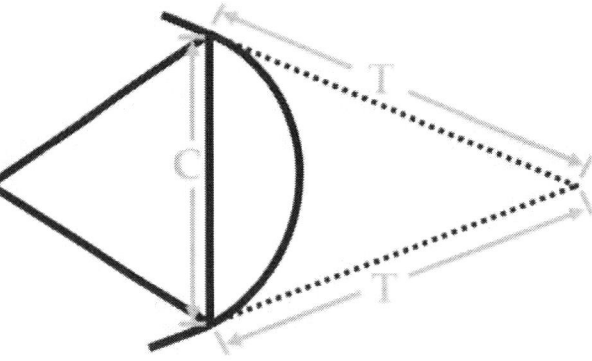

A) 99.4[ft]

B) 99.7[ft]

C) 100.0[ft]

D) 100.3[ft]

Horizontal Curves #6

<u>Find:</u> R[m] ← radius of the curve

<u>Given:</u>

x=65[m] ← tangent distance

distance along the tangent to a particular point

y=25[m] ← tangent offset ← perpendicular distance from an extended tangent to a point on the curve

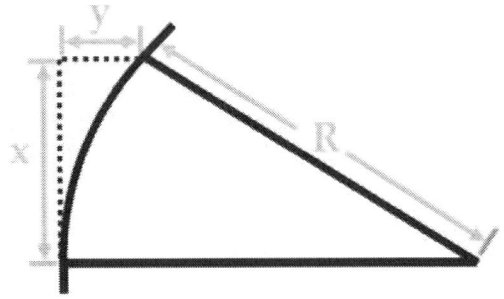

A) 81[m]

B) 97[m]

C) 103[m]

D) 109[m]

4

Horizontal Curves #7

<u>Find</u>: I ← interior angle
<u>Given</u>:

R=215 [m] ← radius of the curve

C=85 [m] ← long chord of the curve

the radius and long chord are
both given in units of meters

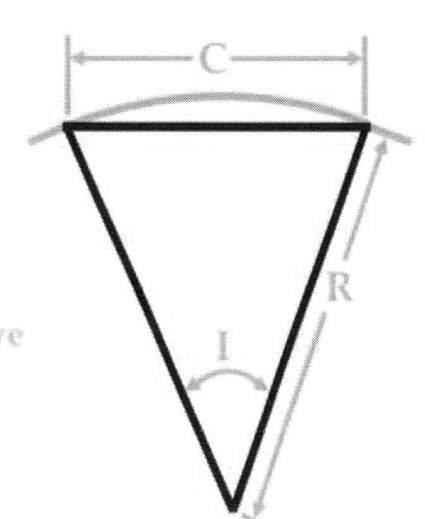

A) 0.4 [rad]
B) 0.8 [rad]
C) 23.0 [rad]
D) 46.0 [rad]

Horizontal Curves #8

<u>Find</u>: STA_B ← the stationing
at point B
<u>Given</u>:

the curve begins
at point A

the curve ends
at point B

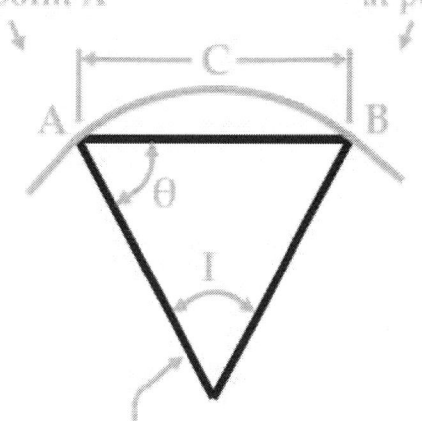

C=200 [ft] ← the long chord
of the curve

θ=78° ← angle theta is not the same
as the "interior angle"

STA_A=3+44
the stationing at point A

the "interior angle" is located
at the center of the curve

A) 3+46
B) 5+43
C) 5+46
D) 5+50

Horizontal Curves #9

<u>Find</u>: L_JH ← the length along curve JK,
from point J to point H
<u>Given</u>:

the back tangent
is parallel to line PH →

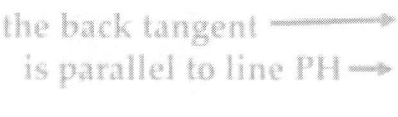
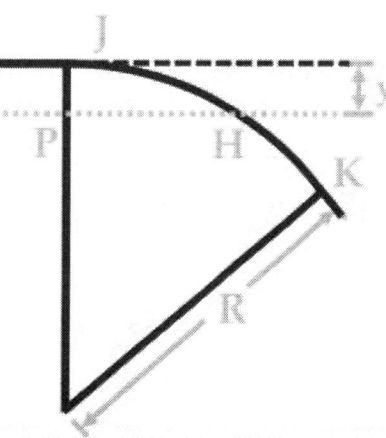

R=700 [ft] ← the radius
of the curve

y=100 [ft] ← the tangent
offset

A) 360 [ft]
B) 370 [ft]
C) 374 [ft]
D) 378 [ft]

Surveying Practice Problems

Horizontal Curves #10

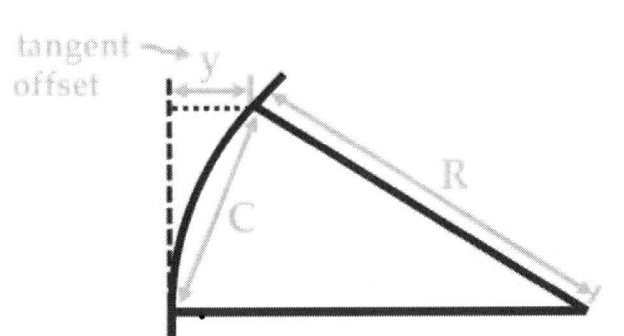

Find: y ← tangent offset

Given:

R=1,000[ft]

↳ the radius of the curve

C=1,800[ft] ← the long chord of the curve

A) 600[ft]
B) 620[ft]
C) 780[ft]
D) 1,620[ft]

Horizontal Curves #11

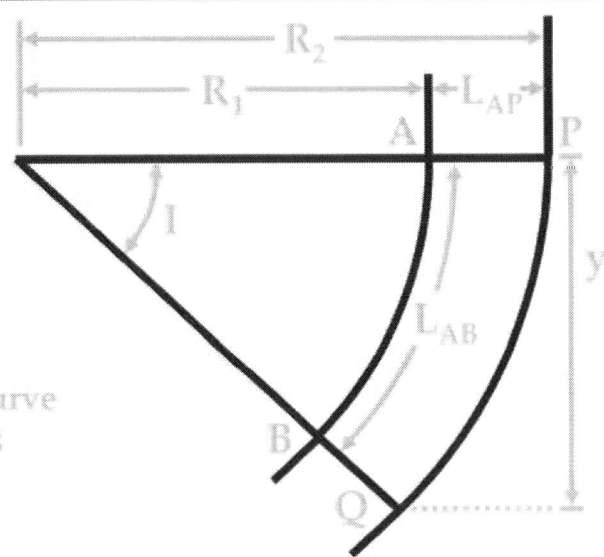

Find: y ← tangent offset

Given:

R_1=400[ft] ← radius of the smaller curve

L_{AB}=150[ft] ← length along the smaller curve from point A from point B

L_{AP}=100[ft]

A) 145[ft]
B) 165[ft]
C) 185[ft]
D) 465[ft]

Horizontal Curves #12

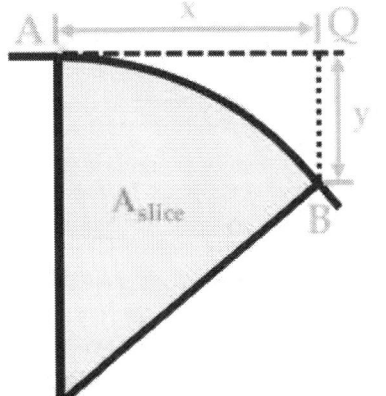

Find: A_{slice} ← the area inside the horizontal curve

Given:

y=75[ft] ← the tangent offset

x=250[ft] ← the tangent distance

The horizontal curve begins at point A, and ends at point B.

A) $6*10^2$[ft^2]
B) $6*10^3$[ft^2]
C) $6*10^4$[ft^2]
D) $6*10^5$[ft^2]

Vertical Curves #1

<u>Find:</u> g_2 [%] ← *departing grade*

<u>Given:</u>

STA_A=0+45
$Elev_A$=143.7 [ft]

STA_B=1+57 ← *station and elevation data for point A and point B*
$Elev_B$=146.0 [ft]

L=300 [ft]
↑
length of the curve

R=-2 [%/STA] ← *rate of grade change*

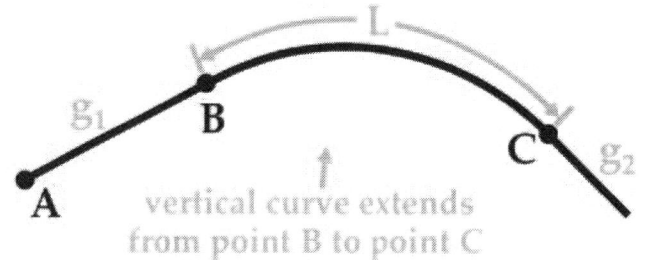

departing grade

g_1 B

C g_2

A   *vertical curve extends from point B to point C*

A) -6%

B) -4%

C) -2%

D) 8%

Vertical Curves #2

<u>Find:</u> STA_B ← *the stationing at point B*

<u>Given:</u>

STA_A=42+00
$Elev_A$=147 [ft]

STA_C=52+00 ← *The station and elevation at point A and point C*
$Elev_C$=143 [ft]

The vertical curve begins at point A and ends at point C.

A g_1=-4% ← *approach grade*

B g_2=2% ← *departing grade*

C

A) 44+00

B) 46+00

C) 48+00

D) 50+00

Vertical Curves #3

<u>Find:</u> $Elev_{min}$ [m] ← *minimum elevation of the curve*

<u>Given:</u>

$R= 4 \left[\dfrac{\%}{100 [m]} \right]$ ← *rate of grade change*

$Elev_C$=727.8 [m] ← *elevation at point C*

g_2=6% ← *departing grade*

L_{AC}=300 [ft] ← *the length of the vertical curve*

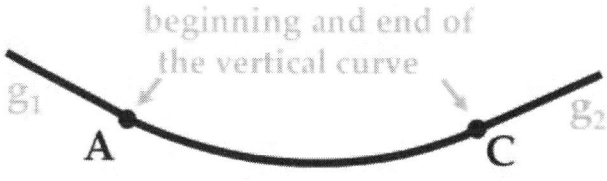

beginning and end of the vertical curve

g_1 A   C g_2

A) 718.8 [m]

B) 723.3 [m]

C) 732.3 [m]

D) 736.8 [m]

Surveying Practice Problems

Vertical Curves #4

Find: g_D ← the grade at point D

Given:

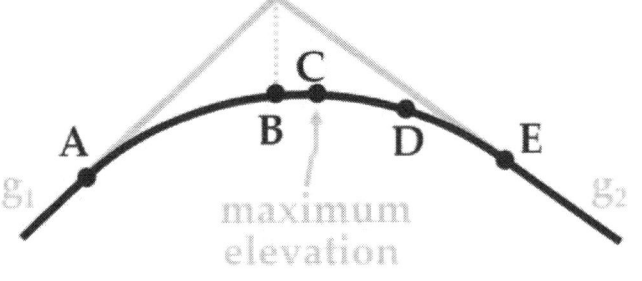

approach grade ↘

$g_1 = 3.5\%$

$g_2 = -2.2\%$

departing grade ↗

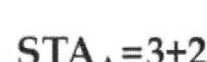

STA$_A$ = 3+22
STA$_B$ = 5+15 ⎫
STA$_C$ = 5+59 ⎬ the stationing for points A, B, C and D
STA$_D$ = 6+00 ⎭

A) -0.6%

B) -1.0%

C) -1.4%

D) -1.8%

Vertical Curves #5

Find: STA$_C$ ← the station at point C

Given:

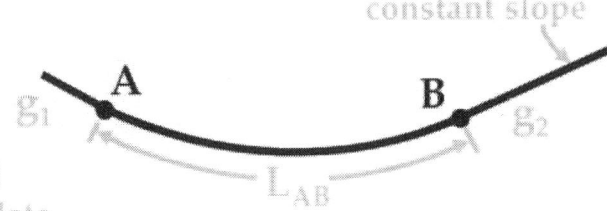

STA$_A$ = 2+54 ← station and
Elev$_A$ = 127.0 [ft] ← elevation data
Elev$_C$ = 127.4 [ft]

$g_1 = -1.8\%$ ← approach grade

$R = 0.6 \left[\dfrac{\%}{STA}\right]$ ← rate of grade change

$L_{AB} = 540$ [ft] ← curve length, from point A to point B

A) 7+45

B) 7+84

C) 8+32

D) 8+91

Vertical Curves #6

Find: Elev$_C$ ← the elevation at point C

Given:

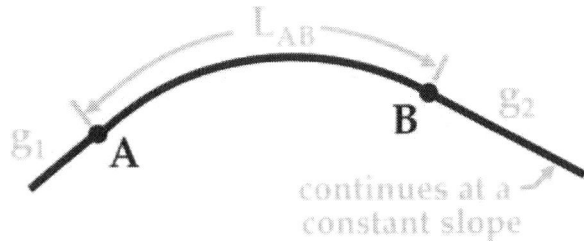

$g_1 = 1.5\%$ ← approach grade

$L_{AB} = 200$ [ft] ← curve length

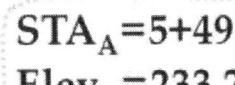

STA$_A$ = 5+49
Elev$_A$ = 233.2 [ft]
STA$_C$ = 7+94 ← station and elevation data

$R = -1$ [%/STA] ← the rate of change of the grade, along the vertical curve

A) 233.0 [ft]

B) 233.2 [ft]

C) 234.0 [ft]

D) 234.2 [ft]

Vertical Curves #7

<u>Find</u>: STA_C ←the stationing, at point C

<u>Given</u>:

g_1=1.5% ←approach grade

g_2=-1.4% ← departing grade

STA_A=1+22 ← the station at point A

$Elev_A$=28.4 [ft] ← the elevation at
$Elev_C$=29.0 [ft] ← point A and point C

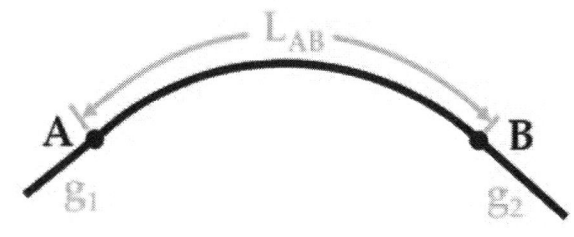

L_{AB}=450 [ft]
↑
curve length

A) 1+66

B) 2+18

C) 3+47

D) 4+17

Vertical Curves #8

<u>Find</u>: **How many times does the curve pass through elevation=150 [ft]**

(no sketch provided)

<u>Given</u>: elevation at point A

point A is located at the beginning of the curve

$Elev_A$=156.2 [ft]

STA_A=44+29 ← stationing at point A

g_1=-3.2% ←approach grade

R=1 [%/STA]
↑
rate change of grade in percent per station

L=250 [ft] ←curve length

A) 0

B) 1

C) 2

D) **not enough information**

Vertical Curves #9

<u>Find</u>: g_1 ←approach grade

<u>Given</u>:

the vertical curve begins at point A and ends at point B.

g_2=-2% ←departing grade

R=-1 [%/STA]
↑
rate of grade change along vertical curve

M=3.125 [ft]
↑
middle ordinate

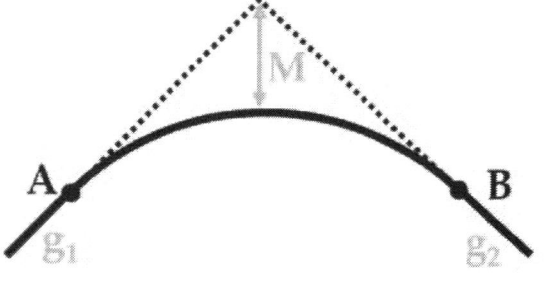

A) 0%

B) 1%

C) 2%

D) 3%

Surveying Practice Problems

Vertical Curves #10

Find: STA_B ← stationing at point B

The vertical curve begins at point B, and ends at point C.

Given:

R=1[%/STA] ← rate of grade change

$STA_A=1+45.2$

$Elev_A=97.60[ft]$ station and elevation data for point A and point C.

$STA_C=4+88.1$

$Elev_C=96.09[ft]$

$g_1=-0.01$ ← approach grade (as a decimal)

A) 2+66

B) 2+92

C) 3+21

D) 3+76

Vertical Curves #11

Find: **Area under the curve and above elevation 50[ft]**

The vertical curve begins at point A and ends at point C.

Given:

R=-0.5[%/STA] ← rate of grade change

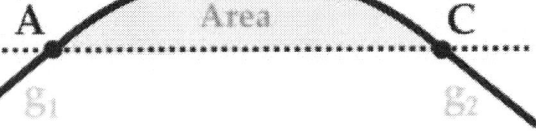

Elev=50[ft] → ....

$Elev_A=50[ft]$ ← The elevation at point A and point C

$Elev_C=50[ft]$

$g_1=1.5\%$ ← The approach grade and departing grade.

$g_2=-1.5\%$

A) 90[ft²]

B) 900[ft²]

C) 9,000[ft²]

D) 90,000[ft²]

Vertical Curves #12

Find: g_B ← The grade at point B

The vertical curve begins at point A and ends at point C.

Given:

The stationing at points A, B and C

$STA_A=1+92$

$STA_B=3+30$

$STA_C=4+22$

$Elev_A=151.7[ft]$ ← The elevation at point A

$g_1=0\%$

$g_2=2.0\%$ The approach grade and departing grade.

A) 0.4%

B) 0.8%

C) 1.2%

D) 1.6%

Distance #1

Find: L_{AC} ← the distance between point A and point C

Given:

$V_{AB}=(4.5, 7.6, 1.9)[m]$

The vector from point A to point B

$V_{BC}=(11.4, -3.1, -0.5)[m]$

The vector from point B to point C

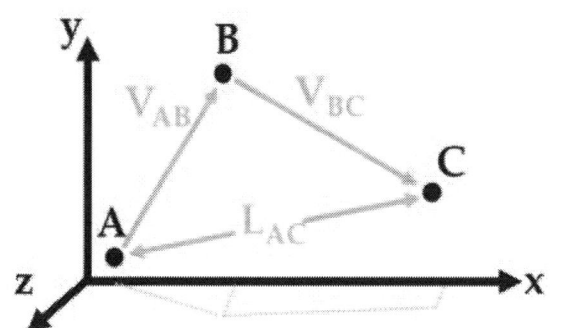

A) 8.4[m]
B) 12.6[m]
C) 16.6[m]
D) 19.3[m]

Distance #2

Find: A_{IJK} ← angle IJK

Given:

$L_{IJ}=135.22[m]$

the distance between point I and point J

$L_{IK}=104.21[m]$

the distance between point I and point K

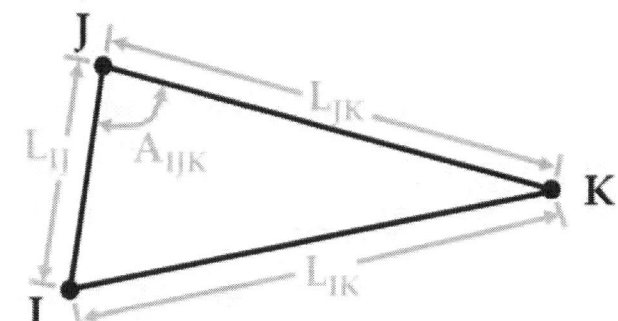

$A_{JIK}=78°47'22''$

angle JIK

A) 40°
B) 50°
C) 60°
D) 70°

Distance #3

Find: $L_{MN,y}$ ← the vertical distance between points M and N

Given:

$L_{MN}=325.11[ft]$

the straight-line distance between point M and point N

$Z_{MN}=67.56°$

the zenith angle from point M to point N

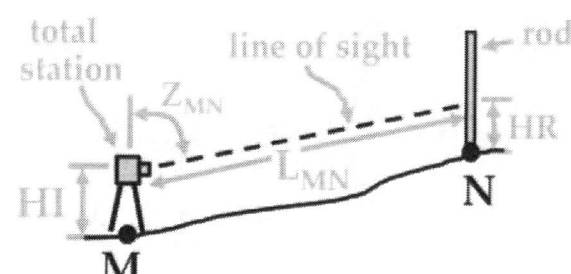

$HR=3.14[ft]$ ← rod height

$HI=5.22[ft]$

height of the total station

A) 122[ft]
B) 126[ft]
C) 298[ft]
D) 303[ft]

Surveying Practice Problems

Distance #4

Find: L_{JK} ← the length of side JK

Given:

$L_{IJ}=86.72\,[ft]$ ← the length, zenith, and

$Z_{IJ}=94°15'00''$ ← azimuth from point I

$Az_{IJ}=0°00'00''$ ← to point J

$L_{IK}=147.65\,[ft]$ ← the length, zenith, and

$Z_{IK}=88°30'00''$ ← azimuth from point I

$Az_{IK}=45°48'00''$ ← to point K

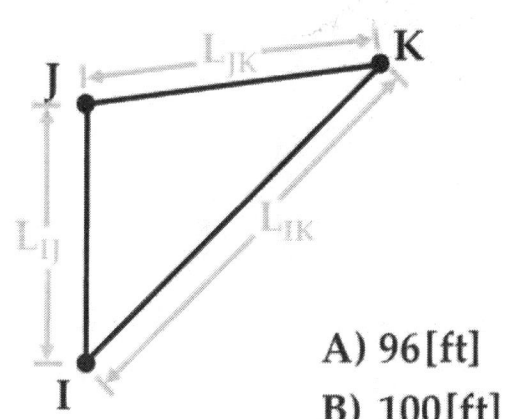

A) 96 [ft]

B) 100 [ft]

C) 104 [ft]

D) 108 [ft]

Distance #5

Find: $L_{JK,x}$ ← the horizontal distance between points J and K

Given:

$L_{IJ}=114.09\,[ft]$

the straight-line distance between point I and point J

$L_{JK}=122.41\,[ft]$

the straight-line distance between point J and point K

$Z_{IJ}=77.21°$ ← zenith angles

$Z_{KJ}=105.84°$

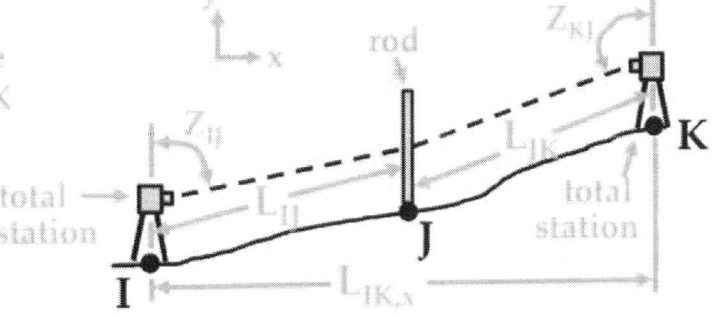

A) 120 [ft]

B) 229 [ft]

C) 236 [ft]

D) 243 [ft]

Distance #6

Find: $L_{IK,x}$ ← the horizontal distance between points I and K

Given:

$L_{IJ}=227.05\,[m]$ ← the distance between point I and point J

$Z_{IK}=114.89°$

the zenith angle of course IK

$\theta=27.41°$

theta equals the measure of interior angle JIK

Triangle IJK is isosceles

Angle IJK is the largest interior angle

The sketch is in profile view

A) 170 [m]

B) 230 [m]

C) 370 [m]

D) 400 [m]

Distance #7

Find: $L_{AB,a}$ ← the actual distance between point A and point B

Given:

$L_{AB,m} = 1{,}411.80\,[\text{ft}]$
  ↑ the measured distance between point A and point B

$T_m = 35^\circ F$ ← the temperature during measurement

$\alpha_{steel} = 6.45 * 10^{-6}\,[^\circ F^{-1}]$ ← thermal expansion coefficient of steel

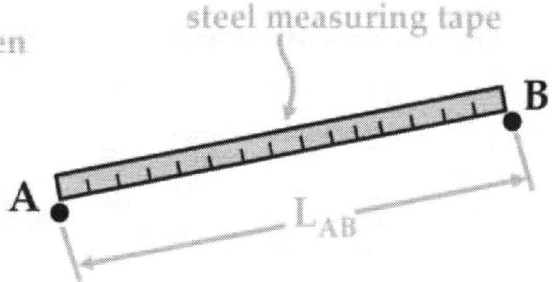
steel measuring tape

A) 1,408.80 [ft]
B) 1,411.50 [ft]
C) 1,411.77 [ft]
D) 1,412.10 [ft]

Distance #8

Find: T_m ← the ambient temperature when $L_{AB,m}$ was measured

Given:

$L_{AB,m} = 455.22\,[\text{ft}]$ ← the measured distance between point A and point B

$L_{AB,a} = 455.28\,[\text{ft}]$
  ↑ the actual distance between points A and B

$\alpha_{steel} = 1.2 * 10^{-5}\,[^\circ C^{-1}]$ ← thermal expansion coefficient of steel

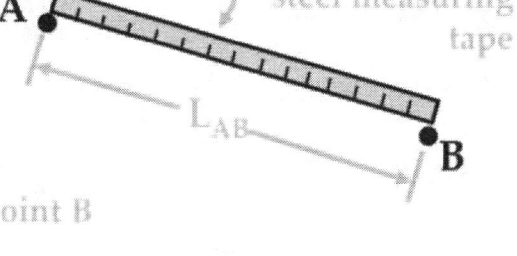
steel measuring tape

T_m? →

A) 11°C
B) 15°C
C) 25°C
D) 31°C

Distance #9

Find: $L_{AC,a}$ ← the actual length between point A and point C

Given:

$\theta = 15^\circ 48' 00''$ ← interior angle CAB

$T_m = 20^\circ F$ ← temperature during measurement

$\alpha_{steel} = 6.45 * 10^{-6}\,[^\circ F^{-1}]$ ← coefficient of thermal expansion (for steel)

$L_{BC,m} = 3{,}519.1\,[\text{ft}]$ ← the measured distance between points B and C

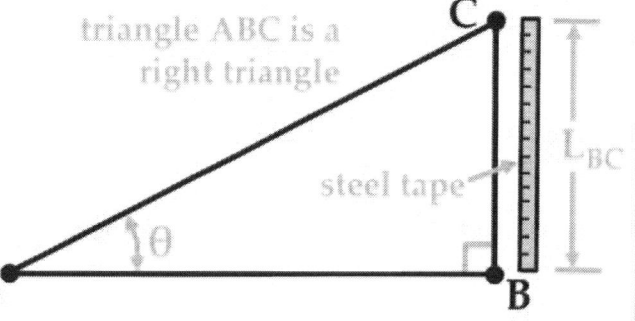
triangle ABC is a right triangle

steel tape

A) 12,921 [ft]
B) 12,925 [ft]
C) 12,929 [ft]
D) 12,933 [ft]

Surveying Practice Problems

Distance #10

<u>Find:</u> α_{steel} ← coefficient of thermal expansion (for steel)

<u>Given:</u>

$T_{m1} = 14.70\,^{\circ}C$ ← temperature during the first measurement

$T_{m2} = 27.10\,^{\circ}C$ ← temperature during the second measurement

$L_{AB,m1} = 227.180\,[m]$ ← the measured lengths between point A and point B for tempera-tures T_{m1} and T_{m2}.

$L_{AB,m2} = 227.145\,[m]$

steel tape $L_{AB,m1}$

A • $L_{AB,a}$ • B

steel tape $L_{AB,m2}$

A) $1.12*10^{-5}\,[^{\circ}C^{-1}]$

B) $1.16*10^{-5}\,[^{\circ}C^{-1}]$

C) $1.20*10^{-5}\,[^{\circ}C^{-1}]$

D) $1.24*10^{-5}\,[^{\circ}C^{-1}]$

Distance #11

triangle ABC is a right triangle

<u>Find:</u> g_{AC} ← the grade from point A to point C

<u>Given:</u>

$L_{AB,a} = 294.15\,[ft]$ ← the actual length between point A and point B

$L_{BC,m} = 95.44\,[ft]$ ← the measured length between poins B and C

g_{AB}

steel tape L_{BC}

A L_{AB} B

the sketch is in profile view

$\alpha_{steel} = 1.2*10^{-5}\,[^{\circ}C^{-1}]$ ← coefficient of thermal expansion (for steel)

$T_m = 28.7\,^{\circ}F$ ← temperature during measurement

A) 0.08

B) 0.16

C) 0.24

D) 0.32

Distance #12

<u>Find:</u> $Elev_C$ ← the elevation at point C

<u>Given:</u>

Course	Length	Zenith
AB	88.66 [ft]	98°17′30″
BC	219.54 [ft]	86°41′00″

$Elev_A = 247.61\,[ft]$ ← the elevation at point A

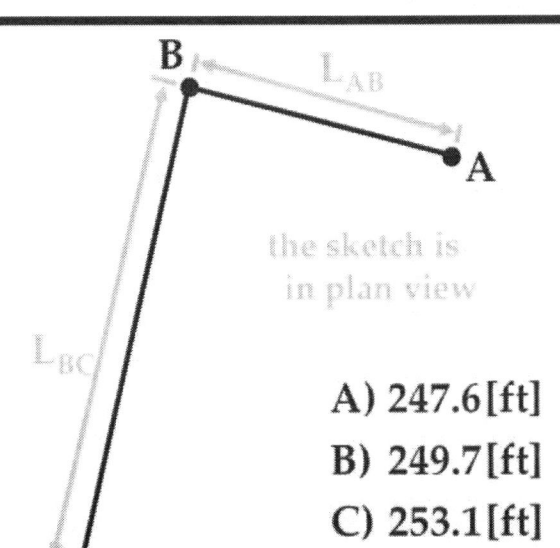

the sketch is in plan view

A) 247.6 [ft]

B) 249.7 [ft]

C) 253.1 [ft]

D) 273.0 [ft]

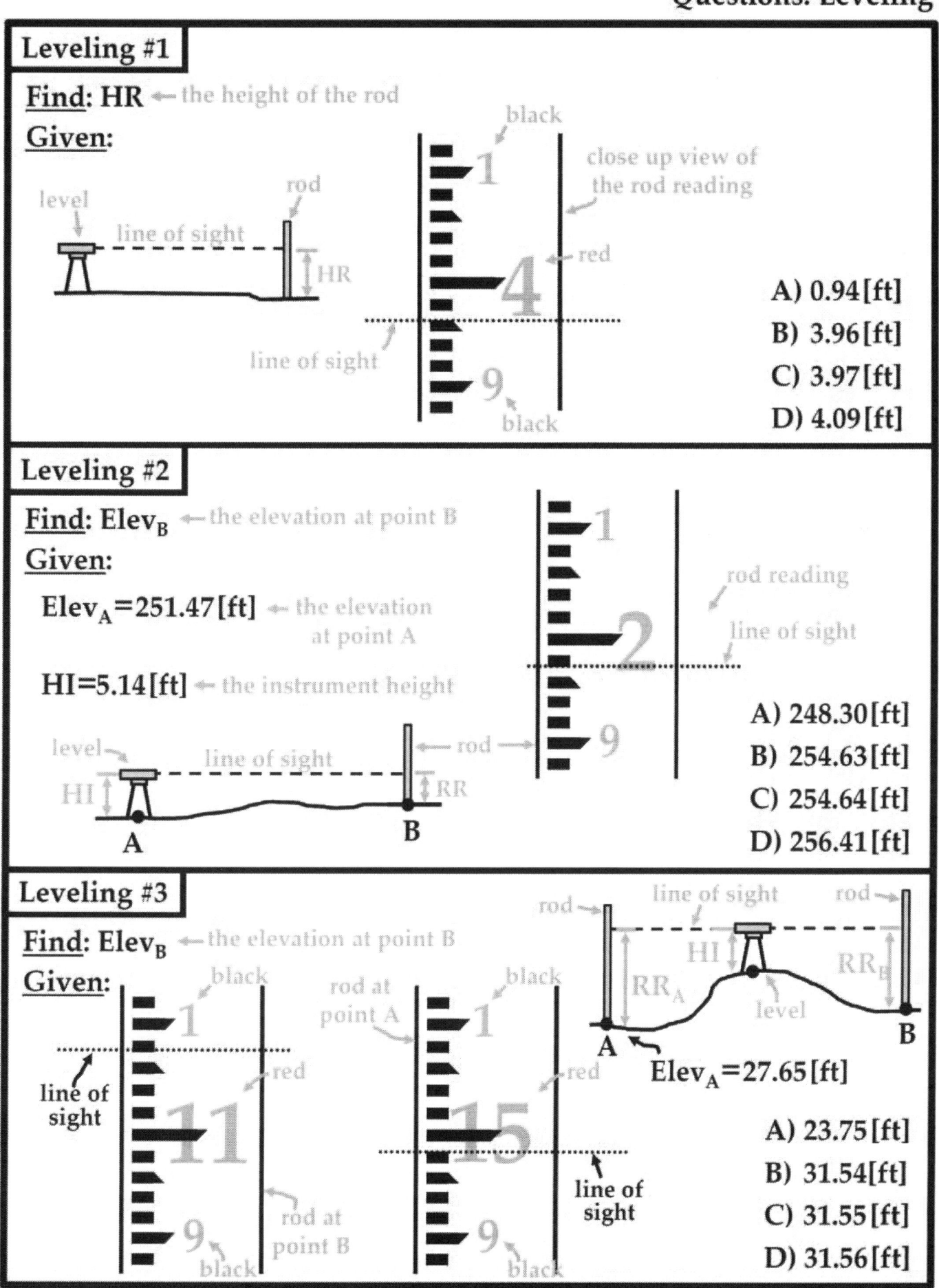

Leveling #1

Find: HR ← the height of the rod
Given:

level
rod
line of sight
HR
line of sight

black
close up view of the rod reading
red
1
4
9
black

A) 0.94 [ft]
B) 3.96 [ft]
C) 3.97 [ft]
D) 4.09 [ft]

Leveling #2

Find: $Elev_B$ ← the elevation at point B
Given:

$Elev_A = 251.47$ [ft] ← the elevation at point A

$HI = 5.14$ [ft] ← the instrument height

level
line of sight
HI
rod
RR
B
A

1
2
9
rod reading
line of sight

A) 248.30 [ft]
B) 254.63 [ft]
C) 254.64 [ft]
D) 256.41 [ft]

Leveling #3

Find: $Elev_B$ ← the elevation at point B
Given:

black
rod at point A
black
line of sight
rod
HI
rod
RR_A
RR_B
level
A
B
$Elev_A = 27.65$ [ft]

1
11
line of sight
red
rod at point B
black

1
15
red
line of sight
9
black

A) 23.75 [ft]
B) 31.54 [ft]
C) 31.55 [ft]
D) 31.56 [ft]

Surveying Practice Problems

Leveling #4

Find: $Elev_K$ ←— the elevation at point K

Given:

the level was at the same location and height when reading the rod at point J and point K.

$Elev_J = 299.51 [ft]$

the elevation at point J

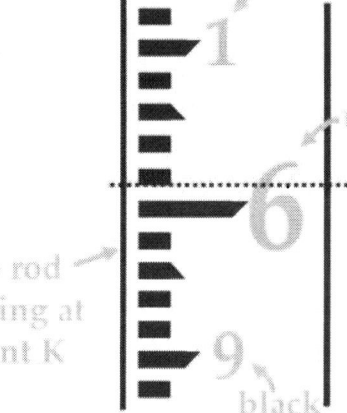

black

line of sight

red

$RR_J = 2.67 [ft]$

the rod reading at point J

the rod reading at point K

black

A) 296.16[ft]

B) 296.17[ft]

C) 302.85[ft]

D) 302.86[ft]

Leveling #5

Find: $Elev_C$ ←— the elevation at point C

Given:

$HI = 5.51 [ft]$ ←— the height of the instrument (above point B)

rod

line of sight

rod

BS_A HI FS_C

A   B level   C

Point	Backsight	Foresight	Elevation
A	4.23		29.71
C		3.76	$Elev_C$

all table values are in units of feet

A) 29.24[ft]

B) 29.71[ft]

C) 30.18[ft]

D) 34.75[ft]

Leveling #6

Find: $Elev_A$ ←— the elevation at point A

Given:

The level was set up at intermediate points B, D and F. For example, the backsight of point A and the foresight of point C were taken from point B.

(no sketch)

Point	BS	FS	Elev
A	3.48		$Elev_A$
C	1.23	19.42	$Elev_C$
E	8.23	6.07	$Elev_E$
G		4.11	225.18

all table values are in units of feet

A) 208.52[ft]

B) 209.15[ft]

C) 241.84[ft]

D) 244.30[ft]

Leveling #7

the ground elevation at point B

Find: Elev$_B$

Given:

the elevation of the instrument

the ground elevation

height of the instrument (above the ground surface)

$$HI=5.26\,[ft]$$

for both setups

Point	BS	ElevI	FS	Elev
D		ElevI$_D$		366.01
C	5.46		8.23	Elev$_C$
B		ElevI$_B$		Elev$_B$
A			1.23	Elev$_A$

all table values are in units of feet

A) 357.98 [ft]
B) 363.24 [ft]
C) 363.52 [ft]
D) 367.27 [ft]

Leveling #8

Find: Elev$_A$ — the elevation at point A

Given:

black

rod reading at point D (backsight of point D)

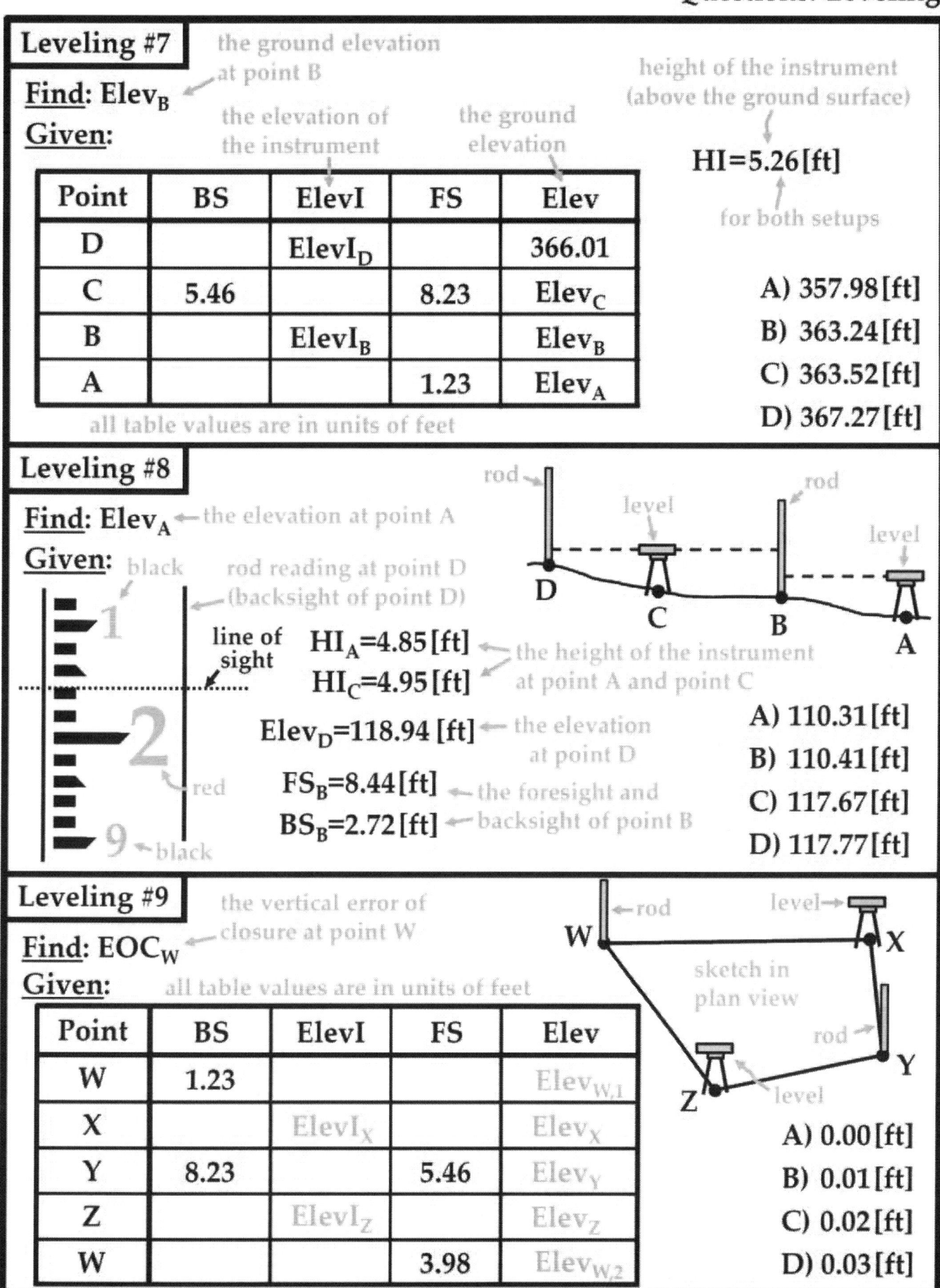

line of sight

$$HI_A=4.85\,[ft]$$
$$HI_C=4.95\,[ft]$$

the height of the instrument at point A and point C

$$Elev_D=118.94\,[ft]$$ — the elevation at point D

$$FS_B=8.44\,[ft]$$ — the foresight and
$$BS_B=2.72\,[ft]$$ — backsight of point B

red

black

A) 110.31 [ft]
B) 110.41 [ft]
C) 117.67 [ft]
D) 117.77 [ft]

Leveling #9

the vertical error of closure at point W

Find: EOC$_W$

Given: all table values are in units of feet

sketch in plan view

Point	BS	ElevI	FS	Elev
W	1.23			Elev$_{W,1}$
X		ElevI$_X$		Elev$_X$
Y	8.23		5.46	Elev$_Y$
Z		ElevI$_Z$		Elev$_Z$
W			3.98	Elev$_{W,2}$

A) 0.00 [ft]
B) 0.01 [ft]
C) 0.02 [ft]
D) 0.03 [ft]

Surveying Practice Problems

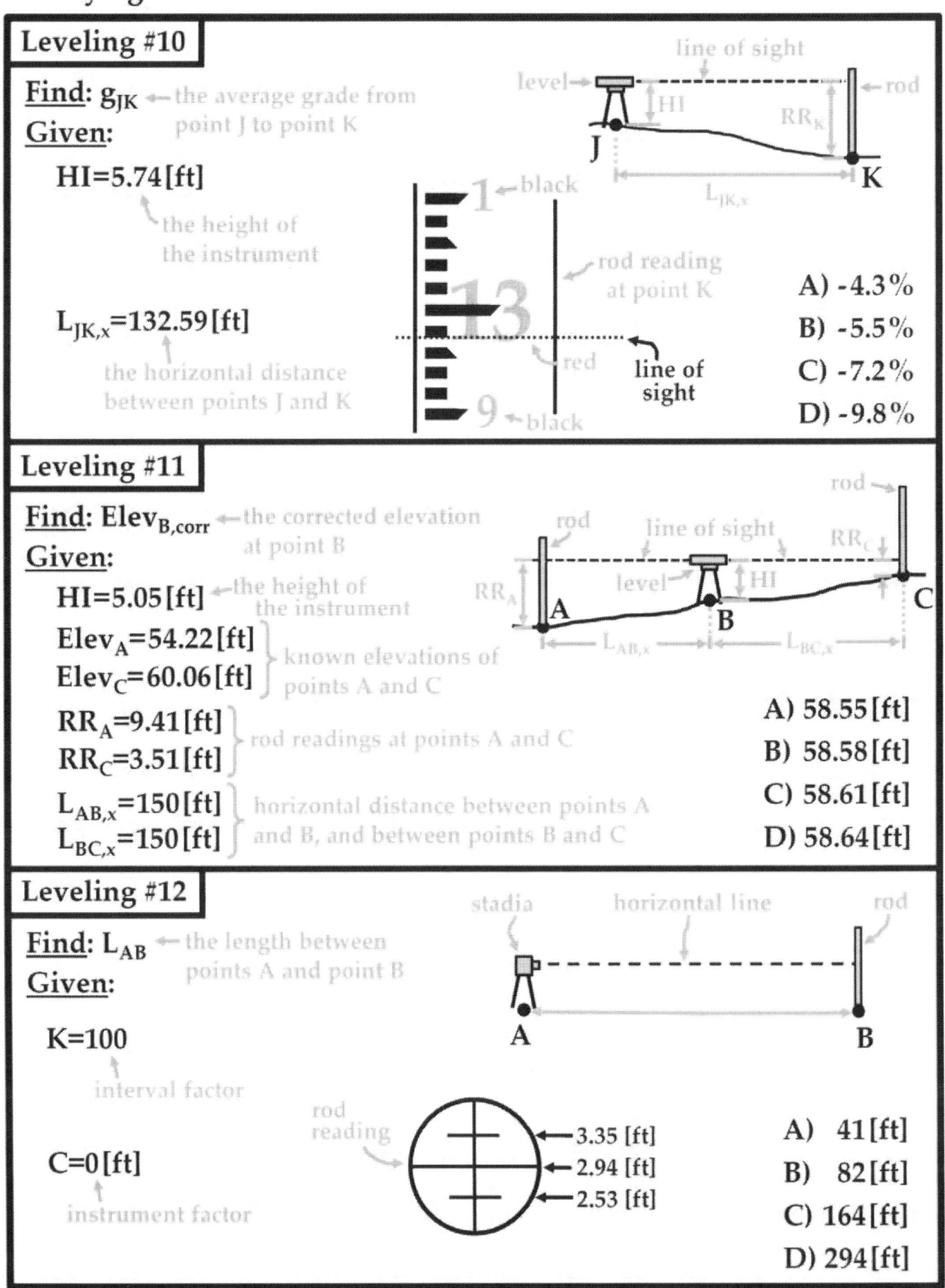

Leveling #10

Find: g_{JK} ← the average grade from point J to point K

Given:

$HI = 5.74\,[ft]$ — the height of the instrument

$L_{JK,x} = 132.59\,[ft]$ — the horizontal distance between points J and K

level line of sight rod
HI RR_K
J K $L_{JK,x}$

1 ← black
rod reading at point K
13
red line of sight
9 ← black

A) -4.3%
B) -5.5%
C) -7.2%
D) -9.8%

Leveling #11

Find: $Elev_{B,corr}$ ← the corrected elevation at point B

Given:

$HI = 5.05\,[ft]$ ← the height of the instrument

$Elev_A = 54.22\,[ft]$
$Elev_C = 60.06\,[ft]$ } known elevations of points A and C

$RR_A = 9.41\,[ft]$
$RR_C = 3.51\,[ft]$ } rod readings at points A and C

$L_{AB,x} = 150\,[ft]$
$L_{BC,x} = 150\,[ft]$ } horizontal distance between points A and B, and between points B and C

rod line of sight rod
RR_A level HI RR_C
A B C
$L_{AB,x}$ $L_{BC,x}$

A) 58.55 [ft]
B) 58.58 [ft]
C) 58.61 [ft]
D) 58.64 [ft]

Leveling #12

Find: L_{AB} ← the length between points A and point B

Given:

$K = 100$ — interval factor

$C = 0\,[ft]$ — instrument factor

stadia horizontal line rod
A B

rod reading
3.35 [ft]
2.94 [ft]
2.53 [ft]

A) 41 [ft]
B) 82 [ft]
C) 164 [ft]
D) 294 [ft]

Leveling #13

Find: $L_{AB,x}$ — the horizontal distance between points A and B.

Given:

  K=200 ← interval factor

  C=0 [ft] ← instrument factor

$\theta=17.4^\circ$

6.25 [ft] →
5.00 [ft] →
3.75 [ft] →

rod reading

HI=5.00 [ft]

height of instrument

stadia

line of sight

HI

θ

A

L_{AB}

rod

B

A) 239 [ft]

B) 455 [ft]

C) 477 [ft]

D) 500 [ft]

Leveling #14

triangle ABC is a right triangle

Find: Z ← the zenith angle

Given:

  L_{AB}=219.50 [ft] ← the length between point A and point B

  K=333 ← interval factor

5.85 [ft] →
5.50 [ft] →
5.15 [ft] →

rod reading

C=0 [ft]

instrument factor

HI=5.50 [ft]

height of instrument

Z

line of sight

stadia

HI

A

L_{AB}

C

B

A) 70°

B) 72°

C) 74°

D) 76°

Leveling #15

Find: Elev$_B$ ← the elevation at point B

Given:

  zenith angle

  Z=108°15′00″

  C=0 [ft] ← instrument factor

6.30 [ft] →
4.50 [ft] →
2.70 [ft] →

rod reading

rod held perpendicular to the line of sight

Elev$_A$=125.47 [ft]

elevation at point A

stadia

Z

HI

line of sight

A

HI=5.40 [ft]

rod

B

height of instrument

K=100 ← interval factor

A) 10.3 [ft]

B) 12.1 [ft]

C) 13.9 [ft]

D) 15.7 [ft]

Surveying Practice Problems

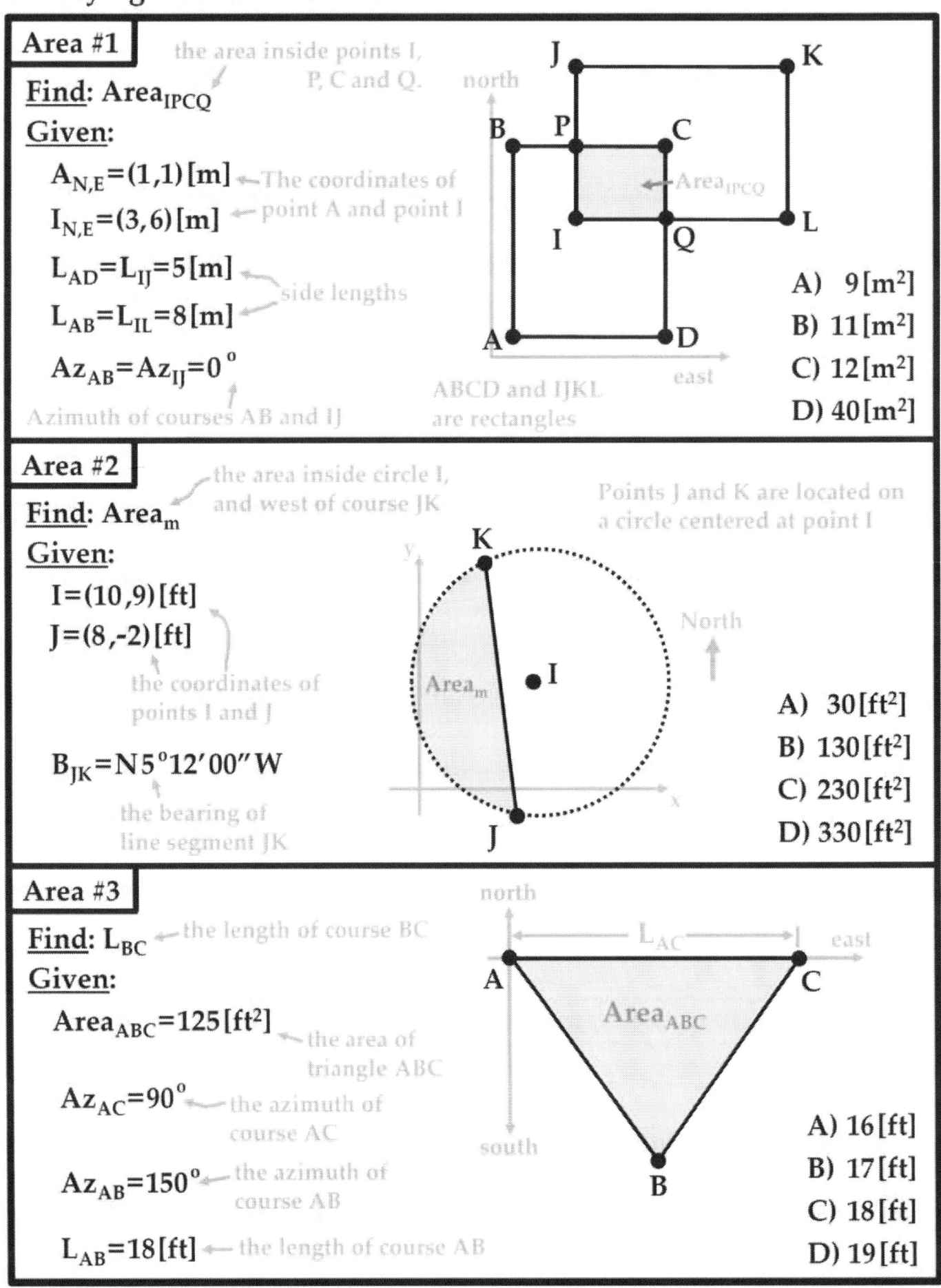

Area #1

Find: Area$_{IPCQ}$ ← the area inside points I, P, C and Q.

Given:

$A_{N,E}=(1,1)\,[m]$ ← The coordinates of point A and point I

$I_{N,E}=(3,6)\,[m]$

$L_{AD}=L_{IJ}=5\,[m]$ ← side lengths

$L_{AB}=L_{IL}=8\,[m]$

$Az_{AB}=Az_{IJ}=0^{\circ}$

Azimuth of courses AB and IJ

ABCD and IJKL are rectangles

A) 9 [m²]
B) 11 [m²]
C) 12 [m²]
D) 40 [m²]

Area #2

Find: Area$_m$ ← the area inside circle I, and west of course JK

Given:

$I=(10,9)\,[ft]$

$J=(8,-2)\,[ft]$

the coordinates of points I and J

$B_{JK}=N\,5^{\circ}12'00''W$

the bearing of line segment JK

Points J and K are located on a circle centered at point I

A) 30 [ft²]
B) 130 [ft²]
C) 230 [ft²]
D) 330 [ft²]

Area #3

Find: L_{BC} ← the length of course BC

Given:

$Area_{ABC}=125\,[ft^2]$ ← the area of triangle ABC

$Az_{AC}=90^{\circ}$ ← the azimuth of course AC

$Az_{AB}=150^{\circ}$ ← the azimuth of course AB

$L_{AB}=18\,[ft]$ ← the length of course AB

A) 16 [ft]
B) 17 [ft]
C) 18 [ft]
D) 19 [ft]

Area #4

Find: Area$_{IJK}$ ← the area of triangle IJK

Given:

L_{IJ}=117.8 [m] ← the length of coruse IJ

A_{IJK}=105° ⟍
A_{JKI}=60° ← the three interior angle measurements of Triangle IJK
A_{KIJ}=15° ⟍

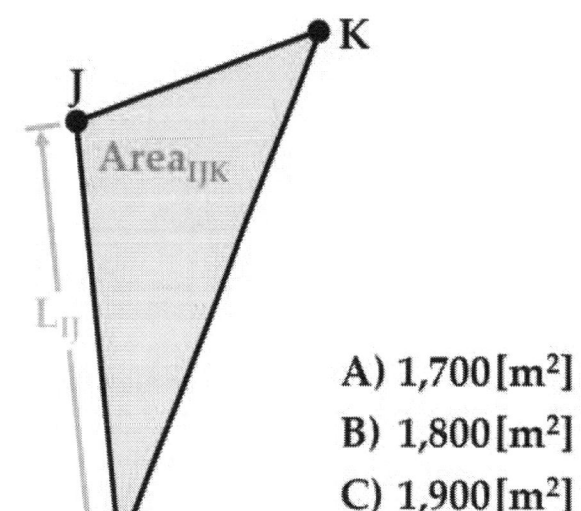

A) 1,700 [m²]
B) 1,800 [m²]
C) 1,900 [m²]
D) 2,000 [m²]

Area #5

Find: L$_{KI}$ ← the length between point K and point I

Given:

L_{IJ}=20.45 [m]

⟍ the length between point J and point K

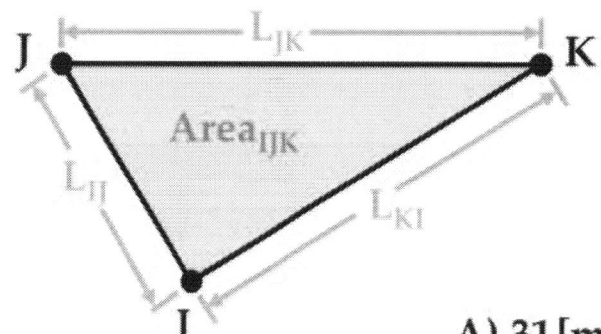

L_{JK}=36.22 [m]   Area$_{IJK}$=334.2 [m²]

⟍ the length between point I and point J   ⟍ the area inside triangle IJK

A) 31 [m]
B) 32 [m]
C) 33 [m]
D) 34 [m]

Area #6

⟍ the area inside triangle ABC

Find: Area$_{ABC}$

the coordinates of points A, B and C

Given:

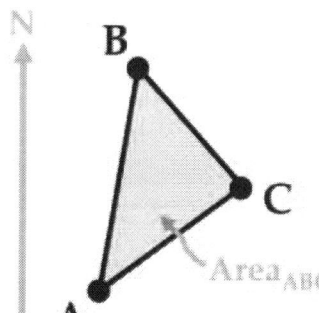

point	Northing	Easting
A	129.7 [ft]	141.8 [ft]
B	517.1 [ft]	167.4 [ft]
C	322.1 [ft]	305.5 [ft]

A) 26,000 [ft²]
B) 27,000 [ft²]
C) 28,000 [ft²]
D) 29,000 [ft²]

Surveying Practice Problems

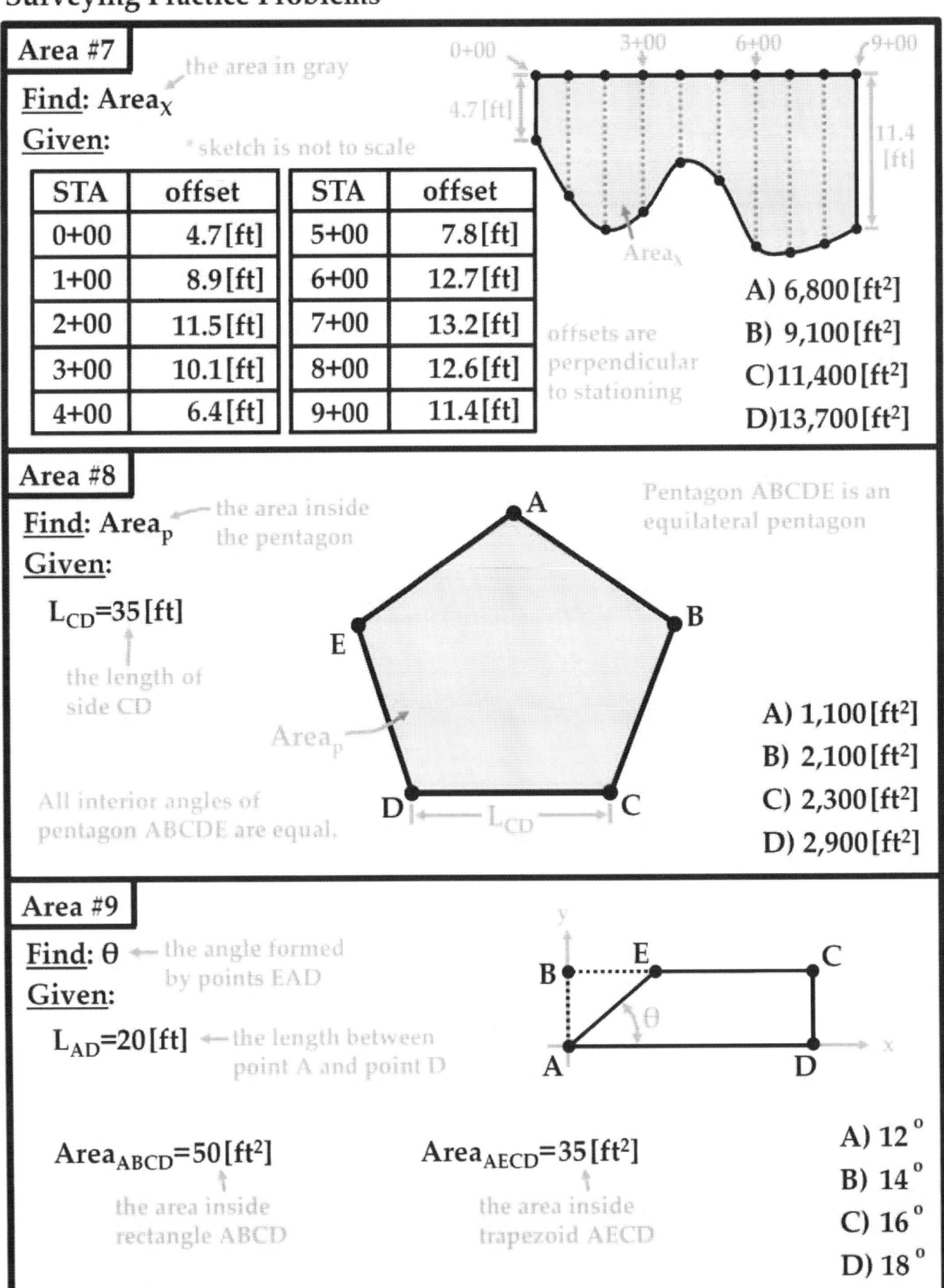

Area #7

Find: Area$_X$ — the area in gray

Given: *sketch is not to scale

STA	offset	STA	offset
0+00	4.7 [ft]	5+00	7.8 [ft]
1+00	8.9 [ft]	6+00	12.7 [ft]
2+00	11.5 [ft]	7+00	13.2 [ft]
3+00	10.1 [ft]	8+00	12.6 [ft]
4+00	6.4 [ft]	9+00	11.4 [ft]

offsets are perpendicular to stationing

A) 6,800 [ft²]

B) 9,100 [ft²]

C) 11,400 [ft²]

D) 13,700 [ft²]

Area #8

Find: Area$_p$ — the area inside the pentagon

Given:

L_{CD}=35 [ft]

the length of side CD

All interior angles of pentagon ABCDE are equal.

Pentagon ABCDE is an equilateral pentagon

A) 1,100 [ft²]

B) 2,100 [ft²]

C) 2,300 [ft²]

D) 2,900 [ft²]

Area #9

Find: θ — the angle formed by points EAD

Given:

L_{AD}=20 [ft] — the length between point A and point D

Area$_{ABCD}$=50 [ft²]

the area inside rectangle ABCD

Area$_{AECD}$=35 [ft²]

the area inside trapezoid AECD

A) 12°

B) 14°

C) 16°

D) 18°

Area #10

<u>Find:</u> maximum Area$_{ABC}$ ← the maximum area of triangle ABC

<u>Given:</u>

L_{AB}=25.4 [m]

length of line segment AB

L_{BC}=37.8 [m]

length of line segment BC

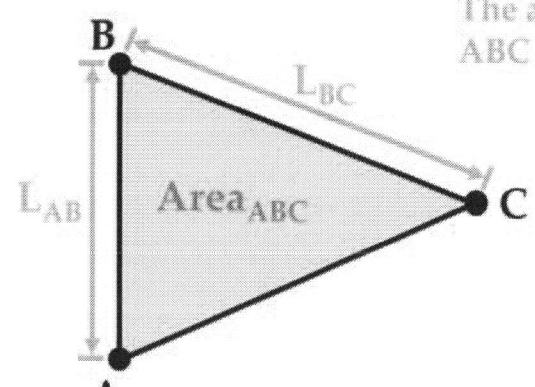

The angles of triangle ABC are not provided

A) 542 [m²]
B) 480 [m²]
C) 488 [m²]
D) 506 [m²]

Area #11

<u>Find:</u> L_{IJ} ← the length of course IJ

<u>Given:</u>

Area$_{IJK}$=1.87 [acres] ← the area of triangle IJK

A_{IJK}=45°

the interior angle formed at point J

A_{KIJ}=100°

the interior angle formed at point I

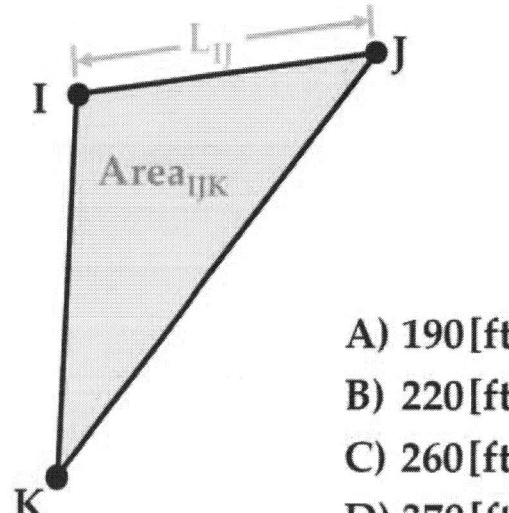

A) 190 [ft]
B) 220 [ft]
C) 260 [ft]
D) 370 [ft]

Area #12

<u>Find:</u> Area$_{ABCD}$ ← the area inside traverse ABCD

<u>Given:</u>

course	Latitude	Departure
AB	157.41	55.89
BC	-23.51	86.22
CD	-174.88	-7.14
DA	40.98	-134.97

all latitude and departure values are in feet

North

traverse has no error of closure

A) 19,000 [ft²]
B) 19,400 [ft²]
C) 19,800 [ft²]
D) 20,200 [ft²]

Surveying Practice Problems

Area #13

Find: Area$_{ABCD}$ ← the area inside traverse ABCDE   (no sketch provided)

Given:

all latitude and departure values are in units of feet

course	Latitude	Departure
AB	95.61	2.25
BC	4.88	47.65
CD	-3.75	50.11
DE	-93.18	-6.42
EA	-3.56	-93.59

A) 5,600 [ft²]

B) 7,400 [ft²]

C) 9,200 [ft²]

D) 11,000 [ft²]

Area #14

Find: Area$_{ABCDE}$ ← the area inside traverse ABCDE

Given:

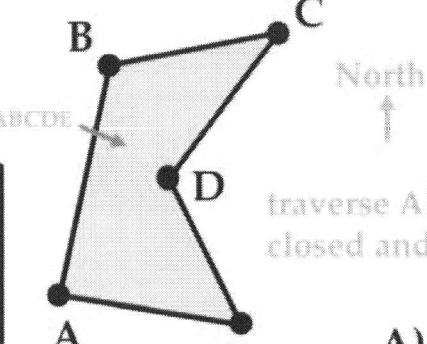

Area$_{ABCDE}$

North

traverse ABCDE is closed and balanced

course	Latitude	Departure
AB	1,428.1	292.8
BC	315.4	1,019.2
CD	-881.5	-749.9
DE	-927.0	515.8
EA	65.0	-1,077.9

← all distances are in feet

A) 23 [acre]

B) 24 [acre]

C) 25 [acre]

D) 26 [acre]

Area #15

Find: Lat$_{AB}$ ← the latitude of course AB

Given: traverse ABCD is balanced

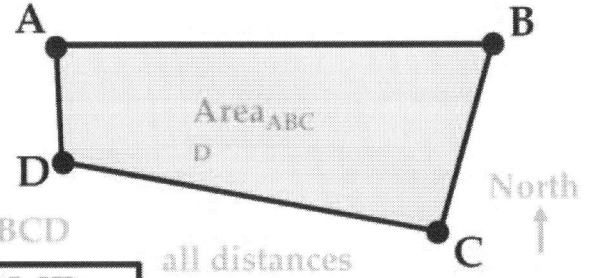

Area$_{ABCD}$

North

all distances are in feet

Area$_{ABCD}$ = 6,015 [ft²] ← the area inside ABCD

course	Latitude	Departure	DMD
AB	Lat$_{AB}$	135.81	135.81
BC	Lat$_{BC}$	-12.40	259.22
CD	24.14	-116.72	130.10
DA	28.08	-6.69	6.69

A) -21.44 [ft]

B) -5.61 [ft]

C) 14.76 [ft]

D) 28.71 [ft]

Area #16

Find: Area$_{ABCD}$ ← area inside closed traverse ABCD

Given:

Point	Northing	Easting
A	218.9	173.4
B	88.4	241.8
C	101.7	121.7
D	197.6	67.9

All northing and easting values are in units of feet

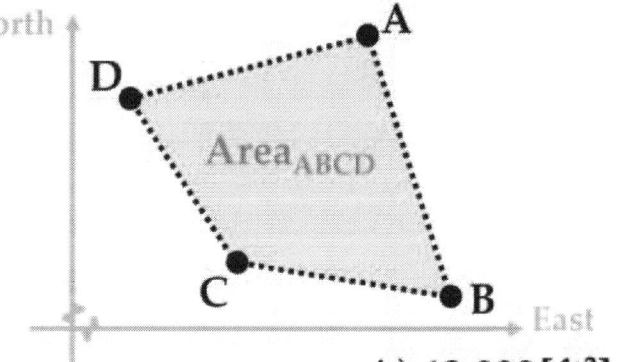

A) 12,000 [ft^2]

B) 13,000 [ft^2]

C) 24,000 [ft^2]

D) 26,000 [ft^2]

Area #17

Find: Area$_{IJK}$ ← the area inside triangle IJK

Given:

point	Northing	Easting
I	151.8 [ft]	47.6 [ft]
J	167.9 [ft]	133.1 [ft]
K	74.1 [ft]	62.0 [ft]

the coordinates of points I, J, K

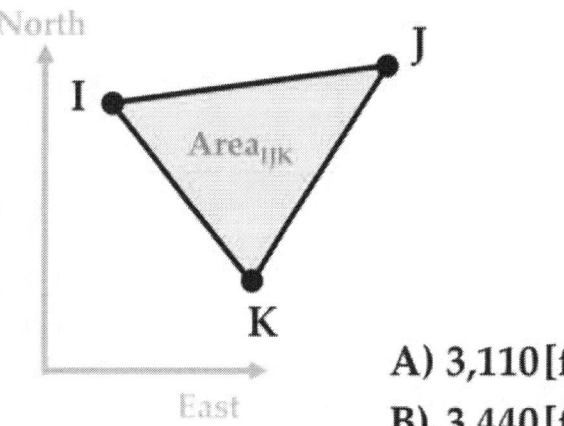

A) 3,110 [ft^2]

B) 3,440 [ft^2]

C) 3,770 [ft^2]

D) 4,010 [ft^2]

Area #18

Find: Area$_{ABCDE}$ ← the area inside pentagon ABCDE

Given:

point	Northing	Easting
A	241.76 [ft]	744.01 [ft]
B	266.05 [ft]	789.54 [ft]
C	238.11 [ft]	841.93 [ft]
D	213.07 [ft]	797.43 [ft]
E	148.62 [ft]	767.92 [ft]

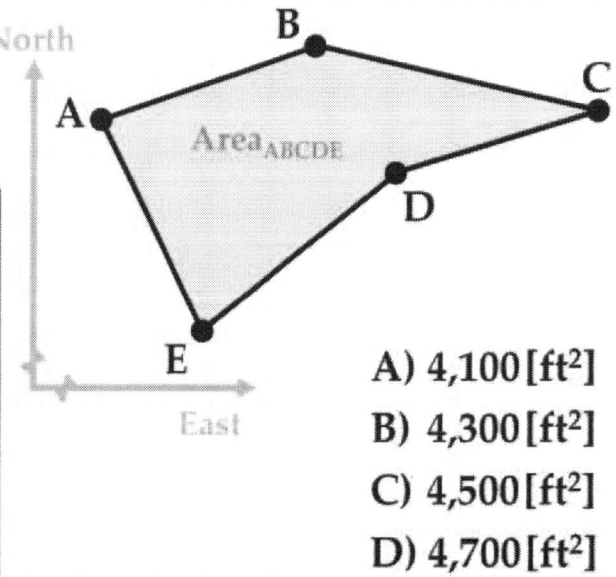

A) 4,100 [ft^2]

B) 4,300 [ft^2]

C) 4,500 [ft^2]

D) 4,700 [ft^2]

Surveying Practice Problems

Angles #1

Find: A_{JKI} ← the angle formed by points J, K and I

Given:

$B_{IJ} = N\,86°30'00''\,E$

$B_{IK} = S\,48°15'00''\,E$ ← the bearing of line segments IJ and IK

$L_{JK} = 95.14\,[ft]$ ← the length of line segments JK and IJ

$L_{IJ} = 102.88\,[ft]$

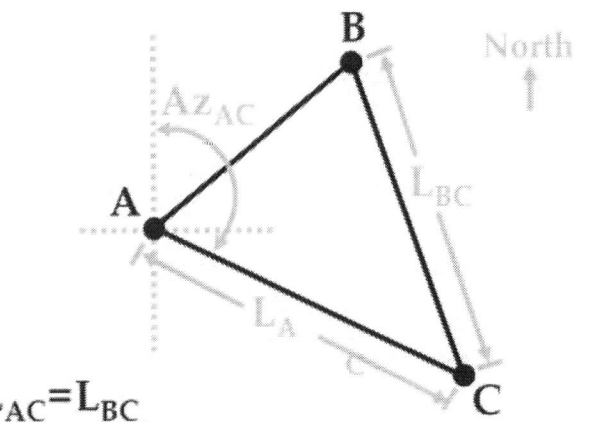

A) 40°

B) 45°

C) 50°

D) 55°

Angles #2

Find: Az_{AC} ← the azimuth of course AC

Given:

$B_{AB} = N\,50°\,E$ ← the bearing of course AB

$B_{BC} = S\,20°\,E$ ← the bearing of course BC

$L_{AC} = L_{BC}$ ← the length of side AC equals the length of side BC.

A) 110°

B) 120°

C) 130°

D) 140°

Angles #3

Find: A_{IJK} ← the angle formed by points I, J and K

Given:

Course	Latitude	Departure
IJ	292.81	77.65
JK	-100.51	211.08
KI	-192.30	-288.73

the latitude and departure of each course is in units of feet.

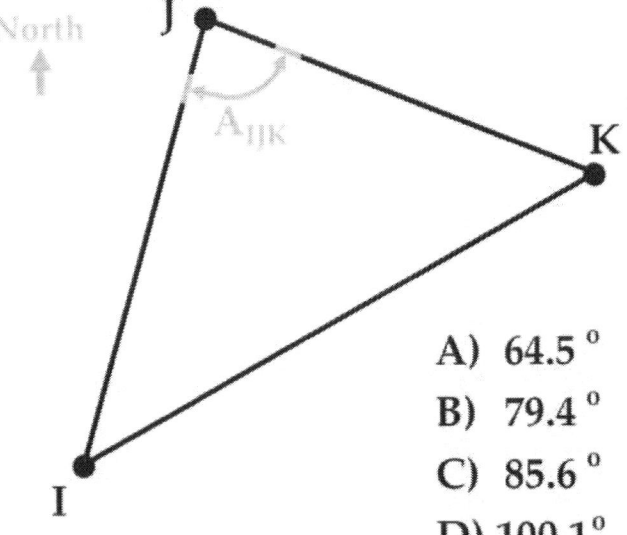

A) 64.5°

B) 79.4°

C) 85.6°

D) 100.1°

Angles #4

Find: Az_{YZ} ← the azimuth angle of course YZ

Given:

$B_{XW} = S\,41°25'00''\,W$

the bearing angle of course XW

$A_{WXY} = 120°00'00''$

the angle formed by points W, X and Y

$A_{XYZ} = 98°17'00''$

the angle formed by points X, Y and Z

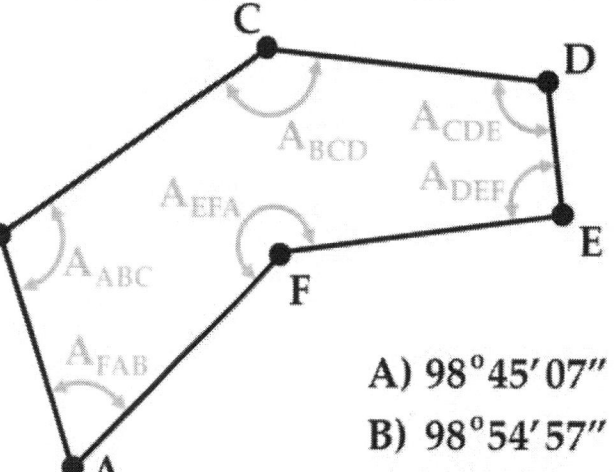

A) 80°
B) 240°
C) 250°
D) 260°

Angles #5

Find: $A_{CDE,\,bal}$ ← the interior angle CDE after closed traverse ABCDEF is balanced

Given:

$A_{FAB,meas} = 48°22'15''$
$A_{ABC,meas} = 103°19'27''$
$A_{BCD,meas} = 157°45'08''$
$A_{CDE,meas} = 98°55'07''$
$A_{DEF,meas} = 88°37'18''$
$A_{EFA,meas} = 222°00'45''$

the measured interior angles of traverse ABCDEF

A) 98°45'07''
B) 98°54'57''
C) 98°55'07''
D) 99°05'07''

Angles #6

Find: A_{AOB} ← the average horizontal angle measured between points A and B, from point O

Given:

Azimuth	Direct	Inverted
Az_{OA}	0°00'00''	180°00'05''
Az_{OB}	37°12'10''	217°12'05''

table of azimuth readings were taken from the total station at point O.

total station set up at point O

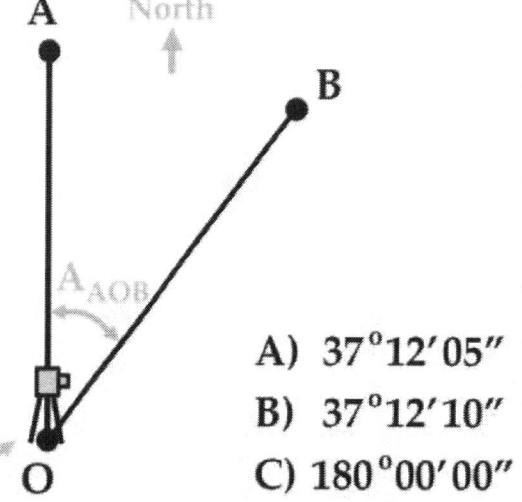

A) 37°12'05''
B) 37°12'10''
C) 180°00'00''
D) 180°00'05''

Surveying Practice Problems

Angles #7

the inverted azimuth from point O, when viewing point N.

Find: $Az_{ON,I}$

Given:

$A_{MON}=203°12'35''$ — the average horizontal angle measured between points M and N, from point O

total station set up at point O

North

M

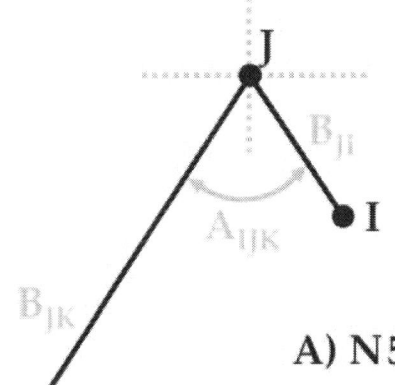

O

A_{MON}

Azimuth	Direct	Inverted
Az_{OM}	$0°00'00''$	$180°00'20''$
Az_{ON}	$203°12'45''$	$Az_{OB,I}$

table of azimuth readings were taken from the total station at point O.

N

A) $23°12'25''$

B) $23°12'35''$

C) $23°12'45''$

D) $203°12'25''$

Angles #8

Find: B_{JK} — the bearing of course JK

Given:

$B_{JI}=S23°23'40''E$

the bearing of course IJ

$A_{IJK}=75°14'25''$

the angle defined by points I, J and K

North

J

B_{JI}

A_{IJK}

I

B_{JK}

K

A) $N51°50'45''E$

B) $N81°21'55''E$

C) $S51°50'45''W$

D) $S81°21'55''W$

Angles #9

the true bearing of course IJ

Find: $B_{IJ,true}$

Given:

$B_{IJ,mag}=N6°12'30''E$

the magnetic bearing of course IJ

$D=12°25'00''E$

the magnetic declination

N_{mag} — the direction of magnetic north

J

$B_{IJ,mag}$

the direction of magnetic east

I

E_{mag}

A) $N6°12'30''W$

B) $N12°25'00''W$

C) $N18°37'30''W$

D) $N18°37'30''E$

Angles #10

Find: D ← the magnetic declination

Given:

$B_{IJ,mag} = N\,85°30'00''\,E$

    the magnetic bearing
    of course IJ

$B_{IJ,true} = S\,87°45'00''\,E$ ← (not shown in sketch)

    the true bearing of course IJ

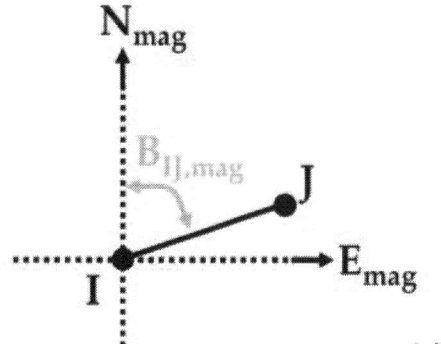

A) $2°15'00''\,E$

B) $2°15'00''\,W$

C) $6°45'00''\,E$

D) $6°45'00''\,W$

Angles #11

Find: E_J ← the easting of point J

Given:

$A_{IJK} = 127°18'25''$ ← angle created by points I, J and K

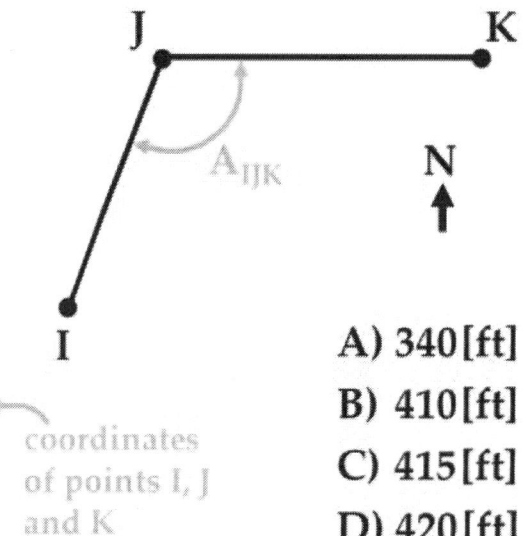

Point	Northing	Easting
I	156.70 [ft]	357.27 [ft]
J	225.91 [ft]	E_J
K	225.91 [ft]	485.19 [ft]

coordinates of points I, J and K

A) 340 [ft]

B) 410 [ft]

C) 415 [ft]

D) 420 [ft]

Angles #12

Find: θ_C ← the interior angle at point C

Given:

$\theta_A = 96.455°$

$\theta_B = 121.809°$

the interior angles at points A, B, D and E

$\theta_D = 198.776°$

$\theta_E = 64.016°$

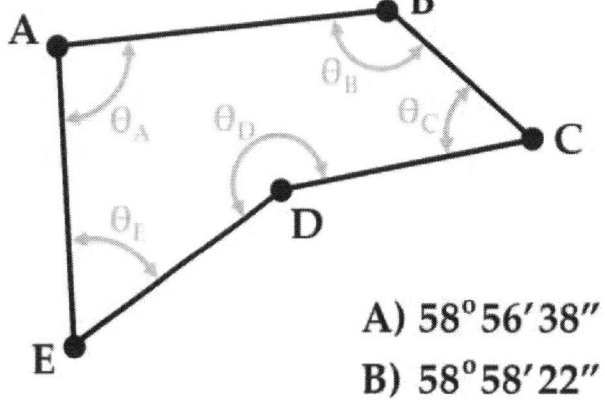

A) $58°56'38''$

B) $58°58'22''$

C) $59°00'14''$

D) $59°01'57''$

Surveying Practice Problems

Angles #13

Find: Az_{AB} ← the azimuth angle of course AB

Given:

Azimuth	Direct	Inverted
Az_{OA}	$105°55'10''$	$285°55'10''$
Az_{OB}	$116°09'25''$	$296°09'15''$

azimuth measurements from point O.

$L_{AB}=265.19[ft]$ ← length of course AB

$L_{OB}=358.21[ft]$ ← length of course OB

A) $116°09'20''$
B) $119°48'30''$
C) $130°02'40''$
D) $166°06'40''$

total station
O ← plan view
A
sketch is in plan view
L_{OB}
L_{AB}
N
B
C

Angles #14

Find: A_{BAG} ← the angle formed by points B, A and G

Given:

$L_{AB}=55[m]$ ← the lengths of
$L_{BC}=55[m]$ ← line segments AB, BC and CE
$L_{CE}=85[m]$

$Area_{BCDG}=Area_{GDEF}$

Area BCDG equals area GDEF

L_A L_B C
A   B
A_{BA} G
rectangle BCEF   G $Area_{BCDG}$ L_C D   E
F $Area_{GDEF}$ E   N

$N_A=N_B=N_C$

the northing of point A equals the northing of points B and C

A) $27°15'$
B) $28°45'$
C) $30°15'$
D) $31°45'$

Angles #15

Find: B_{KM} ← the bearing angle for course KM

Given:

$Az_{IJ}=115.774°$ ← the azimuth angle for course IJ

$A_{IJK}=84.338°$

the angle formed by points I, J and K

$A_{JKM}=82.117°$

the angle formed by points J, K and M

I
J
A_{IJK}
N
K
A_{JKM}
M

A) $S\,62.0°E$
B) $N\,62.0°W$
C) $S\,66.4°E$
D) $N\,66.4°W$

Traverse #1

Find: θ_I ← the interior angle at point I

Given:

$\theta_{I,m}=35°15'47''$ ← the measured interior angles at points I, J and K

$\theta_{J,m}=71°52'41''$

$\theta_{K,m}=72°51'47''$

subscript "m"=measured

balance the closed traverse.

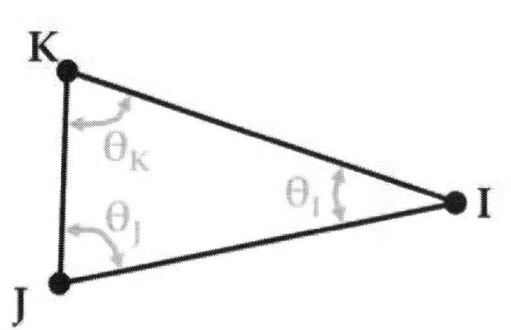

A) 35°15′32″
B) 35°15′42″
C) 35°15′44″
D) 35°15′52″

Traverse #2

Find: L_{AD} ← the distance between point A and point D, on a straight line.

Given:

Course	Latitude	Departure
AB	57.61	-21.19
BC	98.07	-89.62
CD	-12.69	146.55

the latitude and departure of each course is in units of feet.

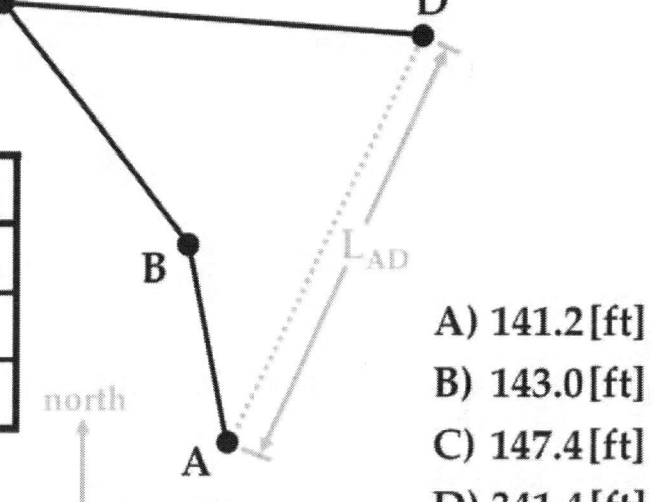

A) 141.2 [ft]
B) 143.0 [ft]
C) 147.4 [ft]
D) 341.4 [ft]

Traverse #3

Find: EOC ← the error of closure

Given:

Course	Latitude	Departure
AB	457.62	-87.65
BC	-115.94	567.81
CA	-342.33	-479.84

the latitude and departure of each course is in units of feet.

ABC is a closed traverse

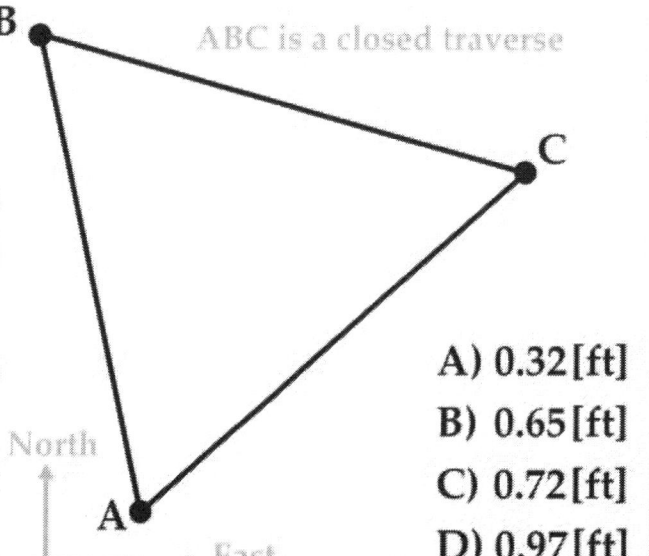

A) 0.32 [ft]
B) 0.65 [ft]
C) 0.72 [ft]
D) 0.97 [ft]

Surveying Practice Problems

Traverse #4

<u>Find:</u> Dep$_{DA}$ ←the departure of course DA

<u>Given:</u> EOC=0.54[ft] ←the error of closure for traverse ABCD

Course	Latitude	Departure
AB	191.86	395.06
BC	245.85	-17.29
CD	-378.99	-297.15
DA	-59.06	Dep$_{DA}$

all lengths are in feet

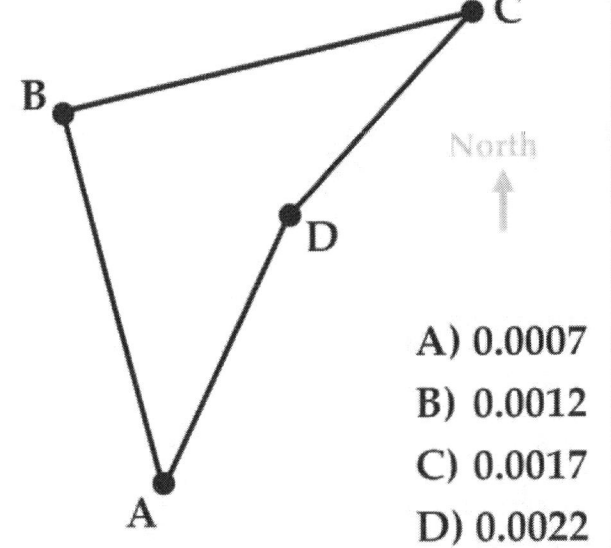

North

A) -80.62[ft]

B) -80.28[ft]

C) -80.20[ft]

D) -80.08[ft]

Traverse #5

<u>Find:</u> ROE$_{ABCD}$ ←the ratio of error of traverse ABCD

<u>Given:</u>

Course	Latitude	Departure
AB	98.17	-21.14
BC	19.59	117.65
CD	-53.22	-69.06
DA	-64.31	-26.87

all latitudes and departures are in feet

North

A) 0.0007

B) 0.0012

C) 0.0017

D) 0.0022

Traverse #6

<u>Find:</u> Dep$_{CA}$ ←the departure of course CA

<u>Given:</u> ROE=0.00124 ←the ratio of error of closed traverse ABC

Course	Latitude	Departure	Length
AB	-295.84	254.76	390.42
BC	267.41	158.91	311.06
CA	29.18	Dep$_{CA}$	L$_{CA}$

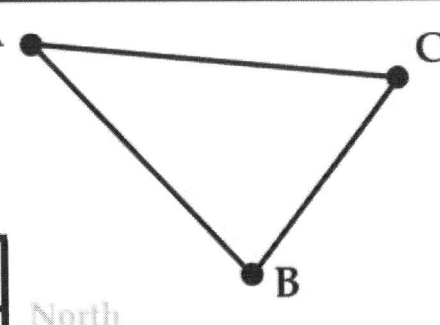

North

A) -412.51[m]

B) -412.17[m]

C) -411.86[m]

D) -411.54[m]

Traverse #7

<u>Find</u>: L_{WXYZ} ← the length of traverse WXYZ

<u>Given</u>:

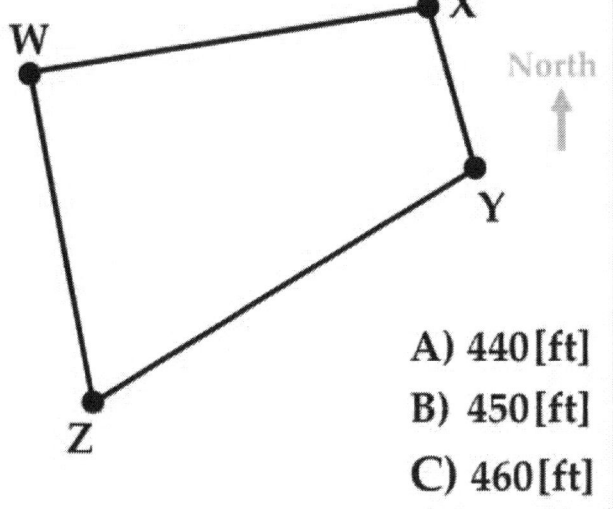

Course	Latitude	Departure
WX	16.49	117.90
XY	-35.18	18.55
YZ	-101.71	-121.54
ZW	120.40	-14.91

all latitudes and departures are in units of feet

A) 440 [ft]
B) 450 [ft]
C) 460 [ft]
D) 470 [ft]

Traverse #8

<u>Find</u>: N_J ← the northing of point J

<u>Given</u>:

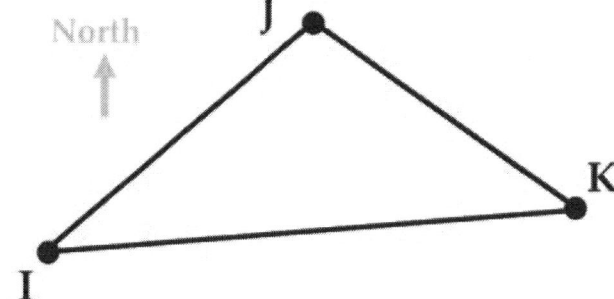

Point	Northing	Easting
I	29.82	65.44
J	N_J	191.40
K	43.11	307.06

measurements for northing and easting are in unit of feet.

L_{IJK}=587 [ft]

perimeter around the traverse IJK

A) 140 [ft]
B) 160 [ft]
C) 180 [ft]
D) 200 [ft]

Traverse #9

<u>Find</u>: $N_{J,bal}$ ← the northing of point J after the traverse is balanced

<u>Given</u>:

Point	Northing	Easting
I	20.71	16.16
L	140.36	125.80

true coordinates

Point	Northing	Easting
I	20.71	16.16
J	81.54	49.11
K	150.88	7.91
L	141.29	124.57

measured coordinates

balance using the compass rule

northing and easting values in meters

A) 80.61 [m]
B) 81.02 [m]
C) 81.30 [m]
D) 81.78 [m]

Surveying Practice Problems

Traverse #10

Find: Lat$_{AB}$ ← the corrected latitude of course AB

Given:

balance traverse using transit rule

known northing and easting values

Course	Latitude	Departure
AB	78.11	-44.60
BC	88.26	31.09
CD	-14.87	104.22

all latitude and departure measurements are in feet.

Point	Northing	Easting
A	31.48	99.71
D	181.58	191.11

A) 77.35 [ft]
B) 77.50 [ft]
C) 78.72 [ft]
D) 78.87 [ft]

Traverse #11

Find: Dep$_{XY}$ ← the corrected departure of course XY

Given:

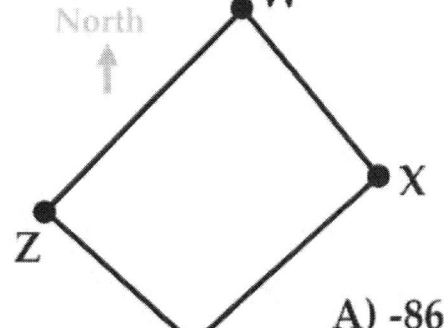

Course	Latitude	Departure
WX	-112.41	67.09
XY	-102.87	-86.22
YZ	89.64	-78.11
ZW	125.07	97.59

all latitude and departure measurements are in feet.

balance the closed traverse WXYZ using the transit rule

A) -86.56 [ft]
B) -86.31 [ft]
C) -86.13 [ft]
D) not enough information

Traverse #12

Find: E$_C$ ← the easting of point C

Given:

all latitude and departure measurements are in feet.

Course	Latitude	Departure
AB	98.71	17.16
BC	72.18	-67.28
CD	58.22	148.96

balance open traverse using the compass rule

known northing and easting values

Point	Northing	Easting
A	21.76	101.70
D	250.07	201.13

A) 51.25 [ft]
B) 51.41 [ft]
C) 51.75 [ft]
D) 51.91 [ft]

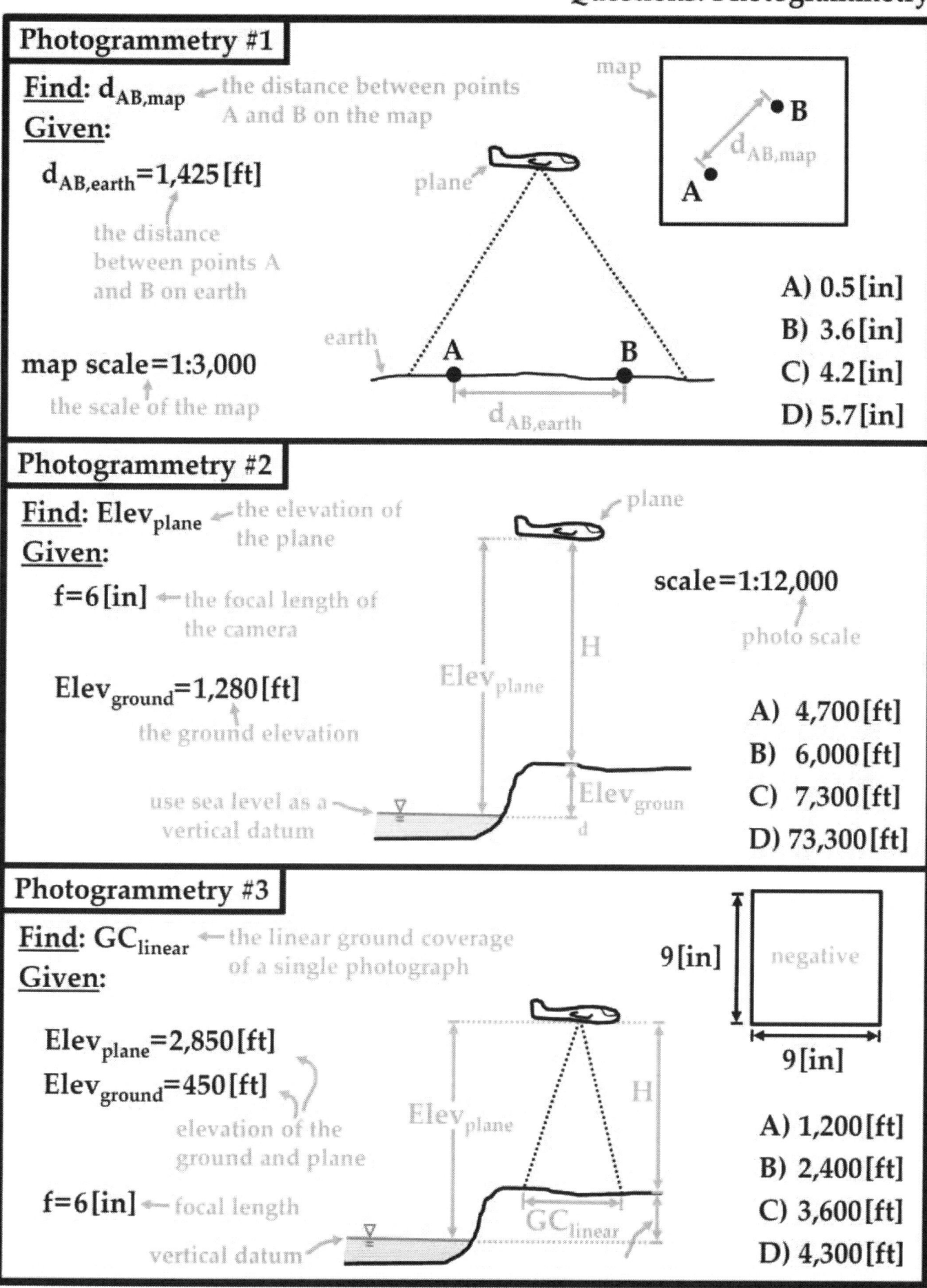

Photogrammetry #1

Find: $d_{AB,map}$ ← the distance between points A and B on the map

Given:

$d_{AB,earth}=1,425\,[ft]$

the distance between points A and B on earth

map scale=1:3,000

the scale of the map

plane

earth

A   B

$d_{AB,earth}$

map

B

$d_{AB,map}$

A

A) 0.5 [in]
B) 3.6 [in]
C) 4.2 [in]
D) 5.7 [in]

Photogrammetry #2

Find: $Elev_{plane}$ ← the elevation of the plane

Given:

$f=6\,[in]$ ← the focal length of the camera

$Elev_{ground}=1,280\,[ft]$

the ground elevation

use sea level as a vertical datum

plane

scale=1:12,000

photo scale

H

$Elev_{plane}$

$Elev_{ground}$

A) 4,700 [ft]
B) 6,000 [ft]
C) 7,300 [ft]
D) 73,300 [ft]

Photogrammetry #3

Find: GC_{linear} ← the linear ground coverage of a single photograph

Given:

$Elev_{plane}=2,850\,[ft]$
$Elev_{ground}=450\,[ft]$

elevation of the ground and plane

$f=6\,[in]$ ← focal length

vertical datum

9 [in]   negative

9 [in]

$Elev_{plane}$

H

GC_{linear}

A) 1,200 [ft]
B) 2,400 [ft]
C) 3,600 [ft]
D) 4,300 [ft]

Surveying Practice Problems

Photogrammetry #4

Find: t ← the time between consecutive photos

Given:

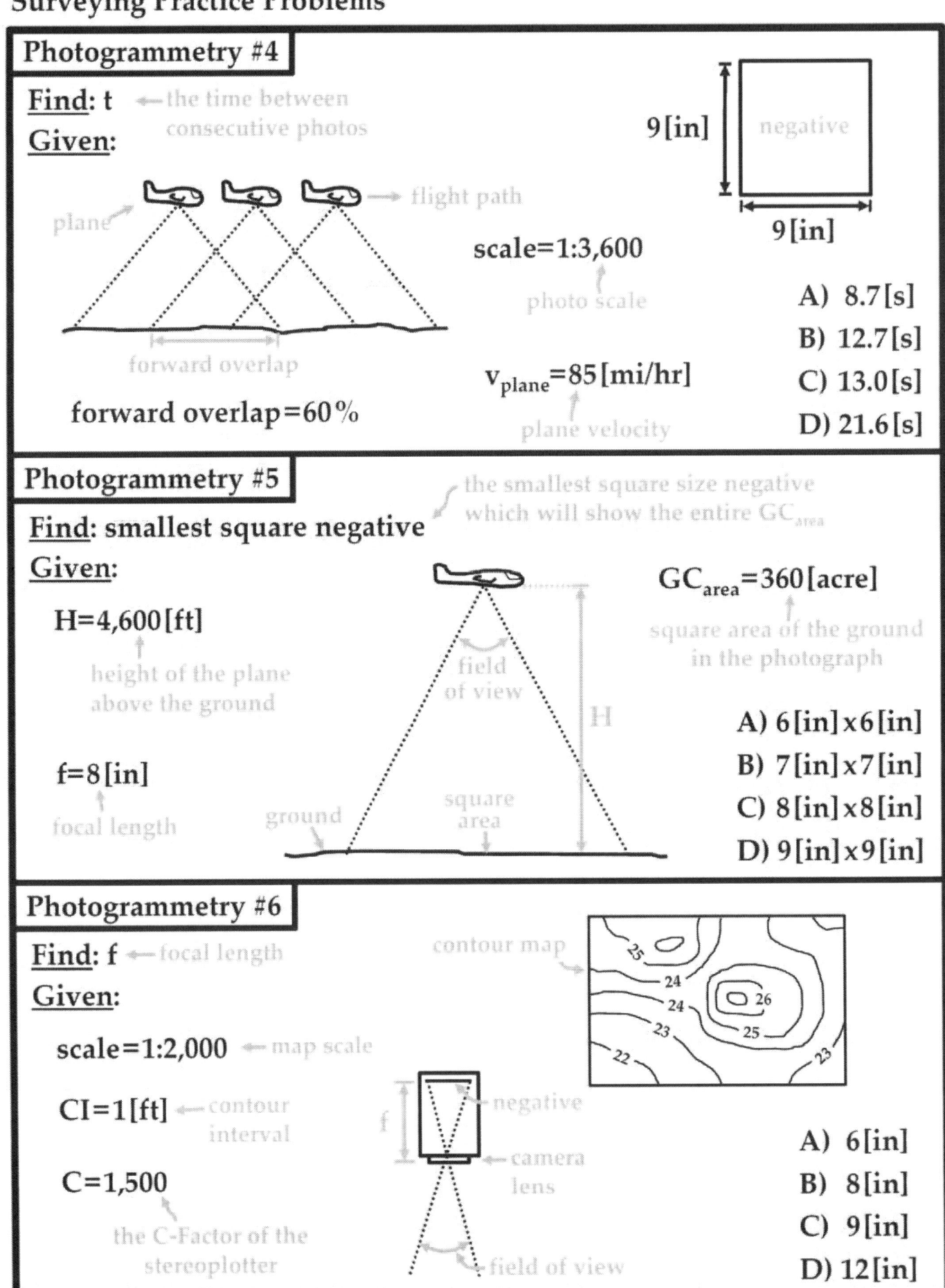

plane → flight path

forward overlap

forward overlap=60%

scale=1:3,600

← photo scale

v_{plane}=85 [mi/hr]

← plane velocity

9 [in] negative
9 [in]

A) 8.7 [s]
B) 12.7 [s]
C) 13.0 [s]
D) 21.6 [s]

Photogrammetry #5

Find: smallest square negative — the smallest square size negative which will show the entire GC_{area}

Given:

H=4,600 [ft]

← height of the plane above the ground

f=8 [in]

← focal length

field of view

ground

square area

GC_{area}=360 [acre]

← square area of the ground in the photograph

A) 6 [in] x 6 [in]
B) 7 [in] x 7 [in]
C) 8 [in] x 8 [in]
D) 9 [in] x 9 [in]

Photogrammetry #6

Find: f ← focal length

Given:

scale=1:2,000 ← map scale

CI=1 [ft] ← contour interval

C=1,500

← the C-Factor of the stereoplotter

contour map

negative

← camera lens

← field of view

A) 6 [in]
B) 8 [in]
C) 9 [in]
D) 12 [in]

Photogrammetry #7

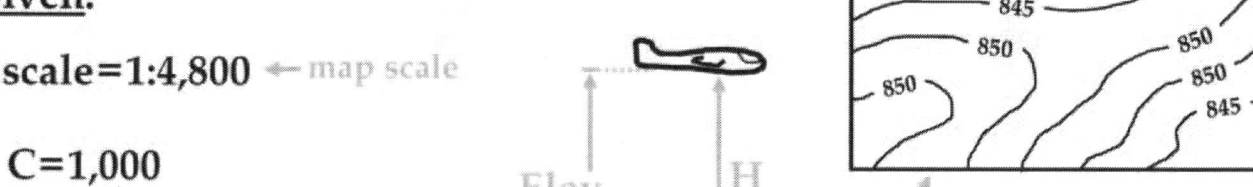

Find: Elev$_{plane}$ ← the elevation of the plane above the ground surface.

Given:

scale=1:4,800 ← map scale

C=1,000

the C-Factor of the stereoplotter

use sea level as a vertical datum

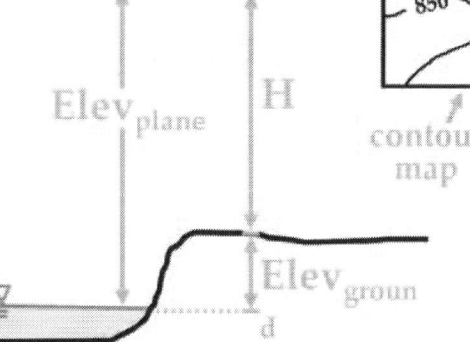

contour map

A) 2,920 [ft]

B) 4,200 [ft]

C) 5,000 [ft]

D) 5,840 [ft]

Photogrammetry #8

Find: FL$_{min}$ ← the minimum number of flight lines to cover the entire area.

Given:

FO=65% ← forward overlap

SO=30% ← side overlap

scale=1:6,000 ← map scale

Area=4[mi]×10[mi]

the total area to be photographed is 10 miles long by 4 miles wide.

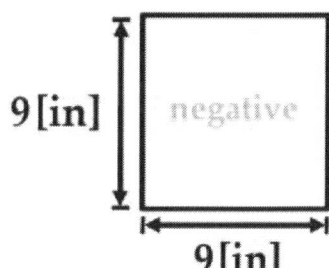

9[in]   negative

9[in]

f=6[in] ← focal length

A) 4

B) 5

C) 6

D) 7

Photogrammetry #9

Find: FO ← forward overlap between consecutive photos on the same flight line.

Given:

H=4,800[ft] ← map scale

f=12[in] ← focal length

air base=1,260[ft]

the distance the plane flies between taking consecutive photos.

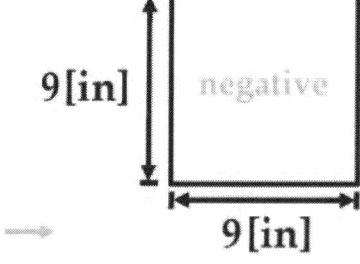

9[in]   negative

9[in]

air base

photo 1   photo 2

A) 60%

B) 65%

C) 70%

D) 75%

(page intentionally left blank)

Section 2: Detailed Solutions

(page intentionally left blank)

Horizontal Curves #1

Find: R [ft] ← the radius of the curve

Given:

L=50 [ft]

the length of the curve

C=45 [ft]

the long chord of the curve

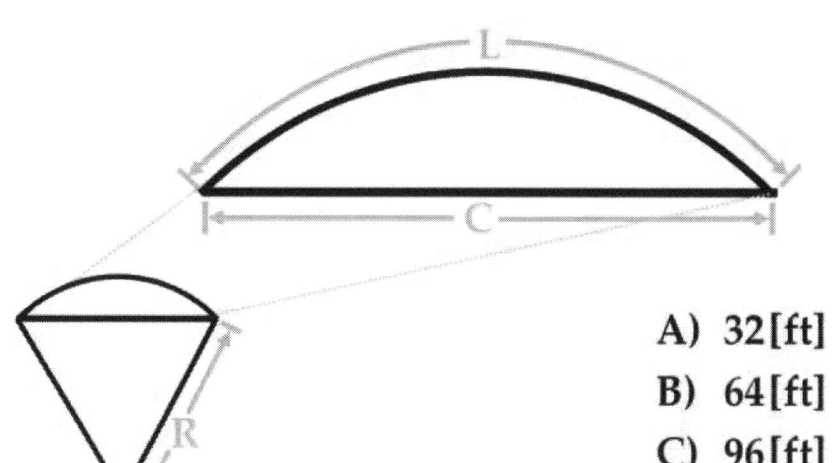

A) 32 [ft]

B) 64 [ft]

C) 96 [ft]

D) 128 [ft]

Analysis:

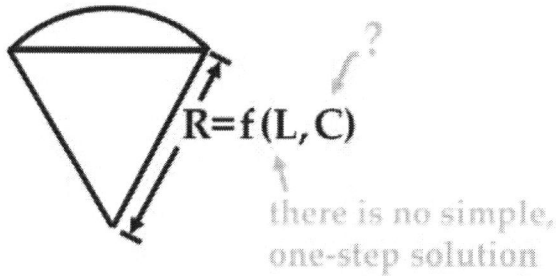

$R=f(L,C)$

?

there is no simple, one-step solution

Figure 1

Ideally, we would have an equation for the radius, as a function of chord length and curve length, but we don't.

Instead, we'll write out equations for curve length (eq.1) and chord length (eq.2), as a function of the radius of the curve.

radius → interior angle (in degrees)

$$L = \frac{2*\pi*R*I}{360°} \leftarrow eq.1$$

curve length

We have two equations (eq. 1 and eq.2) and two unknown variables (R and I)

interior angle

$$C=2*R*\sin\left(\frac{I}{2}\right) \leftarrow eq.2$$

chord length

We'll solve eq. 1 for I (see eq. 3) and then we'll substitute that value of I into eq.2

$$I = \frac{L*360°}{2*\pi*R} \leftarrow eq.3$$

Surveying Practice Problems

Horizontal Curves #1 (cont.)

$$I = \frac{L*360^\circ}{2*\pi*R}$$

$$C = 2*R*\sin\left(\frac{I}{2}\right) \leftarrow eq.2$$

Plug in the chord length and the curve length into eq. 4, and simplify.

$$L = 50\,[ft]$$

$$C = 2*R*\sin\left(\frac{L*360^\circ}{4*\pi*R}\right) \leftarrow eq.4$$

$$C = 45\,[ft]$$

We are left with one equation, and 1 unknown variable, R. However, solving for R may prove difficult.

$$45\,[ft] = 2*R*\sin\left(\frac{4,500\,[ft]}{\pi*R}\right)$$

Plug in each of the possible values of R. We'll choose the value of R which causes the right hand side of eq. 4 to be closest to 45 [ft]

possible solutions for R	the right-hand side of eq. 4 for each possible solution
A) 32 [ft] ⟶	45.1 [ft]
B) 64 [ft] ⟶	48.7 [ft]
C) 96 [ft] ⟶	49.4 [ft]
D) 128 [ft] ⟶	49.7 [ft]

The right hand side is closest to 45 feet when we select R=32 feet. Answer A is correct.

Answer: A

On multiple choice exams, never rule out working backwards from the possible solutions provided.

Horizontal Curves #2

<u>Find:</u> **M** ← middle ordinate, also called the
"horizontal sightline offset" (HSO)

<u>Given:</u>

R = 120 [m] ← the radius
of the curve

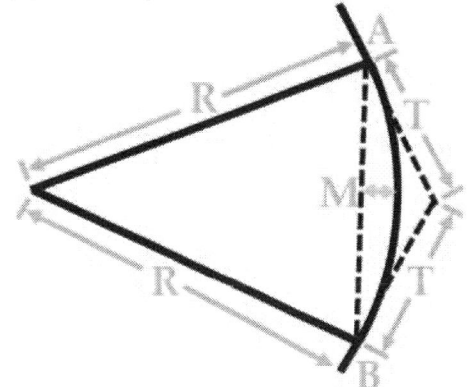

T = 40 [m] ← the tangent
distance

Points A and B represent the
beginning and end of the curve.

A) 2 [m]
B) 4 [m]
C) 6 [m]
D) 8 [m]

Analysis:

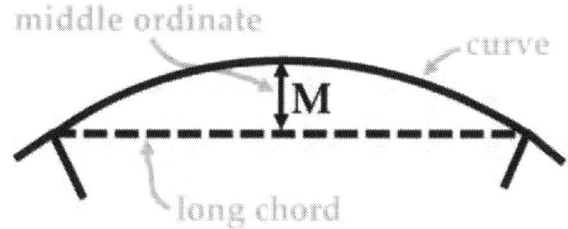

Figure 1

The middle ordinate is the distance
from the midpoint of the curve to the
midpoint of the long chord.

The long chord is the straight line
from the beginning of the curve to
the end of the curve.

$$M = R * \left(1 - \cos\left(\frac{I}{2}\right)\right) \leftarrow eq.\,1$$

We'll first write out the two most
common equations for the middle
ordinate, eq.1 and eq.2.

$$M = \left(\frac{C}{2}\right) * \tan\left(\frac{I}{4}\right) \leftarrow eq.\,2$$

Since we know R = 120 [m], we'll use
eq.1, not eq.2. That way, we only need
to determine the interior angle before
we can solve for M.

$$T = R * \tan\left(\frac{I}{2}\right) \leftarrow eq.\,3$$

Solve eq.3 for the interior angle, I.

Surveying Practice Problems

Horizontal Curves #2 (cont.)

$T=40\,[m]$

$$I = 2 * \tan^{-1}\left(\frac{T}{R}\right) \leftarrow eq.\,4$$

$R=120\,[m]$

Plug in the tangent distance and the radius into eq. 4, then solve for the interior angle.

$$I = 2 * \tan^{-1}\left(\frac{40\,[m]}{120\,[m]}\right)$$

$$I = 36.87^{\circ}$$

Return to eq. 1, plug in the values of I and R, then solve for M.

$R=120\,[m]$ $I=36.87^{\circ}$

$$M = R * \left(1 - \cos\left(\frac{I}{2}\right)\right) \leftarrow eq.\,1$$

$$M = 120\,[m] * \left(1 - \cos\left(\frac{36.87^{\circ}}{2}\right)\right)$$

$$M = 6.16\,[m]$$

When comparing M=6.16 [m] with the four possible solutions, the correct answer is most nearly 6 [m]

Answer: $\boxed{C}$

Horizontal Curves #3

Find: L_{AB} [ft] ← the length along the horizontal curve from point A to point B

Given:

Area=20,000[ft²] ← the area swept out by the curve (the shaded area)

R=200[ft] ← the radius of the curve

points A and B represent the beginning and end of the curve

A) 100[ft]
B) 150[ft]
C) 178[ft]
D) 200[ft]

Analysis:

possible solutions →

A) 100[ft]
B) 150[ft]
C) 178[ft]
D) 200[ft]

It's a good idea to look at the possible solutions before solving the problem.

don't let a "precise-looking" solution, such as 178 [ft], be a distraction.

We may be able to approximate the solution by making scaled drawings

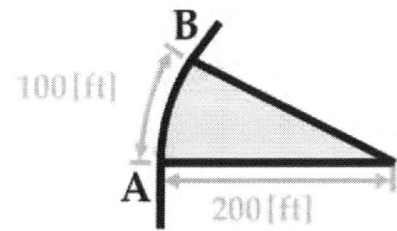

Figure 1

Figure 1 is a scaled drawing of a curve where R=200[ft], and L=100[ft]

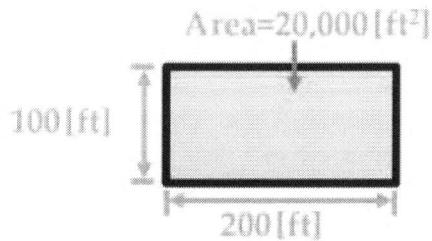

Figure 2

Figure 2 is a scaled drawing of a rectangle whose area is 20,000 square feet, and one side is 200 feet long.

Since the area inside the curve (Figure 1) is less than the area inside the rectangle (Figure 1), we know L is greater than 100[ft].

45

Surveying Practice Problems

Horizontal Curves #3 (cont.)

possible
solutions

~~A) 100[ft]~~

B) 150[ft]

C) 178[ft]

D) 200[ft]

We can rule out L=100 feet (Answer A) as a possible solution.

interior angle, in degrees

$$L = \frac{2*\pi*R*I}{360°} \leftarrow eq.1$$

Use eq. 1 to find the length of the curve. Since we already know the value of the radius, R, we just need to solve for the interior angle, I.

$$Area = A_{slice} = 20,000 [ft^2]$$

For notational convenience, we'll use "A_{slice}" to represent the area.

$$A_{slice} = \left(\frac{I}{360°}\right) * A_{circle} \leftarrow eq.2$$

The area, A_{slice}, equals a fraction of the area of a full circle.

$$I = \frac{A_{slice}*360°}{A_{circle}} \leftarrow eq.3$$

$A_{circle} = \pi * R^2$

Solve eq.2 for I, then plug in $\pi*R^2$ for A_{circle}

$A_{slice} = 20,000 [ft^2]$

$$I = \frac{A_{slice}*360°}{\pi*R^2} \leftarrow eq.4$$

$R = 200 [ft]$

After substituting in A_{slice} and R, solve for the interior angle.

$$I = \frac{20,000*360°}{\pi*(200[ft])^2}$$

Horizontal Curves #3 (cont.)

$$I = 57.3°$$

Return to eq.1, plug in R and I, then solve for the curve length, L

$R = 200 [ft]$

$$L = \frac{2 * \pi * R * I}{360°} \quad \leftarrow eq.1$$

$I = 57.3°$

$$L = \frac{2 * \pi * (200[ft]) * (57.3°)}{360°}$$

$$L = 200.0 [ft]$$

<u>Answer:</u> $\boxed{D}$

Surveying Practice Problems

Horizontal Curves #4

Find: STA$_B$ ← the stationing at point B

Given:

STA$_A$=42+51 ← the stationing at point A

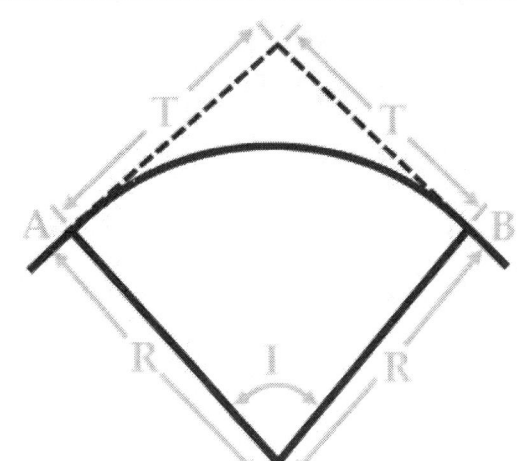

I=15°24′00″ ← interior angle

T=85 [ft] ← tangent distance

points A and B represent the beginning and end of the curve

A) 43+36

B) 44+20

C) 44+36

D) 48+80

Analysis:

$$STA_B = STA_A + L \quad \leftarrow eq.1$$

The stationing at point B equals stationing at point A plus the length of the curve.

$$STA_A = 42+51 = 4,251 \, [ft]$$

42+51 is converted to 4,251 feet.

$$L = \frac{2 * \pi * R * I}{360°} \quad \leftarrow eq.2$$

We'll use eq. 2 to solve for the length of the curve.

DMS notation:

seconds

$$I = 15°24′00″$$

degrees — minutes

Although not necessary, it is sometimes helpful to convert the interior angle, I, from degrees-minutes-seconds (DMS) notation, to decimal-degrees (DD) notation.

DD notation:

$$I = 15.4° \leftarrow degrees$$

where $0.4 = \dfrac{24\,[min]}{60\,[min/deg]} + \dfrac{0\,[sec]}{3,600\,[sec/deg]}$

48

Horizontal Curves #4 (cont.)

$$R = \frac{T}{\tan(I/2)} \leftarrow eq.3$$

T=85 [ft]

I=15.4°

Use eq. 3 to calculate the radius, from the tangent and the interior angle.

$$R = \frac{85\,[ft]}{\tan(15.4/2)^{\circ}}$$

Eq. 3 was derived from: T=R*tan (I/2)

$$R = 629\,[ft]$$

$$L = \frac{2 * \pi * R * I}{360^{\circ}} \leftarrow eq.2$$

R=629 [ft]   I=15.4°

Since we now know R and I, we'll use eq.2 to solve for the length, L.

$$L = \frac{2 * \pi * (629\,[ft]) * (15.4^{\circ})}{360^{\circ}}$$

$$L = 169\,[ft]$$

$$STA_B = STA_A + L \leftarrow eq.1$$

STA_A=4,251 [ft]   L=169 [ft]

Return to eq. 1, substitute in STA_A and L, then solve for STA_B

$$STA_B = 4{,}251\,[ft] + 169\,[ft]$$

$$STA_B = 4{,}420\,[ft]$$

Convert STA_B from feet, back to station notation.

$$STA_B = 44+20$$

Answer: **B**

Surveying Practice Problems

Horizontal Curves #5

<u>Find:</u> C_m (for L=100[ft])

find the minor chord length, for a segment of the curve 100[ft] long

"m" for "minor" chord

<u>Given:</u>

T=800[ft]

the tangent distance (for the entire curve)

C=500[ft]

the long chord (for the entire curve)

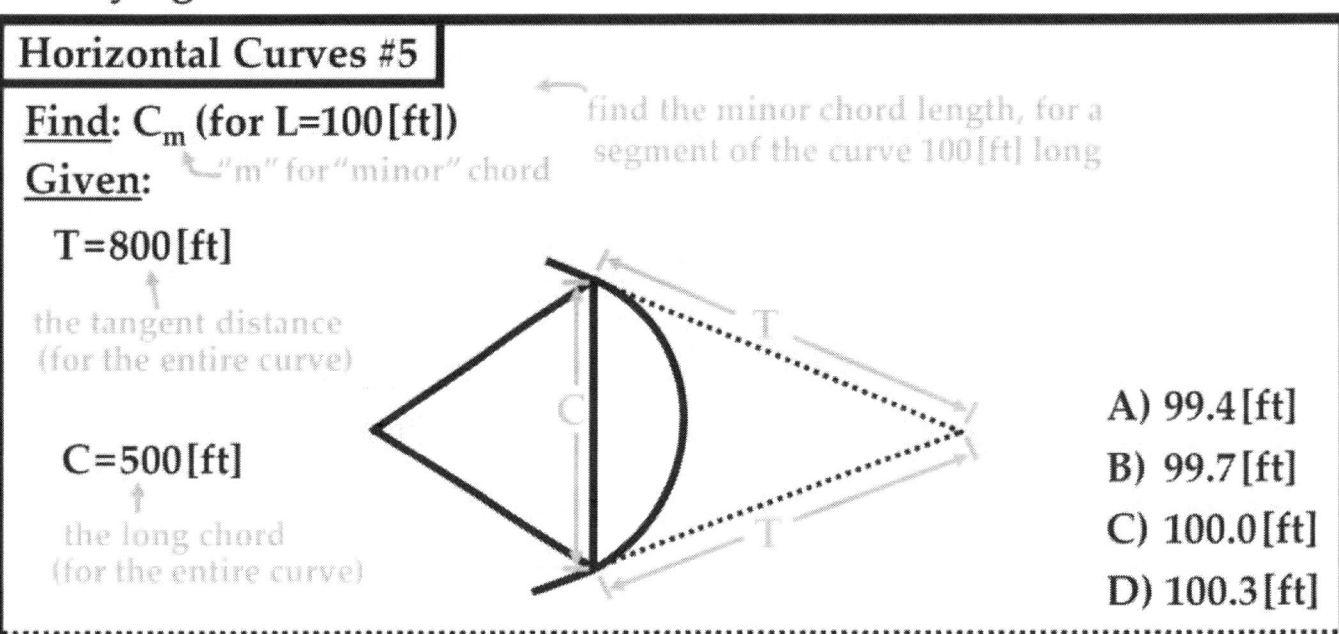

A) 99.4 [ft]
B) 99.7 [ft]
C) 100.0 [ft]
D) 100.3 [ft]

Analysis:

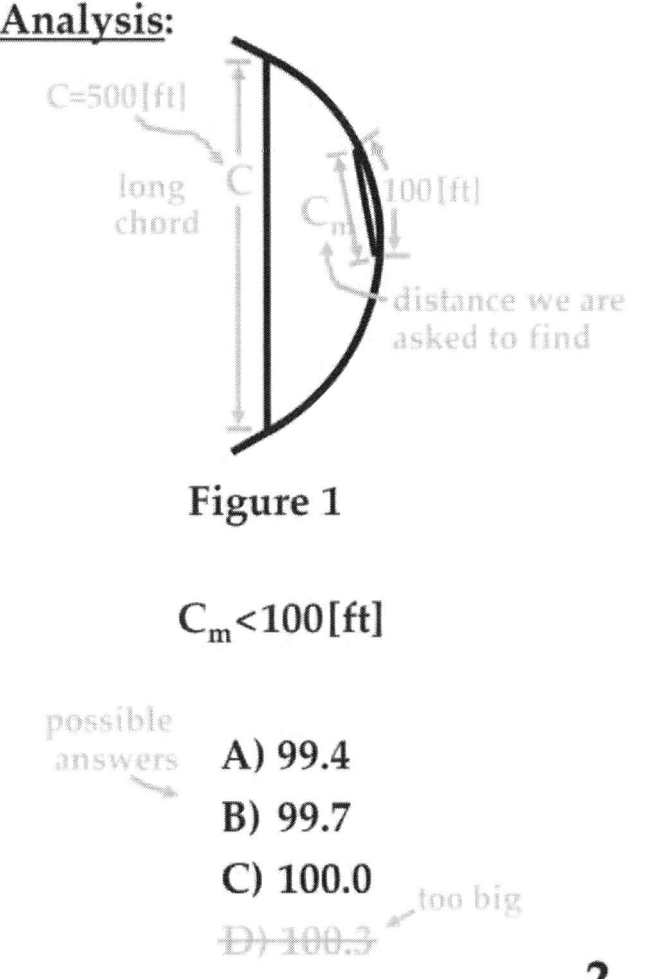

C=500[ft]

long chord

C_m

100[ft]

distance we are asked to find

Figure 1

We can rephrase the question as: "What is the length of a chord, whose endpoints are shared by a segment along the curve measuring 100 feet long."

Sketching out a curve can make it easier to understand exactly what the problem is asking for.

$C_m < 100$[ft]

From observation, the minor chord length, C_m, will be less than the length of the corresponding curve, which eliminates answer D.

possible answers

A) 99.4
B) 99.7
C) 100.0
~~D) 100.3~~ too big

Don't rule out answer C. If, for example, the value of C_m equals 99.95 feet, then we would select answer C, because it would still be the closest possible answer.

?

The value of 99.95 [ft] was chosen arbitrarily.

99.4   99.7   100.0
answer A   answer B   answer C

50

Horizontal Curves #5 (cont.)

chord length   interior angle

$$C = 2 * R * \sin\left(\frac{I}{2}\right) \leftarrow eq.1$$

If there is no subscript "m" on a variable C or I, then these variables refer to the chord length and interior angle for the entire curve.

after adding the subscript "m" to eq.1

$$C_m = 2 * R * \sin\left(\frac{I_m}{2}\right) \leftarrow eq.2$$

If we add the subscript "m", then variables C_m and I_m refer to the chord length and interior angle associated with the 100 foot curve length.

$$R = \frac{T}{\tan\left(\frac{I}{2}\right)} \leftarrow eq.3$$

We need to solve for both R and I_m, we'll first solve for R, using eq.3

In eq.3, we already know T, but we don't yet know I, the interior angle for the entire curve.

C=500[ft]

$$I = 2 * \cos^{-1}\left(\frac{C}{2*T}\right) \leftarrow eq.4$$

T=800[ft]

Use eq.4 to find the interior angle of the entire curve by plugging in the given values of C and T.

$$I = 2 * \cos^{-1}\left(\frac{500[ft]}{2*800[ft]}\right)$$

$$I = 143.6°$$

After solving for I, we'll return to eq. 3 and plug in T, the tangent, and I, the interior angle, to solve for R, the radius.

T=800[ft]

$$R = \frac{T}{\tan\left(\frac{I}{2}\right)} \leftarrow eq.3$$

I=143.6°

Unlike the chord length and interior angle, the radius does not have a subscript "m" because it is constant for all curve lengths and interior angles.

$$R = \frac{800[ft]}{\tan\left(\frac{143.6°}{2}\right)}$$

Surveying Practice Problems

Horizontal Curves #5 (cont.)

$$R = 263.0 \, [\text{ft}]$$

length of the
entire curve

$$I = \frac{L * 360^\circ}{2 * \pi * R} \leftarrow eq.5$$

interior angle
of the entire curve

To solve eq. 2 for C_m, we know R, but we still need to determine I_m.

Variable I_m represents the interior angle associated with an arc length of 100 [ft].

Eq. 5 is used to solve for I, when given variables L and R.

$$L_m = 100 \, [\text{ft}]$$

$$I_m = \frac{L_m * 360^\circ}{2 * \pi * R} \leftarrow eq.6$$

$$R = 263.0 \, [\text{ft}]$$

In eq. 6 we add the subscript "m" to make I_m and L_m. After substituting in the appropriate values, solve for I_m.

$$I_m = \frac{100 \, [\text{ft}] * 360^\circ}{2 * \pi * 263.0 \, [\text{ft}]}$$

$$I_m = 21.79^\circ$$

$$I_m = 21.79^\circ$$

$$C_m = 2 * R * \sin\left(\frac{I_m}{2}\right) \leftarrow eq.2$$

$$R = 263.0 \, [\text{ft}]$$

Return to eq. 2, plug in the radius and the "minor" interior angle, I_m, then solve for C_m

$$C_m = 2 * 263.0 \, [\text{ft}] * \sin\left(\frac{21.79^\circ}{2}\right)$$

Rounding errors may cause slight variations calculated values.

$$C_m = 99.42 \, [\text{ft}]$$

Choosing from the possible solutions, 99.42 [ft] is most nearly 99.4 [ft]. Answer A is correct.

Answer: | A |

Horizontal Curves #6

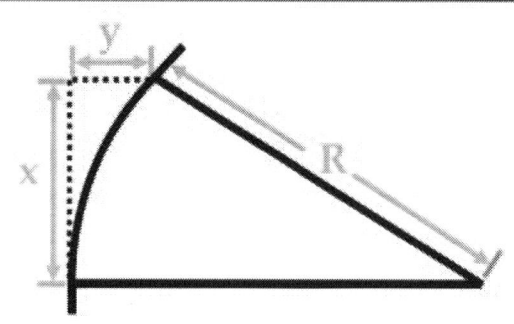

Find: R[m] ←— radius of the curve

Given:

x=65 [m] ←— tangent distance

↑
distance along the tangent
to a particular point

y=25 [m] ←— tangent ←— perpendicular distance
offset   from an extended tangent
to a point on the curve

A) 81 [m]
B) 97 [m]
C) 103 [m]
D) 109 [m]

Analysis:

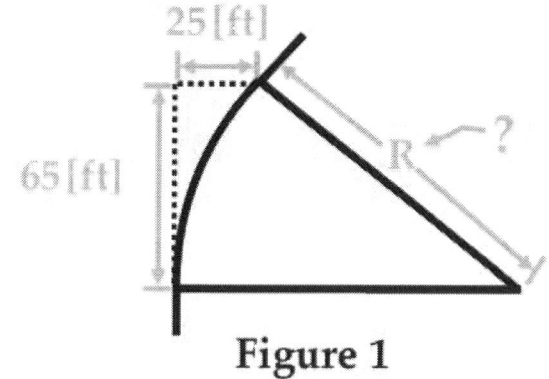

Figure 1

Figure 1 drawn approximately to
scale, but none of the the possible
solutions are obviously correct or
incorrect.

possible
solutions
{
A) 81 [m]
B) 97 [m]
C) 103 [m]
D) 109 [m]
}

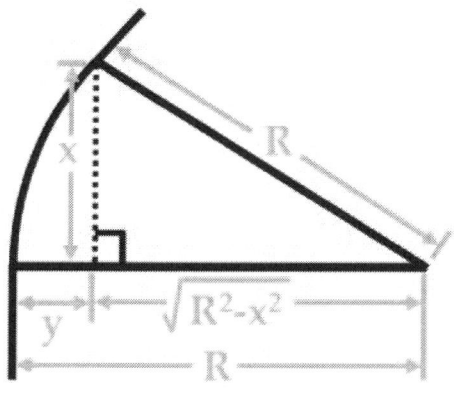

Figure 2

Using the Pythagorean Theorem, we
can solve the unknown side of the
right triangle, which equals $\sqrt{R^2-x^2}$

$R = y + \sqrt{R^2-x^2}$ ←— eq.1

From Figure 2, we can relate all
three variables in a single
equation, eq.1.

Surveying Practice Problems

Horizontal Curves #6 (cont.)

$$(R-y)^2 = R^2 - x^2 \leftarrow eq.2$$

From eq. 1, subtract y, then square both sides of the equation, which is allowed if R>x and R>y.

$$R^2 - 2*R*y + y^2 = R^2 - x^2 \leftarrow eq.3$$

cancel out the R^2 terms

Expand out the left side of eq. 2

Cancel out the R^2 term on each side of eq. 3.

x=65 [m]

$$R = \frac{x^2 + y^2}{2*y} \leftarrow eq.4$$

y=25 [m]

Plug in the given values of x and y into eq. 4, then solve for R.

$$R = \frac{(65\,[m])^2 + (25\,[m])^2}{2*(25\,[m])}$$

$$R = 97\,[m]$$

Answer: $\boxed{B}$

54

Horizontal Curves #7

Find: I ← interior angle

Given:

R=215 [m] ← radius of the curve

C=85 [m] ← long chord of the curve

the radius and long chord are
both given in units of meters

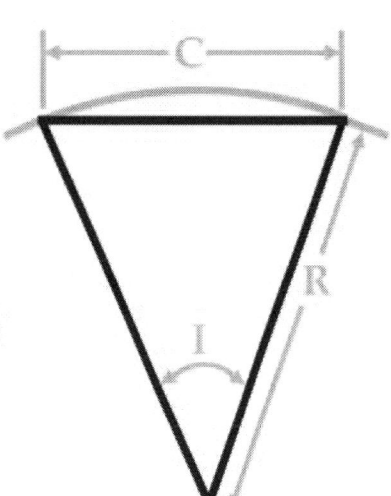

A) 0.4 [rad]

B) 0.8 [rad]

C) 23.0 [rad]

D) 46.0 [rad]

Analysis:

A) 0.4 [rad] ──→ 22.9°

B) 0.8 [rad] ──→ 45.8°

C) 23.0 [rad] ──→ 1318°

D) 46.0 [rad] ──→ 2636°

Looking at the possible solutions, we notice the units are in radians.

$$* \frac{180°}{\pi\,[\text{rad}]}$$ ← we can convert to units of degrees

It's good to be comfortable converting between degrees and radians.

A) 0.4 [rad] ← remaining possible solutions

B) 0.8 [rad] ←

C) 23.0 [rad] ← too large

D) 46.0 [rad] ← too large

We known right away that answers C and D are not correct because those angles are too large.

$$C=2*R*\sin\left(\frac{I}{2}\right) ← eq.1$$

Begin with eq. 1, and solve for I.

C=85 [m]

$$I=2*\sin^{-1}\left(\frac{C}{2*R}\right) ← eq.2$$

R=215 [m]

Plug in the chord length and radius into eq. 2, then solve for the interior angle, I.

Horizontal Curves #7 (cont.)

$$I = 2 * \sin^{-1}\left(\frac{85\,[m]}{2*215\,[m]}\right)$$

we can convert from degrees to radians by multiplying by $\frac{\pi\,[rad]}{180°}$

$$I = 0.398\,[rad]$$

The solution for I is most nearly 0.4 radians.

Answer: $\boxed{A}$

We can also solve this problem by using the law of cosines

Law of Cosines:

$$c^2 = a^2 + b^2 - 2*a*b*\cos C \leftarrow eq.3$$

In eq.3, a, b, and c represent the side lengths of the triangle. C represents the measure of the interior angle opposite side c.

substitute: $a = R$ ⟩ radius
$b = R$

$c = C \leftarrow$ long chord

$C = I \leftarrow$ interior angle

Plug in R, C and I, into eq.3.

$$C^2 = R^2 + R^2 - 2*R*R*\cos I \leftarrow eq.4$$

Solve eq.4 for I

$$I = \cos^{-1}\left(\frac{2*R^2 - C^2}{2*R^2}\right) \leftarrow eq.5$$

$R = 215\,[m]$ $C = 85\,[m]$

Plug in R=215 [m] and C=85 [m], into eq.5, and compute I.

$$I = \cos^{-1}\left(\frac{2*(215\,[m])^2 - (85\,[m])^2}{2*(215\,[m])^2}\right)$$

$$I = 0.398\,[rad]$$

Answer: $\boxed{A}$

Horizontal Curves #8

Find: STA_B ← the stationing at point B

Given:

$C=200[ft]$ ← the long chord of the curve

$\theta=78^{\circ}$ ← angle theta is not the same as the "interior angle"

$STA_A=3+44$

the stationing at point A

the curve begins at point A

the curve ends at point B

the "interior angle" is located at the center of the curve

A) 3+46

B) 5+43

C) 5+46

D) 5+50

Analysis:

$$STA_B=STA_A+L \leftarrow eq.1$$

The stationing at point B equals stationing at point A plus the length of the curve.

$$STA_A=3+44=344[ft]$$

3+44 can be converted to 344[ft], which represents the linear distance away from a datum point.

$$L=\frac{2*\pi*R*I}{360^{\circ}} \leftarrow eq.2$$

Use eq.2, to solve for the length of the curve, L.

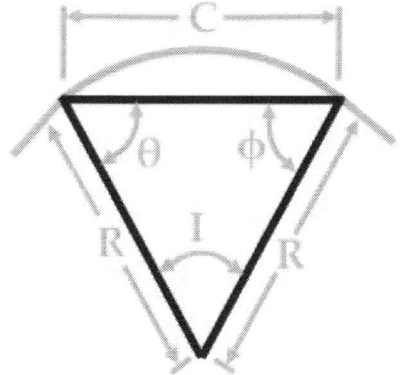

Figure 1

To solve eq.2 for L, we need to determine the radius, R, and the interior angle, I.

We'll define angle phi (ϕ), as the third interior angle in the triangle, as shown in Figure 1.

The sum of the interior angles of a triangle equals 180° degrees.

$$180^{\circ}=I+\phi+\theta \leftarrow eq.3$$

Solve eq.3 for I

Horizontal Curves #8 (cont.)

$$I = 180° - \phi - \theta \leftarrow eq.4$$

We know $\theta = 78°$ but we don't know the value of ϕ yet.

recall the law of sines

$$\frac{\sin A}{a} = \frac{\sin B}{b} = \frac{\sin C}{c} \leftarrow eq.5$$

Using the law of sines, we can prove that angle theta equals angle phi: $\theta = \phi$

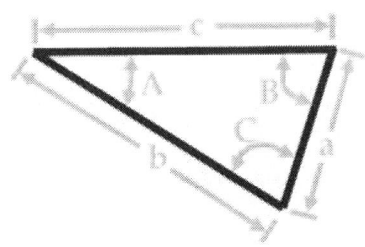

Figure 2

Figure 2 shows a generic triangle with side lengths a, b and c, and interior angles A, B and C.

After substituting in θ, ϕ, and R, into eq. 5, we arrive at eq. 6.

$$\frac{\sin \theta}{R} = \frac{\sin \phi}{R} \leftarrow eq.6$$

After cancelling out the radius term in eq. 6, R, and taking the arcsine of each side, we conclude $\theta = \phi$

$\phi = \theta$

$$I = 180° - \phi - \theta \leftarrow eq.4$$

Substitute θ in for ϕ in eq. 4.

$$I = 180° - 2*\theta \leftarrow eq.7$$

$\theta = 78°$

Plug in the given value of θ into eq. 7, then solve for I.

$$I = 180° - 2*78°$$

$$I = 24°$$

Horizontal Curves #8 (cont.)

Figure 3

Figure 3 shows a more accurate drawing of the triangle we are solving for, where I=24° and θ=78°.

$$C = 2*R*\sin\left(\frac{I}{2}\right) \leftarrow eq.8$$

To find the radius of the curve, start with eq.8, and solve for R.

$$R = \frac{C}{2*\sin\left(\frac{I}{2}\right)} \leftarrow eq.9$$

Plug in the known values of chord length and interior angle, into eq.9, then solve for the radius, R.

$$R = \frac{200\,[\text{ft}]}{2*\sin\left(\frac{24°}{2}\right)}$$

$$R = 481.0\,[\text{ft}]$$

After solving for R, we return to eq.2 to solve for the length of the curve, L.

$$L = \frac{2*\pi*R*I}{360°} \leftarrow eq.2$$

$$L = \frac{2*\pi*(481\,[\text{ft}])*(24°)}{360°}$$

Horizontal Curves #8 (cont.)

$$L = 201.5 \, [ft]$$

$STA_A = 344 \, [ft]$ $L = 201.5 \, [ft]$

$$STA_B = STA_A + L \leftarrow eq.\ 1$$

$$STA_B = 344 \, [ft] + 201.5 \, [ft]$$

$$STA_B = 545.5 \, [ft]$$

$$STA_B = 5+45.5$$

Answer: $\boxed{C}$

Horizontal Curves #9

Find: L_{JH} ← the length along curve JK, from point J to point H

Given:

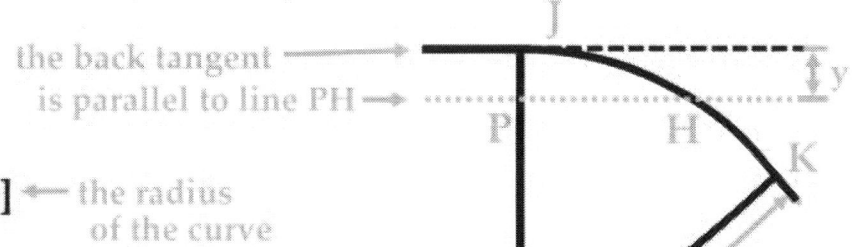

R=700[ft] ← the radius of the curve

y=100[ft] ← the tangent offset

the back tangent is parallel to line PH

A) 360[ft]
B) 370[ft]
C) 374[ft]
D) 378[ft]

Analysis:

$$L = \frac{2*\pi*R*I}{360^\circ} \leftarrow eq.1$$

The length of a horizontal curve is a function of the radius, R, and the interior angle, I.

$$L_{JH} = \frac{2*\pi*R*I_{JH}}{360^\circ} \leftarrow eq.2$$

Since we're looking for the length along the curve from point J to point H, we'll add a subscript "JH" to the L and I terms, in eq.2.

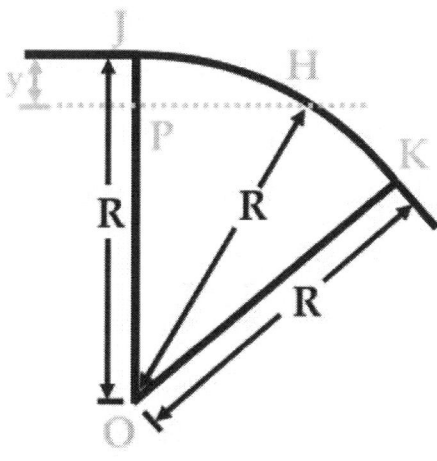

Figure 1

In Figure 1, we'll define the center of the curve as point O.

Horizontal curves have a constant radius, which means the length from point O to any point on the curve equals the radius, R.

Horizontal Curves #9 (cont.)

$$L_{PO} = R - y \leftarrow eq.3$$

From Figure 1, we can solve for the length of line segment PO.

$$L_{PO} = 700 [ft] - 100 [ft]$$

Substitute in the values of R and y, into eq.3, and solve for L_{PO}.

$$L_{PO} = 600 [ft]$$

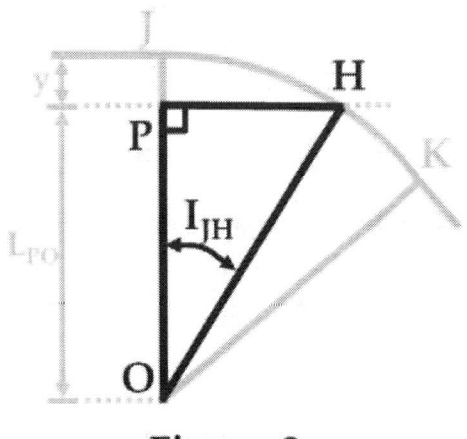

Figure 2

Next we'll draw out triangle POH, and identify angle I_{JH}

Triangle POH is a right triangle, so we can use right triangle trigonometry to solve for angle I_{JH}

$$I_{JH} = \cos^{-1}\left(\frac{L_{PO}}{L_{OH}}\right) \leftarrow eq.4$$

L_{OH} is equivalent to the radius of the curve, 700 feet.

$$I_{JH} = \cos^{-1}\left(\frac{600 [ft]}{700 [ft]}\right)$$

$$I_{JH} = 31.0^{\circ}$$

Next, we'll return to eq.2, plug in R and I_{JH}, and solve for L_{JH}

$$L_{JH} = \frac{2 * \pi * R * I_{JH}}{360^{\circ}} \leftarrow eq.2$$

Horizontal Curves #9 (cont.)

$$L_{JH} = \frac{2 * \pi * (700\,[ft]) * (31.0°)}{360°}$$

$$L_{JH} = 378.8\,[ft]$$

Answer: $\boxed{D}$

Surveying Practice Problems

Horizontal Curves #10

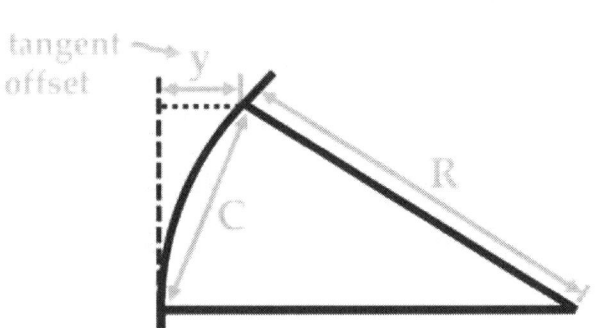

Find: y ← tangent offset

Given:

R=1,000[ft]

↖ the radius
of the curve

C=1,800[ft] ← the long chord
of the curve

A) 600[ft]
B) 620[ft]
C) 780[ft]
D) 1,620[ft]

Analysis:

$$y=R-R*\cos(I) \leftarrow eq.1$$

To find the tangent offset, we'll use eq. 1, which depends on the radius, R, and the interior angle, I.

$$C=2*R*\sin(I/2) \leftarrow eq.2$$

Eq. 2 relates the interior angle to C and R (the two variables provided in the problem statement).

C=1,800[ft]

$$I=2*\sin^{-1}\left(\frac{C}{2*R}\right) \leftarrow eq.3$$

R=1,000[ft]

Solve eq. 2 for I, then plug in the curve length and radius, then solve for the interior angle, I.

$$I=2*\sin^{-1}\left(\frac{1,800[ft]}{2*1,000[ft]}\right)$$

$$I=128.3^{\circ}$$

The calculated interior angle is much larger than drawing provided in the problem statement.

Horizontal Curves #10 (cont.)

tangent offset

y

In Figure 1, the long chord and radius are drawn to scale, and I=128.3° appears correct.

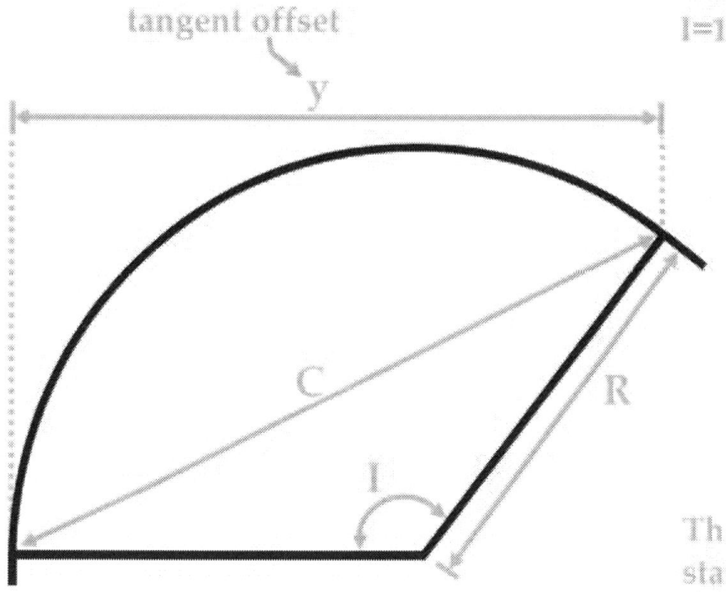

C

R

I

Recall the given values:
C=1,800[ft]
R=1,000[ft]

The sketch in the problem statement may be misleading, because it is not drawn to scale. Trust the numbers first.

Figure 1

I=128.3°

$$y=R-R*\cos(I) \leftarrow eq.1$$

R=1,000[ft]

Substitute in the radius and interior angle into eq.1, then solve for the tangent offset.

$$y=1,000[ft]-1,000[ft]*\cos(128.3°)$$

$$y=1,620[ft]$$

Answer: $\boxed{D}$

Surveying Practice Problems

Horizontal Curves #11

Find: y ← tangent offset

Given:

$R_1 = 400 [ft]$ ← radius of the smaller curve

$L_{AB} = 150 [ft]$

length along the smaller curve from point A from point B

$L_{AP} = 100 [ft]$

A) 145 [ft]
B) 165 [ft]
C) 185 [ft]
D) 465 [ft]

Analysis:

$$y = R_2 * \sin(I) \leftarrow eq.1$$

larger radius   interior angle

The tangent distance equals the larger radius times the sine of the interior angle.

$$L_{AP} = 100 [ft]$$

$$R_2 = R_1 + L_{AP} \leftarrow eq.2$$

$$R_1 = 400 [ft]$$

In this problem both curves share the same interior angle, I.

R_2 represents the radius of the larger curve, and can be calculated using eq.2.

$$R_2 = 400 [ft] + 100 [ft]$$

$$R_2 = 500 [ft]$$

To compute the interior angle, we'll solve eq.3 for I.

$$L = \frac{2 * \pi * R * I}{360°} \leftarrow eq.3$$

In eq.3, the angle I is in units of degrees.

$$L_{AB} = 150 [ft]$$

$$I = \frac{L_{AB} * 360°}{2 * \pi * R_1} \leftarrow eq.4$$

$$R_1 = 400 [ft]$$

Next we'll add the subscript "AB" to the length variable, and the subscript 1 to the radius.

Horizontal Curves #11 (cont.)

$$I = \frac{150 \, [ft] * 360^{\circ}}{2 * \pi * 400 \, [ft]}$$

$$I = 21.49^{\circ}$$

After plugging in the L_{AB} and R_1, we solve for I.

$$y = R_2 * \sin(I) \leftarrow eq.1$$

with $I = 21.49^{\circ}$ and $R_2 = 500 \, [ft]$

Return to eq.1, plug in R_2 and I, then solve for y.

$$y = 500 \, [ft] * \sin(21.49^{\circ})$$

Of the four possible solutions, 183.1 [ft] is most nearly 185 [ft]

$$y = 183.1 \, [ft]$$

Answer: $\boxed{C}$

Surveying Practice Problems

Horizontal Curves #12

Find: A_{slice} ← the area inside the horizontal curve

Given:

$y=75 \, [ft]$ ← the tangent offset

$x=250 \, [ft]$ ← the tangent distance

The horizontal curve begins at point A, and ends at point B.

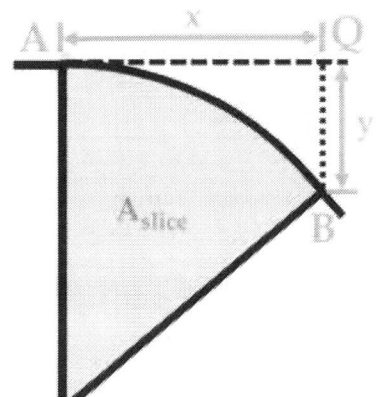

A) $6*10^2 \, [ft^2]$
B) $6*10^3 \, [ft^2]$
C) $6*10^4 \, [ft^2]$
D) $6*10^5 \, [ft^2]$

Analysis:

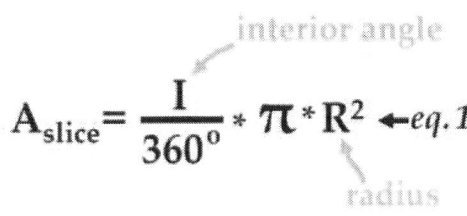

$$A_{slice}= \frac{I}{360^\circ} * \pi * R^2 \leftarrow eq.1$$

interior angle ← I

radius ← R

The area of the slice equals a fraction of the area of a circle, of radius R. See eq. 1.

area of a circle $= \pi * R^2$

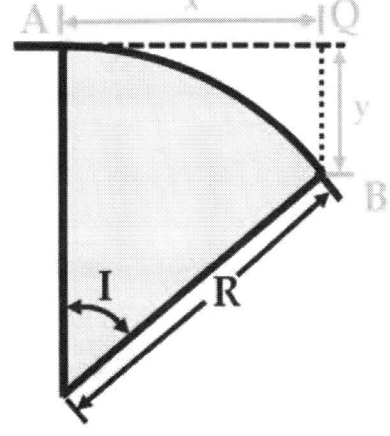

Figure 1

Figure 1 shows the interior angle, I, and the radius, R.

The interior angle and the radius are the two variables we need in eq. 1, to solve for A_{slice}.

$$I=2*\alpha \leftarrow eq.2$$

To solve for angle I, we'll use eq. 2. where angle α is identified in Figure 2.

Horizontal Curves #12 (cont.)

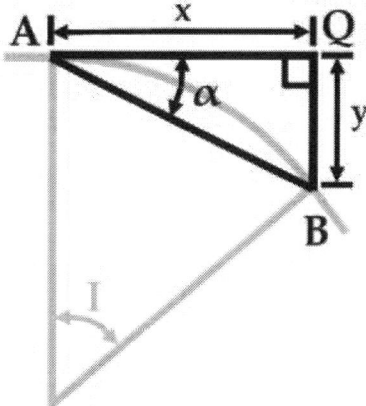

Figure 2

Angle α is the same as Angle QAB, and can be found by using eq.3.

Triangle ABQ is a right triangle, therefore we can use right triangle trigonometry equations to solve for sides and angles.

y=75[ft]   x=250[ft]

$$\alpha=\tan^{-1}(y/x) \leftarrow eq.3$$

Substitute in x and y, into eq.3, then solve for angle α.

$$\alpha=\tan^{-1}(75[ft]/250[ft])$$

$$\alpha=16.70^{\circ}$$

α=16.70°

$$I=2*\alpha \leftarrow eq.2$$

$$I=33.40^{\circ}$$

Return to eq.2, plug in angle α, and solve for the interior angle.

$$C=2*R*\sin(I/2) \leftarrow eq.4$$

To solve for the radius, we'll start with eq.4, and solve for R.

$$R=\frac{C}{2*\sin(I/2)} \leftarrow eq.5$$

Horizontal Curves #12 (cont.)

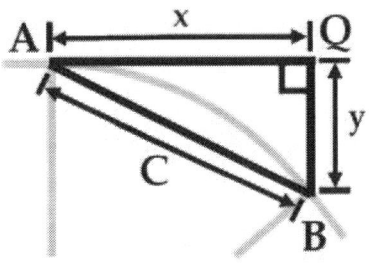

Figure 3

The long chord, C, is the straight line distance between points A and B.

We can solve for C by using the Pythagorean Theorem, in eq. 6.

$$C=\sqrt{x^2+y^2} \leftarrow eq.6$$

x=250 [ft]   y=75 [ft]

Substitute in the values of x and y, then solve for C.

$$C=\sqrt{(250\,[ft])^2+(75\,[ft])^2}$$

$$C=261\,[ft]$$

Return to eq. 5, plug in C and I, then solve for the radius, R.

C=261 [ft]

$$R=\frac{C}{2*\sin(I/2)} \leftarrow eq.5$$

I=33.4°

$$R=\frac{261\,[ft]}{2*\sin(33.4/2)^{\circ}}$$

$$R=454.1\,[ft]$$

Horizontal Curves #12 (cont.)

$$A_{slice} = \frac{I}{360°} * \pi * R^2 \leftarrow eq.1$$

$I=33.4°$

$R=454.1\,[ft]$

Return to eq.1, plug in the values for I and R, then solve for A_{slice}.

$$A_{slice} = \frac{33.4°}{360°} * \pi * (454.1\,[ft])^2$$

$$A_{slice} = 60,103\,[ft^2]$$

$60,103\,[ft^2]$ is approximately $6*10^4\,[ft^2]$, therefore the correct answer is C.

Answer: | C |

When the possible solutions vary by a factor of 10, we can be less precise with our intermediate calculations.

Surveying Practice Problems

Vertical Curves #1

<u>Find:</u> g_2 [%] ← departing grade

<u>Given:</u>

$STA_A=0+45$
$Elev_A=143.7$ [ft]

← station and elevation data for point A and point B

$STA_B=1+57$
$Elev_B=146.0$ [ft]

$L=300$ [ft]
↑
length of the curve

$R=-2$ [%/STA] ← rate of grade change

L

g1

B

vertical curve extends from point B to point C

C   g2

A

A) -6 %

B) -4 %

C) -2 %

D)   8 %

......

Analysis:

approach grade

$g_2=g_1+R*L$ ← eq.1

departing grade

Eq.1 relates the change in grade, the rate of grade change, and the length of the curve.

Since we've been provided the values of R and L, we'll solve for g_1, using eq.2.

$Elev_B=146.0$ [ft] $Elev_A=143.7$ [ft]

$$g_1=\frac{Elev_B-Elev_A}{STA_B-STA_A} \leftarrow eq.2$$

$STA_B=157$ [ft] $STA_A=45$ [ft]

In eq.2, the stationing was converted to feet.

$STA_A=1+57 \longrightarrow 157$ [ft]
$STA_B=0+45 \longrightarrow 45$ [ft]

$$g_1=\frac{146.0 \,[ft]-143.7\,[ft]}{157\,[ft]-45\,[ft]}$$

$g_1=0.0205*100\%$

Convert a decimal to a percent by multiplying by 100%

$g_1=2.05\%$

Vertical Curves #1 (cont.)

$R = -2\,[\%/STA]$

$$g_2 = g_1 + R * L \quad \leftarrow eq.\,1$$

$g_1 = 2.05\,\%$

$3\,[STA]$

$L = 300\,[ft]$

return to eq. 1, substitute in the approach grade, the length of the curve and the rate of grade change, then solve for g_2.

Convert feet to stations before plugging the length into eq. 1.

$$g_2 = 2.05\,\% + (-2\,[\%/STA]) * 3\,[STA]$$

$$g_2 = -3.95\,\%$$

Answer: $\boxed{B}$

-3.95% is most nearly -4%, choose answer B.

Surveying Practice Problems

Vertical Curves #2

<u>Find:</u> STA_B ← the stationing at point B

<u>Given:</u>

$STA_A = 42+00$
$Elev_A = 147 [ft]$

The station and elevation at point A and point C

$STA_C = 52+00$
$Elev_C = 143 [ft]$

The vertical curve begins at point A and ends at point C.

$g_1 = -4\%$

approach grade

$g_2 = 2\%$

departing grade

A) 44+00
B) 46+00
C) 48+00
D) 50+00

....

Analysis:

$$STA_B = STA_A + d_{AB} \leftarrow eq.1$$

The stationing at point B equals the stationing a point A plus the horizontal distance between points A and B.

$$STA_A = 42+00 = 4,200 [ft]$$

$$STA_C = 52+00 = 5,200 [ft]$$

It may be easier to convert the stationing to feet, as we determine the value of d_{AB}.

$$STA_A < STA_B < STA_C \leftarrow ieq.1$$

From observation, the stationing at point B will be between the stationing at points A and C.

A) 44+00 ⟶ 4,400 [ft]
B) 46+00 ⟶ 4,600 [ft]
C) 48+00 ⟶ 4,800 [ft]
D) 50+00 ⟶ 5,000 [ft]

We can also convert the possible solutions to a length.

Since all possible solutions are between STA_A and STA_C, we cannot rule out any answers yet.

Point B is located at the intersection of Line AB and Line BC.

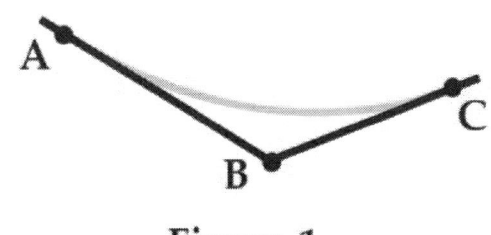

Figure 1

Vertical Curves #2 (cont.)

$$y = m * x + b \leftarrow eq.2$$

slope   y-intercept

Recall the equation of a line.

elevation
of line AB d_{AX}

$$y = m * x + b \leftarrow eq.3$$

g_1 $Elev_A$

Use eq.2 to develop an equation for Line AB, by substituting in the variables shown in eq.3.

Variable d_{AX} is the distance from point A to a point of interest X.

$Elev_A = 147 \,[ft]$

$$Elev_{AB} = g_1 * d_{AX} + Elev_A \leftarrow eq.4$$

$g_1 = -0.04$

Plug in the known values of g_1 and $Elev_A$, into eq.4.

$$Elev_{AB} = -0.04 * d_{AX} + 147 \,[ft] \leftarrow eq.5$$

equation for Line AB

Write a similar equation for line BC

elevation
of line BC d_{CX}

$$y = m * x + b \leftarrow eq.3$$

$-g_2$ $Elev_C$

Return to eq.3. This time plug in $-g_2$, d_{bc} and $Elev_C$.

Use $-g_2$ instead of g_2 for variable m to reverse the station direction.

$Elev_A = 143 \,[ft]$

$$Elev_{BC} = -g_2 * d_{CX} + Elev_C \leftarrow eq.6$$

$g_2 = 0.02$

Variable d_{CX} is the distance from point C to a point of interest X. Where point X is upstation from point C.

$$Elev_{BC} = -0.02 * d_{CX} + 143 \,[ft] \leftarrow eq.7$$

equation for Line BC

Vertical Curves #2 (cont.)

Set eq. 5 and eq. 7 to solve for the elevation at point B by plugging in $Elev_B$, d_{AB} and d_{CB} as shown.

$Elev_B$

d_{AB}

$$Elev_{AB} = -0.04 * d_{AX} + 147 \text{[ft]} \leftarrow eq.5$$

$$Elev_{BC} = -0.02 * d_{CX} + 143 \text{[ft]} \leftarrow eq.7$$

d_{CB}

Equate the right hand sides of eq. 5 and eq. 7, then simplify.

$$-0.04 * d_{AB} + 147 \text{[ft]} = -0.02 * d_{CB} + 143 \text{[ft]} \leftarrow eq.8$$

RHS of eq. 5   RHS of eq. 7

$$0.04 * d_{AB} - 0.02 * d_{CB} = 4 \text{[ft]} \leftarrow eq.9$$

From Figure 2, we know the sum of d_{AB} and d_{CB} equals the difference between STA_A and STA_C.

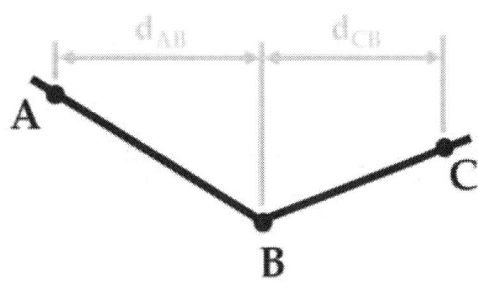

d_{AB} d_{CB}

A

C

B

Figure 2

Substitute in the given values of STA_A and STA_C, then solve for $d_{AB} + d_{BC}$.

$STA_C = 5,200 \text{[ft]}$

$$d_{AB} + d_{BC} = STA_C - STA_A \leftarrow eq.10$$

$STA_A = 4,200 \text{[ft]}$

$$d_{AB} + d_{BC} = 5,200 \text{[ft]} - 4,200 \text{[ft]}$$

At this point we have 2 unknown variables (d_{AB} and d_{BC}), and 2 equations (eq. 9 and eq. 11)

$$d_{AB} + d_{BC} = 1,000 \text{[ft]} \leftarrow eq.11$$

Vertical Curves #2 (cont.)

Solve eq. 11 for d_{BC}.

$$d_{BC} = 1,000\,[ft] - d_{AB} \leftarrow eq.12$$

Substitute the right hand side of eq. 12 into d_{BC} of eq. 9.

$$0.04 * d_{AB} - 0.02 * d_{BC} = 4\,[ft] \leftarrow eq.9$$

$$d_{BC} = \overline{1,000\,[ft] - d_{AB}}$$

Solve eq. 9 for d_{AB}.

$$0.04 * d_{AB} - 0.02 * (1,000\,[ft] - d_{AB}) = 4\,[ft]$$

$$0.06 * d_{AB} = 24\,[ft]$$

$$d_{AB} = 400\,[ft]$$

Point B is 400 feet down-station from point A.

$$d_{AB} = 400\,[ft]$$

$$STA_B = STA_A + d_{AB} \leftarrow eq.1$$

$$STA_A = 4,200\,[ft]$$

Return to eq. 1, plug in STA_A and d_{AB}, then solve for STA_B.

$$STA_B = 4,200\,[ft] + 400\,[ft]$$

$$STA_B = 4,600\,[ft]$$

Convert the units of feet, to stations.

$$STA_B = 46+00$$

Answer: $\boxed{B}$

Surveying Practice Problems

Vertical Curves #3

Find: Elev_{min} [m] ← minimum elevation of the curve

Given:

beginning and end of the vertical curve

g_1 A   C g_2

$R= 4 \left[\dfrac{\%}{100\,[m]} \right]$ ← rate of grade change

$\text{Elev}_C = 727.8\,[m]$ ← elevation at point C

$g_2 = 6\%$ ← departing grade

$L_{AC} = 300\,[ft]$ ← the length of the vertical curve

A) 718.8 [m]
B) 723.3 [m]
C) 732.3 [m]
D) 736.8 [m]

Analysis:

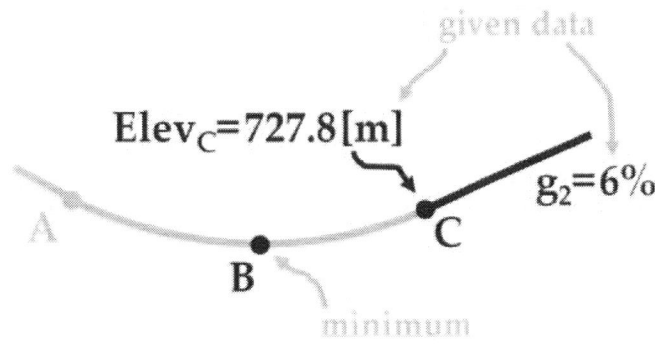

given data

$\text{Elev}_C = 727.8\,[m]$

$g_2 = 6\%$

A

B

C

minimum

The problem provides the departing grade and the elevation at point C.

We'll define a point B, located at the minimum elevation on the curve. Therefore $\text{Elev}_{min} = \text{Elev}_B$.

$\text{Elev}_B < \text{Elev}_C$ ← *ieq. 1*

$\text{Elev}_C = 727.8\,[m]$

Since $g_2 > 0$, then the minimum elevation along the curve (at Elev_B) is less than the the elevation at the end of the curve (at Elev_C).

$\text{Elev}_B < 727.8\,[m]$

possible solutions

A) 718.8 [m]
B) 723.3 [m]
C) 732.3 [m]
D) 736.8 [m]

too big

We can rule out two of the possible solutions because we know Elev_B is less than 727.8 [m].

Vertical Curves #3 (cont.)

A) 718.8 [m]

B) 723.3 [m]

Now we only have to decided between 718.8 [m] and 723.3 [m].

Eq. 1 computes the elevation of point B on vertical curve AC.

$$Elev_B = 0.5*R*x_{BC}^2 - g_2*x_{BC} + Elev_C \leftarrow eq.1$$

rate of grade change

x_{BC} is the distance between points B and C

$g_2 = 6\%$

$$x_{BC} = \frac{g_2}{R} \leftarrow eq.2$$

$R = 4 [\%/100[m]]$

Since we know point B is at the minimum elevation, we can solve for x_{BC} using eq. 2.

$$x_{BC} = \frac{6\%}{4[\%/100[m]]}$$

$$x_{BC} = 150 [m]$$

The distance between point B and point C is 150 meters.

In eq. 1, plug in variables R, x_{BC}, g_2, and $Elev_C$, and solve for $Elev_B$.

$R = 0.0004 [m^{-1}]$ $g_2 = 0.06$

$$Elev_B = 0.5*R*x_{BC}^2 - g_2*x_{BC} + Elev_C \leftarrow eq.1$$

$x_{BC} = 150 [m]$ $Elev_C = 727.8 [m]$

Convert the units of R:
$4[\%/100[m]] = 0.0004 [m^{-1}]$

$$Elev_B = 0.5*0.0004[m^{-1}]*(150[m])^2$$
$$-0.06*150[m] + 727.8[m]$$

g_2 was converted from a percent to a decimal value.

$6\% = 0.06$

$$Elev_B = 723.3 [m] \qquad \underline{Answer:} \quad \boxed{B}$$

Surveying Practice Problems

Vertical Curves #4

Find: g_D ← the grade at point D

Given:

approach grade ⤵

$g_1 = 3.5\%$

$g_2 = -2.2\%$ ⤸ departing grade

$STA_A = 3+22$
$STA_B = 5+15$
$STA_C = 5+59$
$STA_D = 6+00$

the stationing for points A, B, C and D

A) -0.6%

B) -1.0%

C) -1.4%

D) -1.8%

g_1 g_2

maximum elevation

Analysis:

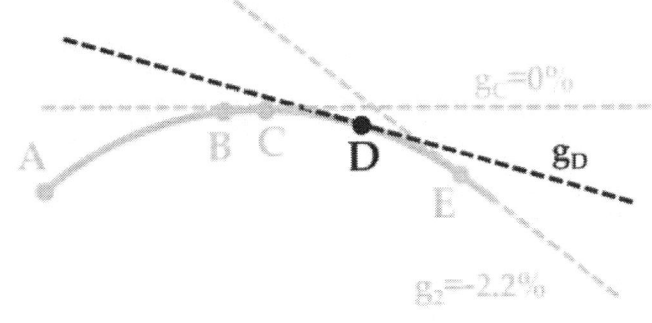

Figure 1

$g_C = 0\%$

g_D

$g_2 = -2.2\%$

From Figure 1, we notice the grade at point D will be between -2.2% and 0%

$$-2.2\% < g_D < 0\%$$

All four possible solutions are between -2.2% and 0%.

approach grade ⤸

$$g_D = g_1 + L_{AD} * R \;\leftarrow eq.1$$

rate of grade change

From eq.1, we can find the grade at point D by knowing g_1, L_{AD} and R.

$STA_D = 600[ft]$ ↓

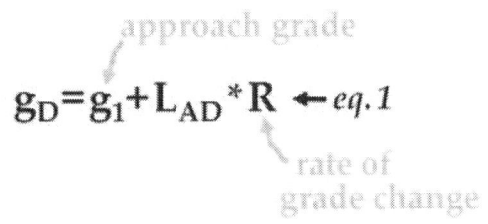

$$L_{AD} = STA_D - STA_A \leftarrow eq.2$$

$STA_A = 322[ft]$

Use eq.2, to find L_{AD}.

$$L_{AD} = 600[ft] - 322[ft]$$

Convert the station units of 3+22 and 6+00, to lengths of 322[ft] and 600[ft], and solve for L_{AD}.

$$L_{AD}=278[ft]$$

$$g_D=g_1+L_{AD}*R \leftarrow eq.1$$

Next we'll solve for R, the rate of grade change. Solve eq.1 for R.

$$R= \frac{g_2-g_1}{L_{AE}} \leftarrow eq.3$$

In eq.3, we'll add a subscript "AE" to the length term, L, to specify the entire length of the curve.

$$STA_B=515[ft]$$

$$L_{AE}=2*(STA_B-STA_A) \leftarrow eq.4$$

$$STA_A=322[ft]$$

Since we know $g_C=0$, we could have also found R by using $R=-g_1/L_{AC}$

Solve eq.4 for length L_{AE}

$$L_{AE}=2*(515[ft]-322[ft])$$

$$L_{AE}=386[ft]$$

$$g_2=-2.2\% \qquad g_1=3.5\%$$

$$R= \frac{g_2-g_1}{L_{AE}} \leftarrow eq.3$$

$$L_{AE}=386[ft]$$

Return to eq.3, and solve for R, the rate of grade change.

$$R= \frac{-2.2\%-(3.5\%)}{386[ft]}$$

$$R=-0.0148[\%/ft]$$

-0.0148[%/ft] means that for every foot along the vertical curve, the grade decreases by 0.0148%

Surveying Practice Problems

Vertical Curves #4 (cont.)

$g_1 = 3.5\%$ $R = -0.0148\,[\%/ft]$

$$g_D = g_1 + L_{AD} * R \leftarrow eq.1$$

$L_{AD} = 278\,[ft]$

Return to eq.1, plug in g_1, L_{AD} and R, then solve for g_D.

$$g_D = 3.5\% + 278\,[ft] * (-0.0148\,[\%/ft])$$

$$g_D = -0.61\%$$

-0.61% is most nearly -0.6%

Answer: $\boxed{A}$

Select answer A.

Vertical Curves #5

<u>Find:</u> STA_C ← the station at point C

<u>Given:</u>

STA_A=2+54 ← station and

$Elev_A$=127.0 [ft] ← elevation data

$Elev_C$=127.4 [ft]

g_1=-1.8% ← approach grade

R=0.6 $\left[\dfrac{\%}{STA}\right]$ ← rate of grade change

L_{AB}=540 [ft] ← curve length, from point A to point B

continues at a constant slope

A

B

g_1 g_2

L_{AB}

A) 7+45

B) 7+84

C) 8+32

D) 8+91

Analysis:

$Elev_C$=127.4 [ft]

Find the station at point C. Since we already know $Elev_C$, we'll write out the equations for $Elev_C$.

if $STA_C \leq STA_B$:

$Elev_C$=0.5*R*L_{AC}^2+g_1*L_{AC}+$Elev_A$ ← *eq.1*

STA_C=STA_A+L_{AC} ← *eq.2*

if $STA_C \geq STA_B$:

$Elev_C$=$Elev_B$+g_2*L_{BC} ← *eq.3*

STA_C=STA_B+L_{BC} ← *eq.4*

To find STA_C, we should use either eq.2 or eq.4, depending on whether or not STA_C is less than or greater than STA_B.

We can solve for L_{AC} using eq.1, or L_{BC} using eq.2.

STA_A=254 [ft]

STA_B=STA_A+L_{AB} ← *eq.5*

Use eq.5 to solve for STA_B.

L_{AB}=540 [ft]

STA_B=254 [ft]+540 [ft]

Vertical Curves #5 (cont.)

$$STA_B=794\,[\text{ft}]$$

$$STA_B=7+94$$

Next we'll compare $STA_B=7+94$, with the four possible solutions for STA_C.

possible solutions
for STA_C
_____

A) 7+45 ⎫
        ⎬ $STA_C \leq STA_B$
B) 7+84 ⎭

←7+94 ←STA_B

C) 8+32 ⎫
        ⎬ $STA_C \geq STA_B$
D) 8+89 ⎭

If we assume STA_C is either answer A or answer B, then $STA_C < STA_B$, and we would use eq.1 and eq.2.

If we assume STA_C is either answer C or answer D, then $STA_C > STA_B$, and we would use eq.3 and eq.4.

To start, we'll assume either answer C or answer D is correct.

if $STA_C \geq STA_B$:

$$STA_C=STA_B+L_{BC} \quad \leftarrow eq.4$$

Solve eq.4 for L_{BC}.

$$L_{BC}=STA_C-STA_B \quad \leftarrow eq.6$$

$L_{BC}=STA_C-STA_B$

Plug in L_{BC} into eq.3.

$$Elev_C=Elev_B+g_2 {}^*L_{BC} \quad \leftarrow eq.3$$

$$Elev_C=Elev_B+g_2 {}^*(STA_C-STA_B) \quad \leftarrow eq.7$$

In eq.7, we need to solve for $Elev_B$ and g_2, before we can check if 8+32 (answer C) or 8+89 (answer D) are solutions for STA_C.

$L_{AB}=540\,[\text{ft}]$

$$g_2=g_1+L_{AB} {}^*R \quad \leftarrow eq.8$$

$g_1=-1.8\%$ $R=0.006\%\,[\text{ft}^{-1}]$

Use eq.8 to solve for g_2.

Vertical Curves #5 (cont.)

$g_2 = -1.8\% + 540[ft] * 0.006\%[ft^{-1}]$

$g_2 = 1.44\%$

Be comfortable converting the units for R, the rate change of grade:

$0.6[\%/STA] = 0.006\%[ft^{-1}]$
$= 0.006[STA^{-1}]$
$= 0.00006[ft^{-1}]$

$g_1 = -0.018$ $Elev_A = 127[ft]$

$Elev_B = 0.5 * R * L_{AB}^2 + g_1 * L_{AB} + Elev_A \leftarrow eq.9$

$R = 0.00006[ft^{-1}]$ $L_{AB} = 540[ft]$

Next we'll use eq.9 to solve for $Elev_B$.

$Elev_B = 0.5 * 0.00006[ft^{-1}] * (540[ft])^2 + (-0.018) * 540[ft] + 127[ft]$

$Elev_B = 126.0[ft]$

Solve eq.7 for STA_C. Plug in the variables on the right hand side of eq.10. Then calculate STA_C.

$Elev_C = 127.4[ft]$ $STA_B = 794[ft]$

$$STA_C = \frac{Elev_C - Elev_B + g_2 * STA_B}{g_2} \leftarrow eq.10$$

$Elev_B = 126.0[ft]$ $g_2 = 0.0144$

$$STA_C = \frac{127.4[ft] - 126.0[ft] + 0.0144 * 794[ft]}{0.0144}$$

$STA_C = 981.2[ft]$

$STA_C = 9+81.2$

<u>Answer:</u> $\boxed{D}$

Vertical Curves #6

<u>Find:</u> $Elev_C$ ← the elevation at point C

<u>Given:</u>

$g_1 = 1.5\%$ ← approach grade

$L_{AB} = 200 [ft]$ ← curve length

$STA_A = 5+49$
$Elev_A = 233.2 [ft]$
$STA_C = 7+94$ ← station and elevation data

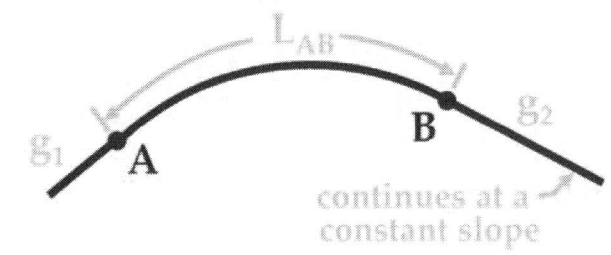

$R = -1 [\%/STA]$

the rate of change of the grade, along the vertical curve

A) 233.0 [ft]
B) 233.2 [ft]
C) 234.0 [ft]
D) 234.2 [ft]

<u>Analysis:</u>

if $STA_C \leq STA_B$:

$$Elev_C = 0.5*R*L_{AC}^2 + g_1*L_{AC} + Elev_A \leftarrow eq.1$$

if $STA_C \geq STA_B$:

$$Elev_C = g_2*L_{BC} + Elev_B \leftarrow eq.2$$

Eq.1 computes the elevation of point C if STA_C is on the vert-ical curve (if $STA_C \leq STA_B$).

Eq.2 computes the elevation of point C if STA_C is not on the vertical curve (if $STA_C > STA_B$).

use eq.1 if point C is in this range → ← use eq.2 if point C is in this range →

We'll first solve for STA_B to determine if we should use eq.1 or eq.2 to calculate $Elev_C$.

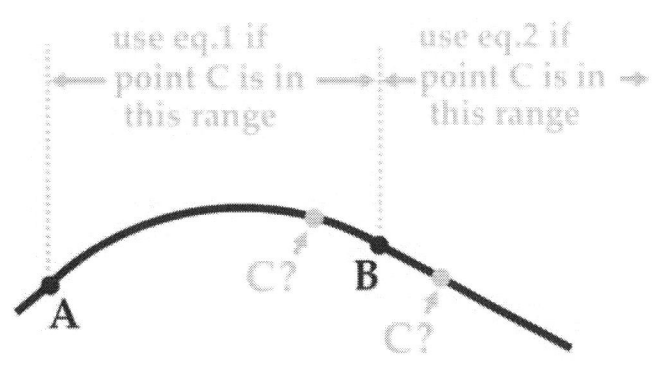

Figure 1

$STA_A = 549 [ft]$ $L_{AB} = 200 [ft]$

$$STA_B = STA_A + L_{AB} \leftarrow eq.3$$

Use eq.3 to solve for STA_B.

$$STA_B = 549[ft] + 200[ft]$$

Vertical Curves #6 (cont.)

$STA_B = 749 [ft]$

$STA_B = 7+49$

Since $STA_C > STA_B$, we'll use eq.2 to solve for $Elev_C$.

Figure 2

$Elev_C = g_2 * L_{BC} + Elev_B \quad \leftarrow eq.2$

Before we can use eq.2 to solve for $Elev_C$, we first need to determine the values of g_2, L_{BC} and $Elev_B$.

$g_1 = 1.5\%$ $\qquad L_{AB} = 2[STA]$

$g_2 = g_1 + R * L_{AB} \leftarrow eq.4$

$R = -1\%[STA^{-1}]$

Use eq.4. to compute g_2.

In eq.4, the units of length, L_{AB}, were converted from feet to stations: $200[ft] = 2[STA]$

$g_2 = 1.5\% + (-1\%[STA^{-1}]) * 2[STA]$

$g_2 = -0.5\%$

$STA_C = 794[ft]$

$L_{BC} = STA_C - STA_B \leftarrow eq.5$

$STA_B = 749[ft]$

In eq.5, plug in STA_C and STA_B, then solve for L_{BC}.

Convert stations units to feet:
$STA_C = 7+94 \longrightarrow 794[ft]$
$STA_B = 7+49 \longrightarrow 749[ft]$

$L_{BC} = 794[ft] - 749[ft]$

$L_{BC} = 45[ft]$

Surveying Practice Problems

Vertical Curves #6 (cont.)

$L_{AB}=200[ft]$

Use eq.6 to solve for $Elev_B$.

$$Elev_B = 0.5 * R * L_{AB}^2 + g_1 * L_{AB} + Elev_A \leftarrow eq.6$$

$R = -0.0001[ft^{-1}]$

$g_1 = 0.015$

$Elev_A = 233.2[ft]$

$$Elev_B = 0.5 * (-0.0001[ft^{-1}]) * (200[ft])^2 + 0.015 * 200[ft] + 233.2[ft]$$

$$Elev_B = 234.2[ft]$$

$L_{BC} = 45[ft]$

$$Elev_C = g_2 * L_{BC} + Elev_B \leftarrow eq.2$$

Return to eq.2, and solve for $Elev_C$.

$g_2 = -0.005$

$Elev_B = 234.2[ft]$

In eq.2, g_2 is converted from percent to decimal: $-0.5\% = -0.005$

$$Elev_C = -0.005 * 45[ft] + 234.2[ft]$$

$$Elev_C = 234.0[ft]$$

Answer: $\boxed{C}$

Vertical Curves #7

Find: STA_C ←the stationing, at point C

Given:

g_1=1.5% ←approach grade

g_2=-1.4% ←departing grade

STA_A=1+22 ←the station at point A

$Elev_A$=28.4[ft] ←the elevation at
$Elev_C$=29.0[ft] ←point A and point C

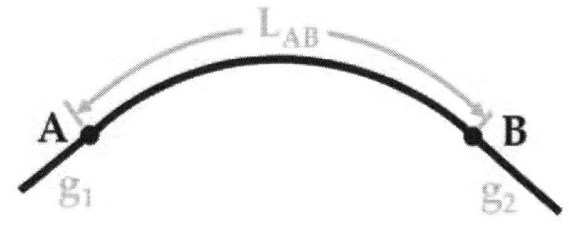

L_{AB}=450[ft]
↑
curve
length

A) 1+66

B) 2+18

C) 3+47

D) 4+17

Analysis:

Figure 1 shows the general shape of the vertical curve. The curve may cross $Elev_C$ twice, as pictured.

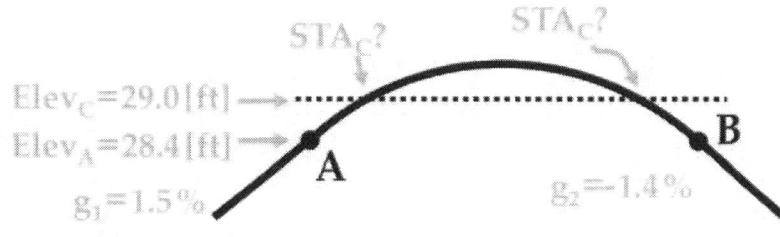

Figure 1

$$STA_C=STA_A+L_{AC} \leftarrow eq.1$$

Station C equals Station A plus the length between stations A and C.

Solve eq.2 and solve for L_{AC}.

$$Elev_C=0.5*R*L_{AC}^2+g_1*L_{AC}+Elev_A \leftarrow eq.2$$

Since eq.2 is quadratic, L_{AC} in eq.3 will have 2 solutions.

$$L_{AC}=\frac{-g_1 \pm \sqrt{g_1^2-4*(0.5*R)*(Elev_A-Elev_C)}}{2*(0.5*R)} \leftarrow eq.3$$

To solve eq.3, we need to determine R, the rate change in grade.

Surveying Practice Problems

Vertical Curves #7 (cont.)

$g_2 = -1.4\%$ $g_1 = 1.5\%$

$$R = \frac{g_2 - g_1}{L_{AB}} \leftarrow eq.4$$

$L_{AB} = 450\,[ft]$

Plug in g_1, g_2 and L_{AB} into eq.4, then solve for R.

$$R = -0.00644\,[\%/ft]$$

It's good practice to preserve at least 3 significant figures at all intermediate steps. Preserve at least 4 significant figures if the first significant figure is 1.

$$R = -6.44*10^{-5}\,[ft^{-1}]$$

Convert R to units of (decimal) change in grade per foot.

$R = -6.44*10^{-5}\,[ft^{-1}]$

Return to eq.3, plug in the known values, then solve for L_{AC}.

$$L_{AC} = \frac{-g_1 \pm \sqrt{g_1^2 - 4*(0.5*R)*(Elev_A - Elev_C)}}{2*(0.5*R)} \leftarrow eq.3$$

$g_1 = 0.015$

$Elev_A = 28.4\,[ft]$

$Elev_C = 29.0\,[ft]$

$$L_{AC} = \frac{-(0.015) \pm \sqrt{\begin{array}{c}(0.015)^2 - 4*(0.5*(-6.44*10^{-5}\,[ft^{-1}])) \\ *(28.4\,[ft] - 29.0\,[ft])\end{array}}}{2*(0.5*(-6.44*10^{-5}\,[ft^{-1}]))}$$

$$L_{AC} = 44.3\,[ft],\ 421.6\,[ft]$$

The vertical curve passes through $Elev_C = 29.0\,[ft]$ twice, because both computed values of L_{AC} are less than L_{AB}.

$STA_A = 122\,[ft]$ $L_{AC} = 44.3\,[ft]$

$$STA_C = STA_A + L_{AC} \leftarrow eq.1$$

$$STA_C = 122\,[ft] + 44.3\,[ft]$$

Returning to eq.1, we'll first try $L_{AC} = 44.3\,[ft]$ as the correct distance between station A and station C.

$$STA_C = 166.3\,[ft] \longrightarrow 1+66.3$$

<u>Answer:</u> $\boxed{A}$

Vertical Curves #8

Find: How many times does the curve pass through elevation=150[ft]

(no sketch provided)

Given: elevation at
point A — point A is located at the beginning of the curve

$Elev_A=156.2[ft]$

$STA_A=44+29$ — stationing at point A

$g_1=-3.2\%$ — approach grade

$R=1[\%/STA]$
rate change of grade
in percent per station

$L=250[ft]$ — curve length

A) 0

B) 1

C) 2

D) not enough
information

. . . .

Analysis:

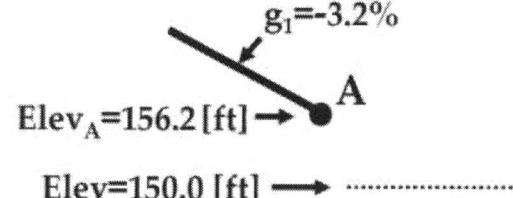

$g_1=-3.2\%$

$Elev_A=156.2[ft] \rightarrow$ A

$Elev=150.0[ft] \longrightarrow$ ....

Figure 1

Figure 1 shows the elevation of point A, and the elevation of 150.0 feet.

It can be helpful to make a sketch of the problem, when no sketch is provided.

Find: n

We'll define n as the number of times the curve passes through elevation 150[ft].

case 1:

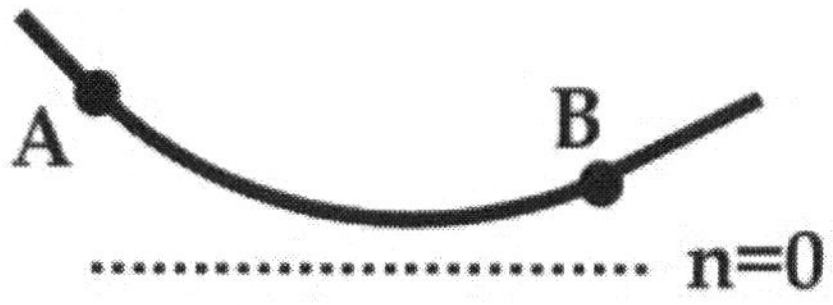

A   B

.... n=0

Figure 2

Define point B as the point at the end of the curve.

Brainstorm all the ways the curve could look and the corresponding value of n.

case 2:

A   B

.... n=1

Figure 3

In case 2, the minimum elevation of the curve is exactly 150.0 feet.

Surveying Practice Problems

Vertical Curves #8 (cont.)

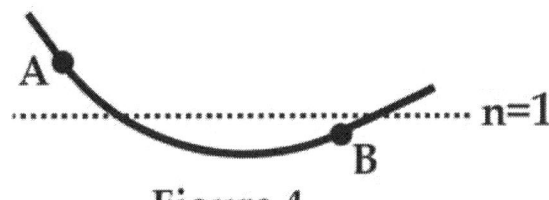

Figure 4

Figure 5

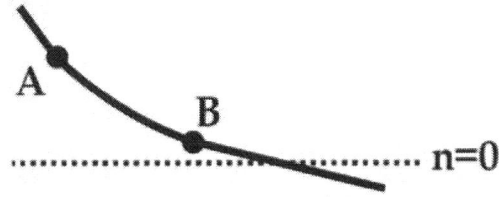

Figure 6

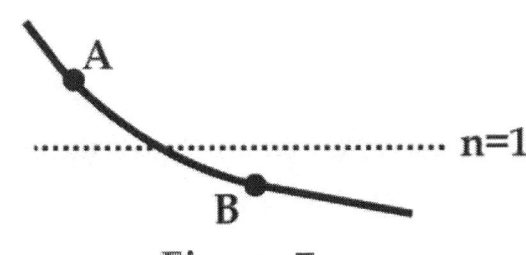

Figure 7

$g_1=-3.2\%$ $R=1\,[\%/STA]$

$$g_2=g_1+L*R \leftarrow eq.1$$

$L=2.5\,[STA]$

Using eq. 1, plug in the approach grade, the curve length and the rate grade of change, then solve for the departing grade.

Convert $L=250\,[ft]$ to $L=2.5\,[STA]$

$$g_2=-3.2\%+2.5\,[STA]*1\%\,[STA^{-1}]$$

$$g_2=-0.7\%$$

Since $g_2<0$, we know the curve looks like either case 5 or case 6 (see Figure 6 and Figure 7, above).

A) 0

B) 1

~~C) 2~~

D) **not enough
information**

We can eliminate answer C from the possible solutions.

Next, we must determine the elevation at the end of the vertical curve, at point B.

Vertical Curves #8 (cont.)

If $Elev_B > 150.0$ [ft], then $n=0$
If $Elev_B \leq 150.0$ [ft], then $n=1$

$L_{AC} = 250$ [ft]

$$Elev_B = 0.5*R*L_{AC}^2 + g_1*L_{AC} + Elev_A \leftarrow eq.2$$

0.0001 [ft^{-1}]

$g_1 = -0.032$

$Elev_A = 156.2$ [ft]

$$Elev_B = 0.5*0.0001 [ft^{-1}]*(250 [ft])^2$$
$$+ (-0.032)*250 [ft] + 156.2 [ft]$$

Use eq.2 to calculate $Elev_B$, the elevation at the end of the curve.

$$Elev_B = 151.3 [ft]$$

The vertical curve ends above 150 [ft], therefore the curve never passes through elevation 150 [ft], and $n=0$.

Case 5:

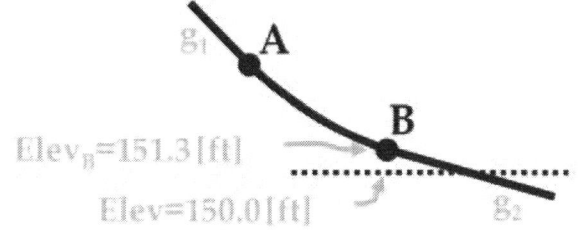

g_1

A

B

$Elev_B = 151.3$ [ft]

$Elev = 150.0$ [ft]

g_2

Figure 8

$n=0$

Answer: $\boxed{A}$

Surveying Practice Problems

Vertical Curves #9

Find: g_1 ← approach grade

Given:

$g_2 = -2\%$ ← departing grade

$R = -1[\%/STA]$
↑ rate of grade change along vertical curve

$M = 3.125[ft]$
↑ middle ordinate

the vertical curve begins at point A and ends at point B.

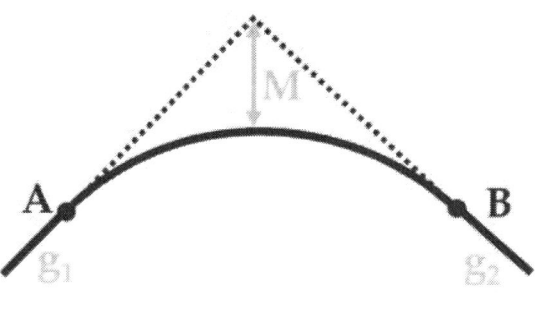

A) 0%
B) 1%
C) 2%
D) 3%

Analysis:

absolute value bars

$$M = \frac{|g_2 - g_1| * L}{8} \leftarrow eq.1$$
↑ middle ordinate

Eq.1 computes the middle ordinate based on the approach grade, departing grade and curve length.

Since R<0, we know g_1>g_2 and we can remove the absolute value bars in eq. 1, if we switch the variables g_1 and g_2.

$$M = \frac{(g_1 - g_2) * L_{AB}}{8} \leftarrow eq.2$$

In eq.2, we'll add the subscript "AB" to the length to specify the entire length of the curve.

$$L_{AB} = \frac{g_2 - g_1}{R} \leftarrow eq.3$$

Plug in the value of L_{AB} (from eq.3) into eq.2, and simplify.

$$M = \frac{(g_1 - g_2) * (g_2 - g_1)}{8 * R} \leftarrow eq.4$$

Write out eq.4 as a quadratic equation with respect to g_1.

$$0 = g_1^2 - 2 * g_2 * g_1 + g_2^2 + 8 * M * R \leftarrow eq.5$$

Vertical Curves #9 (cont.)

Use the quadratic equation to solve for g_1.

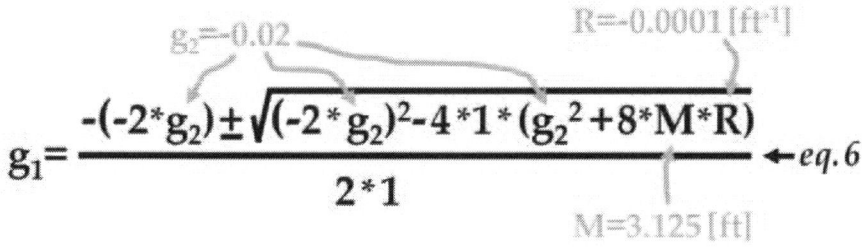

$$g_1 = \frac{-(-2*g_2) \pm \sqrt{(-2*g_2)^2 - 4*1*(g_2^2 + 8*M*R)}}{2*1} \leftarrow eq.6$$

$g_2 = -0.02$

$R = -0.0001\,[\text{ft}^{-1}]$

$M = 3.125\,[\text{ft}]$

$$g_1 = \frac{-(-2*(-0.02)) \pm \sqrt{\begin{array}{l}(-2*(-0.02))^2 - \{4*1*((-0.02)^2 \\ \qquad + 8*3.125\,[\text{ft}]*(-0.0001\,[\text{ft}^{-1}]))\}\end{array}}}{2*1}$$

$g_1 = -7\%, 3\%$

too small

We know -7% is not the correct answer because if R<0, then $g_1 > g_2$.

$g_1 = 3\%$

Choose answer D for $g_1 = 3\%$.

Answer: $\boxed{\text{D}}$

Surveying Practice Problems

Vertical Curves #10

<u>Find:</u> STA_B ← stationing at point B

<u>Given:</u>

$R=1[\%/STA]$ ← rate of grade change

$STA_A=1+45.2$
$Elev_A=97.60[ft]$ } station and elevation data for point A and point C.
$STA_C=4+88.1$
$Elev_C=96.09[ft]$

$g_1=-0.01$ ← approach grade (as a decimal)

The vertical curve begins at point B, and ends at point C.

A) 2+66

B) 2+92

C) 3+21

D) 3+76

Analysis:

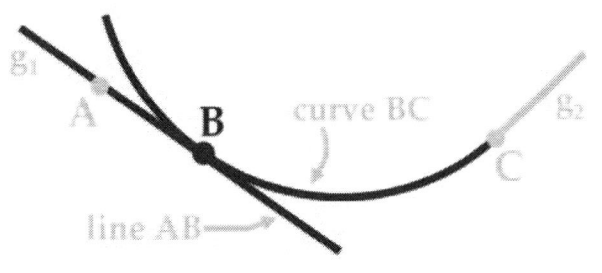

Figure 1

Station B is located at the intersection of line AB, and curve BC.

We can solve for STA_B by defining equations for line AB and curve BC, and then solving for the two unknown variables, STA_B and $Elev_B$.

$L_{AB}=STA_B-STA_A$

$Elev_B=Elev_A+g_1*L_{AB}$ ←eq.1

Plug in the elevation of point A, the approach grade, and the stationing at point A, into eq. 1.

$Elev_B=Elev_A+g_1*(STA_B-STA_A)$

Solve for the elevation at point B, in terms of the stationing at point B.

$Elev_B=97.60[ft]-0.01*(STA_B-145.2[ft])$

Vertical Curves #10 (cont.)

$Elev_B = 99.05\,[ft] - 0.01 * STA_B \leftarrow eq.2$

Eq. 3 is the equation for curve BC.

$Elev_C = 0.5 * R * L_{BC}^2 + g_1 * L_{BC} + Elev_B \leftarrow eq.3$

Rather than solve eq.2 and eq.3 simultaneously, we'll guess one of the four solutions, use eq.2 to solve for $Elev_B$, then check $Elev_C$ using eq.3.

A) 2+66

B) 2+92 ← **our first guess**

C) 3+21

D) 3+76

When guessing and checking on a multiple choice exam, it may be best to first guess one of the middle solutions from a sorted list. (i.e. choose B or C)

(assumed)
$STA_B = 2+92 \rightarrow 292\,[ft]$

$STA_B = 292\,[ft]$

$Elev_B = 99.05\,[ft] - 0.01 * STA_B \leftarrow eq.2$

After converting units from stations to feet, we plug in our assumed STA_B into eq.2 and solve for $Elev_B$.

$Elev_B = 99.05\,[ft] - 0.01 * 292\,[ft]$

$Elev_B = 96.13\,[ft]$

$STA_B = 292\,[ft]$

$L_{BC} = STA_C - STA_B \leftarrow eq.4$

$STA_C = 488.1\,[ft]$

Use eq.4 to solve for L_{BC}, the length of the vertical curve (assuming $STA_C = 2+92$).

$L_{BC} = 488.1\,[ft] - 292\,[ft]$

Vertical Curves #10 (cont.)

$$L_{BC} = 196.1 [ft]$$

$g_1 = -0.01$ $Elev_A = 96.13 [ft]$

$$Elev_C = 0.5 * R * L_{BC}^2 + g_1 * L_{BC} + Elev_B \leftarrow eq.3$$

$R = 0.0001 [ft^{-1}]$ $L_{BC} = 196.1 [ft]$

Plug in R, g_1, L_{BC} and $Elev_B$ into eq.3, then solve for $Elev_C$ (based on our assumption that $STA_B = 2+92$).

$$Elev_C = 0.5 * (0.0001 [ft^{-1}]) * (196.1 [ft])^2 + (-0.01) * 196.1 [ft] + 96.13 [ft]$$

$$Elev_C = 96.09 [ft]$$

Our calculated $Elev_C$ matches the given $Elev_C$ value of 96.09 feet. Our first guess of $STA_C = 2+92$ was correct. Select answer B.

Answer: B

If the calculated value of $Elev_C$ from eq.3 was less than 96.09 feet, we would choose a smaller STA_B to check.

STA=2+66
STA=2+92
STA=3+21
STA=3+76

If the calculated value of $Elev_C$ from eq.3 was greater than 96.09 feet, we would choose a larger STA_B to check.

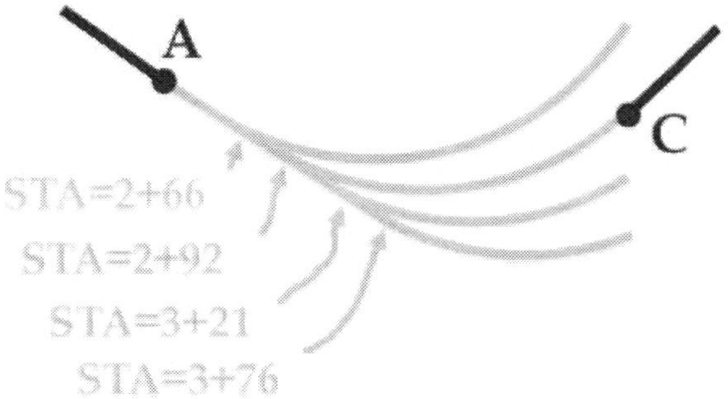

Figure 2

Vertical Curves #11

Find: Area under the curve and above elevation 50 [ft]

Elev=50 [ft] →

A   Area   **C**

The vertical curve begins at point A and ends at point C.

g_1 g_2

Given:

$R=-0.5 [\%/STA]$ ← rate of grade change

$Elev_A=50 [ft]$ — The elevation at point
$Elev_C=50 [ft]$ — A and point C

$g_1=1.5\%$ — The approach grade
$g_2=-1.5\%$ — and departing grade.

A) 90 [ft²]
B) 900 [ft²]
C) 9,000 [ft²]
D) 90,000 [ft²]

Analysis:

A) 90 [ft²]
B) 900 [ft²]
C) 9,000 [ft²]
D) 90,000 [ft²]

The possible solutions differ by a factor of 10, therefore we can approximate the area.

Approximate solutions are usually easier and quicker to compute than exact solutions.

Find: A_{curve}

For notation convenience, we'll define "A_{curve}" as the area we are solving for.

maximum elevation — **B**

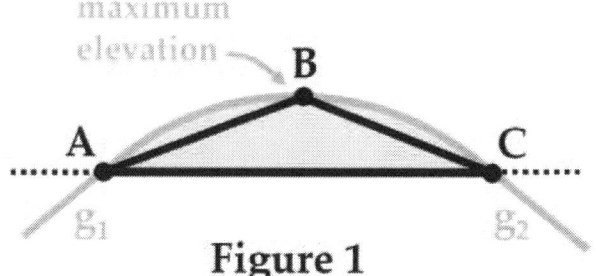

A   **C**

g_1 g_2

Figure 1

Define point B as the point on the curve having the maximum elevation and draw triangle ABC.

$A_{triangle} < A_{curve}$ ← *ieq.1*

A_{curve} is greater than $A_{triangle}$ (the area of triangle ABC).

Vertical Curves #11 (cont.)

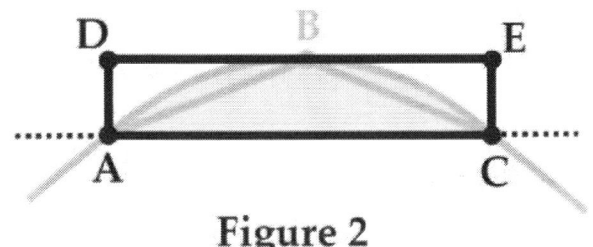

Figure 2

Define points D and E as the points above A and E, and at the same elevation as point B.

Draw out rectangle ADEC.

$$A_{curve} < A_{rectangle} \leftarrow ieq.2$$

A_{curve} is less than $A_{rectangle}$ (the area of rectangle ADEC).

$$A_{triangle} < A_{curve} < A_{rectangle} \leftarrow ieq.3$$

Combining ieq. 1 and ieq. 2, we have defined upper and lower bounds for A_{curve}.

base = L_{AC}

$$A_{triangle} = 0.5 * base * height \leftarrow eq.1$$

Define the area of triangle ABC.

height = $Elev_B$-50[ft]

$$A_{triangle} = 0.5 * L_{AC} * (Elev_B - 50[ft]) \leftarrow eq.2$$

Use eq. 3 to find L_{AC}.

$g_2 = -1.5\%$ $g_1 = 1.5\%$

$$L_{AC} = \frac{g_2 - g_1}{R} \leftarrow eq.3$$

Convert R, the rate of grade change: -0.5 [%/STA]=-0.005% [ft^{-1}]

$R = -0.005\% [ft^{-1}]$

$$L_{AC} = \frac{(-1.5\%) - 1.5\%}{-0.005\% [ft^{-1}]}$$

The "%" symbols in the numerator and denominator cancel out, so the units of L_{AC} are in feet.

Vertical Curves #11 (cont.)

$$L_{AC}=600\,[\text{ft}]$$

We'll find the elevation at point B using eq. 4.

$$Elev_B=0.5*R*L_{AB}{}^2+g_1*L_{AB}+Elev_A \leftarrow eq.4$$

$g_1=1.5\%$

$$L_{AB}=\frac{-g_1}{R} \leftarrow eq.5$$

$R=-0.005\%\,[\text{ft}^{-1}]$

Substitute in the approach grade and rate change of slope into eq. 5, then solve for the length between point A and point B.

$$L_{AB}=\frac{-1.5\%}{-0.005\%\,[\text{ft}^{-1}]}$$

Since $g_1=-g_2$, then $L_{AB}=0.5*L_{AC}$

$$L_{AB}=300\,[\text{ft}]$$

Return to eq. 4, substitute in the known variables, then solve for the elevation at point B.

$L_{AB}=300\,[\text{ft}]$ $Elev_A=50\,[\text{ft}]$

$$Elev_B=0.5*R*L_{AB}{}^2+g_1*L_{AB}+Elev_A \leftarrow eq.4$$

$R=-0.00005\,[\text{ft}^{-1}]$ $g_1=0.015$

$$Elev_B=0.5*(-0.0005\,[\text{ft}^{-1}])*(300\,[\text{ft}])^2+(0.015)*300\,[\text{ft}]+50\,[\text{ft}]$$

$$Elev_B=52.25\,[\text{ft}]$$

Next, we'll use eq. 2 to solve for the area inside triangle ABC.

$Elev_B=52.5\,[\text{ft}]$

$$A_{triangle}=0.5*L_{AC}*(Elev_B-50\,[\text{ft}]) \leftarrow eq.2$$

$L_{AC}=600\,[\text{ft}]$

Vertical Curves #11 (cont.)

$$A_{triangle}=0.5*600[ft]*(52.5[ft]-50[ft])$$

$$A_{triangle}=675[ft^2]$$

$$A_{rectangle}=L_{AC}*(Elev_B-50[ft]) \leftarrow eq.6$$

Use eq.6 to compute the area of rectangle ADEC.

$$A_{rectangle}=600[ft]*(52.5[ft]-50[ft])$$

$$A_{rectangle}=1,350[ft^2]$$

$$A_{triangle}<A_{curve}<A_{rectangle} \leftarrow ieq.3$$

From ieq.3, we know A_{curve} is between 675 square feet and 1,350 square feet.

$$675[ft^2]<A_{curve}<1,350[ft^2]$$

The only solution between 675 square feet and 1,350 square feet is 900 square feet.

A) 90[ft²]

B) 900[ft²]   <u>Answer:</u> B

C) 9,000[ft²]

D) 90,000[ft²]

Solving this problem for an exact solution would require taking the integral shown in eq.7.

$$A_{curve}=\int_0^{L_{AC}}(0.5*R*x^2+g_1*x+Elev_A-50.0[ft])*dx \leftarrow eq.7$$

Vertical Curves #12

Find: g_B ←The grade at point B

The vertical curve begins at point A and ends at point C.

Given:

$STA_A = 1+92$ ←The stationing at points A, B and C

$STA_B = 3+30$

$STA_C = 4+22$

$Elev_A = 151.7 [ft]$ ←The elevation at point A

$g_1 = 0\%$ ←

$g_2 = 2.0\%$ ← The approach grade and departing grade.

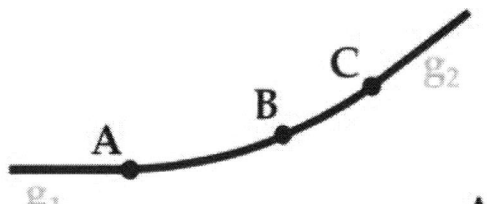

A) 0.4%

B) 0.8%

C) 1.2%

D) 1.6%

Analysis:

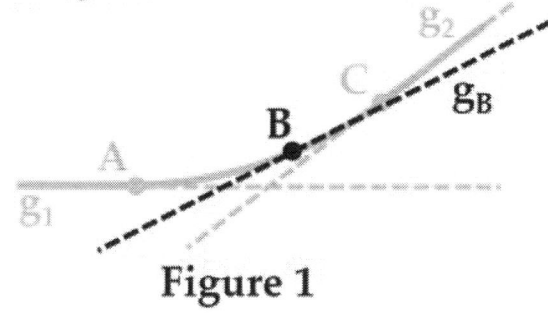

Figure 1

Figure 1 shows the grade at point B.

From Figure 1, we realize the grade at point B is greater than g_1 and less than g_2.

$$g_1 < g_B < g_2 \quad ←ieq.1$$

$g_1 = 0\% \qquad g_2 = 2.0\%$

$$0\% < g_B < 2.0\%$$

Since all possible solutions are between 0% and 2.0% we cannot rule out any solutions yet.

Since the rate change in grade is constant, the change in grade is linear with the change in stationing.

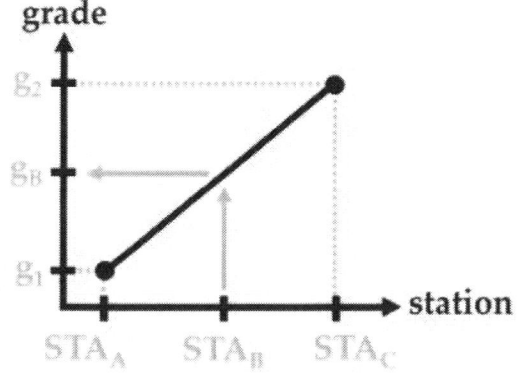

Figure 2

Substitute in g_1, g_2, STA_A, STA_B and STA_C into Figure 2.

Surveying Practice Problems

Vertical Curves #12 (cont.)

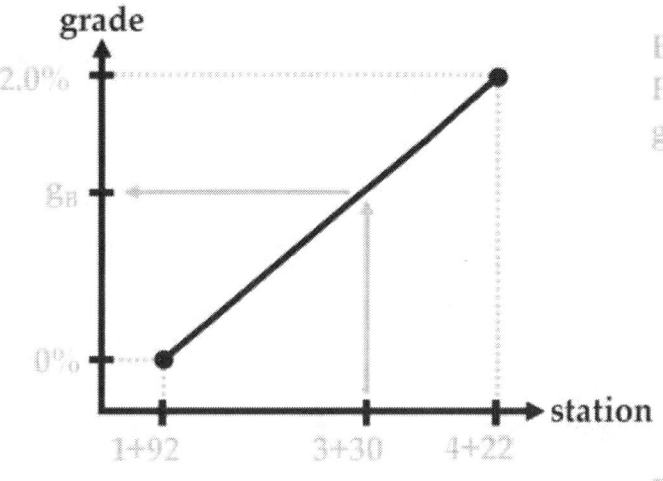

Figure 3

Based on the scaled drawing in Figure 3 and the possible solutions, g_B appears closest to 1.2%

A) 0.4%

B) 0.8%

C) 1.2% ←?

D) 1.6%

By sketching out the problem, we have a good idea of the solution before writing our first equation.

Use eq.1 to solve for g_B, by linear interpolation.

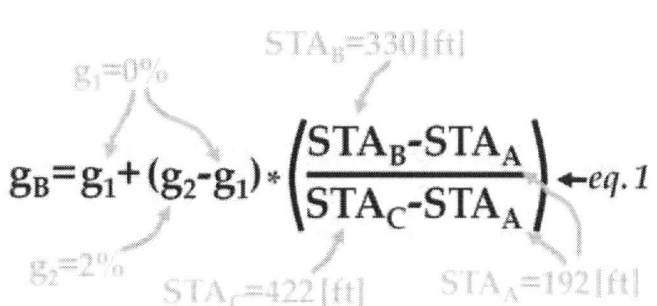

$$g_B = g_1 + (g_2 - g_1) * \left(\frac{STA_B - STA_A}{STA_C - STA_A} \right) \leftarrow eq.1$$

Convert the station units to length values before substituting into eq.1.

$$g_B = 0\% + (2\% - 0\%) * \left(\frac{330[ft] - 192[ft]}{422[ft] - 192[ft]} \right)$$

$$g_B = 1.20\%$$

We never used $Elev_A = 151.7[ft]$ to solve for g_B. Sometimes the problem will provide extra data.

Answer: $\boxed{C}$

Distance #1

Find: L_{AC} ← the distance between point A and point C

Given:

$V_{AB}=(4.5, 7.6, 1.9)\,[m]$

The vector from point A to point B

$V_{BC}=(11.4, -3.1, -0.5)\,[m]$

The vector from point B to point C

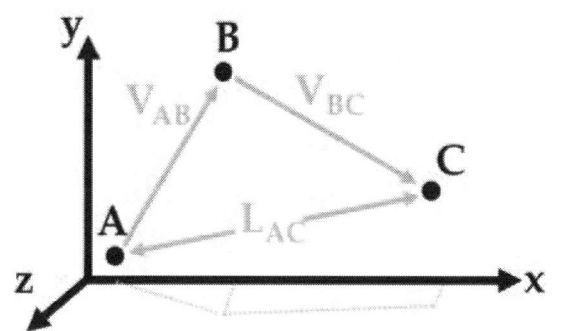

A) $8.4\,[m]$

B) $12.6\,[m]$

C) $16.6\,[m]$

D) $19.3\,[m]$

Analysis:

$$L_{AC}=\sqrt{L_{AC,x}^2+L_{AC,y}^2+L_{AC,z}^2} \leftarrow eq.1$$

Eq. 1 calculates the distance between point A and point C.

$L_{AC,x}$, $L_{AC,y}$ and $L_{AC,z}$ equal the distances between point A and point C, in the x, y and z directions, respectively.

$V_{BC,x}=11.4\,[m]$

$$L_{AC,x}=V_{AB,x}+V_{BC,x} \leftarrow eq.2$$

$V_{AB,x}=4.5\,[m]$

$$L_{AC,x}=4.5\,[m]+11.4\,[m]$$

$$L_{AC,x}=15.9\,[m]$$

We can compute $L_{AC,x}$, $L_{AC,y}$ and $L_{AC,z}$ by summing the x, y and z vector components of vectors V_{AB} and V_{AC}, as shown in eq. 2, eq. 3 and eq. 4, respectively.

$V_{BC,y}=-3.1\,[m]$

$$L_{AC,y}=V_{AB,y}+V_{BC,y} \leftarrow eq.3$$

$V_{AB,y}=7.6\,[m]$

$$L_{AC,y}=7.6\,[m]+(-3.1)\,[m]$$

$$L_{AC,y}=4.5\,[m]$$

Since we know $L_{AC,x}=15.9\,[m]$, we know from eq.1, that $L_{AC}\geq15.9\,[m]$, which rules out solutions A and B.

A) 8.4 [m]

B) 12.6 [m]

C) 16.6 [m]

D) 19.3 [m]

Surveying Practice Problems

Distance #1 (cont.)

$V_{BC,z} = -0.5 \, [m]$

$$L_{AC,z} = V_{AB,z} + V_{BC,z} \leftarrow eq.4$$

$V_{AB,z} = 1.9 \, [m]$

Vector V_{AB} and vector V_{AC} are represented as distances in the x, y and z directions.

$$L_{AC,z} = 1.9 \, [m] + (-0.5) \, [m]$$

$$L_{AC,z} = 1.4 \, [m]$$

Now that we know the value of vector $V_{AC} = (15.9, 4.5, 1.4) \, [m]$, we'll return to eq.1, plug in $L_{AC,x}$, $L_{AC,y}$ and $L_{AC,z}$ then solve for L_{AC}.

$L_{AC,y} = 4.5 \, [m]$

$$L_{AC} = \sqrt{L_{AC,x}^2 + L_{AC,y}^2 + L_{AC,z}^2} \leftarrow eq.1$$

$L_{AC,x} = 15.9 \, [m]$ $L_{AC,z} = 1.4 \, [m]$

$$L_{AC} = \sqrt{(15.9 \, [m])^2 + (4.5 \, [m])^2 + (1.4 \, [m])^2}$$

$$L_{AC} = 16.58 \, [m]$$

Of the four possible solutions, the answer is most nearly 16.6 [m]. Answer C is correct.

Answer: $\boxed{C}$

Distance #2

<u>Find:</u> A_{IJK} ←—— angle IJK

<u>Given:</u>

L_{IJ}=135.22[m]

the distance between
point I and point J

L_{IK}=104.21[m]

the distance between
point I and point K

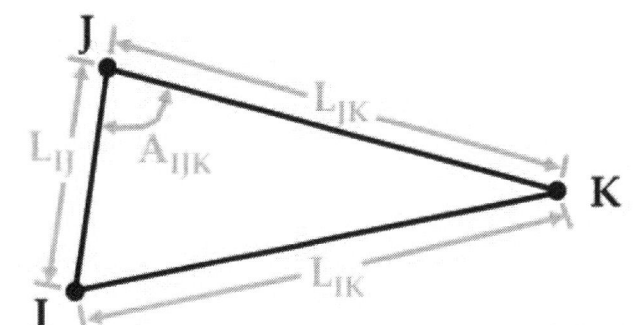

A_{JIK}=78°47′22″

angle JIK

A) 40°

B) 50°

C) 60°

D) 70°

....

Analysis:

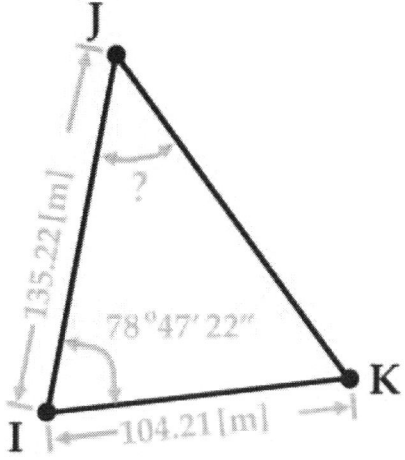

Figure 1

In Figure 1, triangle IJK is drawn
to scale. A_{IJK} appears smaller
than 70° and smaller than 60°.

    A) 40°

    B) 50°

    C) 60° ←—probably not

    D) 70° ←—probably not

The problem statement will not
always provide a scaled drawing.
Making a scaled drawing can help
us approximate the correct answer.

Use the Law of Cosines (eq.1), to find
L_{JK}, the length between point J and
point K.

Law of Cosines:

$$a^2 = b^2 + c^2 - 2*b*c*\cos(A) ←eq.1$$

$a=L_{JK}$ $b=L_{IK}$ $c=L_{IJ}$ $A=A_{JIK}$

Plug in the variables L_{JK}, L_{IK}, L_{IJ}
and A_{JIK}, into eq.1.

$$L_{JK}^2 = L_{IK}^2 + L_{IJ}^2 - 2*L_{IK}*L_{IJ}*\cos(A_{JIK}) ←eq.2$$

Solve eq.2 for L_{JK}

Surveying Practice Problems

Distance #2 (cont.)

Plug in the values of L_{IK}, L_{IJ} and A_{JIK}, into eq.3, then solve for L_{JK}.

$$L_{JK} = \sqrt{L_{IK}^2 + L_{IJ}^2 - 2*L_{IK}*L_{IJ}*\cos(A_{JIK})} \leftarrow eq.3$$

$L_{IK} = 104.21\,[m]$ $L_{IJ} = 135.22\,[m]$ $A_{JIK} = 78°\,47'\,22''$

$$L_{JK} = \sqrt{\begin{array}{l} (104.21\,[m])^2 + (135.22\,[m])^2 \\ -2*104.21[m]*135.22[m]*\cos(78°\,47'\,22'') \end{array}}$$

$$L_{JK} = 153.83\,[m]$$

Use the Law of Sines, eq.4, to compute A_{IJK}

$$\frac{\sin(A_{JIK})}{L_{JK}} = \frac{\sin(A_{IJK})}{L_{IK}} \leftarrow eq.4$$

Solve eq.4 for A_{IJK}

Plug in A_{JIK}, L_{IK}, and L_{JK} into eq.5, then solve for A_{IJK}.

$A_{JIK} = 78°\,47'\,22''$

$$A_{IJK} = \sin^{-1}\left(\frac{\sin(A_{JIK})*L_{IK}}{L_{JK}}\right) \leftarrow eq.5$$

$L_{JK} = 153.83\,[m]$ $L_{IK} = 104.21\,[m]$

$$A_{IJK} = \sin^{-1}\left(\frac{\sin(78°\,47'\,22'')*104.21\,[m]}{153.83\,[m]}\right)$$

$$A_{IJK} = 41°\,38'\,41''$$

The calculated value of A_{IJK} is closer to $40°$ than to $50°$. Select answer A.

Answer: | A |

Distance #3

Find: $L_{MN,y}$ ← the vertical distance between points M and N

Given:

L_{MN}=325.11[ft]

↑ the straight-line distance between point M and point N

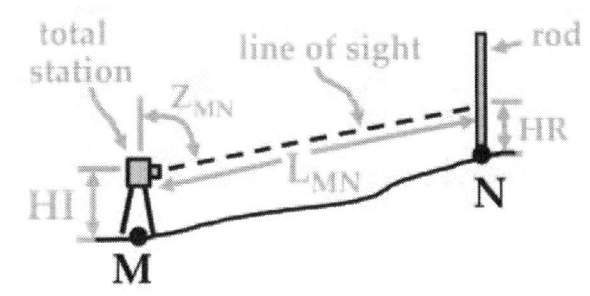

Z_{MN}=67.56°

↑ the zenith angle from point M to point N

HR=3.14[ft] ← rod height

HI=5.22[ft]

↑ height of the total station

A) 122[ft]
B) 126[ft]
C) 298[ft]
D) 303[ft]

Analysis:

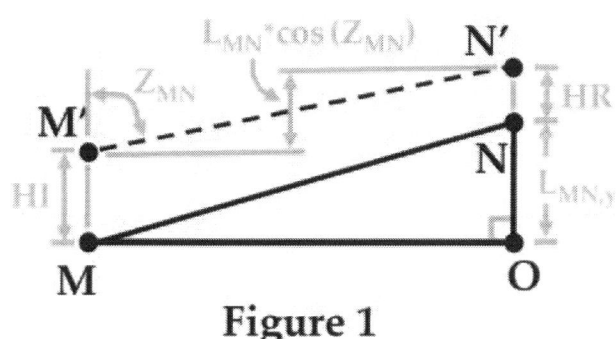

Figure 1

Figure 1 identifies $L_{MN,y}$, and the other vertical distances in eq.1.

The zenith angle is a vertical angle measured from a point directly above the observer to the target point.

Use eq.1 to compute $L_{MN,y}$

$$L_{MN,y}=L_{MN}*\cos(Z_{MN})+HI-HR \leftarrow eq.1$$

Substitute in the values for variables L_{MN}, Z_{MN}, HR and HI, then solve for $L_{MN,y}$.

$$L_{MN,y}=325.11[ft]*\cos(67.56°)+5.22[ft]-3.14[ft]$$

$$L_{MN,y}=126.18[ft]$$

Answer: $\boxed{B}$

Distance #4

<u>Find:</u> L_{JK} ← the length of side JK
<u>Given:</u>

$L_{IJ}=86.72\,[ft]$ ← the length, zenith, and
$Z_{IJ}=94°15'00''$ ← azimuth from point I
$Az_{IJ}=0°00'00''$ ← to point J

$L_{IK}=147.65\,[ft]$ ← the length, zenith, and
$Z_{IK}=88°30'00''$ ← azimuth from point I
$Az_{IK}=45°48'00''$ ← to point K

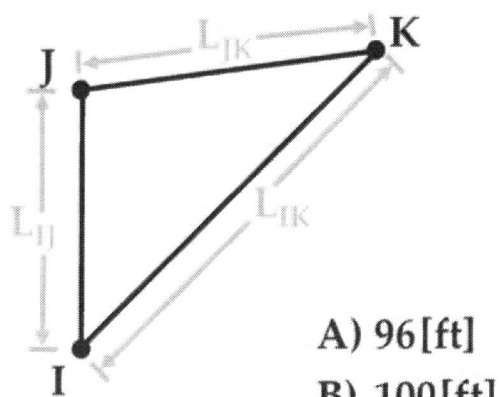

A) 96 [ft]
B) 100 [ft]
C) 104 [ft]
D) 108 [ft]

Analysis:

Eq. 1 calculates the distance between point J and point K.

point K   point J

$$L_{JK}=\sqrt{(K_x-J_x)^2+(K_y-J_y)^2+(K_z-J_z)^2} \leftarrow eq.1$$

x coordinate   z coordinate

y coordinate

To solve eq. 1, we must compute the x, y and z coordinates of point J and point K.

assumed → $I=(0,0,0)\,[ft]$
coordinate I_x I_y I_z

For convenience, we'll define point I to be located at the origin.

Use eq. 2, to solve for J_x.

$Az_{IJ}=0°00'00''$ $I_x=0\,[ft]$

$$J_x=L_{IJ}*\sin(Az_{IJ})*\sin(Z_{IJ})+I_x \leftarrow eq.2$$

$L_{IJ}=86.72\,[ft]$ $Z_{IJ}=94°15'00''$

$$J_x=86.72[ft]*\sin(0°00'00'')*\sin(94°15'00'')+0\,[ft]$$

$$J_x=0\,[ft]$$

Since $Az_{IJ}=0°00'00''$, then $I_x=J_x$.

Distance #4 (cont.)

Use eq. 3, to solve for J_y.

$Az_{IJ}=0°00'00''$ $I_x=0$ [ft]

$$J_y=L_{IJ}*\cos(Az_{IJ})*\sin(Z_{IJ})+I_y \leftarrow eq.3$$

$L_{IJ}=86.72$ [ft] $Z_{IJ}=94°15'00''$

$$J_y=86.72[ft]*\cos(0°00'00'')*\sin(94°15'00'')+0[ft]$$

$$J_y=86.48[ft]$$

$Z_{IJ}=94°15'00''$

Use eq. 4, to solve for J_z.

$$J_z=L_{IJ}*\cos(Z_{IJ})+I_z \qquad \leftarrow eq.4$$

$L_{IJ}=86.72$ [ft] $I_x=0$ [ft]

$$J_z=86.72[ft]*\cos(94°15'00'')+0[ft]$$

$$J_z=-6.43[ft]$$

Use eq. 5, to solve for K_x.

$Az_{IK}=45°48'00''$ $I_x=0$ [ft]

$$K_x=L_{IK}*\sin(Az_{IK})*\sin(Z_{IK})+I_x \leftarrow eq.5$$

$L_{IK}=147.65$ [ft] $Z_{IK}=88°30'00''$

$$K_x=147.65[ft]*\sin(45°48'00'')*\sin(88°30'00'')+0[ft]$$

$$K_x=105.82[ft]$$

Use eq. 6, to solve for K_y.

$Az_{IK}=45°48'00''$ $I_x=0$ [ft]

$$K_y=L_{IK}*\cos(Az_{IK})*\sin(Z_{IK})+I_y \leftarrow eq.6$$

$L_{IK}=147.65$ [ft] $Z_{IK}=88°30'00''$

Surveying Practice Problems

Distance #4 (cont.)

$K_y = 147.65\,[\text{ft}] * \cos(45\,°48'00'') * \sin(88\,°30'00'') + 0\,[\text{ft}]$

$K_y = 102.90\,[\text{ft}]$

$Z_{IK} = 88\,°30'00''$

Use eq. 7, to solve for K_z.

$K_z = L_{IK} * \cos(Z_{IK}) + I_z \leftarrow eq.\,7$

$L_{IK} = 147.65\,[\text{ft}]$ $I_z = 0\,[\text{ft}]$

$K_z = 147.65\,[\text{ft}] * \cos(88\,°30'00'') + 0\,[\text{ft}]$

$K_z = 3.87\,[\text{ft}]$

After solving for the x, y and z coordinates of point J and point K, we return to eq.1 and solve for L_{JK}.

$K_x = 105.82\,[\text{ft}]$ $K_y = 102.90\,[\text{ft}]$ $K_z = 3.87\,[\text{ft}]$

$L_{JK} = \sqrt{(K_x-J_x)^2 + (K_y-J_y)^2 + (K_z-J_z)^2} \leftarrow eq.\,1$

$J_x = 0\,[\text{ft}]$ $J_y = 86.48\,[\text{ft}]$ $J_z = -6.43\,[\text{ft}]$

$L_{JK} = \sqrt{(105.82\,[\text{ft}]-0\,[\text{ft}])^2 + (102.90\,[\text{ft}]-86.48\,[\text{ft}])^2 + (3.87\,[\text{ft}]-(-6.43\,[\text{ft}]))^2}$

$L_{JK} = 107.58\,[\text{ft}]$

Since 107.58 [ft] is most nearly 108 [ft], answer D is correct.

Answer: $\boxed{D}$

Distance #5

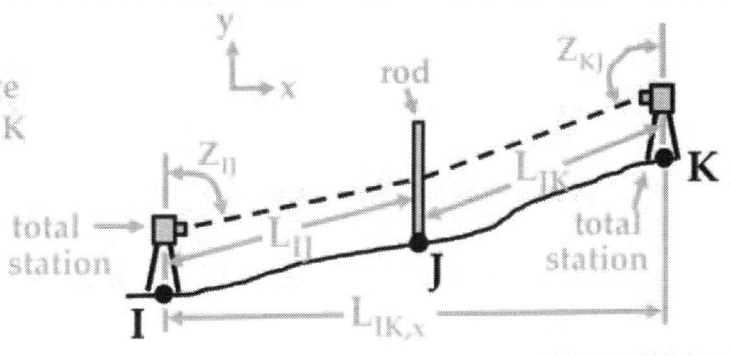

Find: $L_{JK,x}$ ← the horizontal distance between points J and K

Given:

$L_{IJ}=114.09\,[ft]$

the straight-line distance between point I and point J

$L_{JK}=122.41\,[ft]$

the straight-line distance between point J and point K

$Z_{IJ}=77.21°$ ← zenith angles

$Z_{KJ}=105.84°$

A) 120 [ft]

B) 229 [ft]

C) 236 [ft]

D) 243 [ft]

Analysis:

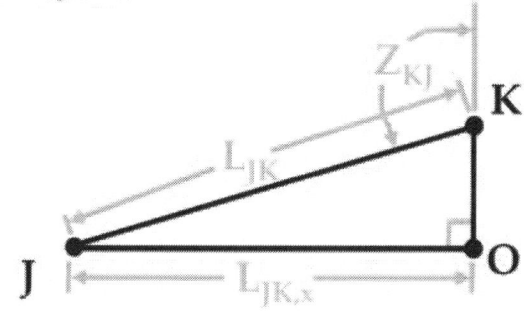

Figure 1

Figure 1 identifies $L_{JK,x}$, the horizontal distance between point J and point K.

Some problems will provide more information than required.

$L_{JK}=122.41\,[ft]$

$$L_{JK,x}=L_{JK}*\sin(Z_{KJ}) \leftarrow eq.1$$

$Z_{KJ}=105.84°$

Using eq.1, plug in variables L_{JK} and Z_{KJ}, then solve for $L_{JK,x}$.

$$L_{JK,x}=122.41\,[ft]*\sin(105.84°)$$

$$L_{JK,x}=117.76\,[ft]$$

117.76 [ft] is closest to 120 [ft]. Answer A is correct.

Answer: $\boxed{A}$

Surveying Practice Problems

Distance #6

Find: $L_{IK,x}$ ← the horizontal distance between points I and K

Given:

$L_{IJ}=227.05\,[m]$ ← the distance between point I and point J

$Z_{IK}=114.89\,°$ ← the zenith angle of course IK

$\theta=27.41°$

↑ theta equals the measure of interior angle JIK

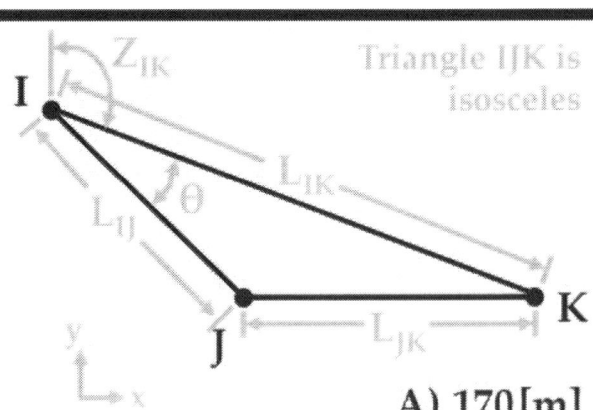

Triangle IJK is isosceles

Angle IJK is the largest interior angle

The sketch is in profile view

A) 170 [m]
B) 230 [m]
C) 370 [m]
D) 400 [m]

Analysis:

$$L_{IK,x}=L_{IK}*\sin(Z_{IK}) \quad \leftarrow eq.1$$

The horizontal distance between points I and K equals the total distance between points I and K times the sine of Z_{IK}.

$$\frac{\sin(A_{IJK})}{L_{IK}}=\frac{\sin(A_{IKJ})}{L_{IJ}} \quad \leftarrow eq.2$$

Use law of sines to solve for L_{IK}. Solve eq.2 for L_{IK}.

$$L_{IK}=\frac{\sin(A_{IJK})*L_{IJ}}{\sin(A_{IKJ})} \quad \leftarrow eq.3$$

In eq.3, the problem provides L_{IJ}, but we don't know A_{IJK} or A_{IKJ}.

$L_{IJ}=227.05\,[m]$

$$L_{JK}=L_{IJ} \quad \leftarrow eq.4$$

$$L_{JK}=227.05\,[m]$$

Since Triangle IJK is isosceles, two of the side lengths are equal, and two of the interior angles are equal.

Since angle IJK is the largest interior angle, we know which side lengths are equal (see eq.4) and which angles are equal (see eq.5).

$\theta=27.41°$

$$A_{IKJ}=A_{JIK} \quad \leftarrow eq.5$$

$$A_{IKJ}=27.41°$$

Recall A_{JIK} is given as θ in the problem statement.

Distance #6 (cont.)

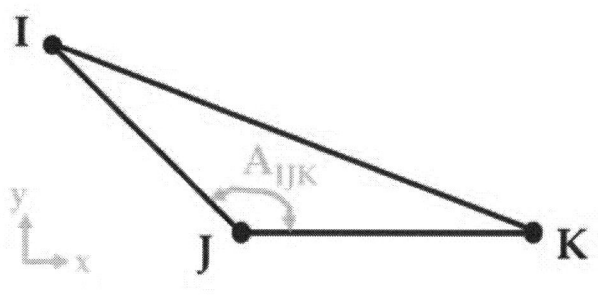

Figure 1

Figure 1 shows Triangle IJK and labels A_{IJK}.

We can compute A_{IJK} because the sum of the interior angles of a triangle equals 180.°

$A_{JIK}=27.41°$

$A_{IJK}=180°-A_{JIK}-A_{IKJ}$ ←*eq.6*

$A_{IKJ}=27.41°$

Plug in A_{IKJ} and A_{JIK} into eq 6, then solve for A_{IJK}.

$A_{IJK}=180°-27.41°-27.41°$

$A_{IJK}=125.18°$

In Figure 2, Line segment IJ is rotated to be parallel to the x axis. Figure 2 is drawn (nearly) to scale.

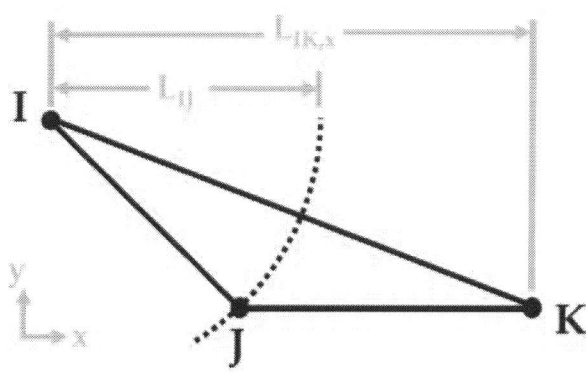

Figure 2

In Figure 2, we observe $L_{IK,x}>L_{IJ}$. This sets a minimum on our value for $L_{IK,x}$, so we can eliminate answer A as a possible solution.

A) ~~170 [m]~~

B) 230 [m]

C) 370 [m]

D) 400 [m]

$L_{IJ}=227.05 [m]$

$L_{IK,x}>L_{IJ}$ ←*ieq.1*

$L_{IK,x}>227.05 [m]$

The correct value for $L_{IK,x}$ appears to be either 370 [m] or 400 [m].

Distance #6 (cont.)

$A_{IJK}=125.18°$ $L_{IJ}=227.05\,[m]$

$$L_{IK}= \frac{\sin (A_{IJK})*L_{IJ}}{\sin (A_{IKJ})} \leftarrow eq.3$$

$A_{IKJ}=27.41°$

Plug in A_{IJK}, A_{IKJ} and L_{IJ} into eq.3, then solve for L_{IK}.

$$L_{IK}= \frac{\sin (125.18°)*227.05\,[m]}{\sin (27.41°)}$$

$$L_{IK}=403.12\,[m]$$

$L_{IK}=403.12\,[m]$

$$L_{IK,x}=L_{IK}*\sin (Z_{IK}) \leftarrow eq.1$$

$Z_{IK}=114.89°$

Lastly, plug in L_{IK} and Z_{IK} into eq.1, then solve for $L_{IK,x}$.

$$L_{IK,x}=403.12\,[m]*\sin (114.89°)$$

$$L_{IK,x}=365.67\,[m]$$

Of the four possible solutions, 365.67 [m] is most nearly 370 [m]. Answer C is correct.

Answer: $\boxed{C}$

Distance #7

<u>Find:</u> $L_{AB,a}$ ← the actual distance between
point A and point B

<u>Given:</u>

$L_{AB,m}=1{,}411.80 \text{[ft]}$

the measured distance
between point A and point B

$T_m=35^\circ \text{F}$ ← the temperature
during measurement

$\alpha_{steel}=6.45{*}10^{-6} \text{[}^\circ\text{F}^{-1}\text{]}$ ← thermal expansion
coefficient of steel

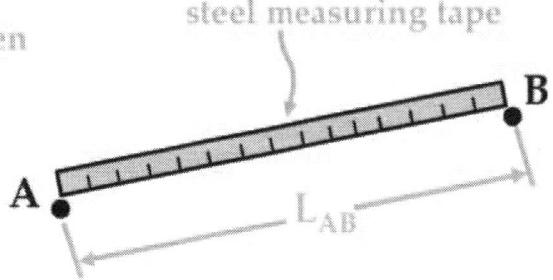

steel measuring tape

A) 1,408.80 [ft]
B) 1,411.50 [ft]
C) 1,411.77 [ft]
D) 1,412.10 [ft]

<u>Analysis:</u>

higher temperatures

↘

shorter measurements

First, we know that as the
temperature increases, the
measuring tape gets longer and
measured lengths appear shorter.

lower temperatures

↘

longer measurements

Similarly, lower temperatures lead to
longer apparent measurements.

$T_o=68\,^\circ\text{F}$

calibrated
temperature

Unless otherwise noted, assume the
measuring tape is calibrated at 68°F
(standard temperature)

Since the measured temperature
is lower than the calibrated
temperature, the actual length is
shorter than the measured length.

if $T_m<T_o$ → then $L_{AB,a}<L_{AB,m}$

$L_{AB}=1{,}411.80\text{[ft]}$

$L_{AB,a}<1{,}411.80\text{[ft]}$ ← *ieq. 1*

Surveying Practice Problems

Distance #7 (cont.)

A) 1,408.80 [ft]

B) 1,411.50 [ft]

C) 1,411.77 [ft]

~~D) 1,412.10 [ft]~~

Since the actual length is shorter than the measured length, we can rule out answer D.

temperature correction

$$L_{AB,a} = L_{AB,m} + c \leftarrow eq.1$$

We'll use eq.1 to solve for, $L_{AB,a}$, the actual length between points A and B.

$\alpha_{steel} = 6.45 * 10^{-6} [°F^{-1}]$

$$c = \alpha_{steel} * (T_m - T_o) * L_{AB,m} \leftarrow eq.2$$

$T_m = 35 [°F]$

$T_o = 68 [°F]$

$L_{AB,m} = 1,411.80 [ft]$

Using eq.2, we can plug in α_{steel}, T_m, T_o, and $L_{AB,m}$, to solve for the temperature correction, c.

$$c = 6.45 * 10^{-6} [°F^{-1}] * (35 [°F] - 68 [°F]) * 1,411.80 [ft]$$

$$c = -0.30 [ft]$$

$c = -0.30 [ft]$ means we need to correct the measured length by adding -0.30 [ft], to obtain the actual length.

$c = -0.30 [ft]$

$$L_{AB,a} = L_{AB,m} + c \leftarrow eq.1$$

$L_{AB,m} = 1,411.80 [ft]$

Return to eq.1, and solve for $L_{AB,a}$

$$L_{AB,a} = 1,411.80 [ft] + (-0.30 [ft])$$

$$L_{AB,a} = 1,411.50 [ft]$$

Answer: B

Distance #8

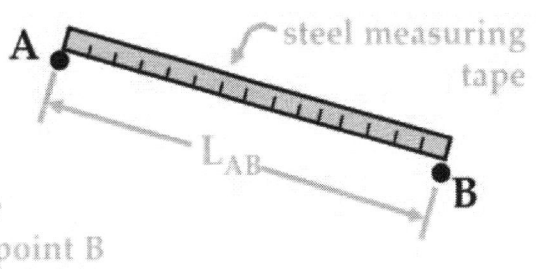

Find: T_m ← the ambient temperature
      when $L_{AB,m}$ was measured

Given:

$L_{AB,m}=455.22\,[ft]$ ← the measured distance
      between point A and point B

$L_{AB,a}=455.28\,[ft]$

      the actual distance
      between points A and B

$\alpha_{steel}=1.2*10^{-5}\,[°C^{-1}]$ ← thermal expansion
      coefficient of steel

T_m? →

A) 11°C
B) 15°C
C) 25°C
D) 31°C

Analysis:

since $L_{AB,m}<L_{AB,a}$

then, $T_m>T_o$

$T_o=20°C$

Since the measured distance is less than the actual distance, we know the measured temperature is hotter than the standard temperature.

$T_m>20°C$

~~A) 11°C~~

~~B) 15°C~~

C) 25°C

D) 31°C

After plugging in the standard temperature, $T_o=20°C$, we know answer A and answer B cannot be correct.

By remembering the steel tape expands as the temperature increases, we can quickly rule out 2 of the possible answers.

temperature
correction

$c=\alpha_{steel}*(T_m-T_o)*L_{AB,m}$ ← eq. 1

Eq. 1 computes the temperature correction.

$T_m=\left(\dfrac{c}{\alpha_{steel}*L_{AB,m}}\right)+T_o$ ← eq. 2

Eq. 2, solves eq. 1 for the measured temperature, T_m.

Surveying Practice Problems

Distance #8 (cont.)

$$c = L_{AB,a} - L_{AB,m} \leftarrow eq.3$$

Solve for the temperature correction by plugging in the values of $L_{AB,a}$ and $L_{AB,m}$ into eq.3.

$$c = 455.28\,[ft] - 455.22\,[ft]$$

$$c = 0.06\,[ft]$$

Using eq. 2, plug in c, α_{steel}, $L_{AB,m}$, and T_o, then solve for T_m.

$$T_m = \left(\frac{c}{\alpha_{steel} * L_{AB,m}}\right) + T_o \leftarrow eq.2$$

$$T_m = \left(\frac{0.06\,[ft]}{1.2*10^{-5}\,[°C^{-1}] * 455.22\,[ft]}\right) + 20\,[°C]$$

$$T_m = 31.0\,°C$$

The units of α_{steel}, $[°C^{-1}]$, in eq. 2, is read as "per degree Celsius."

<u>Answer:</u> $\boxed{D}$

Distance #9

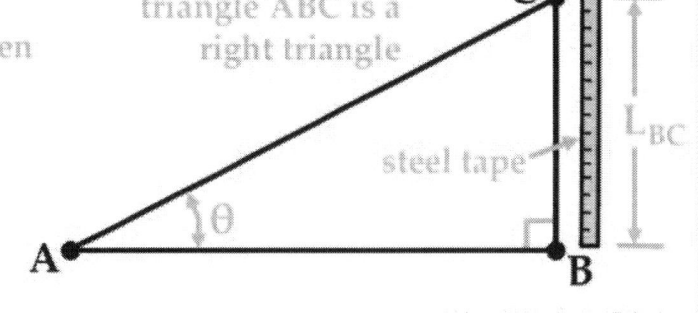

triangle ABC is a right triangle

steel tape

L_{BC}

Find: $L_{AC,a}$ ← the actual length between point A and point C

Given:

$\theta=15°48'00''$ ← interior angle CAB

$T_m=20°F$ ← temperature during measurement

$\alpha_{steel}=6.45*10^{-6}[°F^{-1}]$ ← coefficient of thermal expansion (for steel)

$L_{BC,m}=3,519.1[ft]$ ← the measured distance between points B and C

A) 12,921 [ft]

B) 12,925 [ft]

C) 12,929 [ft]

D) 12,933 [ft]

Analysis:

$$L_{AC,a}=L_{AC,m}+c \leftarrow eq.1$$

temperature correction

We'll use eq.1 to calculate $L_{AC,a}$. We first need to determine the values of variables $L_{AC,m}$ and c.

$\theta=15.8°$

$$L_{AC,m}=L_{BC,m}/\sin\theta \leftarrow eq.2$$

$L_{BC,m}=3,519.1[ft]$

In eq.2, we'll use right triangle trigonometry to solve for $L_{AC,m}$, the measured length between point A and point C.

$$L_{AC,m}=(3,519.1[ft])/\sin(15.8°)$$

$$L_{AC,m}=12,924.55[ft]$$

It may be easier to convert angle θ from "degrees minutes seconds" notation to "decimal degrees" notation.

$\theta=15°48'00''=15.8°$

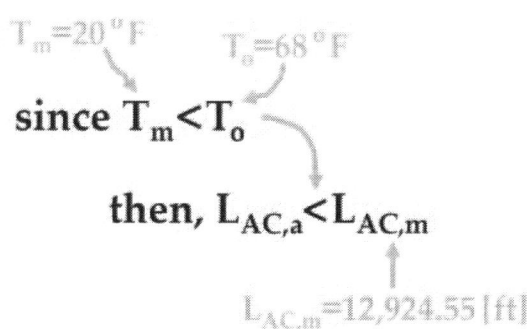

$T_m=20°F$ $T_o=68°F$

since $T_m<T_o$

then, $L_{AC,a}<L_{AC,m}$

$L_{AC,m}=12,924.55[ft]$

Since the measured temperature is less than the calibrated temperature, we know the actual length is less than the measured length.

Surveying Practice Problems

Distance #9 (cont.)

$$L_{AC,a} < 12,924.55 \, [ft] \leftarrow ieq.1$$

From ieq.1, we can rule out answer C and answer D.

A) 12,921 [ft]
B) 12,925 [ft]
~~C) 12,929 [ft]~~
~~D) 12,933 [ft]~~

Although, answer B is greater than 12,924.55 [ft], answer B can be the correct answer. The correct answer is the answer "most nearly" the exact solution.

To solve for $L_{AC,a}$, we still need to compute the temperature correction, c. Use eq.3 to compute c.

$$\alpha_{steel} = 6.45 \times 10^{-6} \, [°F^{-1}]$$

$$c = \alpha_{steel} \ast (T_m - T_o) \ast L_{AB,m} \leftarrow eq.3$$

$$T_m = 20 \, [°F]$$
$$L_{AB,m} = 12,924.55 \, [ft]$$
$$T_o = 68 \, [°F]$$

It can be helpful to memorize the standard temperature.
$$T_o = 68° F = 20°C$$

$$c = 6.45 \times 10^{-6} \, [°F^{-1}] \ast (20 \, [°F] - 68 \, [°F]) \ast 1,411.80 \, [ft]$$

$$c = -4.00 \, [ft]$$

The temperature correction, c, accounts for the contraction or expansion of the measuring tape due to changes in temperature.

$$c = -4.00 \, [ft]$$

$$L_{AC,a} = L_{AC,m} + c \leftarrow eq.1$$

$$L_{AC,m} = 12,924.55 \, [ft]$$

Return to eq.1, plug in $L_{AC,m}$, and c, then solve for $L_{AC,a}$.

$$L_{AC,a} = 12,924.55 \, [ft] + (-4.00 \, [ft])$$

$$L_{AC,a} = 12,920.55 \, [ft]$$

The exact solution is most nearly answer A.

Answer: $\boxed{A}$

Distance #10

<u>Find:</u> α_{steel} ← coefficient of thermal expansion (for steel)

<u>Given:</u>

$T_{m1} = 14.70\,°C$ ← temperature during the first measurement

$T_{m2} = 27.10\,°C$ ← temperature during the second measurement

$L_{AB,m1} = 227.180\,[m]$ ← the measured lengths between point A and point B for tempera-tures T_{m1} and $T_{m2.}$

$L_{AB,m2} = 227.145\,[m]$

A) $1.12*10^{-5}\,[°C^{-1}]$

B) $1.16*10^{-5}\,[°C^{-1}]$

C) $1.20*10^{-5}\,[°C^{-1}]$

D) $1.24*10^{-5}\,[°C^{-1}]$

Analysis:

$$L_{AB,a} = L_{AC,m1} + c_1 \quad ←eq.1$$

Eq.1 shows the equation for the actual length from point A to point B, using the first measurement.

$$c_1 = \alpha_{steel}*(T_{m1}-T_o)*L_{AB,m1}$$

Substitute in c_1 into eq.1.

$$L_{AB,m1} = 227.180\,[m]$$

$$L_{AB,a} = L_{AC,m1} + \alpha_{steel}*(T_{m1}-T_o)*L_{AB,m1} \quad ←eq.2$$

$$T_{m1} = 14.70\,°C \qquad T_o = 20\,°C$$

Plug in $L_{AC,m1}$, T_{m1}, and T_o into eq.2. Standard temperature, T_o, is 20°C.

$$L_{AB,a} = 227.180\,[m] + \alpha_{steel}*(14.70\,[°C]-20\,[°C])*227.180\,[m] ←eq.3$$

Simplify eq.3.

$$L_{AB,a} = 227.180\,[m] - 1,204.054\,[m*°C]*\alpha_{steel} ←eq.4$$

From eq.4, we notice our units for α_{steel} will be $[°C^{-1}]$, which we would expect from the possible solutions.

$$L_{AC,a} = L_{AC,m2} + c_2 ←eq.5$$

$$c_2 = \alpha_{steel}*(T_{m2}-T_o)*L_{AB,m2}$$

Eq.5 shows the equation for the actual length from point A to point B, using the second measurement.

Surveying Practice Problems

Distance #10 (cont.)

$L_{AB,m2} = 227.145 \, [m]$

Plug in $L_{AC,m2}$, T_{m2}, and T_o into eq.6, and simplify

$$L_{AB,a} = L_{AC,m2} + \alpha_{steel} * (T_{m2} - T_o) * L_{AB,m2} \leftarrow eq.6$$

$T_{m2} = 27.10 \, °C \qquad T_o = 20 \, °C$

$$L_{AB,a} = 227.145 \, [m] + \alpha_{steel} * (27.10 \, [°C] - 20 \, [°C]) * 227.145 \, [m] \leftarrow eq.7$$

$$L_{AB,a} = 227.145 \, [m] + 1{,}612.730 \, [m * °C] * \alpha_{steel} \leftarrow eq.8$$

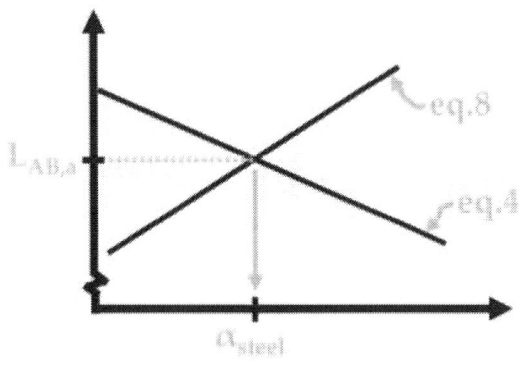

Figure 1

At this point we have 2 equations (eq.4 and eq.8) and 2 unknown variables ($L_{AB,a}$ and α_{steel}).

We can plot eq.4 and eq.8 on the same coordinate system. The intersecting point is the solution.

Equate the right-hand side of eq.4 with the right-hand of eq.8, and solve for α_{steel}.

$$227.180 \, [m] - 1{,}204.054 \, [m * °C] * \alpha_{steel}$$
$$= 227.145 \, [m] + 1{,}612.730 \, [m * °C] * \alpha_{steel} \leftarrow eq.9$$

$$\alpha_{steel} = 1.242 * 10^{-5} \, [C^{-1}]$$

$1.242 * 10^{-5} \, [°C^{-1}]$ is most nearly $1.24 * 10^{-5} \, [°C^{-1}]$. Choose Answer D.

Answer: $\boxed{D}$

Distance #11

Find: g_{AC} ←the grade from point A to point C

Given:

$L_{AB,a}$=294.15[ft] ← the actual length between point A and point B

$L_{BC,m}$=95.44[ft]

the measured length between poins B and C

α_{steel}=1.2*10⁻⁵[°C⁻¹]

coefficient of thermal expansion (for steel)

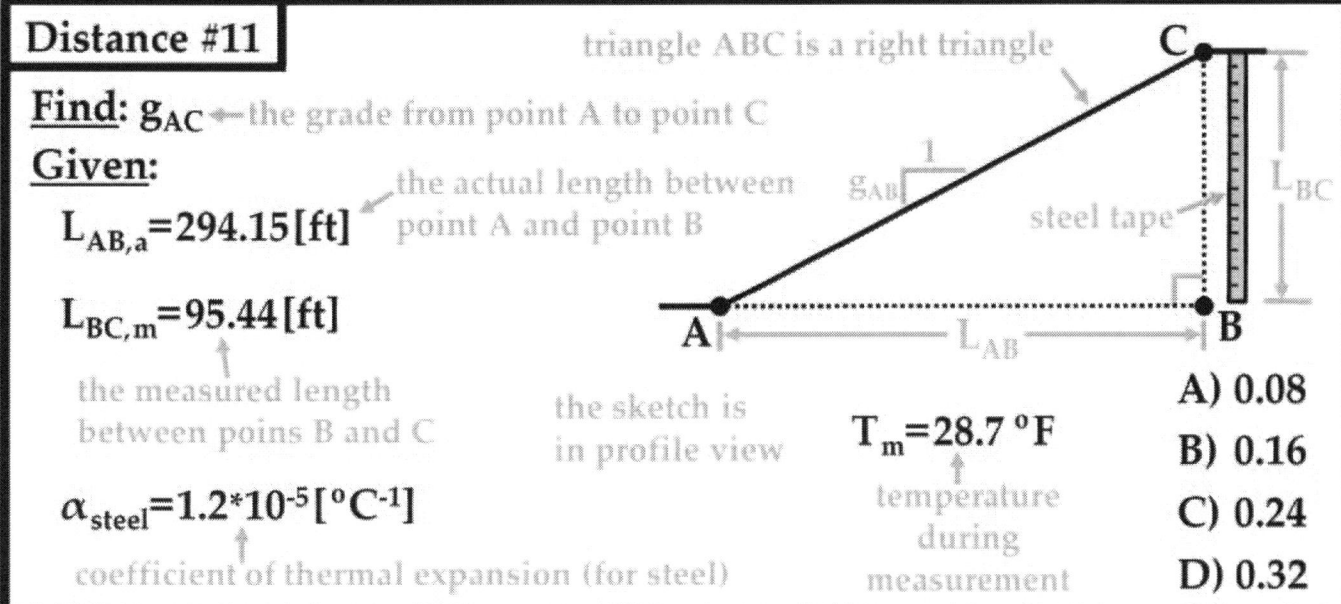

triangle ABC is a right triangle

the sketch is in profile view

T_m=28.7 °F

temperature during measurement

A) 0.08

B) 0.16

C) 0.24

D) 0.32

Analysis:

$$g_{AC}=\frac{L_{BC,a}}{L_{AB,a}} \leftarrow eq.1$$

a="actual"

From eq. 1, g_{AC} equals the actual distance between points B and C, divided by the actual distance between points A and B.

wide range of possible solutions

A) 0.08

B) 0.16

C) 0.24

D) 0.32

Due to the wide range of possible solutions, we may be able to determine the correct solution by approximating g_{AC}, by using the measured value of length BC, $L_{BC,m}$, instead of the actual value of length BC, $L_{BC,a}$.

$L_{BC,m}$=95.44[ft]

measured

$$g_{AC} \approx \frac{L_{BC,m}}{L_{AB,a}} \leftarrow approx.1$$

actual

$L_{AB,a}$=294.15[ft]

The "actual" distance is the true distance, or length, when a measurement is taken at the calibrated temperature of the measuring tape.

$$g_{AC} \approx \frac{95.44[ft]}{294.15[ft]}$$

Approx. 1 is an approximation. The measured value is not exactly the same as the actual value.

Surveying Practice Problems

Distance #11 (cont.)

$$g_{AC} \approx 0.324$$

Since $g_{AC} \approx 0.324$, we strongly
suspect answer D ($g_{AC}=0.32$) is
the correct solution.

A) 0.08
B) 0.16
C) 0.24
? → D) 0.32

temperature
correction
↓

$$L_{BC,a}=L_{BC,m}+c \leftarrow eq.2$$

↑   ↑

actual   measured

Use eq.2 to solve for $L_{BC,a}$

$\alpha_{steel}=1.2*10^{-5}\,[^\circ C^{-1}]$ $L_{BC,m}=95.44\,[ft]$

$$c=\alpha_{steel}*(T_m-T_o)*L_{BC,m} \leftarrow eq.3$$

$T_m=28.7\,[^\circ C]$ $T_o=20\,[^\circ C]$

Use eq.3 to solve for the
temperature correction, c.

Substitute the known values
into eq.3, then calculate c.

$$c=1.2*10^{-5}[^\circ C^{-1}]*(28.7[^\circ C]-20[^\circ C])*95.44[ft]$$

$$c=0.010[ft]$$

It is not always necessary to
convert all variables in the same
equation to the same system of
measurement.

$L_{BC,m}=95.44\,[ft]$ $c=0.010\,[ft]$

$$L_{BC,a}=L_{BC,m}+c \leftarrow eq.2$$

Return to eq. 2, substitute in $L_{BC,m}$
and c, then solve for $L_{BC,a}$.

$$L_{BC,a}=95.44[ft]+0.01[ft]$$

$$L_{BC,a}=95.45[ft]$$

$L_{BC,a}=95.45\,[ft]$

$$g_{AC}=\frac{L_{BC,a}}{L_{AB,a}} \leftarrow eq.1$$

$L_{AB,a}=294.15\,[ft]$

Return to eq.1, plug in $L_{BC,a}$ and
$L_{AB,a}$, then solve for g_{AC}.

Distance #11 (cont.)

$$g_{AC,a} = \frac{95.45 \,[\text{ft}]}{294.15 \,[\text{ft}]}$$

$$g_{AC,a} = 0.324$$

Answer: $\boxed{D}$

The temperature correction had a negligible affect on the grade from point A to point C.

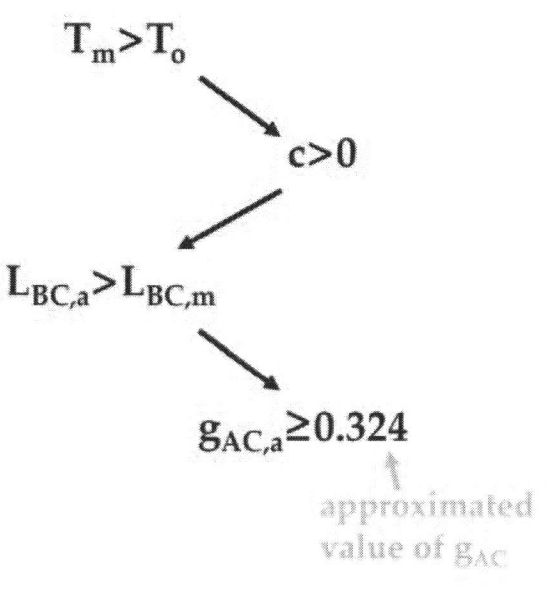

Also note, since $T_m > T_o$, the temperature correction is positive, and $L_{BC,a} > L_{BC,m}$. Therefore, our approximation of $g_{AC} \approx 0.324$ serves as a lower bound for the grade. ($g_{AC} \geq 0.324$)

$T_m > T_o$

$c > 0$

$L_{BC,a} > L_{BC,m}$

$g_{AC,a} \geq 0.324$

approximated value of g_{AC}

The correct answer is D.

Surveying Practice Problems

Distance #12

<u>Find:</u> Elev$_C$ ←the elevation at point C

<u>Given:</u>

Course	Length	Zenith
AB	88.66 [ft]	98°17′30″
BC	219.54 [ft]	86°41′00″

Elev$_A$=247.61 [ft]

the elevation at point A

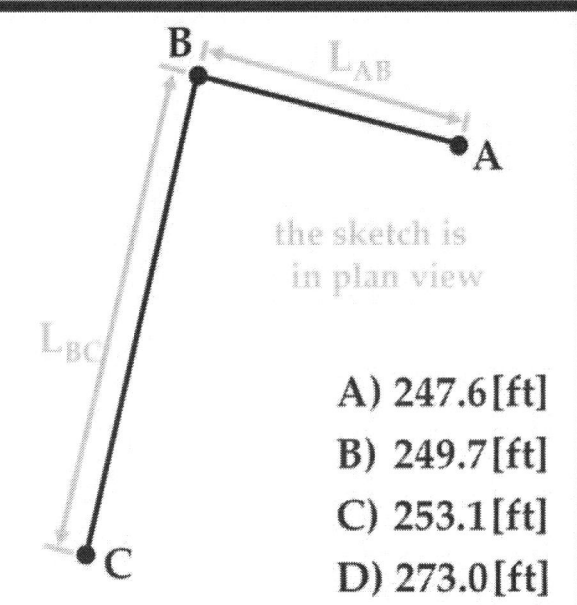

the sketch is in plan view

A) 247.6 [ft]
B) 249.7 [ft]
C) 253.1 [ft]
D) 273.0 [ft]

Analysis:

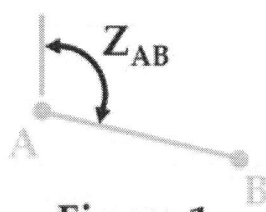

Figure 1

Figure 1 shows the zenith angle is a vertical angle measured from a line through the first point, straight up in the air, to the line connecting the first and second points.

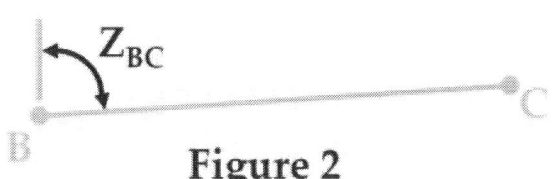

Figure 2

In profile view, Figure 1 shows zenith angle AB and Figure 2 shows zenith angle BC.

Plug in the zenith angles, the lengths and elevation at point A into eq. 1, then solve for the elevation at point C.

L_{AB}=88.66 [ft] L_{BC}=219.54 [ft]

$$Elev_C = Elev_A + L_{AB}*\cos(Z_{AB}) + L_{BC}*\cos(Z_{BC}) \leftarrow eq.1$$

Elev$_A$=247.61 [ft] Z_{AB}=98°17′30″ Z_{BC}=86 41′00″

$$Elev_C = 247.61\,[ft] + 88.66\,[ft]*\cos(98°17′30″)$$
$$+ 219.54\,[ft]*\cos(86°41′00″)$$

Elev$_C$=247.52 [ft]   <u>Answer:</u> A

Leveling #1

Find: HR ← the height of the rod
Given:

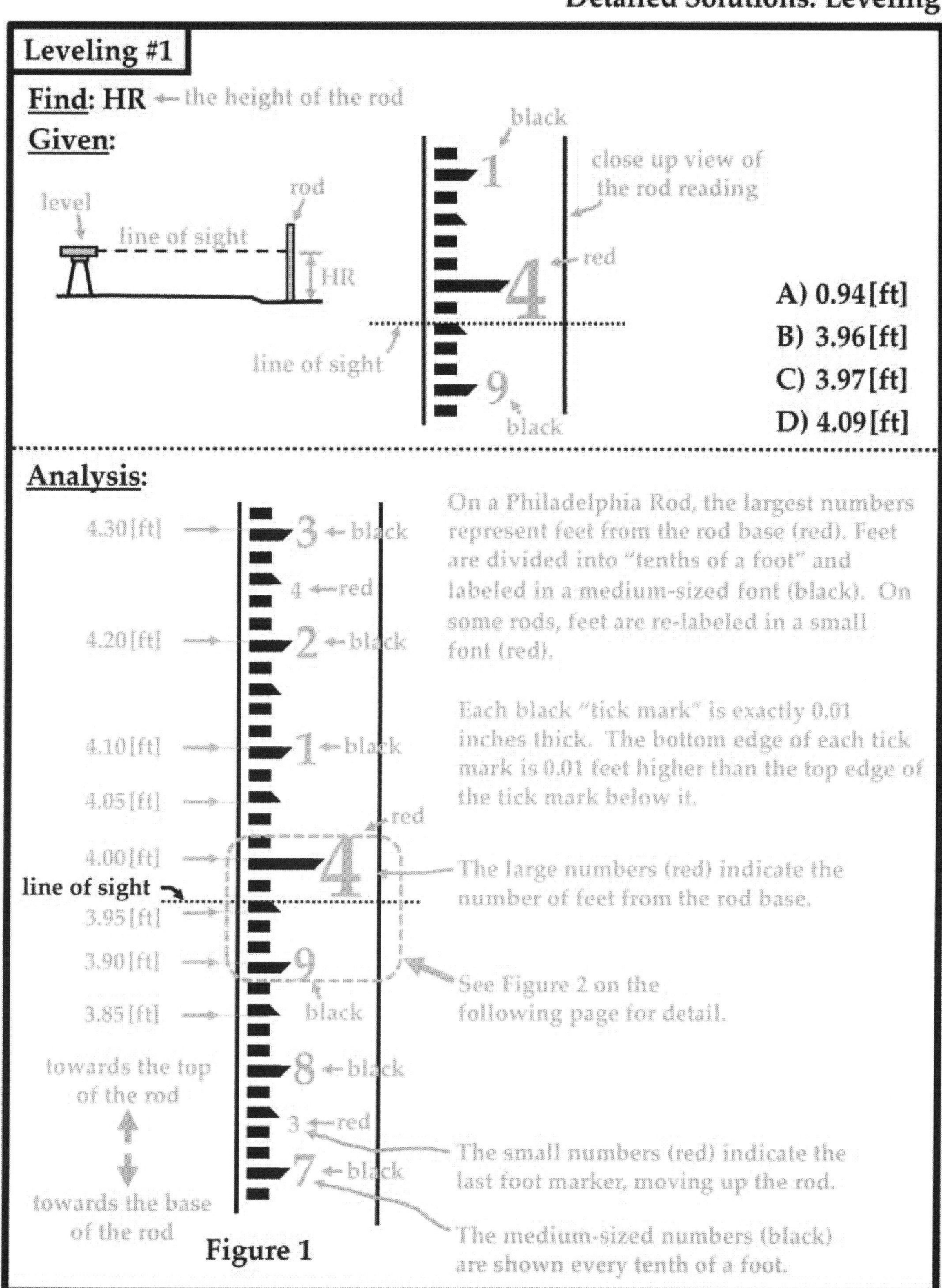

A) 0.94 [ft]

B) 3.96 [ft]

C) 3.97 [ft]

D) 4.09 [ft]

Analysis:

On a Philadelphia Rod, the largest numbers represent feet from the rod base (red). Feet are divided into "tenths of a foot" and labeled in a medium-sized font (black). On some rods, feet are re-labeled in a small font (red).

Each black "tick mark" is exactly 0.01 inches thick. The bottom edge of each tick mark is 0.01 feet higher than the top edge of the tick mark below it.

The large numbers (red) indicate the number of feet from the rod base.

See Figure 2 on the following page for detail.

The small numbers (red) indicate the last foot marker, moving up the rod.

The medium-sized numbers (black) are shown every tenth of a foot.

Figure 1

Leveling #1 (cont)

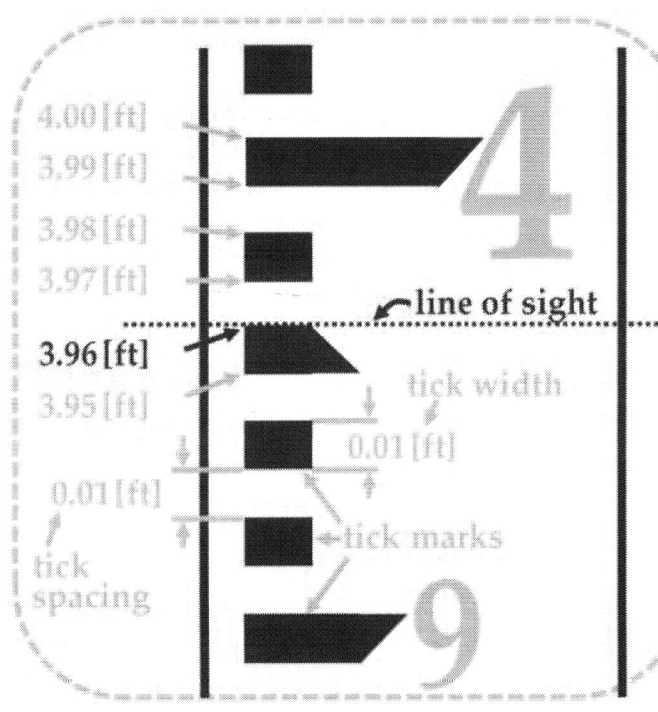

Figure 2

HR=3.96 [ft]

Answer: | B |

Figure 2 is a zoomed portion of Figure 1, from the previous page.

Each black tick mark is exactly 0.01 feet thick. Tick marks are spaced exactly 0.01 feet apart.

The sharp edge of the tick mark is the edge which represents the whole inch, the tenth of an inch, or the twentieth of an inch.

The Philadelphia rod should be held plumb when measurements are read.

Leveling #2

<u>Find</u>: $Elev_B$ ← the elevation at point B

<u>Given</u>:

$Elev_A = 251.47[ft]$ ← the elevation at point A

$HI = 5.14[ft]$ ← the instrument height

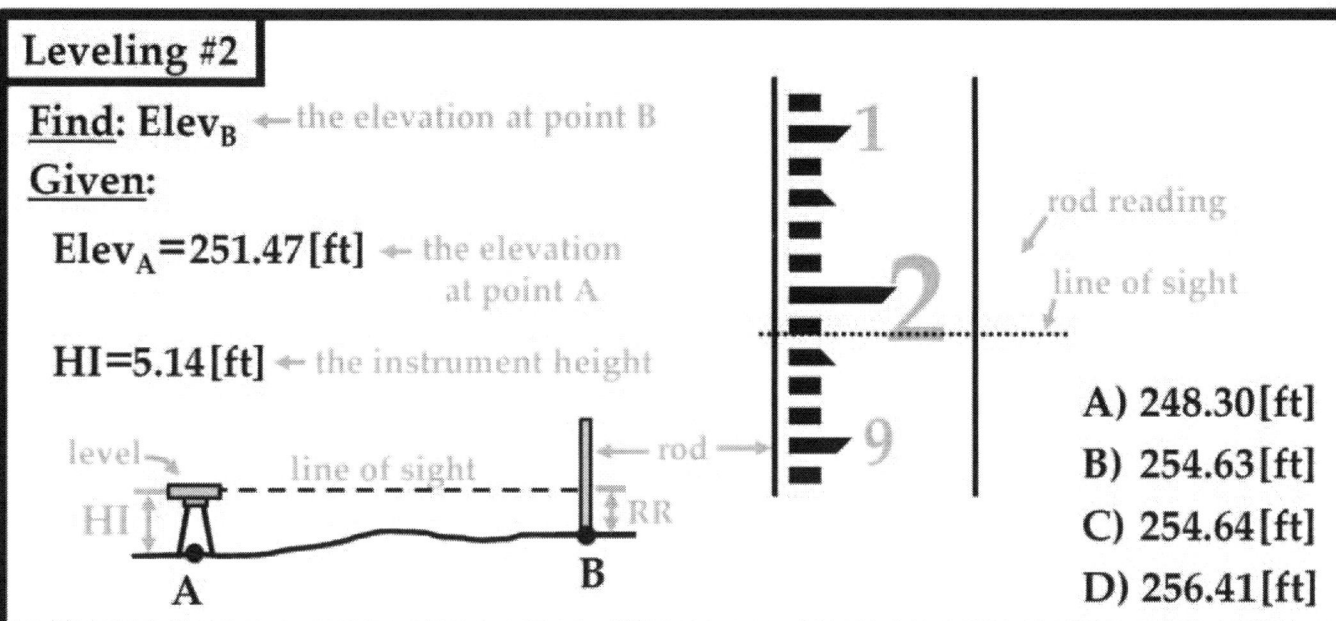

rod reading

line of sight

level

line of sight ← rod →

HI

RR

A

B

A) 248.30[ft]
B) 254.63[ft]
C) 254.64[ft]
D) 256.41[ft]

Analysis:

$$Elev_B = Elev_A + HI - RR \leftarrow eq.1$$

height of the instrument

rod reading, height of rod

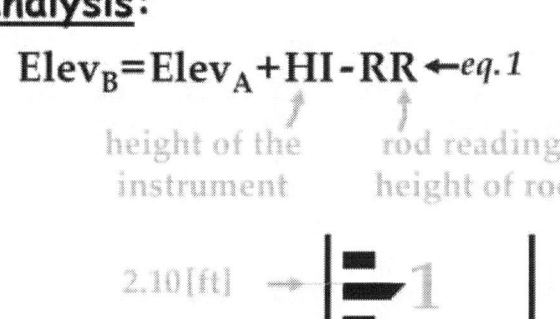

2.10[ft] →

2.05[ft] →

line of sight

2.00[ft] →

RR=1.97[ft]

1.90[ft] →

Figure 1

The elevation at point B equals the elevation at point A, plus the height of the instrument, HI, minus the rod reading, RR.

The terms 'height of rod' and 'rod reading' are used interchangeably.

The rod reading is the length from the base of the rod to the line of sight, when the rod his held plumb.

The rod reading is 1.97 feet.

Philadelphia rods measure to the nearest hundredth of an foot. (0.01[ft])

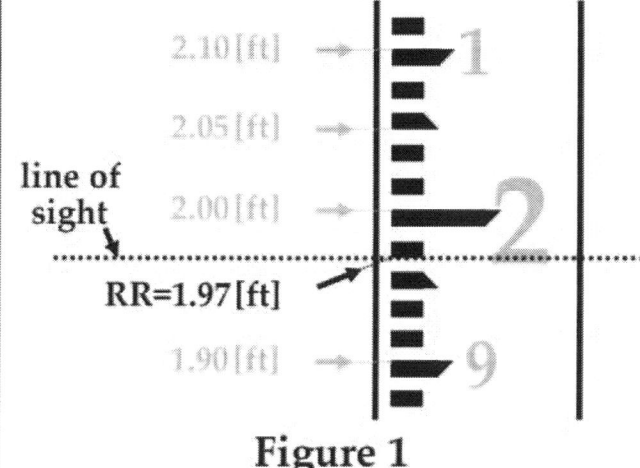

$Elev_A = 251.47[ft]$ $RR = 1.97[ft]$

$$Elev_B = Elev_A + HI - RR \leftarrow eq.1$$

$HI = 5.14[ft]$

In eq.1, substitute in $Elev_A$, HI, and RR, then solve for $Elev_B$.

$$Elev_B = 251.47[ft] + 5.14[ft] - 1.97[ft]$$

$$Elev_C = 254.64[ft]$$ <u>Answer</u>: $\boxed{C}$

Surveying Practice Problems

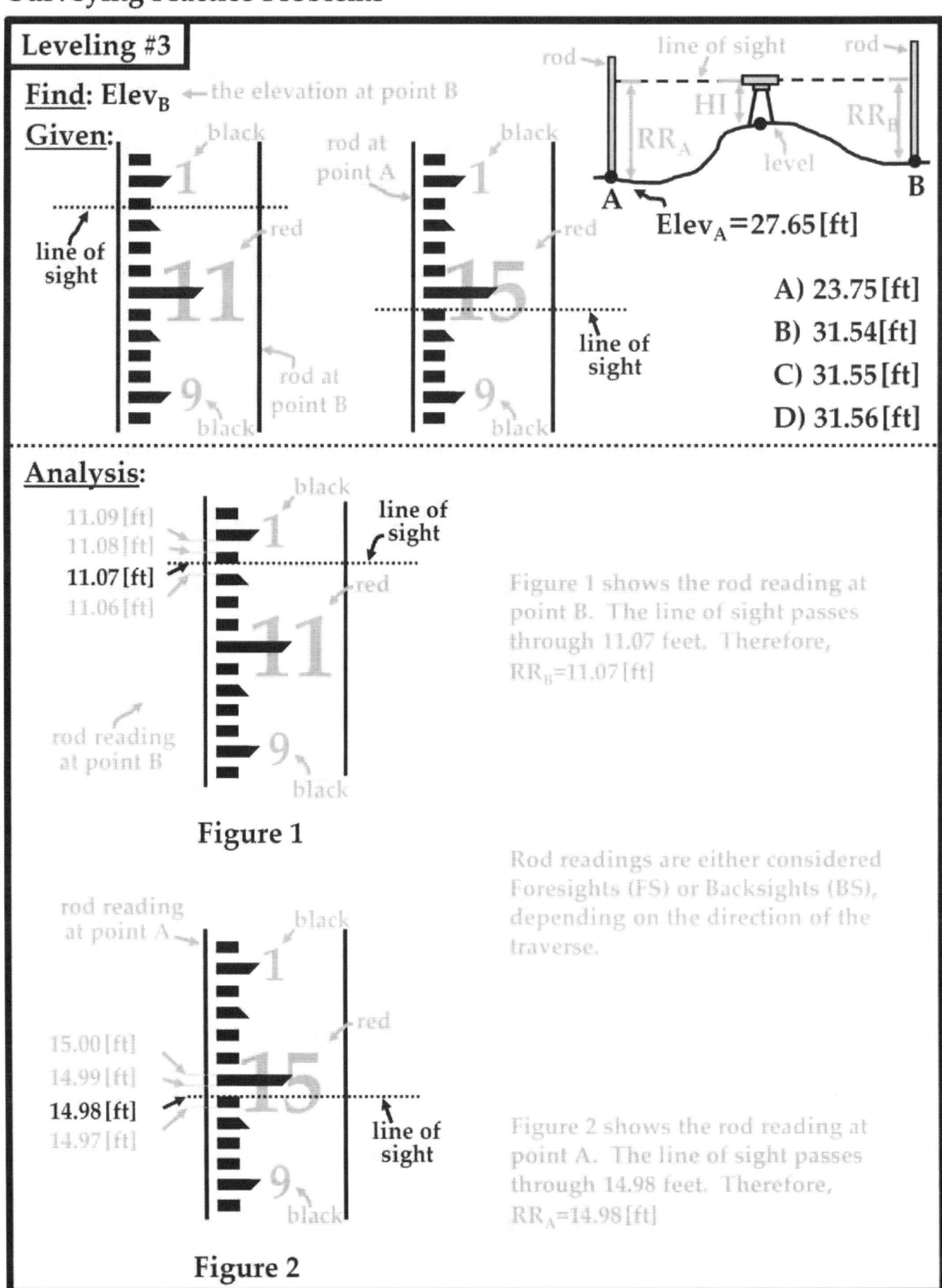

Leveling #3

Find: Elev_B ← the elevation at point B

Given:

Elev$_A$=27.65 [ft]

A) 23.75 [ft]

B) 31.54 [ft]

C) 31.55 [ft]

D) 31.56 [ft]

Analysis:

11.09 [ft]
11.08 [ft]
11.07 [ft]
11.06 [ft]

Figure 1 shows the rod reading at point B. The line of sight passes through 11.07 feet. Therefore, RR$_B$=11.07 [ft]

Figure 1

Rod readings are either considered Foresights (FS) or Backsights (BS), depending on the direction of the traverse.

15.00 [ft]
14.99 [ft]
14.98 [ft]
14.97 [ft]

Figure 2 shows the rod reading at point A. The line of sight passes through 14.98 feet. Therefore, RR$_A$=14.98 [ft]

Figure 2

Leveling #3 (cont)

$$RR_A = 14.98 \, [\text{ft}]$$

$$RR_B = 11.07 \, [\text{ft}]$$

The elevation at point B equals the elevation at point A, plus the rod reading at point A, RR_A, minus the rod reading at point B, RR_B.

$$RR_A = 14.98 \, [\text{ft}]$$

$$Elev_B = Elev_A + RR_A - RR_B \leftarrow eq.1$$

$$Elev_A = 27.65 \, [\text{ft}] \qquad RR_B = 11.07 \, [\text{ft}]$$

Substitute in RR_A, RR_B and $Elev_A$ into eq.1, then solve for $Elev_B$.

$$Elev_B = 27.65 \, [\text{ft}] + 14.98 \, [\text{ft}] - 11.07 \, [\text{ft}]$$

$$Elev_B = 31.56 \, [\text{ft}]$$

In this problem, we don't need to know the height of the instrument.

Answer: $\boxed{D}$

The correct answer is D.

Surveying Practice Problems

Leveling #4

Find: $Elev_K$ ←the elevation at point K

Given:

$Elev_J=299.51\,[ft]$

↑ the elevation at point J

$RR_J=2.67\,[ft]$

↑ the rod reading at point J

the level was at the same location and height when reading the rod at point J and point K.

black

red — line of sight

the rod reading at point K

A) 296.16 [ft]
B) 296.17 [ft]
C) 302.85 [ft]
D) 302.86 [ft]

Analysis:

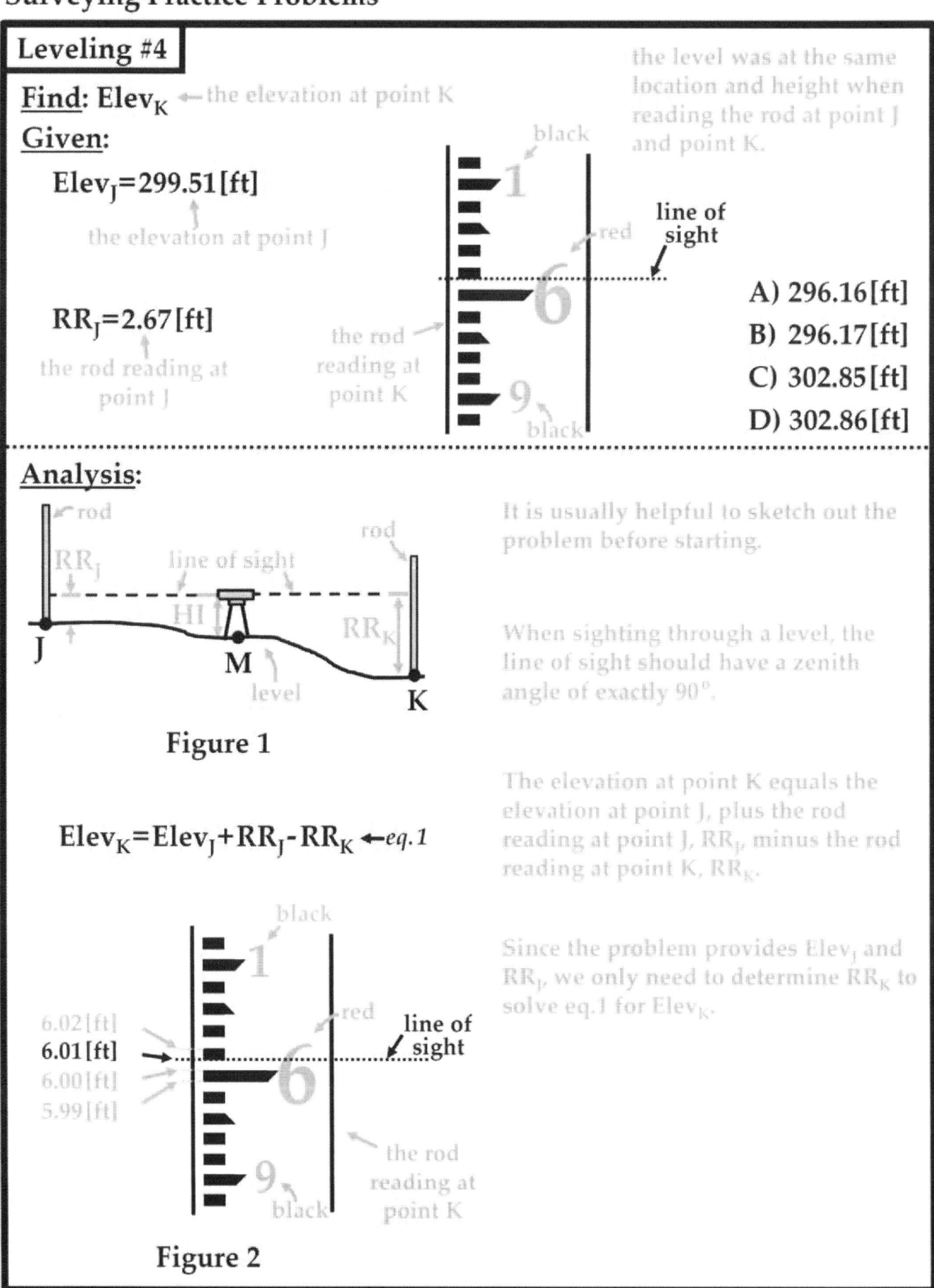

Figure 1

It is usually helpful to sketch out the problem before starting.

When sighting through a level, the line of sight should have a zenith angle of exactly 90°.

$$Elev_K=Elev_J+RR_J-RR_K \leftarrow eq.1$$

The elevation at point K equals the elevation at point J, plus the rod reading at point J, RR_J, minus the rod reading at point K, RR_K.

Since the problem provides $Elev_J$ and RR_J, we only need to determine RR_K to solve eq.1 for $Elev_K$.

black

6.02 [ft]
6.01 [ft]
6.00 [ft]
5.99 [ft]

red — line of sight

the rod reading at point K

black

Figure 2

Leveling #4 (cont)

$$RR_K = 6.01 \, [ft]$$

Plug in the variables on the right side of eq. 1, then solve for $Elev_K$.

$$RR_J = 2.67 \, [ft]$$

$$Elev_K = Elev_J + RR_J - RR_K \; \leftarrow eq.1$$

$$Elev_J = 299.51 \, [ft] \qquad RR_K = 6.01 \, [ft]$$

$$Elev_K = 299.51 \, [ft] + 2.67 \, [ft] - 6.01 \, [ft]$$

$$Elev_K = 296.17 \, [ft]$$

Answer: $\boxed{B}$

From Figure 1, we noticed that $Elev_K < Elev_J$, therefore, we could have ruled out answer C and answer D immediately.

Surveying Practice Problems

Leveling #5

the elevation at
Find: Elev$_C$ ← point C
Given:
the height of the
HI=5.51 [ft] ← instrument
(above point B)

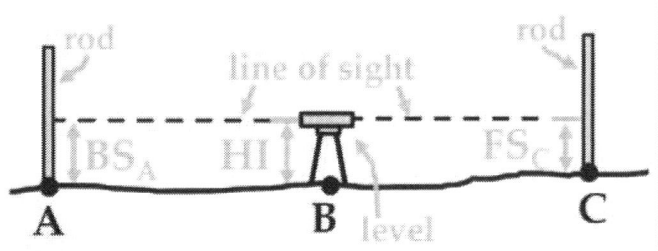

Point	Backsight	Foresight	Elevation
A	4.23		29.71
C		3.76	Elev$_C$

all table values are in units of feet

A) 29.24 [ft]
B) 29.71 [ft]
C) 30.18 [ft]
D) 34.75 [ft]

Analysis:

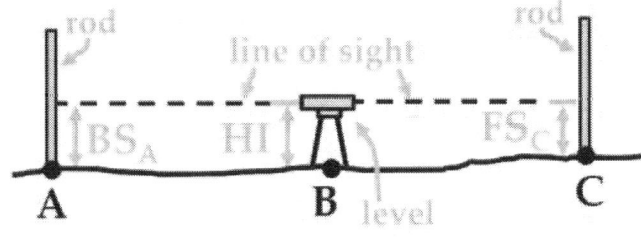

Figure 1

Backsight and foresight values are
rod readings. In this problem, the
backsight is the rod reading at point
A and the foresight is the rod reading
at point C.

Backsight and foresight are
usually abbreviated BS and FS.

Elev$_A$=29.71[ft]   FS$_C$=3.76[ft]

$$Elev_C = Elev_A + BS_A - FS_C \leftarrow eq.1$$

BS$_A$=4.23[ft]

Substitute in Elev$_A$, BS$_A$ and FS$_C$
into eq.1, then solve for Elev$_C$.

$$Elev_C = 29.71 [ft] + 4.23 [ft] - 3.76 [ft]$$

$$Elev_C = 30.18 [ft]$$

Answer: $\boxed{C}$

Since we're not interested in point B,
we don't use HI in this problem.

Leveling #6

<u>Find:</u> $Elev_A$ ← the elevation
at point A

<u>Given:</u>

The level was set up at intermediate points B, D and F. For example, the backsight of point A and the foresight of point C were taken from point B.

Point	BS	FS	Elev
A	3.48		$Elev_A$
C	1.23	19.42	$Elev_C$
E	8.23	6.07	$Elev_E$
G		4.11	225.18

all table values are in units of feet

(no sketch)

A) 208.52 [ft]

B) 209.15 [ft]

C) 241.84 [ft]

D) 244.30 [ft]

<u>Analysis:</u>

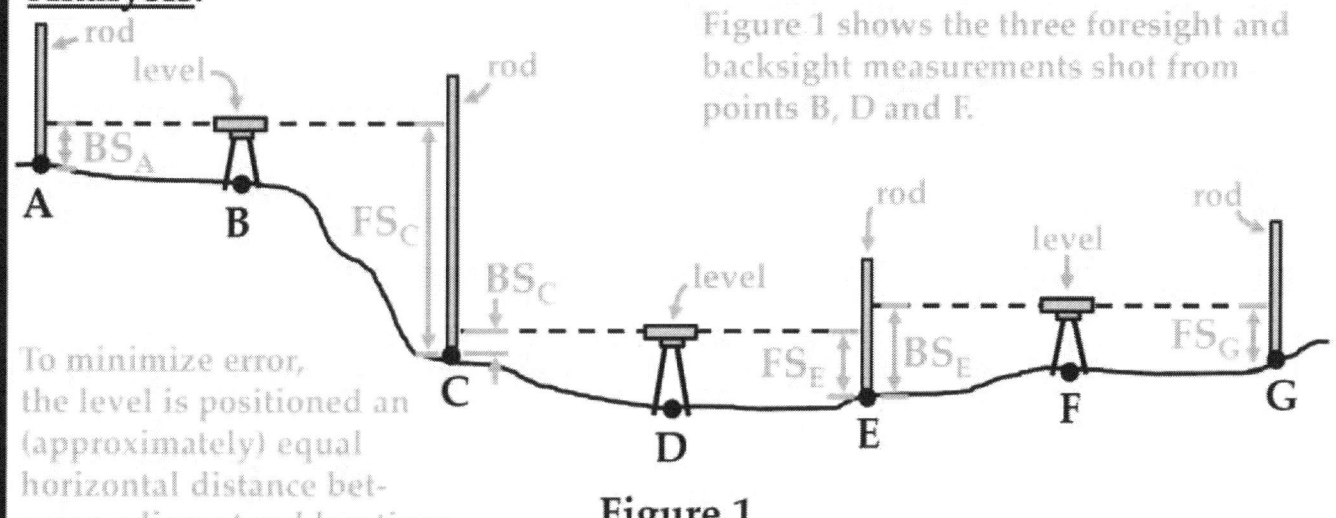

Figure 1 shows the three foresight and backsight measurements shot from points B, D and F.

To minimize error, the level is positioned an (approximately) equal horizontal distance between adjacent rod locations.

Figure 1

In eq. 1, the elevation at point G equals the elevation at point E plus the backsight at point E, minus the foresight at point G.

$$Elev_G = Elev_E + BS_E - FS_G \leftarrow eq.1$$

$FS_G = 4.11 \,[ft]$

$$Elev_E = Elev_G + FS_G - BS_E \leftarrow eq.2$$

$Elev_G = 225.18 \,[ft]$ $BS_E = 8.23 \,[ft]$

After solving eq. 1 for $Elev_E$, we plug in $Elev_G$, FS_G, and BS_E, and solve for $Elev_E$.

$$Elev_E = 225.18 \,[ft] + 4.11 \,[ft] - 8.23 \,[ft]$$

Surveying Practice Problems

Leveling #6 (cont)

$$\text{Elev}_E = 221.06 \, [\text{ft}]$$

$$\text{Elev}_E = \text{Elev}_C + \text{BS}_C - \text{FS}_E \leftarrow eq.3$$

In eq.3, the elevation at point E equals the elevation at point C plus the backsight at point C, minus the foresight at point E.

$$\text{FS}_E = 6.07 \, [\text{ft}]$$
$$\text{Elev}_C = \text{Elev}_E + \text{FS}_E - \text{BS}_C \leftarrow eq.4$$
$$\text{Elev}_E = 221.06 \, [\text{ft}] \qquad \text{BS}_C = 1.23 \, [\text{ft}]$$

After solving eq.3 for Elev_C, we plug in Elev_E, FS_E, and BS_C, and solve for Elev_C.

$$\text{Elev}_C = 221.06 \, [\text{ft}] + 6.07 \, [\text{ft}] - 1.23 \, [\text{ft}]$$

$$\text{Elev}_C = 225.90 \, [\text{ft}]$$

$$\text{Elev}_C = \text{Elev}_A + \text{BS}_A - \text{FS}_C \leftarrow eq.5$$

In eq.5, the elevation at point C equals the elevation at point A plus the backsight at point A, minus the foresight at point C.

$$\text{FS}_C = 19.42 \, [\text{ft}]$$
$$\text{Elev}_A = \text{Elev}_C + \text{FS}_C - \text{BS}_A \leftarrow eq.6$$
$$\text{Elev}_C = 225.90 \, [\text{ft}] \qquad \text{BS}_A = 3.48 \, [\text{ft}]$$

After solving eq.5 for Elev_A, we plug in Elev_C, FS_C, and BS_A, and solve for Elev_A.

$$\text{Elev}_A = 225.90 \, [\text{ft}] + 19.42 \, [\text{ft}] - 3.48 \, [\text{ft}]$$

$$\text{Elev}_A = 241.84 \, [\text{ft}]$$

Answer: $\boxed{\text{C}}$

Leveling #7

<u>Find:</u> Elev$_B$ ← the ground elevation at point B

<u>Given:</u>

the elevation of the instrument

the ground elevation

height of the instrument (above the ground surface)

HI=5.26[ft]

for both setups

Point	BS	ElevI	FS	Elev
D		ElevI$_D$		366.01
C	5.46		8.23	Elev$_C$
B		ElevI$_B$		Elev$_B$
A			1.23	Elev$_A$

all table values are in units of feet

A) 357.98[ft]

B) 363.24[ft]

C) 363.52[ft]

D) 367.27[ft]

<u>Analysis:</u>

Sketching a figure can help us understand the problem.

Figure 1 shows the level is located at points B and D, and the rod is located at points A and C.

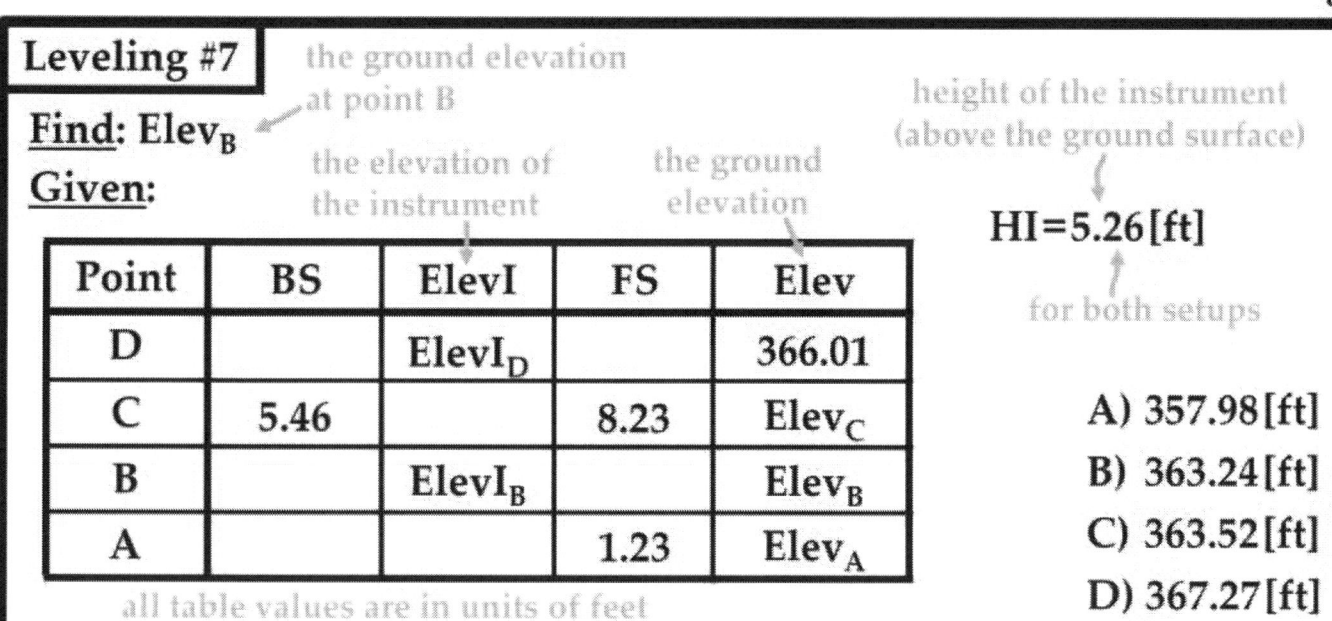

rod

FS$_C$=1.23[ft]

level

rod

5.46[ft]

8.23[ft]

level

HI

BS$_C$

FS$_C$

HI

A

B   5.26[ft]

C

5.26[ft]

D

Figure 1

possible solutions

A) 357.98[ft]

B) 363.24[ft]

C) 363.52[ft]

D) 367.27[ft] ← too large?

From Figure 1, the elevation at point B appears lower than the elevation at point D. Therefore, answer D is probably too large.

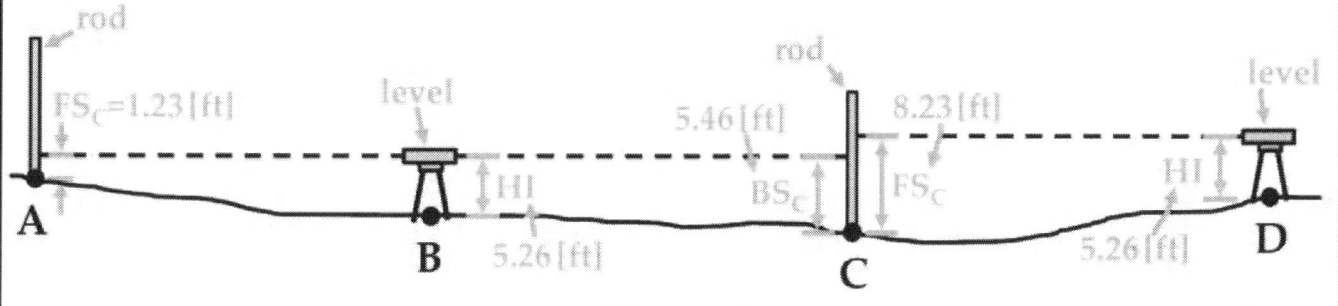

The elevation at point B equals the elevation at point C plus the backsight of point C, minus the height of the instrument.

$$\text{Elev}_B=\text{Elev}_C+\text{BS}_C-\text{HI} \quad \leftarrow eq.\,1$$

Surveying Practice Problems

Leveling #7 (cont)

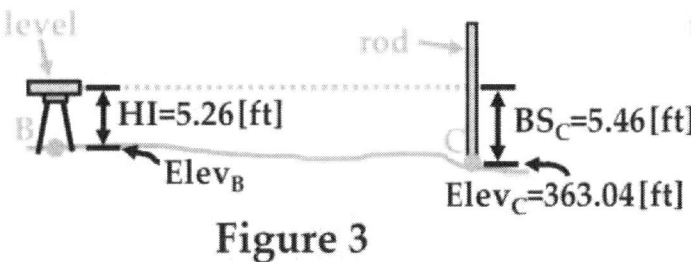

Figure 2 identifies the variables used in eq.2.

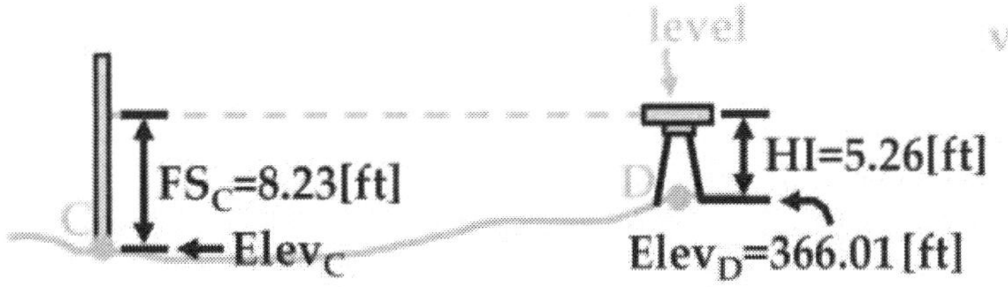

$$FS_C = 8.23 \, [ft]$$
$$HI = 5.26 \, [ft]$$
$$\leftarrow Elev_C$$
$$Elev_D = 366.01 \, [ft]$$

Figure 2

$Elev_D = 366.01 \, [ft]$

$$Elev_C = Elev_D + HI - FS_C \leftarrow eq.2$$

$HI = 5.26 \, [ft] \quad FS_C = 8.23 \, [ft]$

In eq.2, we calculate the elevation at point C, which equals the elev-ation at point D plus the height of the instrument, minus the foresight at point C.

$$Elev_C = 366.01 \, [ft] + 5.26 \, [ft] - 8.23 \, [ft]$$

$$Elev_C = 363.04 \, [ft]$$

level

$$HI = 5.26 \, [ft]$$
$$Elev_B$$
rod
$$BS_C = 5.46 \, [ft]$$
$$Elev_C = 363.04 \, [ft]$$

Figure 3 identifies the variables used in eq.3.

Figure 3

Return to eq.1, plug in $Elev_C$, BS_C, and HI, then solve for $Elev_B$.

$BS_C = 5.46 \, [ft] \quad HI = 5.26 \, [ft]$

$$Elev_B = Elev_C + BS_C - HI \leftarrow eq.1$$

$Elev_C = 363.04 \, [ft]$

Remember the problem states the HI value is the same for set ups at point B and at point D.

$$Elev_B = 363.04 \, [ft] + 5.46 \, [ft] - 5.26 \, [ft]$$

$$Elev_B = 363.24 \, [ft]$$

Answer: $\boxed{B}$

The correct answer is B.

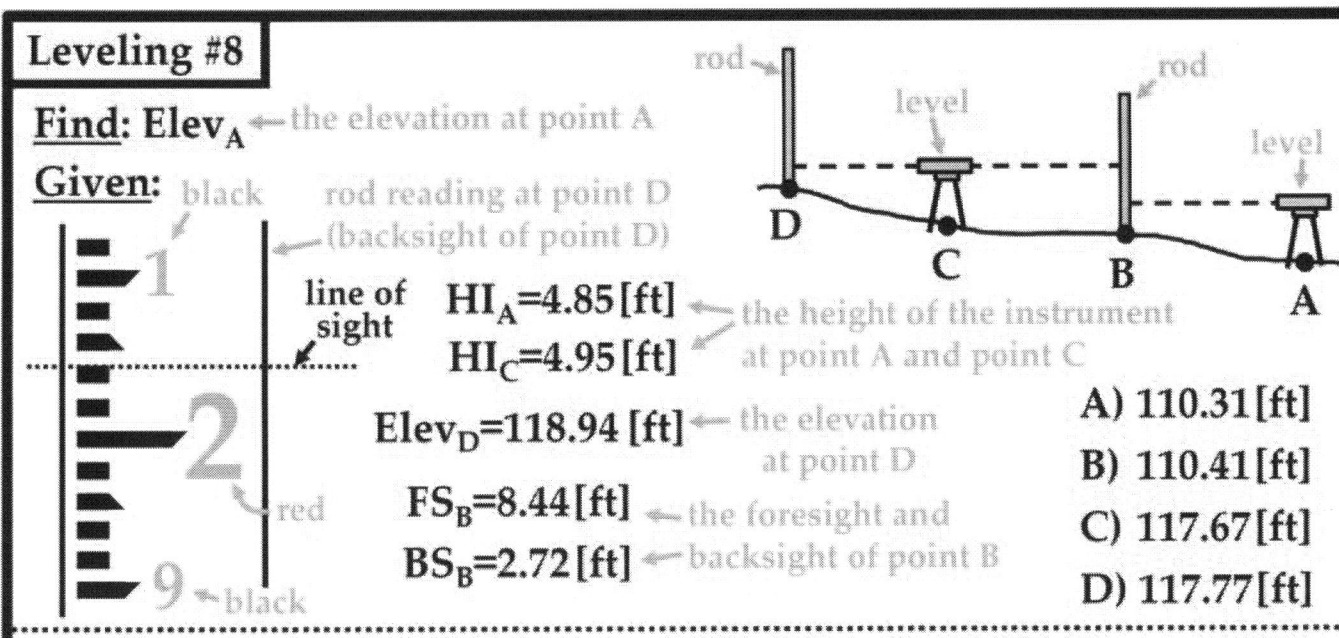

Leveling #8

Find: Elev$_A$ ←the elevation at point A

Given: black   rod reading at point D
(backsight of point D)

line of sight

HI_A=4.85 [ft] ←the height of the instrument
HI_C=4.95 [ft]   at point A and point C

$Elev_D$=118.94 [ft] ←the elevation
at point D

FS_B=8.44 [ft] ←the foresight and
BS_B=2.72 [ft] ←backsight of point B

A) 110.31 [ft]

B) 110.41 [ft]

C) 117.67 [ft]

D) 117.77 [ft]

Analysis:

Figure 1 identifies the given variables

HI_A and HI_C represent the height of the instrument above the surface of the ground at points A and C, respectively.

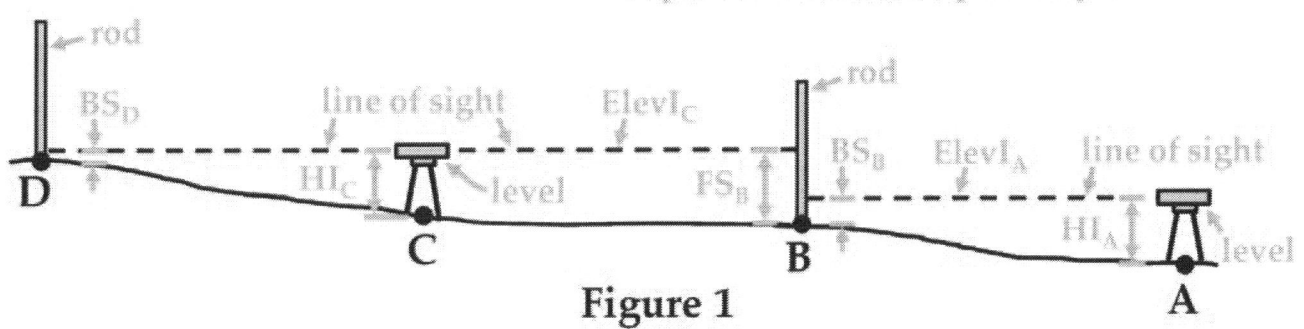

Figure 1

Point	BS	ElevI	FS	Elev
D	BS_D			$Elev_D$
C		$ElevI_C$		$Elev_C$
B	BS_B		FS_B	$Elev_B$
A		$ElevI_A$		$Elev_A$

Table 1

We'll organize our data into Table 1.

Elev=ground elevation

ElevI=elevation of the instrument

ElevI is also the elevation of the line of sight.

$Elev_D$=118.94 [ft]

FS_B=8.44 [ft]

BS_B=2.72 [ft]

we will update Table 1 with the given values

Surveying Practice Problems

Leveling #8 (cont)

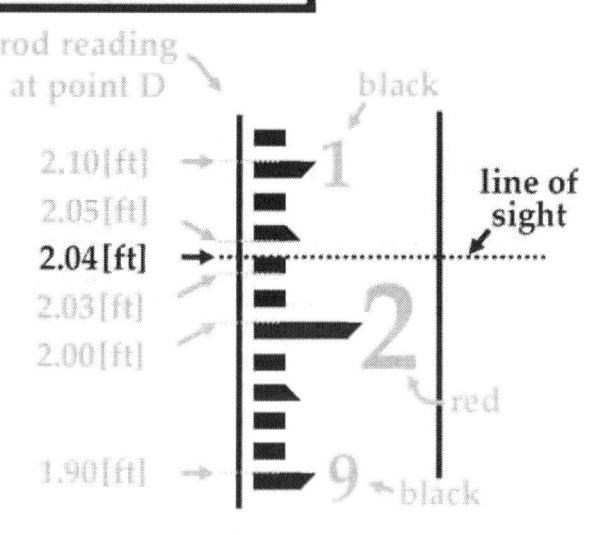

rod reading at point D

2.10[ft]
2.05[ft]
2.04[ft]
2.03[ft]
2.00[ft]

1.90[ft]

black

line of sight

red

black

Figure 2

Figure 2 shows the rod reading at point D, which is the backsight, shot from point C.

In Figure 2, the big "red" 2 represents a rod reading of 2.00 feet. The "black" 1 and "black" 9 represent rod readings of 2.10 feet and 1.90 feet, respectively.

$$BS_D=2.04\,[ft]$$

From Figure 2, we determine the backsight of point D equals 2.04 feet.

Point	BS	ElevI	FS	Elev
D	2.04			118.94
C		$ElevI_C$		$Elev_C$
B	2.72		8.44	$Elev_B$
A		$ElevI_A$		$Elev_A$

Table 2   ?

Table 2 includes the values of the known variables.

Remember we want to solve for the elevation at point A, $Elev_A$.

$$Elev_A=Elev_B+BS_B-HI_A \leftarrow eq.1$$

The ground elevation at point A equals the ground elevation at point B plus the backsight at point B, minus the height of the instrument of point A.

$$Elev_B=Elev_D+BS_D-FS_B \leftarrow eq.2$$

The ground elevation at point B equals the ground elevation at point D plus the backsight of point D, minus the foresight of point B.

Leveling #8 (cont)

$Elev_B = Elev_D + BS_D - FS_B$

$Elev_A = Elev_B + BS_B - HI_A \leftarrow eq.1$

Substitute the right hand side of eq. 2 into variable $Elev_B$ of eq. 1.

Plug in variables $Elev_D$, BS_D, FS_B, BS_B and HI_A, into eq.3, then solve for $Elev_A$.

$Elev_D = 118.94 \, [ft]$ $BS_B = 2.72 \, [ft]$

$$Elev_A = Elev_D + BS_D - FS_B + BS_B - HI_A \leftarrow eq.3$$

$BS_D = 2.04 \, [ft]$ $FS_B = 8.44 \, [ft]$ $HI_A = 4.85 \, [ft]$

$$Elev_A = 118.94 \, [ft] + 2.04 \, [ft] - 8.44 \, [ft] + 2.72 \, [ft] - 4.85 \, [ft]$$

$$Elev_A = 110.41 \, [ft]$$

Answer: **B**

Surveying Practice Problems

Leveling #9

the vertical error of closure at point W

Find: EOC_W

Given: all table values are in units of feet

Point	BS	ElevI	FS	Elev
W	1.23			$Elev_{W,1}$
X		$ElevI_X$		$Elev_X$
Y	8.23		5.46	$Elev_Y$
Z		$ElevI_Z$		$Elev_Z$
W			3.98	$Elev_{W,2}$

sketch in plan view

rod → W   level → X

rod →

Z   level   Y

A) 0.00 [ft]

B) 0.01 [ft]

C) 0.02 [ft]

D) 0.03 [ft]

Analysis:

$$EOC_W = Elev_{W,2} - Elev_{W,1} \leftarrow eq.1$$

The vertical error of closure equals the vertical difference between a known elevation and a measured elevation.

$$Elev_{W,2} = Elev_{W,1} + BS_W - FS_Y + BS_Y - FS_W \leftarrow eq.2$$

Solve eq. 2 for $Elev_{W,2} - Elev_{W,1}$.

$$Elev_{W,2} - Elev_{W,1} = BS_W - FS_Y + BS_Y - FS_W \leftarrow eq.3$$

$$Elev_{W,2} - Elev_{W,1} = \underbrace{BS_W - FS_Y + BS_Y - FS_W}$$

$$EOC_W = \overbrace{Elev_{W,2} - Elev_{W,1}} \leftarrow eq.1$$

Substitute in the right hand side of eq. 3 in for the right hand side of eq. 1.

$BS_W = 1.23 [ft]$ $BS_Y = 8.23 [ft]$

$$EOC_W = BS_W - FS_Y + BS_Y - FS_W \leftarrow eq.4$$

$FS_W = 5.46 [ft]$ $FS_Y = 3.98 [ft]$

Plug in variables BS_W, FS_Y, BS_Y and FS_W, into eq.4, then solve for EOC_W.

$EOC_W = 1.23[ft] - 5.46[ft] + 8.23[ft] - 3.98[ft]$

$EOC_W = 0.02[ft]$

In this problem we don't need to solve for the elevation of the points or the elevation instrument.

Answer: $\boxed{C}$

Surveying Practice Problems

Leveling #10

Find: g_{JK} ← the average grade from point J to point K

Given:

$HI = 5.74$ [ft]
the height of the instrument

$L_{JK,x} = 132.59$ [ft]
the horizontal distance between points J and K

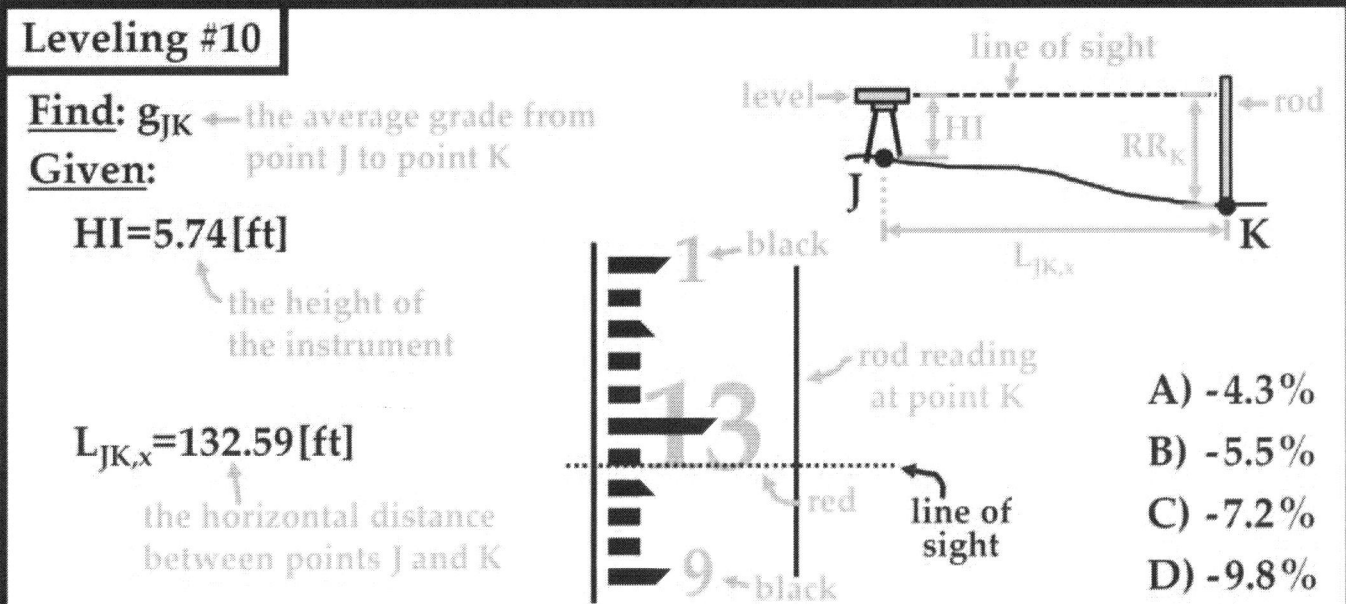

A) -4.3%

B) -5.5%

C) -7.2%

D) -9.8%

Analysis:

$$g_{JK} = \frac{Elev_K - Elev_J}{L_{JK,x}} \leftarrow eq.1$$

The average grade between two points is the change in elevation between the two points, divided by the horizontal distance between the two points.

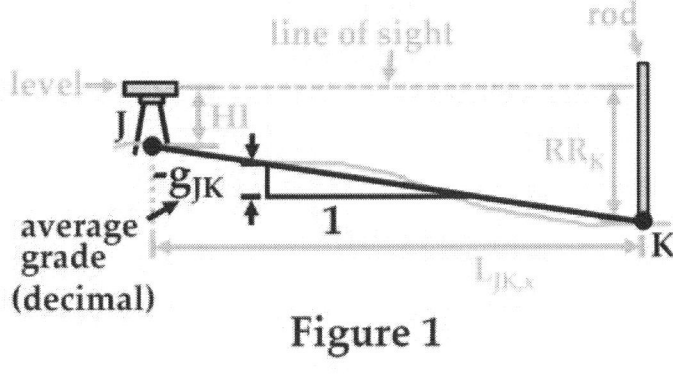

Figure 1

Figure 1 identifies the average grade between points J and K.

If the elevation of point K is less than the elevation of point J (as shown in Figure 1), then the average grade will be negative.

$$Elev_K = Elev_J + HI - RR_K \leftarrow eq.2$$

The elevation of point K equals the elevation of point J, plus the height of the instrument, minus the rod reading at point K.

$$Elev_K - Elev_J = HI - RR_K \leftarrow eq.3$$

Subtract $Elev_J$ from both sides of eq.2. The left hand side of eq.3 is the same as the numerator of eq.1.

Leveling #10 (cont.)

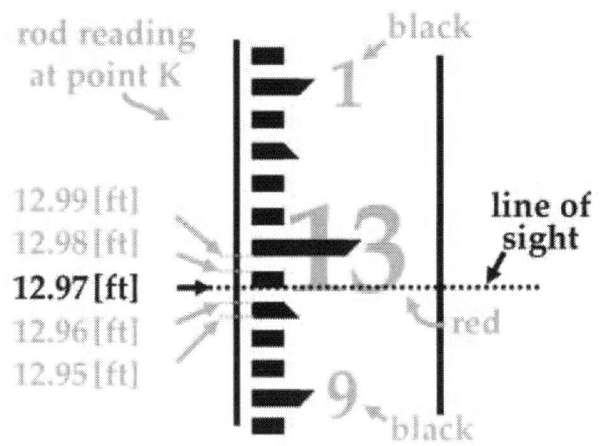

rod reading at point K

black

12.99 [ft]
12.98 [ft]
12.97 [ft]
12.96 [ft]
12.95 [ft]

line of
sight

red

black

Figure 2

Figure 2 shows the rod reading at point K and identifies the rod reading equals 12.97 [ft].

$$RR_K = 12.97 \, [ft]$$

$$HI = 5.74 \, [ft] \quad RR_K = 12.97 \, [ft]$$

$$Elev_K - Elev_J = HI - RR_K \leftarrow eq.3$$

Return to eq.3, plug in HI and RR_K, and solve for the elevation difference between point K and point J.

$$Elev_K - Elev_J = 5.74 \, [ft] - 12.97 \, [ft]$$

$$Elev_K - Elev_J = -7.23 \, [ft]$$

Point K is 7.23 feet lower than point J.

$$Elev_K - Elev_J = -7.23 \, [ft]$$

$$g_{JK} = \frac{Elev_K - Elev_J}{L_{JK,x}} \leftarrow eq.1$$

$$L_{JK,x} = 132.59 \, [ft]$$

In eq.1, plug in $Elev_K - Elev_J$ and $L_{JK,x}$, then solve for g_{JK}.

$$g_{JK} = \frac{-7.23 \, [ft]}{132.59 \, [ft]}$$

Surveying Practice Problems

Leveling #10 (cont.)

$g_{JK} = -0.0545$

$*100\%$

Convert the decimal value of -0.0545 to a percentage by multiplying by 100%

$g_{JK} = -5.45\%$

A) -4.3%

B) -5.5%

C) -7.2%

D) -9.8%

Of the possible solutoins, our calculated value of g_{JK} is most nearly answer B.

Notice how we don't need to know the actual elevation of points J or K, we only need to know the elevation difference.

<u>Answer:</u> B

Leveling #11

Find: $Elev_{B,corr}$ ←the corrected elevation at point B

Given:

$HI = 5.05 [ft]$ ←the height of the instrument

$Elev_A = 54.22 [ft]$
$Elev_C = 60.06 [ft]$ } known elevations of points A and C

$RR_A = 9.41 [ft]$
$RR_C = 3.51 [ft]$ } rod readings at points A and C

$L_{AB,x} = 150 [ft]$
$L_{BC,x} = 150 [ft]$ } horizontal distance between points A and B, and between points B and C

A) $58.55 [ft]$

B) $58.58 [ft]$

C) $58.61 [ft]$

D) $58.64 [ft]$

Analysis:

$$Elev_{B,corr} = Elev_{B,meas} + c_B \quad \leftarrow eq.1$$

elevation correction

The corrected elevation at point B equals the measured elevation at point B, plus the elevation correction at point B.

$Elev_A = 54.22 [ft]$ $HI = 5.05 [ft]$

$$Elev_{B,meas} = Elev_A + RR_A - HI \quad \leftarrow eq.2$$

$RR_A = 9.41 [ft]$

$$Elev_{B,meas} = 54.22 [ft] + 9.41 [ft] - 5.05 [ft]$$

$$Elev_{B,meas} = 58.58 [ft]$$

The measured elevation at point B equals 58.58 feet.

$$c_B = \left(\frac{L_{AB}}{L_{AB} + L_{BC}}\right) * (Elev_C - Elev_{C,meas}) \quad \leftarrow eq.3$$

elevation correction at point B

In eq.3, $Elev_{C,meas}$ is the elevation of point C based on the known elevation at point A, and the rod readings at point A and point C.

Surveying Practice Problems

Leveling #11 (cont.)

Use eq. 4 to compute the measured elevation at point C.

$Elev_A = 54.22 [ft]$ $RR_C = 3.51 [ft]$

$$Elev_{C,meas} = Elev_A + RR_A - RR_C \leftarrow eq.4$$

$RR_A = 9.41 [ft]$

$$Elev_{C,meas} = 54.22 [ft] + 9.41 [ft] - 3.51 [ft]$$

$$Elev_{C,meas} = 60.12 [ft]$$

Return to eq. 3, substitute in L_{AB}, L_{BC}, $Elev_C$, and $Elev_{C,meas}$, then solve for c_B.

$L_{AB} = 150 [ft]$ $Elev_C = 60.06 [ft]$

$$c_B = \left(\frac{L_{AB}}{L_{AB} + L_{BC}} \right) * (Elev_C - Elev_{C,meas}) \leftarrow eq.3$$

$L_{BC} = 150 [ft]$ $Elev_{C,meas} = 60.12 [ft]$

The measured elevation at point C is 0.06 feet higher than the true elevation at point C.

$$c_B = \left(\frac{150 [ft]}{150 [ft] + 150 [ft]} \right) * (60.06 [ft] - 60.12 [ft])$$

$$c_B = -0.03 [ft]$$

Since point B is an equal horizontal distance from points A and C, the elevation correction at point B will equal half the elevation difference at point C.

$c_B = -0.03 [ft]$

$$Elev_{B,corr} = Elev_{B,meas} + c_B \leftarrow eq.1$$

$Elev_{B,meas} = 58.58 [ft]$

Return to eq. 1, plug in $Elev_{B,meas}$ and c_B, then solve for $Elev_{B,corr}$.

$$Elev_{B,corr} = 58.58 [ft] + (-0.03 [ft])$$

$$Elev_{B,corr} = 58.55 [ft]$$

If we began at point C, we would compute $Elev_{A,meas} = 54.16 [ft]$, then $c_B = 0.03 [ft]$, and also determine $Elev_{B,corr} = 58.55 [ft]$.

Answer: A

Leveling #12

Find: L_{AB} ← the length between points A and point B

Given:

K=100

↑ interval factor

C=0 [ft]

↑ instrument factor

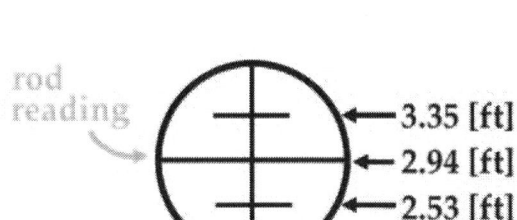

stadia   horizontal line   rod

A   B

rod reading →

← 3.35 [ft]
← 2.94 [ft]
← 2.53 [ft]

A) 41 [ft]

B) 82 [ft]

C) 164 [ft]

D) 294 [ft]

Analysis:

$$L_{AB}=K*S+C \leftarrow eq.1$$

↳ stadia intercept

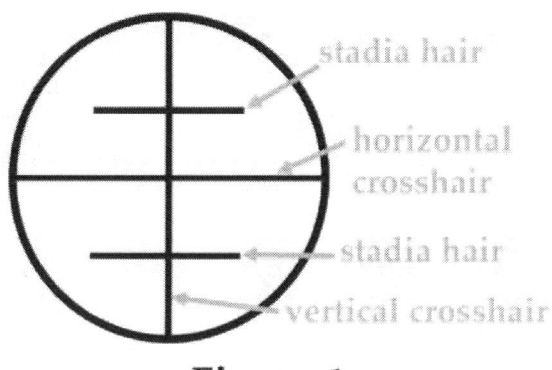

stadia hair

horizontal crosshair

stadia hair

vertical crosshair

Figure 1

Use eq.1 to compute the distance between point A and point B.

The stadia intercept, S, is the distance between the stadia hairs on the rod, when the rod is angled perpendicular to the line of sight.

Figure 1 identifies the crosshairs and stadia hairs of the stadia.

Unless otherwise noted, assume the rod is held vertical (plumb).

$$S=3.35 [ft]-2.53 [ft] \leftarrow eq.2$$

$$S=0.82 [ft]$$

Use eq.2 to compute S.

$$L_{AB}=K*S+C \leftarrow eq.1$$

K=100   S=0.82 [ft]   C=0 [ft]

Return to eq.1, plug in K, S, and C, then solve for L_{AB}.

$$L_{AB}=100*0.82 [ft]+0 [ft]$$

$$L_{AB}=82 [ft]$$ **Answer:** | B |

Surveying Practice Problems

Leveling #13

Find: $L_{AB,x}$ — the horizontal distance between points A and B.

Given:

K=200 ← interval factor

C=0 [ft] ← instrument factor

$\theta=17.4°$

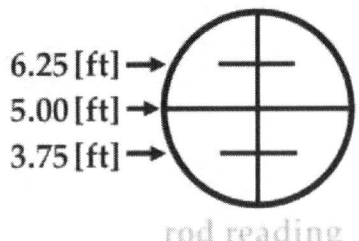

6.25 [ft] →
5.00 [ft] →
3.75 [ft] →

rod reading

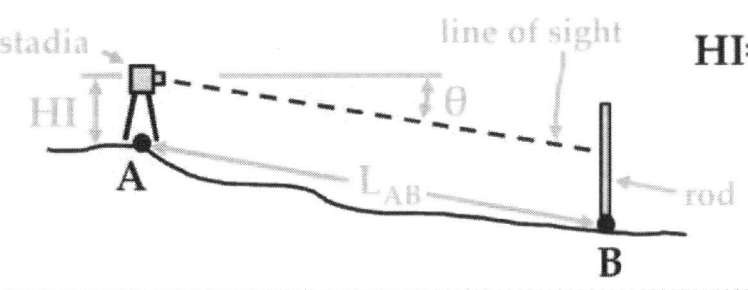

stadia

line of sight

HI

θ

A

L_{AB}

rod

B

HI=5.00 [ft]

height of instrument

A) 239 [ft]

B) 455 [ft]

C) 477 [ft]

D) 500 [ft]

Analysis:

$$L_{AB,x}=L_{AB}*\cos(\theta) \leftarrow eq.1$$

We'll use eq.1 to find $L_{AB,x}$. Since the problem provides θ, we just need to determine L_{AB}.

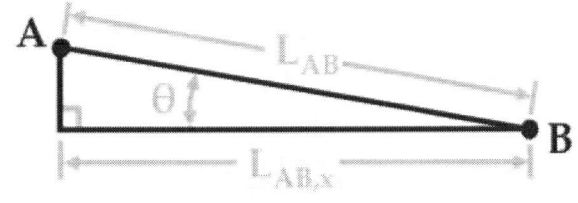

A

L_{AB}

θ

B

$L_{AB,x}$

Figure 1

Figure 1 shows $L_{AB,x}$, the horizontal distance between points A and B, and L_{AB}, the straight-line distance between points A and B.

Eq.2 computes the straight-line distance between points A and B.

$$L_{AB}=K*S+C \leftarrow eq.2$$

stadia intercept

Since HI equals the horizontal crosshair reading, no additional adjustment is necessary to eq.2.

$$S=S_i*\cos(\theta) \leftarrow eq.3$$

inclined stadia intercept

Eq.3 computes the stadia intercept.

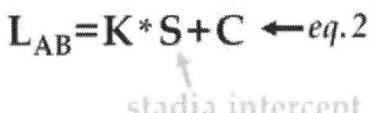

$$S_i=6.25[ft]-3.75[ft]$$

The inclined stadia intercept is the distance between the stadia hairs on the rod reading when the line of sight is not perpendicular to the rod

$$S_i=2.50[ft]$$

Leveling #13 (cont.)

$\theta = 17.4°$

$$S = S_i * \cos(\theta) \leftarrow eq.3$$

$S_i = 2.50 [ft]$

Return to eq.3, plug in S_i and θ, then solve for S.

$$S = 2.50 [ft] * \cos(17.4°)$$

$$S = 2.386 [ft]$$

$S = 2.386 [ft]$

$$L_{AB} = K * S + C \leftarrow eq.2$$

$K = 200 \qquad C = 0 [ft]$

In eq.2, plug in K, S and C, then solve for L_{AB}.

$$L_{AB} = 200 * 2.386 [ft] + 0 [ft]$$

$$L_{AB} = 477.2 [ft]$$

$L_{AB} = 477.2 [ft]$

$$L_{AB,x} = L_{AB} * \cos(\theta) \leftarrow eq.1$$

$\theta = 17.4°$

Solve for $L_{AB,x}$ using eq.1.

$$L_{AB,x} = 477.2 [ft] * \cos(17.4°)$$

$$L_{AB,x} = 455.4 [ft]$$

Answer: $\boxed{B}$

Surveying Practice Problems

Leveling #14

Find: Z ← the zenith angle

triangle ABC is a right triangle

5.85 [ft] →
5.50 [ft] →
5.15 [ft] →

rod reading

Given:

L_{AB}=219.50[ft] ← the length between point A and point B

K=333 ← interval factor

C=0[ft]

instrument factor

A) 70°

B) 72°

C) 74°

D) 76°

HI=5.50[ft]

height of instrument

Z — line of sight — stadia — HI — A — L_{AB} — B — C

Analysis:

height of rod

HR=5.50[ft]

From the rod reading, we notice HR=5.50[ft]. Since HR=HI, we know L_{AC} equals the length of the line of sight.

HR=HI

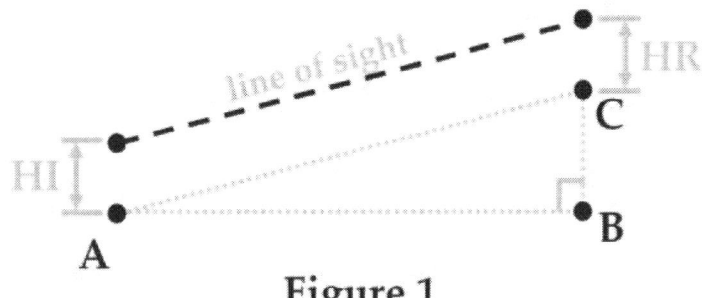

In Figure 1, notice how shows how the length of the line of sight equals the length between point A and point C, when HI=HR.

Figure 1

L_{AB}=L_{AC}*sin(Z) ←eq.1

Since we know triangle ABC is a right triangle, we can relate L_{AB}, L_{AC} and angle Z, in eq.1.

$$\sin(Z)=\left(\frac{L_{AB}}{L_{AC}}\right) \leftarrow eq.2$$

Isolate the sin(Z) term from eq.1

Leveling #14 (cont.)

$$L_{AC} = K * S + C \leftarrow eq.3$$

We already know L_{AB}. Use eq.3 to find L_{AC}.

$$S = S_1 * \sin(Z) \leftarrow eq.4$$

$$S_1 = 5.85 [ft] - 5.15 [ft]$$

In eq.3 and eq.4, variable S refers to the distance between the two stadia hairs when the rod is held perpendicular to the line of sight.

$$S = (5.85 [ft] - 5.15 [ft]) * \sin(Z)$$

$$S = 0.7 [ft] * \sin(Z)$$

In eq.4, variable S_1 refers to the observed distance between the two stadia hairs when the rod is held vertically.

$$S = 0.7 [ft] * \sin(Z)$$

$$L_{AC} = K * S + C \leftarrow eq.3$$

$$K = 333 \qquad C = 0 [ft]$$

Plug in K, S and C into eq.3, then solve for L_{AC}.

$$L_{AC} = 333 * 0.7 [ft] * \sin(Z) + 0 [ft]$$

$$L_{AC} = 233.1 [ft] * \sin(Z)$$

$$\sin(Z) = \left(\frac{L_{AB}}{L_{AC}}\right) \leftarrow eq.2$$

$$L_{AC} = 233.1 [ft] * \sin(Z)$$

Plug in L_{AC} into eq.2.

$$\sin(Z) = \left(\frac{L_{AB}}{233.1 [ft] * \sin(Z)}\right) \leftarrow eq.5$$

Isolate the zenith angle, Z, in eq.5, plug in L_{AB}, then solve for Z.

Leveling #14 (cont.)

$L_{AB}=219.50\,[ft]$

$$Z=\sin^{-2}\left(\frac{L_{AB}}{233.1\,[ft]}\right) \leftarrow eq.6$$

In eq.6, Z equals the arcsine of the square root of the quotient inside the parenthesis.

$$Z=\sin^{-2}\left(\frac{219.50\,[ft]}{233.1\,[ft]}\right)$$

$$Z=76.02°$$

Answer: $\boxed{D}$

Leveling #15

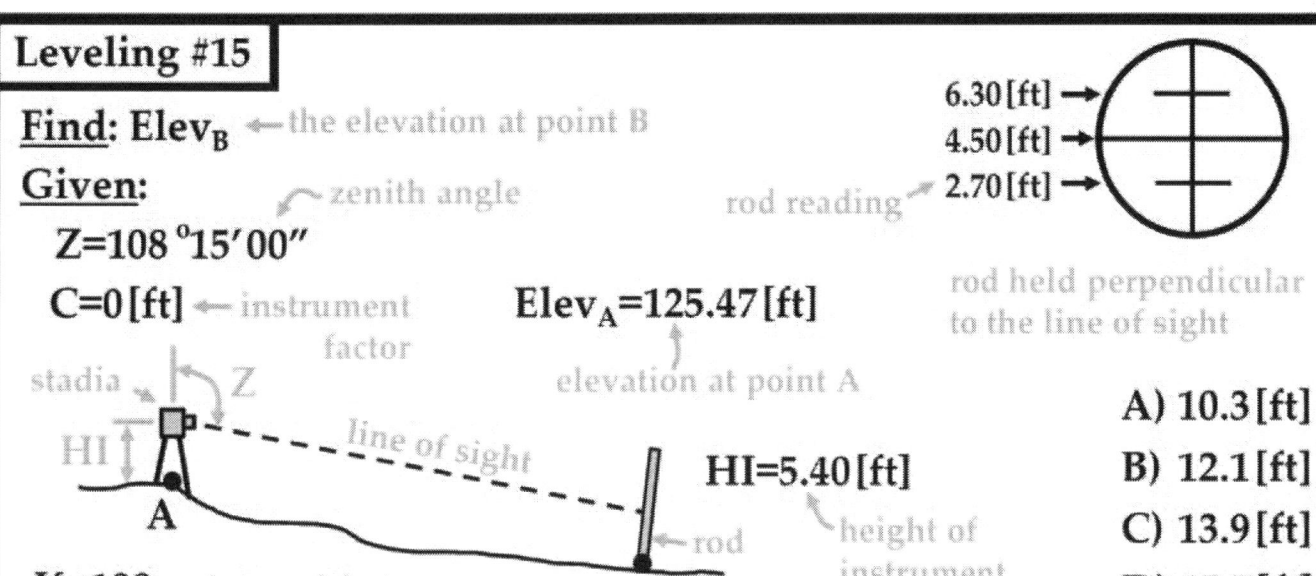

Find: $Elev_B$ ← the elevation at point B

Given: ← zenith angle

$Z=108°15'00''$

$C=0\,[ft]$ ← instrument factor

$Elev_A=125.47\,[ft]$ ← elevation at point A

rod reading ← 6.30 [ft] →
4.50 [ft] →
2.70 [ft] →

rod held perpendicular to the line of sight

stadia

HI

Z

line of sight

A

$HI=5.40\,[ft]$ ← height of instrument

rod

A) 10.3 [ft]

B) 12.1 [ft]

C) 13.9 [ft]

D) 15.7 [ft]

$K=100$ ← interval factor

B

Analysis:

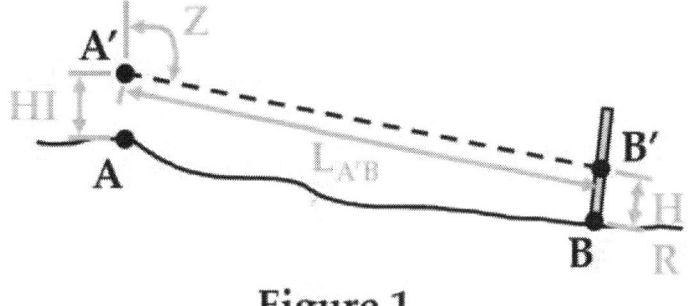

Figure 1

In Figure 1, we define point A' at the stadia lens, and point B' on the rod at the horizontal crosshair.

$L_{A'B'}$ is the straight-line distance between point A' and point B'.

$$Elev_B=Elev_A+HI+L_{A'B'}*\cos(Z)-HR*\sin(Z) \leftarrow eq.1$$

Use eq.1 to solve for $Elev_B$. The only variables we need to compute before we can solve eq.1 is HR and $L_{A'B'}$.

rod reading

$$HR=4.50\,[ft]$$

The height of the rod is the rod reading at the horizontal crosshair.

$$L_{A'B'}=K*S+C \leftarrow eq.2$$

$L_{A'B'}$ can be computed using eq.2.

$$S=6.30\,[ft]-2.70\,[ft] \leftarrow eq.3$$

Compute S as the difference between the two stadia hairs.

$$S=3.6\,[ft]$$

Surveying Practice Problems

Leveling #15 (cont.)

$S=3.6\,[\text{ft}]$

$$L_{A'B'}=K*S+C \leftarrow eq.2$$

$K=100 \qquad C=0\,[\text{ft}]$

Plug in K, S and C into eq.2, then solve for $L_{A'B'}$.

$$L_{A'B'}=100*3.6\,[\text{ft}]+0\,[\text{ft}]$$

$$L_{A'B'}=360\,[\text{ft}]$$

Plug in all the variables on the right-hand side of eq.1, then solve for $Elev_B$.

$Elev_A=125.47\,[\text{ft}] \qquad HR=4.5\,[\text{ft}]$

$$Elev_B=Elev_A+HI+L_{A'B'}*\cos(Z)-HR*\sin(Z) \leftarrow eq.1$$

$HI=5.40\,[\text{ft}] \qquad L_{A'B'}=360\,[\text{ft}] \qquad Z=108°15'00''$

$$Elev_B=125.47\,[\text{ft}]+5.40\,[\text{ft}]+360\,[\text{ft}]*\cos(108°15'00'')$$
$$-4.5\,[\text{ft}]*\sin(108°15'00'')$$

$$Elev_B=13.86\,[\text{ft}]$$

Answer: $\boxed{C}$

Area #1

Find: Area_{IPCQ} — the area inside points I, P, C and Q.

Given:

$A_{N,E}=(1,1)\,[m]$ ← The coordinates of point A and point I

$I_{N,E}=(3,6)\,[m]$

$L_{AD}=L_{IJ}=5\,[m]$ ← side lengths

$L_{AB}=L_{IL}=8\,[m]$

$Az_{AB}=Az_{IJ}=0\,^\circ$ — Azimuth of courses AB and IJ

ABCD and IJKL are rectangles

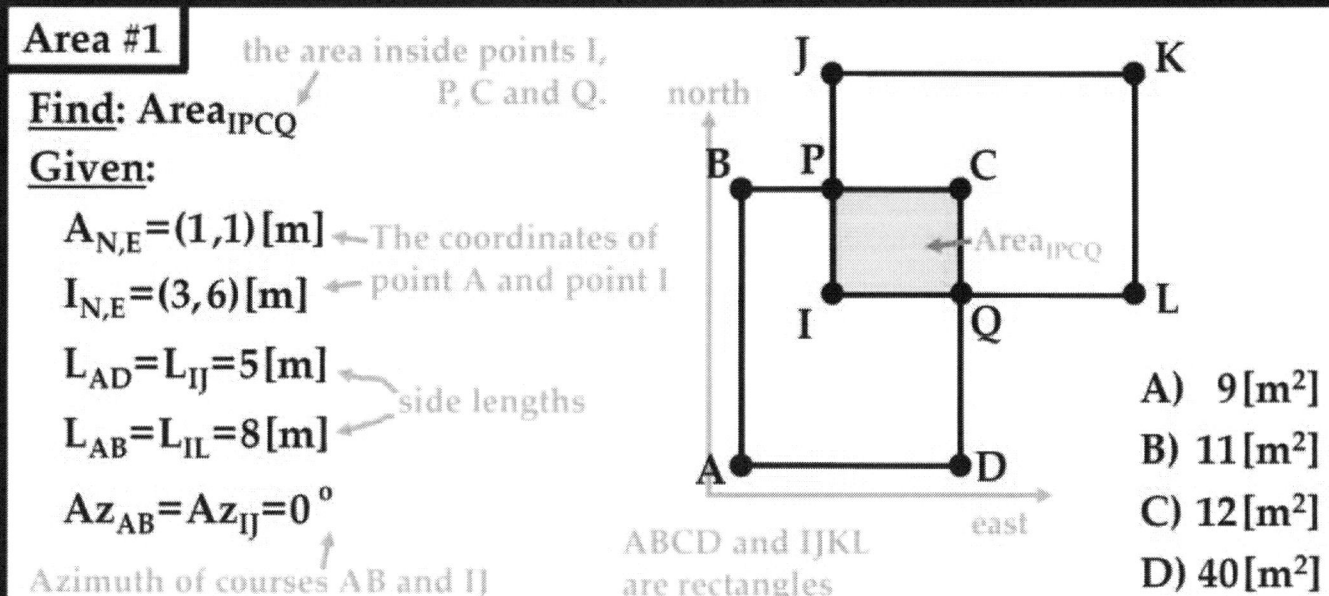

A) 9 [m²]

B) 11 [m²]

C) 12 [m²]

D) 40 [m²]

Analysis:

$$\text{Area}_{IPCQ}=L_{IP}*L_{IQ} \leftarrow eq.1$$

Use eq.1 to compute Area_{IPCQ}.

Since both ABCD and IJKL are rectangles aligned in the same direction, the union of these two rectangles results in a rectangle.

Figure 1 identifies L_{IP}, which is one of the two variables we will need for eq.1. Figure 1 also identifies L_{AB}, A_N and I_N.

Subscripts N and E refer to northing and easting, respectively.

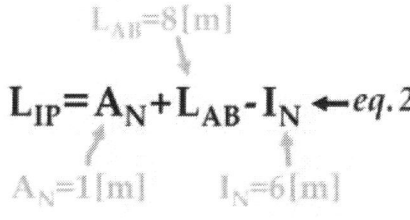

Figure 1

$$L_{IP}=A_N+L_{AB}-I_N \leftarrow eq.2$$

$L_{AB}=8\,[m]$

$A_N=1\,[m]$ $I_N=6\,[m]$

From Figure 1, we derive eq.2 to find L_{IP}, the length from point I to point P.

$$L_{IP}=1\,[m]+8\,[m]-6\,[m]$$

Area #1 (cont.)

$$L_{IP}=3[m]$$

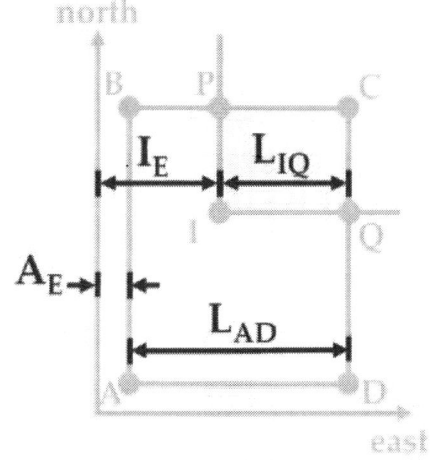

Figure 2

Figure 2 identifies variables L_{IQ}, L_{AD}, A_E and I_E.

A_E refers to the easting coordinate of point A.

$L_{AB}=5[m]$

$$L_{IQ}=A_E+L_{AD}-I_E \leftarrow eq.3$$

$A_N=1[m] \qquad I_N=3[m]$

From Figure 2, we derive eq.3 to find L_{IQ}, the length from point I to point Q.

$$L_{IQ}=1[m]+5[m]-3[m]$$

$$L_{IQ}=3[m]$$

$L_{IP}=3[m] \qquad L_{IQ}=3[m]$

$$Area_{IPCQ}=L_{IP}*L_{IQ} \leftarrow eq.1$$

Return to eq.1, plug in variables L_{IP} and L_{IQ}, then solve for $Area_{IPCQ}$.

$$Area_{IPCQ}=3[m]*3[m]$$

$$Area_{IPCQ}=9[m^2] \qquad \underline{\textbf{Answer:}} \boxed{A}$$

Area #2

Find: $Area_m$ — the area inside circle I, and west of course JK

Given:

$I = (10, 9)$ [ft]

$J = (8, -2)$ [ft]

the coordinates of points I and J

$B_{JK} = N\,5°12'00''\,W$

the bearing of line segment JK

Points J and K are located on a circle centered at point I

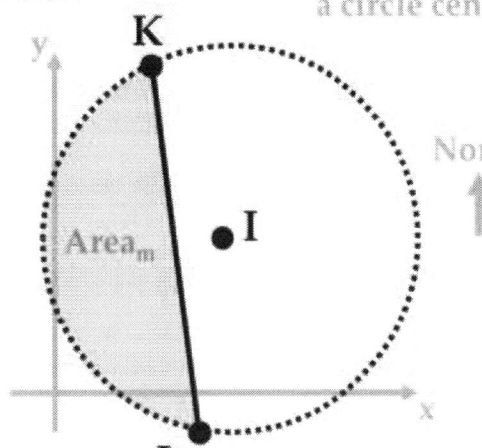

A) 30 [ft²]

B) 130 [ft²]

C) 230 [ft²]

D) 330 [ft²]

Analysis:

$$Area_m < 0.5 * Area_I \leftarrow ieq.1$$

area of circle I

$$Area_I = \pi * R_I^2 \leftarrow eq.1$$

radius of circle I

$$R_I = \sqrt{(J_x - I_x)^2 + (J_y - I_y)^2} \leftarrow eq.2$$

$J_x = 8$ [ft] $J_y = -2$ [ft]

$I_x = 10$ [ft] $I_y = 9$ [ft]

$$R_I = \sqrt{(8\,[ft] - 10\,[ft])^2 + ((-2\,[ft]) - 9\,[ft])^2}$$

$$R_I = 11.18\,[ft]$$

$$Area_I = \pi * R_I^2 \leftarrow eq.1$$

$R_I = 11.18$ [ft]

The sketch in the problem statement is drawn (nearly) to scale. Therefore, we know $Area_m$ is less than half the area of the circle centered at point I, $Area_I$.

Use eq. 1 to compute $Area_I$.

Find the radius of circle I by computing the distance between point I and point J, using eq.2.

J_x, I_x, J_y and I_y refer to the x and y coordinates of points J and I

Return to eq.1, plug in R_I, then solve for the area of circle I.

Surveying Practice Problems

Area #2 (cont.)

$$\text{Area}_I = \pi * (11.18\,[\text{ft}])^2$$

$$\text{Area}_I = 392.7\,[\text{ft}^2]$$

$$\text{Area}_I = 392.7\,[\text{ft}^2]$$

$$\text{Area}_m < 0.5 * \text{Area}_I \leftarrow ieq.1$$

$$\text{Area}_m < 196.4\,[\text{ft}^2]$$

After returning to ieq.1 and plugging in Area_I, we realize Area_m is less than $196.4\,[\text{ft}^2]$

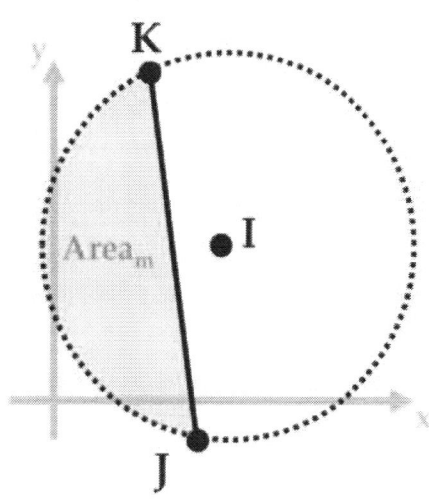

Figure 1

Answer D is too big, and Answer C is probably too big as well.

A) 30 [ft²]
B) 130 [ft²]
C) 230 [ft²] ← probably too big?
D) 330 [ft²] ← too big!

From Figure 1 we can approximate Area_m is about one third the area of the circle centered at point I.

$$\text{Area}_I = 392.7\,[\text{ft}^2]$$

$$\text{Area}_m \approx (1/3) * \text{Area}_I \leftarrow approx.1$$

$$\text{Area}_m \tilde{} \sim 130.9\,[\text{ft}^2]$$

Answer: $\boxed{\text{B}}$

When calculated out, the value of Area_m is closer to $130.5\,[\text{ft}^2]$. However, computing an exact value for Area_m would take longer and is not necessary to correctly answer the question.

Area #3

Find: L_{BC} ←the length of course BC

Given:

$Area_{ABC} = 125 [ft^2]$ ←the area of triangle ABC

$Az_{AC} = 90°$ ←the azimuth of course AC

$Az_{AB} = 150°$ ←the azimuth of course AB

$L_{AB} = 18 [ft]$ ←the length of course AB

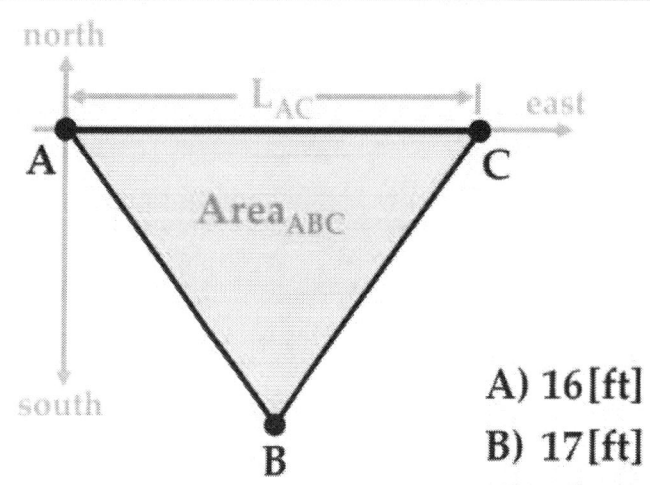

A) 16 [ft]
B) 17 [ft]
C) 18 [ft]
D) 19 [ft]

Analysis:

Eq.1 computes the area of triangle ABC, when given L_{AB}, L_{AC} and A_{BAC}.

$$Area_{ABC} = 0.5 * L_{AB} * L_{AC} * \sin(A_{BAC}) \leftarrow eq.1$$

Solve eq.1 for L_{AC}.

$$L_{AC} = \frac{Area_{ABC}}{0.5 * L_{AB} * \sin(A_{BAC})} \leftarrow eq.2$$

We can solve for L_{AC}, by first plugging in Az_{AB} and Az_{AC} into eq.3, then solving for A_{BAC}.

$Az_{AB} = 150°$ $Az_{AC} = 90°$

$$A_{BAC} = Az_{AB} - Az_{AC} \leftarrow eq.3$$

$$A_{BAC} = 150° - 90°$$

$$A_{BAC} = 60°$$

Return to eq.2, plug in the known variables, then solve for L_{AC}.

$Area_{ABC} = 125 [ft^2]$

$$L_{AC} = \frac{Area_{ABC}}{0.5 * L_{AB} * \sin(A_{BAC})} \leftarrow eq.2$$

$L_{AB} = 18 [ft]$ $A_{BAC} = 60°$

Surveying Practice Problems

Area #3 (cont.)

$$L_{AC} = \frac{125[ft^2]}{0.5 * 18[ft] * \sin(60°)}$$

$$L_{AC} = 16.0[ft]$$

Use the law of cosines, eq.4, to solve for the length of course BC.

$$L_{BC}^2 = L_{AB}^2 * L_{AC}^2 - 2 * L_{AB} * L_{AC} * \cos(A_{BAC}) \leftarrow eq.4$$

After taking the square root of both sides of eq.4, plug in L_{AB}, L_{AC} and A_{BAC}, then solve for L_{BC}.

$L_{AB} = 18[ft]$

$$L_{BC} = \sqrt{L_{AB}^2 * L_{AC}^2 - 2 * L_{AB} * L_{AC} * \cos(A_{BAC})} \leftarrow eq.5$$

$L_{AC} = 16.0[ft]$ $A_{BAC} = 60°$

$$L_{BC} = \sqrt{(18[ft])^2 * (16.0[ft])^2 - 2 * (18[ft]) * (16.0[ft]) * \cos(60°)}$$

$$L_{BC} = 17.10[ft]$$

Answer: $\boxed{B}$

Area #4

Find: Area_{IJK} ← the area of triangle IJK

Given:

$L_{IJ} = 117.8\,[m]$ ← the length of coruse IJ

$A_{IJK} = 105°$

$A_{JKI} = 60°$ ← the three interior angle measurements of Triangle IJK

$A_{KIJ} = 15°$

A) $1,700\,[m^2]$
B) $1,800\,[m^2]$
C) $1,900\,[m^2]$
D) $2,000\,[m^2]$

Analysis:

Use eq.1. Substitute in the given angles and course length, then solve for Area_{IJK}

$L_{IJ} = 117.8\,[m]$ $A_{KIJ} = 15°$

$$\text{Area}_{IJK} = \frac{L_{IJ}^2 * \sin(A_{IJK}) * \sin(A_{KIJ})}{2 * \sin(A_{JKI})} \leftarrow eq.1$$

$A_{IJK} = 105°$ $A_{JKI} = 60°$

$$\text{Area}_{IJK} = \frac{(117.8\,[m])^2 * \sin(105°) * \sin(15°)}{2 * \sin(60°)}$$

$$\text{Area}_{IJK} = 2002.9\,[m^2]$$

Answer: ⬚ D

Notice the area of triangle IJK is independent of its orientation

Surveying Practice Problems

Area #5

Find: L_{KI} — the length between point K and point I

Given:

$L_{IJ} = 20.45 \, [m]$ — the length between point J and point K

$L_{JK} = 36.22 \, [m]$ — the length between point I and point J

$Area_{IJK} = 334.2 \, [m^2]$ — the area inside triangle IJK

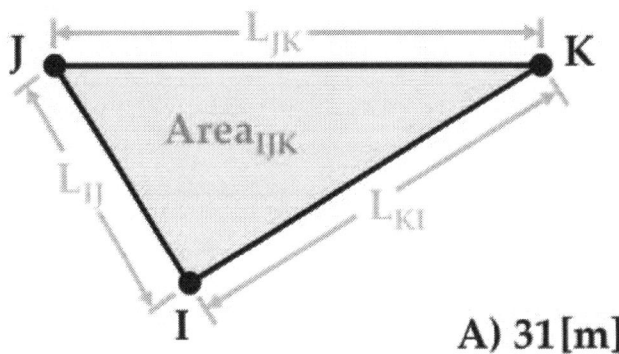

A) 31 [m]
B) 32 [m]
C) 33 [m]
D) 34 [m]

Analysis:

Law of Cosines:

$$a^2 = b^2 + c^2 - 2*b*c*\cos(A) \leftarrow eq.1$$

$a = L_{KI} \qquad b = L_{IJ} \qquad c = L_{JK} \qquad A = A_{IJK}$

Use the law of cosines to find L_{KI}.

In eq.1, capital A equals the interior angle opposite side a. Variables a, b and c represent the side lengths of the triangle.

$$L_{KI}{}^2 = L_{IJ}{}^2 + L_{JK}{}^2 - 2*L_{IJ}*L_{JK}*\cos(A_{IJK}) \leftarrow eq.2$$

Plug in variables L_{KI}, L_{IJ}, L_{JK} and A_{IJK} into eq.1, then solve for L_{KI}.

$$L_{KI} = \sqrt{L_{IJ}{}^2 + L_{JK}{}^2 - 2*L_{IJ}*L_{JK}*\cos(A_{IJK})} \leftarrow eq.3$$

To solve eq.3, we need to compute A_{IJK}. Use eq.4 to relate variables A_{IJK}, $Area_{IJK}$, L_{IJ} and L_{JK}.

$$Area_{IJK} = 0.5*L_{IJ}*L_{JK}*\sin(A_{IJK}) \leftarrow eq.4$$

$Area_{IJK} = 334.2 \, [m^2]$

$$A_{IJK} = \sin^{-1}\left(\frac{Area_{IJK}}{0.5*L_{IJ}*L_{JK}} \right)$$

$L_{IJ} = 20.45 \, [m] \qquad L_{JK} = 36.22 \, [m]$

Solve eq.4 for A_{IJK}. Then plug in variables L_{IJ}, L_{JK} and $Area_{IJK}$, and solve for A_{IJK}.

Area #5 (cont.)

$$A_{IJK}=\sin^{-1}\left(\frac{334.2\,[m^2]}{0.5*20.45\,[m]*36.22\,[m]}\right)$$

$$A_{IJK}=\sin^{-1}(0.9024)$$

From Figure 1, we notice $\sin^{-1}(0.9024)$ can equal either $64.47\,^\circ$ or $115.53\,^\circ$.

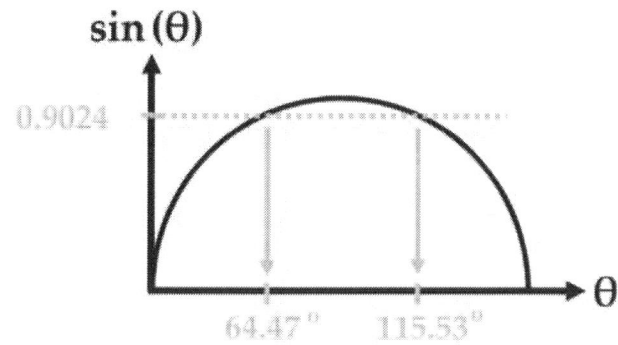

We'll assume Triangle IJK is an acute triangle, and $A_{IJK}=64.47\,^\circ$.

Figure 1

assumed value $\longrightarrow A_{IJK}=64.47\,^\circ$

Return to eq.3, plug in A_{IJK}, L_{IJ} and L_{JK}, then solve for L_{KI}.

$$L_{KI}=\sqrt{L_{IJ}^2+L_{JK}^2-2*L_{IJ}*L_{JK}*\cos(A_{IJK})}\quad\leftarrow eq.3$$

$A_{IJK}=64.47^\circ$

$L_{IJ}=20.45\,[m]$ $L_{JK}=36.22\,[m]$

$$L_{KI}=\sqrt{(20.45\,[m])^2+(36.22\,[m])^2-2*20.45\,[m]*36.22\,[m]*\cos(64.47^\circ)}$$

$$L_{KI}=33.04\,[m]$$

33.04 [m] is most nearly 33 [m]. Answer C is correct.

<u>Answer:</u> $\boxed{\text{C}}$

Surveying Practice Problems

Area #6

the area inside triangle ABC

Find: Area$_{ABC}$

the coordinates of points A, B and C

Given:

point	Northing	Easting
A	129.7 [ft]	141.8 [ft]
B	517.1 [ft]	167.4 [ft]
C	322.1 [ft]	305.5 [ft]

A) 26,000 [ft²]
B) 27,000 [ft²]
C) 28,000 [ft²]
D) 29,000 [ft²]

Analysis:

$$Area_{ABC}= \sqrt{S*(S-L_{AB})*(S-L_{BC})*(S-L_{CA})} \leftarrow eq.1$$

semi-perimeter

Use eq.1 (Heron's formula) to find the area of triangle ABC.

$$S=0.5*(L_{AB}+L_{BC}+L_{CA}) \leftarrow eq.2$$

Eq.2 calculates the semi-perimeter which is equal to one half the perimeter of the triangle.

$B_N=517.1 [ft]$ $B_E=167.4 [ft]$

$$L_{AB}= \sqrt{(B_N-A_N)^2+(B_E-A_E)^2} \leftarrow eq.3$$

$A_N=129.7 [ft]$ $A_E=141.8 [ft]$

Using the coordinates of points A, B and C, we can compute the side lengths between these three points, L_{AB}, L_{BC} and L_{CA}, using eq.3, eq.4 and eq.5.

$$L_{AB}= \sqrt{(517.1 [ft]-129.7 [ft])^2+(167.4 [ft]-141.8 [ft])^2}$$

$$L_{AB}=388.2 [ft]$$

In eq.3, eq.4 and eq.5, the subscripts "N" and "E" refer to northing and easting of each point

Area #6 (cont.)

$C_N=322.1\,[ft]$ $C_E=305.5\,[ft]$

$$L_{BC}=\sqrt{(C_N-B_N)^2+(C_E-B_E)^2} \leftarrow eq.4$$

$B_N=517.1\,[ft]$ $B_E=167.4\,[ft]$

Eq. 4 computes the length between points B and C.

$$L_{BC}=\sqrt{(322.1\,[ft]-517.1\,[ft])^2+(305.5\,[ft]-167.4\,[ft])^2}$$

$$L_{BC}=238.9\,[ft]$$

$A_N=129.7\,[ft]$ $A_E=141.8\,[ft]$

$$L_{CA}=\sqrt{(A_N-C_N)^2+(A_E-C_E)^2} \leftarrow eq.5$$

$C_N=322.1\,[ft]$ $C_E=305.5\,[ft]$

Eq. 5 computes the length between points C and A.

$$L_{CA}=\sqrt{(129.7\,[ft]-322.1\,[ft])^2+(141.8\,[ft]-305.5\,[ft])^2}$$

$$L_{CA}=252.6\,[ft]$$

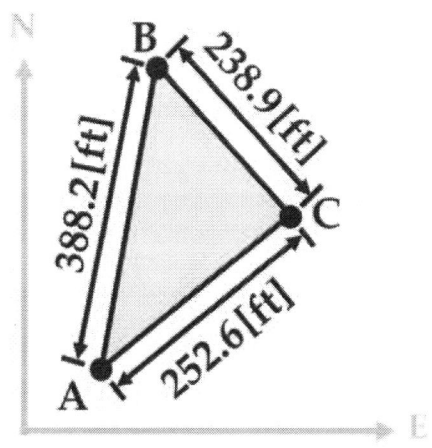

Figure 1 shows Triangle ABC with the side lengths labeled.

Figure 1

Surveying Practice Problems

Area #6 (cont.)

L_{BC}=238.9 [ft]

$$S=0.5*(L_{AB}+L_{BC}+L_{CA}) \leftarrow eq.2$$

L_{AB}=388.2 [ft] L_{CA}=252.6 [ft]

Return to eq. 2 and compute the semi-perimeter, S.

$$S=0.5*(388.2[ft]+238.9[ft]+252.6[ft])$$

$$S=439.85[ft]$$

S=439.85 [ft]

Plug in variables S, L_{AB}, L_{BC} and L_{CA} into eq.1, then solve for $Area_{ABC}$.

$$Area_{ABC}=\sqrt{S*(S-L_{AB})*(S-L_{BC})*(S-L_{CA})} \leftarrow eq.1$$

L_{AB}=388.2 [ft] L_{BC}=238.9 [ft] L_{CA}=252.6 [ft]

$$Area_{ABC}=\sqrt{\begin{array}{l}439.85[ft]*(439.85[ft]-388.2[ft])\\ *(439.85[ft]-238.9[ft])*(439.85[ft]-252.6[ft])\end{array}}$$

$$Area_{ABC}=29,238[ft^2]$$

Answer: ☐ D

Heron's formula (eq.1) is limited to finding the area of a triangle. Other methods are used to find areas bound by more than 3 sides.

Area #7

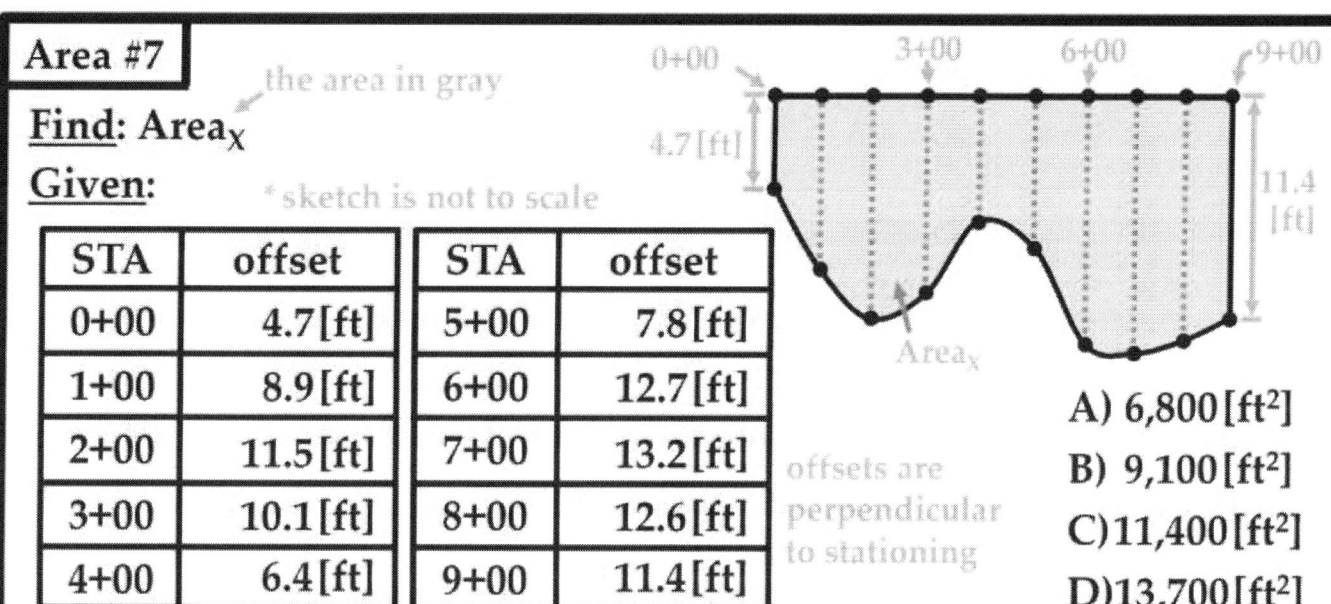

Find: Area$_X$ the area in gray

Given: * sketch is not to scale

STA	offset	STA	offset
0+00	4.7 [ft]	5+00	7.8 [ft]
1+00	8.9 [ft]	6+00	12.7 [ft]
2+00	11.5 [ft]	7+00	13.2 [ft]
3+00	10.1 [ft]	8+00	12.6 [ft]
4+00	6.4 [ft]	9+00	11.4 [ft]

offsets are perpendicular to stationing

A) 6,800 [ft²]

B) 9,100 [ft²]

C) 11,400 [ft²]

D) 13,700 [ft²]

Analysis:

$$\text{Area}_{LER} \leq \text{Area}_X \leq \text{Area}_{SER} \leftarrow ieq.1$$

largest enclosed rectangle   smallest enclosing rectangle

We can quickly determine the upper and lower limits of Area$_X$ by computing the area of the largest enclosed rectangle and the area of the smallest enclosing rectangle.

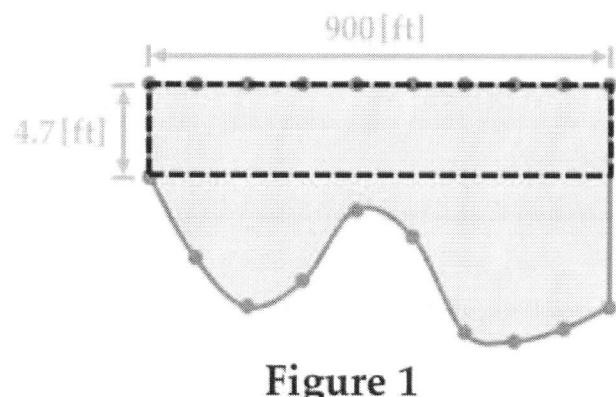

Figure 1

Figure 1 shows the outline of the largest enclosed rectangle.

Use eq.1 to find the area of the largest enclosed rectangle.

length=900 [ft]   min offset=4.7 [ft]

$$\text{Area}_{LER} = \text{length} * \text{min offset} \leftarrow eq.1$$

The length of the stationing is the final station minus the first station.

900 [ft]-0 [ft]=900 [ft]

$$\text{Area}_{LER} = 900 \,[\text{ft}] * 4.7 \,[\text{ft}]$$

Surveying Practice Problems

Area #7 (cont.)

$$\text{Area}_{\text{LER}}=4{,}230\,[\text{ft}^2]$$

The largest enclosed rectangle inside Area$_X$ is 4,230 square feet.

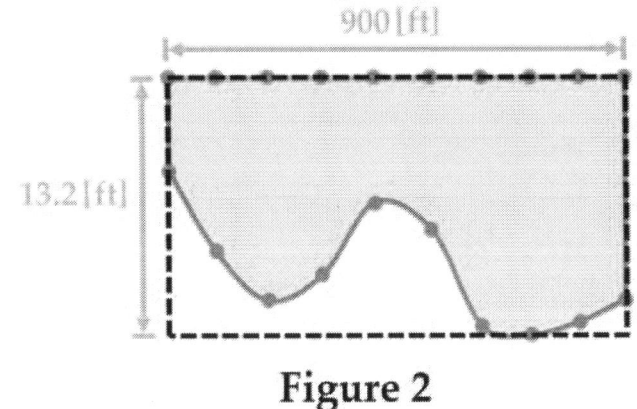

Figure 2

Figure 2 shows the outline of the smallest enclosing rectangle.

Use eq.2 to find the area of the smallest enclosing rectangle.

length=900[ft]   max offset=13.2[ft]

$$\text{Area}_{\text{SER}}=\text{length}*\text{max offset} \leftarrow eq.2$$

$$\text{Area}_{\text{SER}}=900\,[\text{ft}]*13.2\,[\text{ft}]$$

The maximum offset of 13.2[ft] occurs at station = 7+00

$$\text{Area}_{\text{SER}}=11{,}880\,[\text{ft}]$$

The smallest rectangle enclosing Area$_X$ is 11,880 square feet.

Area$_{\text{LER}}$=4,230[ft^2]   Area$_{\text{SER}}$=11,880[ft^2]

$$\text{Area}_{\text{LER}} \leq \text{Area}_X \leq \text{Area}_{\text{SER}} \leftarrow ieq.1$$

Substitute in Area$_{\text{LER}}$ and Area$_{\text{SER}}$ into ieq.1.

$$4{,}230\,[\text{ft}^2] \leq \text{Area}_X \leq 11{,}880\,[\text{ft}^2]$$

A) 6,800 [ft^2]

B) 9,100 [ft^2]

C) 11,400 [ft^2]

too large → ~~D) 13,700 [ft^2]~~

Based on our rough approximation, we can rule out answer D, because 13,700[ft^2] > Area$_{\text{SER}}$

This primary approximation can be helpful, but is not necessary.

Area #7 (cont.)

We'll approximate the area using the trapezoidal rule.

$$\text{Area}_X \approx \sum_{i=0}^{N-1} \frac{(\text{offset}_i + \text{offset}_{i+1})}{2} * dx \quad \leftarrow approx.1$$

distance between offsets

In approx.1, dx refers to the perpendicular distance between consecutive offset measurements.

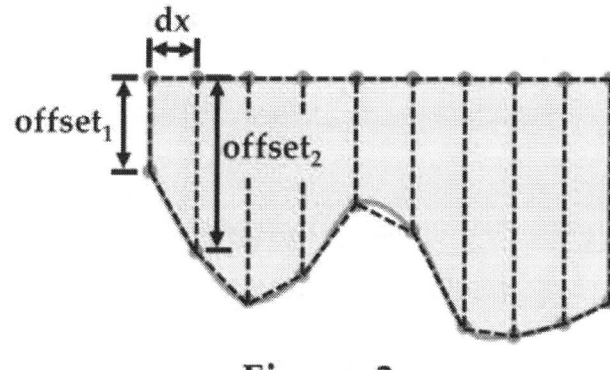

Figure 3

The trapezoidal rule approximates Area_X by dividing Area_X into multiple trapezoids, and then summing those trapezoids.

In Figure 3, the dimensions of the first term of the summation in approx 1 are identified.

Below, we write out the first four terms of approx 1.

offset$_0$=4.7[ft]　　i=0　　offset$_1$=8.9[ft]　　i=1　　offset$_2$=11.5[ft]

$$\text{Area}_X \approx \frac{(\text{offset}_0 + \text{offset}_1)}{2} * dx + \frac{(\text{offset}_1 + \text{offset}_2)}{2} * dx$$

dx=100[ft]　　　　　　dx=100[ft]

$$+ \frac{(\text{offset}_2 + \text{offset}_3)}{2} * dx + \frac{(\text{offset}_3 + \text{offset}_4)}{2} * dx + ...$$

offset$_2$=11.5[ft]　　i=2　　offset$_3$=10.1[ft]　　i=3　　offset$_4$=6.4[ft]

$$\text{Area}_X \approx \frac{(4.7[ft] + 8.9[ft])}{2} * 100[ft] + \frac{(8.9[ft] + 11.5[ft])}{2} * 100[ft]$$

$$+ \frac{(11.5[ft] + 10.1[ft])}{2} * 100[ft] + \frac{(10.1[ft] + 6.4[ft])}{2} * 100[ft] + \cdots$$

Surveying Practice Problems

Area #7 (cont.)

$$\overset{i=0}{\downarrow} \qquad \overset{i=1}{\downarrow} \qquad \overset{i=2}{\downarrow} \qquad \overset{i=3}{\downarrow}$$

$$\text{Area}_X \approx 680\,[\text{ft}^2] + 1{,}020\,[\text{ft}^2] + 1{,}080\,[\text{ft}^2] + 825\,[\text{ft}^2] + 710\,[\text{ft}^2]$$
$$+ 1{,}025\,[\text{ft}^2] + 1{,}295\,[\text{ft}^2] + 1{,}290\,[\text{ft}^2] + 1{,}200\,[\text{ft}^2]$$

$$\text{Area}_X \approx 9{,}125\,[\text{ft}^2]$$

Using the trapezoidal rule, Area_X equals approximately $9{,}125\,[\text{ft}^2]$

A) 6,800 [ft²]

B) 9,100 [ft²]

C) 11,400 [ft²]

D) 13,700 [ft²]

From Figure 3, we notice the trapezoidal approximation is fairly accurate.

$9{,}125\,[\text{ft}^2]$ is closer to $9{,}100\,[\text{ft}^2]$ than it is to the other possible answers. Choose answer B.

<u>Answer:</u> $\boxed{\text{B}}$

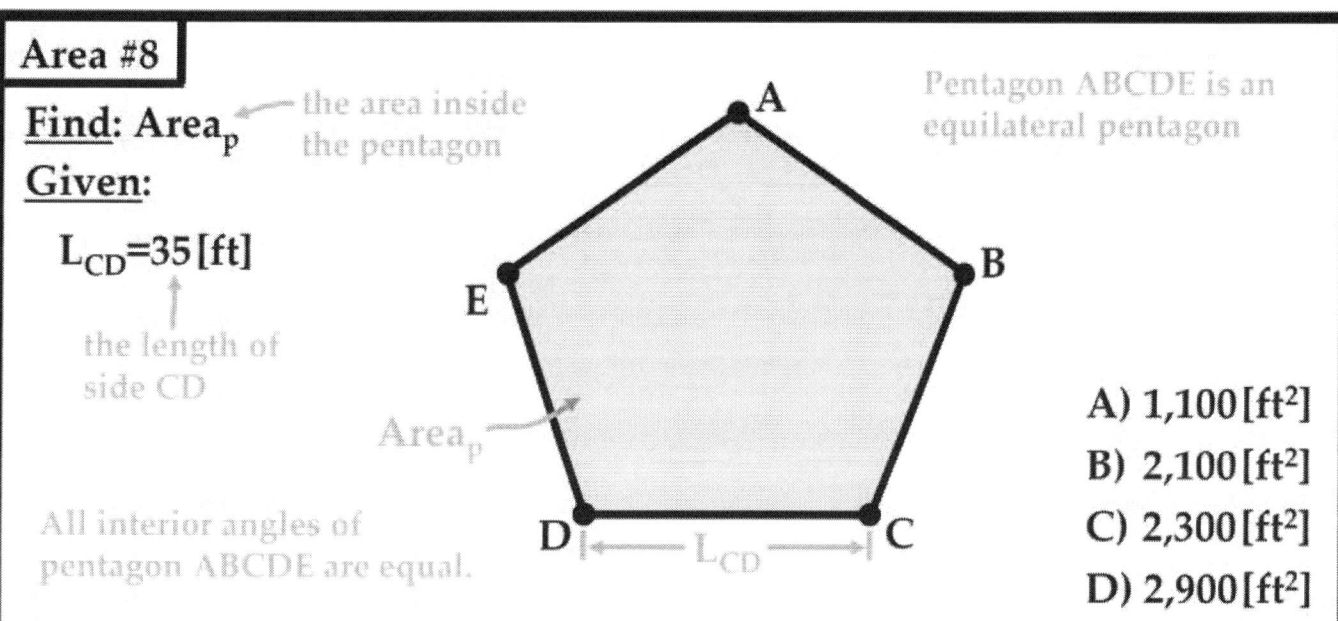

Area #8

Find: Area$_p$ ← the area inside the pentagon

Given:

$L_{CD} = 35\,[\text{ft}]$

↑ the length of side CD

Area$_p$

All interior angles of pentagon ABCDE are equal.

Pentagon ABCDE is an equilateral pentagon

A) 1,100 [ft²]
B) 2,100 [ft²]
C) 2,300 [ft²]
D) 2,900 [ft²]

Analysis:

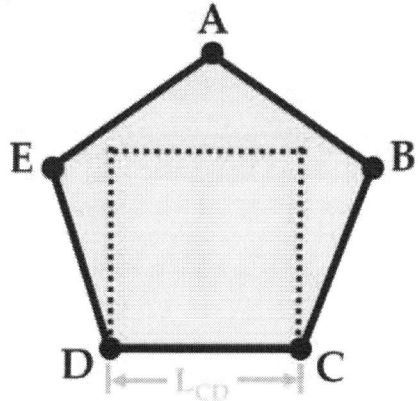

Figure 1

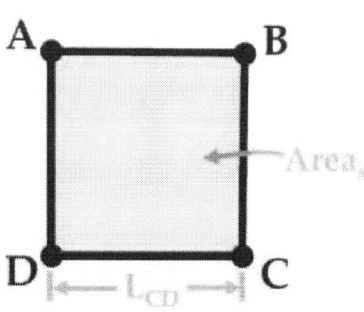

Figure 2

$$\text{Area}_s = L_{CD}^2 \leftarrow eq.1$$

$L_{CD} = 35\,[\text{ft}]$

An equilateral pentagon is a 5-sided polygon having 5 equal side lengths.

We can quickly compute a lower bound on Area$_p$ by computing the area of a square having a side length of L_{CD}.

Figure 1 shows the area of a square is less than the area of our equilateral pentagon having the same side length.

Figure 2 shows square ABCD. We'll define the area inside the square as Area$_s$.

Use eq.1 to compute Area$_s$. Plug in L_{CD}, then solve for Area$_s$.

Area #8 (cont.)

$$Area_s = (35[ft])^2$$

$$Area_s = 1,225[ft^2]$$

$$Area_s = 1,225[ft^2]$$

$$Area_p > Area_s \leftarrow ieq.1$$

$$Area_p > 1,225[ft^2]$$

Making sketches and approximations at the beginning are not necessary, but they can help quickly estimate the exact solution and eliminate incorrect solutions.

Since we know $Area_p$ is greater than $1,225[ft^2]$, we can probably rule out answer A as the solution.

A) $1,100[ft^2]$

B) $2,100[ft^2]$

C) $2,300[ft^2]$

D) $2,900[ft^2]$

From Figure 1, it appears $Area_p$ is about twice the area of $Area_s$. Therefore, we'll suspect the correct answer is either B or C.

In Figure 3, pentagon ABCDE is divided into 5 equal isosceles triangles. Point O is located at the center of Pentagon ABCDE.

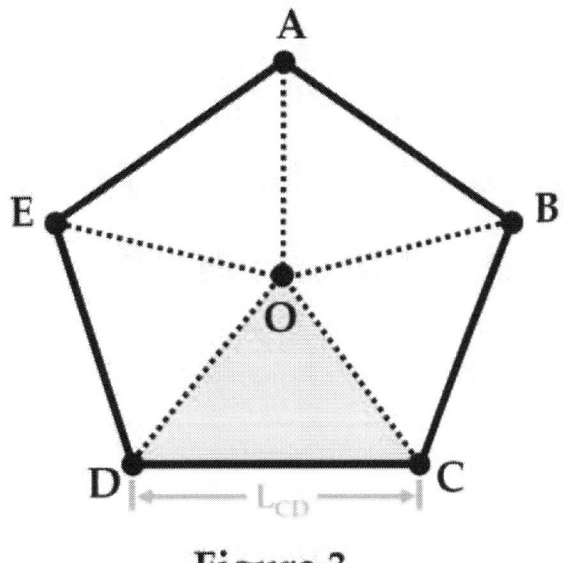

Figure 3

$$Area_p = 10 * Area_{DOO'} \leftarrow eq.2$$

the area of triangle DOO'

Eq. 2 equates the area of pentagon ABCDE to 10 times the area of triangle DOO'.

Triangle DOO' is shown in Figure 4.

Area #8 (cont.)

$$Area_{DOO'}=0.5*L_{DO'}*L_{OO'} \leftarrow eq.3$$

Eq.3 solves for the area of triangle DOO', as a function of $L_{DO'}$ and $L_{OO'}$.

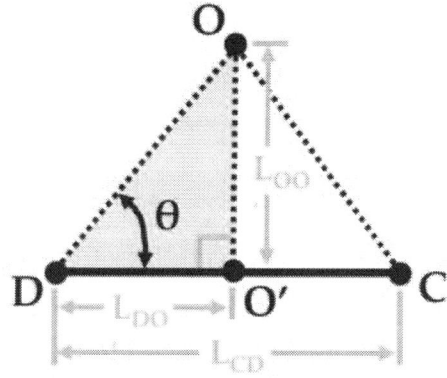

Figure 4

Since line segment OO' is perpendicular to line segment DO, triangle DOO' a right triangle.

$$L_{DO'}=0.5*L_{CD} \leftarrow eq.4$$

Use eq.4 to solve for $L_{DO'}$, which is half of L_{DC}.

$$L_{DO'}=0.5*(35[ft])$$

$$L_{DO'}=17.5[ft]$$

$$L_{OO'}=L_{DO'}*tan(\theta) \leftarrow eq.5$$

We'll use eq.5 to solve for $L_{OO'}$. We first need to solve for angle θ, shown in Figure 4.

m=sum of the interior angles.

$$m=180°*(n-2[sides]) \leftarrow eq.6$$

n=5[sides]

Eq.6 computes the sum of the interior angles of an n sided polygon.

$$m=180°*(5[sides]-2[sides])$$

Surveying Practice Problems

Area #8 (cont.)

$$m = 540°$$

Using n=5 [sides], we find the sum of the interior angles equals 540°.

$$m = 540°$$
$$\downarrow$$
$$\theta = m/10 \leftarrow eq.7$$

Use eq.7 to compute θ.

$$\theta = 540°/10$$

$$\theta = 54°$$

Since all interior angles of pentagon ABCDE are equal, we know $A_{CDE} = 540°/5$, and we also know $\theta = 540°/10$.

$$\theta = 54°$$
$$\downarrow$$
$$L_{OO'} = L_{DO'} * \tan(\theta) \leftarrow eq.5$$
$$\uparrow$$
$$L_{DO'} = 17.5 [ft]$$

Return to eq.5, plug in $L_{DO'}$ and θ, then solve for $L_{OO'}$.

$$L_{OO'} = 17.5 [ft] * \tan(54°)$$

$$L_{OO'} = 24.09 [ft]$$

$$L_{OO'} = 24.09 [ft]$$
$$\downarrow$$
$$Area_{DOO'} = 0.5 * L_{DO'} * L_{OO'} \leftarrow eq.3$$
$$\uparrow$$
$$L_{DO'} = 17.5 [ft]$$

Return to eq.3, substitute in $L_{DO'}$ and $L_{OO'}$, then solve for the area of triangle DOO'.

$$Area_{DOO'} = 0.5 * 17.5 [ft] * 24.09 [ft]$$

$$Area_{DOO'} = 210.8 [ft^2]$$

Area #8 (cont.)

$$\text{Area}_p = 10 * \text{Area}_{DOO'} \leftarrow eq.2$$

$$\text{Area}_{DOO'} = 210.8 \, [\text{ft}^2]$$

Finally, plug in $\text{Area}_{DOO'}$ into eq. 2, and solve for Area_p.

$$\text{Area}_p = 10 * 210.8 \, [\text{ft}^2]$$

$$\text{Area}_p = 2{,}108 \, [\text{ft}^2]$$

Answer: $\boxed{B}$

$2{,}108 \, [\text{ft}^2]$ is most nearly $2{,}100 \, [\text{ft}^2]$. Answer B is correct.

Surveying Practice Problems

Area #9

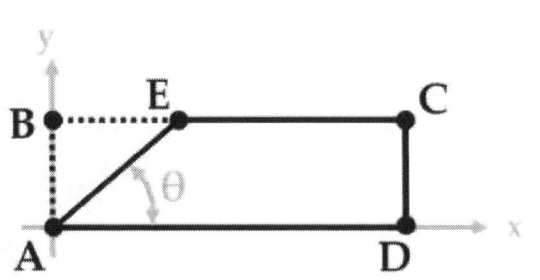

Find: θ ← the angle formed
by points EAD
Given:

L_{AD}=20[ft] ← the length between
point A and point D

$Area_{ABCD}$=50[ft²]

the area inside
rectangle ABCD

$Area_{AECD}$=35[ft²]

the area inside
trapezoid AECD

A) 12°

B) 14°

C) 16°

D) 18°

- -

Analysis:

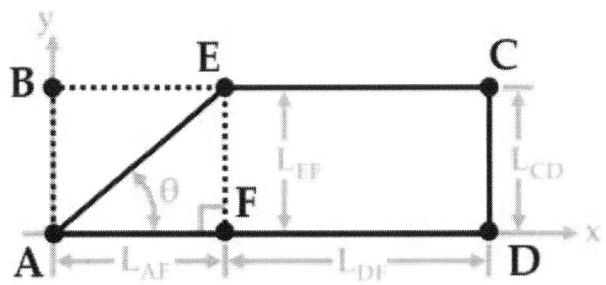

Figure 1

In Figure 1, we define point F.
AEF forms a right triangle.
FECD forms a rectangle.

From Figure 1, we derive eq.1 to find
θ. To solve eq.1, we need to solve for
the values of L_{EF} and L_{AF}.

$$θ=\tan^{-1}(L_{EF}/L_{AF}) ←eq.1$$

$Area_{ABCD}$=50[ft²]

$$L_{EF}=\frac{Area_{ABCD}}{L_{AD}} ←eq.2$$

L_{AD}=20[ft]

Since we know L_{AD} and $Area_{ABCD}$,
we can compute L_{EF} using eq.2.

$$L_{EF}=\frac{50[ft²]}{20[ft]}$$

$$L_{EF}=2.5[ft]$$

Since L_{ABCD} is a rectangle,
$L_{EF}=L_{CD}=L_{AB}=2.5$[ft]

Area #9 (cont.)

$$Area_{FECD}=L_{FD}*L_{CD}$$

In eq.3, we equate the area of trapezoid AECD to the area of right triangle AEF, plus the area of rectangle FECD.

$$Area_{AECD}=Area_{AEF}+Area_{FECD} \leftarrow eq.3$$

$$Area_{AEF}=0.5*L_{AF}*L_{EF}$$

$$Area_{AECD}=0.5*L_{AF}*L_{EF}+L_{FD}*L_{CD} \leftarrow eq.4$$

$$L_{AF}+L_{FD}=L_{AD} \leftarrow eq.5$$

From Figure 1, we know the sum of L_{AF} and L_{FD} equals L_{AD}.

$$L_{FD}=L_{AD}-L_{AF} \leftarrow eq.6$$

Solve eq.5 for L_{FD}.

$$L_{FD}=L_{AD}-L_{AF}$$

Plug in L_{FD} into eq.4, then solve for L_{AF}.

$$Area_{AECD}=0.5*L_{AF}*L_{EF}+L_{FD}*L_{CD} \leftarrow eq.4$$

$$Area_{AECD}=0.5*L_{AF}*L_{EF}+(L_{AD}-L_{AF})*L_{CD}$$

$$Area_{AECD}=35[ft^2] \qquad L_{AD}=20[ft]$$

$$L_{AF}=\frac{Area_{AECD}-L_{AD}*L_{CD}}{0.5*L_{EF}-L_{CD}} \leftarrow eq.5$$

Plug in $Area_{AECD}$, L_{AD}, L_{CD} and L_{EF} into eq.5, then solve for L_{AF}.

$$L_{EF}=2.5[ft] \qquad L_{CD}=2.5[ft]$$

$$L_{AF}=\frac{35[ft^2]-20[ft]*2.5[ft]}{0.5*2.5[ft]-2.5[ft]}$$

Surveying Practice Problems

Area #9 (cont.)

$$L_{AF}=12\,[ft]$$

$L_{AF}=12\,[ft]$

$$\theta=\tan^{-1}(L_{EF}/L_{AF}) \leftarrow eq.1$$

$L_{EF}=2.5\,[ft]$

Plug in L_{EF} and L_{AF} into eq.1, then solve for θ

$$\theta=\tan^{-1}(2.5\,[ft]/12\,[ft])$$

$$\theta=11.8\,^{\circ}$$

11.8° is most nearly 12°. Answer A is the correct.

Answer: $\boxed{A}$

Area #10

<u>Find</u>: maximum Area$_{ABC}$ ← the maximum area of triangle ABC

<u>Given</u>:

L$_{AB}$=25.4[m]

length of line
segment AB

L$_{BC}$=37.8[m]

length of line
segment BC

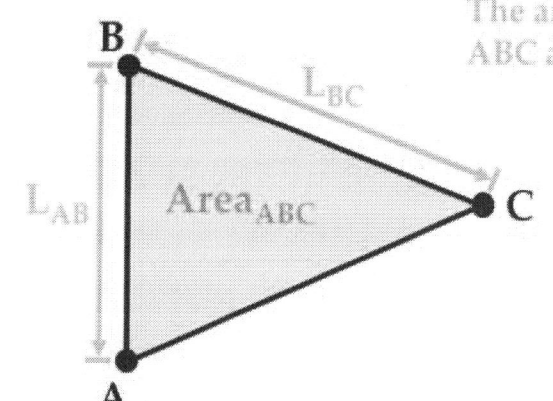

The angles of triangle
ABC are not provided

A) 542[m^2]

B) 480[m^2]

C) 488[m^2]

D) 506[m^2]

<u>Analysis</u>:

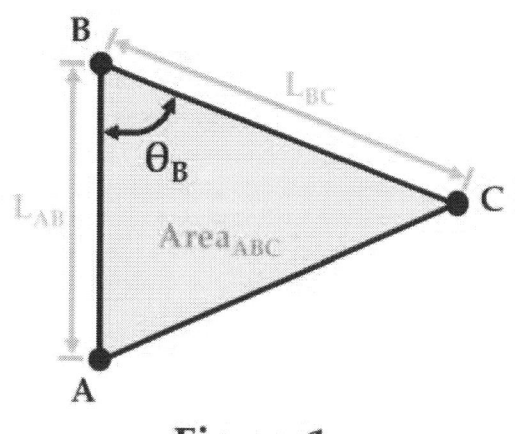

Figure 1

In Figure 1, we redraw triangle ABC,
and define angle θ_B.

In Eq. 1, we define the area of triangle
ABC as a function of angle θ_B and the
side lengths L$_{AB}$ and L$_{BC}$.

We can simplify eq. 1, by plugging in
the length of line segment AB and
the length of line segment BC.

L$_{AB}$=25.4[m]   L$_{BC}$=37.8[m]

Area$_{ABC}$=0.5*L$_{AB}$*L$_{BC}$*sin(θ_B) ←eq. 1

unknown

Area$_{ABC}$=0.5*25.4[m]*37.8[m]*sin(θ_B)

Area$_{ABC}$=480.06[m^2]*sin(θ_B) ←eq. 2

To maximize Area$_{ABC}$, we should
choose a value for θ_B which results
in the largest value of sin(θ_B).

Area #10 (cont.)

$$0° < \theta_B < 180°$$

Since the interior angle of a triangle cannot be more than 180, we know the bounds of θ_B.

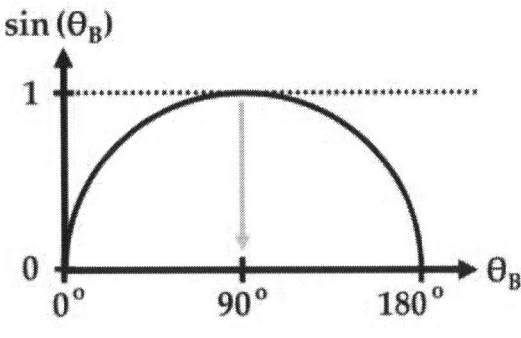

Figure 2

Figure 2 shows the graph of $\sin(\theta_B)$ as a function of θ_B.

From Figure 2, we notice $\theta_B = 90°$ maximizes $\sin(\theta_B)$, for the range of θ_B values.

We can confirm $\theta_B = 90°$ maximizes $\sin(\theta_B)$ by setting the derivative of $\sin(\theta_B)$, which is $\cos(\theta_B)$, equal to 0, and then solving for θ_B. $\theta_B = 90°$.

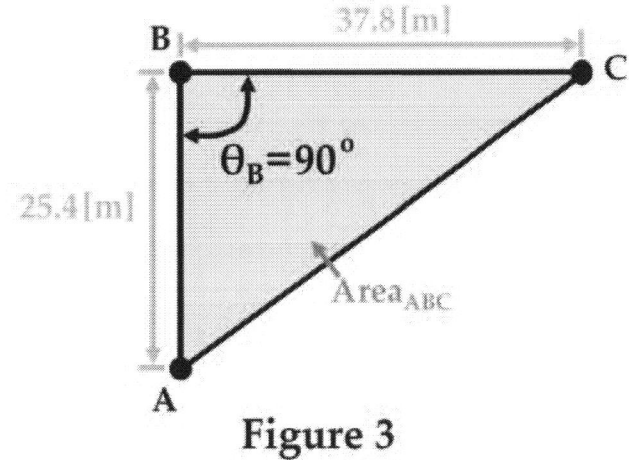

Figure 3

Figure 3 shows triangle ABC with angle θ_B drawn at it's optimal value of 90°.

Plug in 90° for θ_B and solve eq.3 for the maximum area of triangle ABC.

maximum Area$_{ABC}$ = 480.06 [m^2] * $\sin(\theta_B)$ ←*eq. 3*

$\theta_B = 90°$

maximum Area$_{ABC}$ = 480.06 [m^2] * $\sin(90°)$ $\sin(90°) = 1$

maximum Area$_{ABC}$ = 480.06 [m^2]

Answer: B

Area #11

<u>Find:</u> L_{IJ} ← the length of course IJ

<u>Given:</u>

Area$_{IJK}$=1.87 [acres] ← the area of triangle IJK

A$_{IJK}$=45°

the interior angle formed at point J

A$_{KIJ}$=100°

the interior angle formed at point I

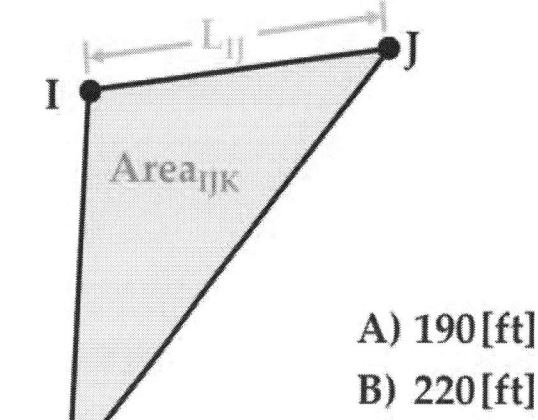

A) 190 [ft]

B) 220 [ft]

C) 260 [ft]

D) 370 [ft]

<u>Analysis:</u>

Start with eq.1, and solve for L_{IJ}.

$$Area_{IJK}=\frac{L_{IJ}^{2}*\sin(A_{IJK})*\sin(A_{KIJ})}{2*\sin(A_{JKI})} \leftarrow eq.1$$

$$L_{IJ}=\sqrt{\frac{Area_{IJK}*2*\sin(A_{JKI})}{\sin(A_{IJK})*\sin(A_{KIJ})}} \leftarrow eq.2$$

The sum of the interior angles of a triangle equals 180°.

$$180°=A_{IJK}+A_{JKI}+A_{KIJ} \leftarrow eq.3$$

Solve eq.3 for A_{JKI}, plug in A_{IJK} and A_{KIJ}, then calculate A_{JKI}.

$A_{IJK}=45°$

$$A_{JKI}=180°-A_{IJK}-A_{KIJ} \leftarrow eq.4$$

$A_{KIJ}=100°$

$$A_{JKI}=180°-45°-100°$$

$$A_{JKI}=35°$$

Surveying Practice Problems

Area #11 (cont.)

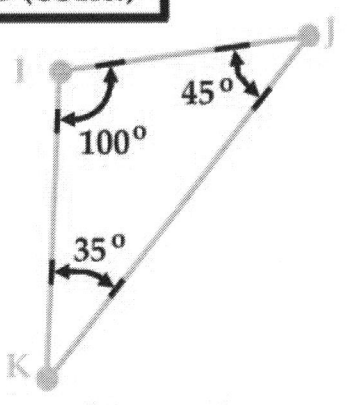

Figure 1

Figure 1 shows triangle IJK with all three interior angles labeled.

We noticed the possible solutions for L_{IJ} are in units of feet.

Convert the area from units of acres to units of square feet, using eq.5.

$$\text{Area}_{IJK}\,[\text{ft}^2] = \text{Area}\,[\text{acre}] * \frac{43{,}560\,[\text{ft}^2]}{1\,[\text{acre}]} \leftarrow eq.5$$

$$\text{Area}_{IJK} = 1.87\,[\text{acres}] * \frac{43{,}560\,[\text{ft}^2]}{1\,[\text{acre}]}$$

$$\text{Area}_{IJK} = 81{,}457\,[\text{ft}^2]$$

It makes more sense to take the square root of an area in units of ft², than to take the square root of an area in units of acres.

$$L_{IJ} = \sqrt{\frac{\text{Area}_{IJK} * 2 * \sin(A_{JKI})}{\sin(A_{IJK}) * \sin(A_{KIJ})}} \leftarrow eq.2$$

Return to eq.2, plug in the known variables, then solve for L_{IJ}.

$$L_{IJ} = \sqrt{\frac{81{,}457\,[\text{ft}^2] * 2 * \sin(35°)}{\sin(45°) * \sin(100°)}}$$

$$L_{IJ} = 366.3\,[\text{ft}]$$

Answer: $\boxed{\text{D}}$

Area #12

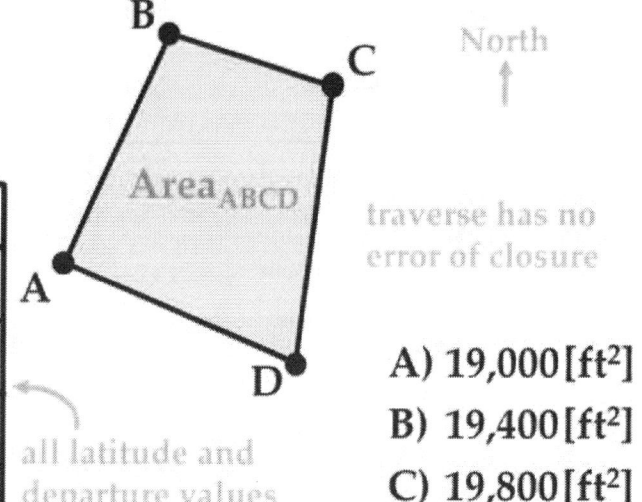

Find: Area$_{ABCD}$ ← the area inside traverse ABCD

Given:

course	Latitude	Departure
AB	157.41	55.89
BC	-23.51	86.22
CD	-174.88	-7.14
DA	40.98	-134.97

traverse has no error of closure

all latitude and departure values are in feet

A) 19,000 [ft²]

B) 19,400 [ft²]

C) 19,800 [ft²]

D) 20,200 [ft²]

Analysis:

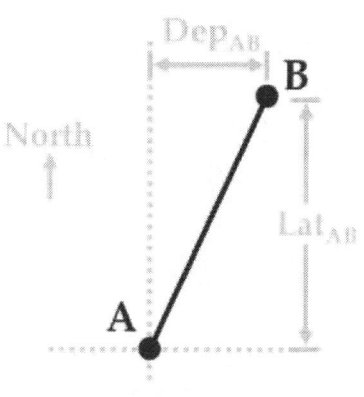

Figure 1

Figure 1 shows the latitude of a course is the distance the course traverses in the northward direction. The departure of a course is the distance the course traverses in the eastward direction.

Latitude is occasionally abbreviated "Lat." Departure is occasionally abbreviated "Dep."

absolute value bar

Double Meridian Distance, "DMD"

We'll use the double meridian distance method to solve for Area$_{ABCD}$.

$$\text{Area}_{ABCD} = \frac{|\Sigma(DMD * Lat)|}{2} \leftarrow eq.1$$

Use eq.1 to find Area$_{ABCD}$

course	Lat	Dep	DMD	DMD*Lat
AB	157.41	55.89	DMD$_{AB}$	DMD$_{AB}$*157.41
BC	-23.51	198.00	DMD$_{BC}$	DMD$_{BC}$*-23.51
CD	-174.88	277.08	DMD$_{CD}$	DMD$_{CD}$*-174.88
DA	40.98	134.97	DMD$_{DA}$	DMD$_{CD}$*40.98
				Σ(DMD*LAT)

Copy the structure of Table 1 and add the given Lat and Dep values.

Remember we are working in units of ft and ft²

Table 1

Surveying Practice Problems

Area #12 (cont.)

$$DEP_{AB} = 55.89 \, [ft]$$

$$DMD_{AB} = DEP_{AB} \leftarrow eq.2$$

$$DMD_{AB} = 55.89 \, [ft]$$

We need to calculate the double meridian distances before we can solve for $\Sigma(DMD*Lat)$.

Step 1: The DMD of the first course equals the departure of the first course. (eq. 2)

$$DMD_{AB} = 55.89 \, [ft] \qquad DEP_{BC} = 86.22 \, [ft]$$

$$DMD_{BC} = DMD_{AB} + DEP_{AB} + DEP_{BC} \leftarrow eq.3$$

$$DEP_{AB} = 55.89 \, [ft]$$

$$DMD_{BC} = 55.89 \, [ft] + 55.89 \, [ft] + 86.22 \, [ft]$$

$$DMD_{BC} = 198.00 \, [ft]$$

Step 2: Compute the other DMD values, which equal the DMD of the previous course, plus the departure of the previous course, plus the departure of the current course. (eq. 3, eq. 4, eq. 5).

Compute the DMD values in order around the traverse because each DMD value depends on the previous DMD value.

$$DEP_{BC} = 86.22 \, [ft]$$

$$DMD_{CD} = DMD_{BC} + DEP_{BC} + DEP_{CD} \leftarrow eq.4$$

$$DMD_{BC} = 198.00 \, [ft] \qquad DEP_{CD} = -7.14 \, [ft]$$

$$DMD_{CD} = 198.00 \, [ft] + 86.22 \, [ft] + (-7.14 \, [ft])$$

$$DMD_{CD} = 277.08 \, [ft]$$

We can add the DMD values to Table 1 as we calculate them.

$$DMD_{CD} = 277.08 \, [ft] \qquad DEP_{DA} = -134.97 \, [ft]$$

$$DMD_{DA} = DMD_{CD} + DEP_{CD} + DEP_{DA} \leftarrow eq.5$$

$$DEP_{CD} = -7.14 \, [ft]$$

Area #12 (cont.)

$$DMD_{DA}=277.08[ft]+(-7.14[ft])+(-134.97[ft])$$

$$DMD_{DA}=134.97[ft]$$

As a check, the DMD of the final course should have the opposite sign (+/-), and same magnitude as the departure of the final course.

Step 3: Multiply the DMD length and the latitude, for each course.

$DMD_{AB}=55.89[ft]$ $Latitude_{AB}=157.41[ft]$

$$DMD_{AB}*Latitude_{AB}=55.89[ft]*157.41[ft]=8,797.6[ft^2]$$

$DMD_{BC}=198.00[ft]$ $Latitude_{BC}=-23.51[ft]$

$$DMD_{BC}*Latitude_{BC}=198.00[ft]*(-23.51[ft])=-4,655.0[ft^2]$$

$DMD_{CD}=277.08[ft]$ $Latitude_{CD}=-174.88[ft]$

$$DMD_{CD}*Latitude_{CD}=277.08[ft]*(-174.88[ft])=-48,455.8[ft^2]$$

$DMD_{DA}=134.97[ft]$ $Latitude_{DA}=40.98[ft]$

$$DMD_{DA}*Latitude_{DA}=134.97[ft]*40.98[ft]=5,531.1[ft^2]$$

Once calculated, add the DMD *Lat values to the last column of Table 1.

Surveying Practice Problems

Area #12 (cont.)

Step 4: Sum the product of DMD*Lat for all courses in the traverse (eq.6)

$DMD_{AB}*Lat_{AB}=8,797.6\,[ft^2]$ $DMD_{BC}*Lat_{BC}=-4,655.0\,[ft^2]$

$$\Sigma(DMD*Lat)=DMD_{AB}*Lat_{AB}+DMD_{BC}*Lat_{BC}$$
$$+DMD_{CD}*Lat_{CD}+DMD_{DA}*Lat_{DA}$$

$DMD_{CD}*Lat_{CD}=-48,455.8\,[ft^2]$ $DMD_{DA}*Lat_{DA}=5,531.1\,[ft^2]$

$$\Sigma(DMD*Lat)=8,797.4\,[ft^2]+(-4,655.0\,[ft^2])+(-48,455.8\,[ft^2])+5,531.1\,[ft^2]$$

$$\Sigma(DMD*Lat)=-38,782\,[ft^2]$$

The area $-38,782\,[ft^2]$ can be added to the bottom right corner of Table 1.

$\Sigma(DMD*Lat)=-38,782\,[ft^2]$

Step 5: Plug in $\Sigma(DMD*Lat)$ into eq.1, then solve for $Area_{ABCD}$.

$$Area_{ABCD}=\frac{\left|\Sigma(DMD*Lat)\right|}{2} \leftarrow eq.1$$

$$Area_{ABCD}=\frac{\left|-38,782\,[ft^2]\right|}{2}$$

$$Area_{ABCD}=19,391\,[ft^2]$$

Answer: $\boxed{B}$

Area #13

Find: Area$_{ABCD}$ ← the area inside traverse ABCDE

Given:

(no sketch provided)

course	Latitude	Departure
AB	95.61	2.25
BC	4.88	47.65
CD	-3.75	50.11
DE	-93.18	-6.42
EA	-3.56	-93.59

all latitude and departure values are in units of feet

A) 5,600 [ft^2]

B) 7,400 [ft^2]

C) 9,200 [ft^2]

D) 11,000 [ft^2]

Analysis:

error of closure (in latitude)

If necessary, we first need to balance the traverse. A balanced traverse has no error of closure.

$$EOC_{LAT} = \sum_{i=1}^{N} LAT_i \leftarrow eq.1$$

Use eq.1 to compute the error in closure of the latitude measurements.

$$EOC_{LAT} = 95.61\,[ft] + 4.88\,[ft] + (-3.75\,[ft]) + (-93.18\,[ft]) + (-3.56\,[ft])$$

$$EOC_{LAT} = 0.00\,[ft]$$

Expand eq.1, plug in the given latitude measurements, then solve for EOC_{LAT}.

error of closure (in departure)

Use eq.2 to compute the error in closure for the departure measurements, similar to eq.1.

$$EOC_{DEP} = \sum_{i=1}^{N} DEP_i \leftarrow eq.2$$

Remember, all latitude and departure values are in feet.

$$EOC_{DEP} = 2.25\,[ft] + 47.65\,[ft] + (50.11\,[ft]) + (-6.42\,[ft]) + (-93.59\,[ft])$$

$$EOC_{DEP} = 0.00\,[ft]$$

Since there is no error of closure in latitude or departure, no correction is necessary.

Surveying Practice Problems

Area #13 (cont.)

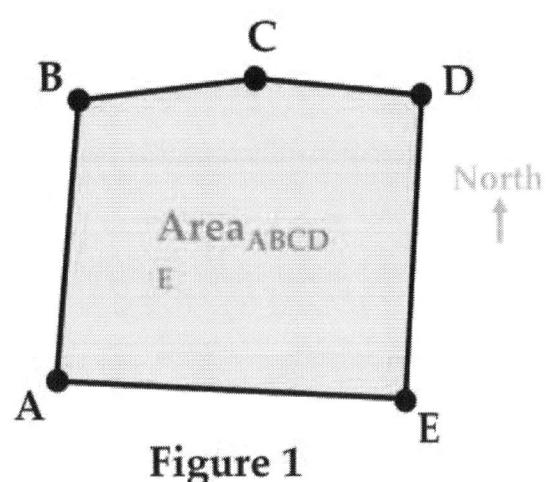

Figure 1

Figure 1 is a sketch of Area_ABCDE.

From Figure 1, we notice the outline of traverse ABCDE is roughly rectangular.

We may be able to approximate Area_ABCDE by assuming the area is rectangular.

course	Latitude	Departure
AB	**95.61**	2.25
BC	4.88	**47.65**
CD	-3.75	**50.11**
DE	**-93.18**	-6.42
EA	-3.56	**-93.59**

Looking back at the table of latitudes and departures, we approximate the average height to be 94 [ft] and the average width to be 96 [ft]

If our approximation doesn't yield an answer sufficiently close to one of the possible solutions, we'll use the double meridian distance method to find Area_ABCDE.

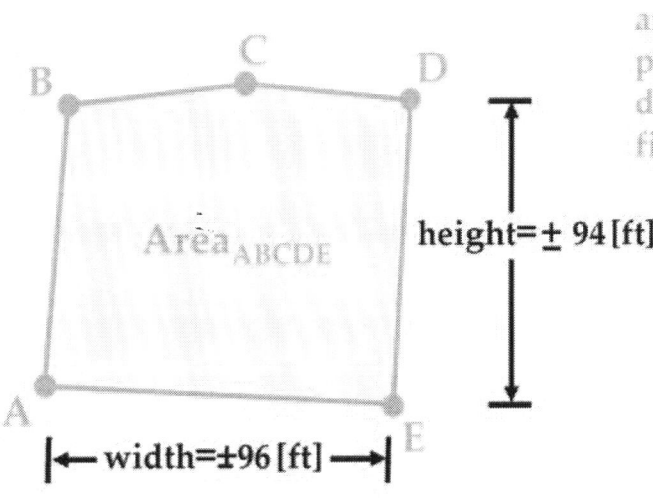

height=± 94 [ft]

|← width=±96 [ft] →|

Figure 2

an approximation

$$Area_{ABCDE} \approx average\ width * average\ height \leftarrow approx.\ 1$$

average width=96 [ft]

average height=94 [ft]

Area #13 (cont.)

$$\text{Area}_{ABCDE} \approx 96 \, [ft] * 94 \, [ft]$$

$$\text{Area}_{ABCDE} \approx 9{,}024 \, [ft^2]$$

Answer: $\boxed{A}$

Since 9,024 [ft²] is much closer to 9,200 [ft²] (answer C) than to 7,400 [ft²] (answer B) we assume our approximation is close enough, and we do not need to perform a more rigorous calculation.

If we solved for Area$_{ABCDE}$ using the double meridian distance method we would find Area$_{ABCDE}$=9,232.7 [ft²]

Surveying Practice Problems

Area #14

Find: Area_{ABCDE} — the area inside traverse ABCDE

Given:

course	Latitude	Departure
AB	1,428.1	292.8
BC	315.4	1,019.2
CD	-881.5	-749.9
DE	-927.0	515.8
EA	65.0	-1,077.9

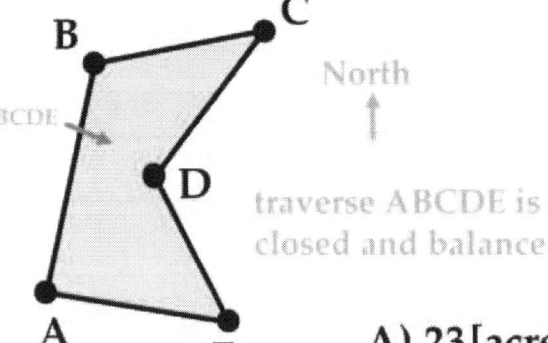

Area_{ABCDE}

North

traverse ABCDE is closed and balanced

← all distances are in feet

A) 23 [acre]
B) 24 [acre]
C) 25 [acre]
D) 26 [acre]

Analysis:

Double Meridian Distance, "DMD"

Use eq.1 from the double meridian distance method to find Area_{ABCDE}.

$$\text{Area}_{ABCDE} = \frac{|\Sigma(DMD*Lat)|}{2} \quad \leftarrow eq.1$$

Since we know ABCDE is a balanced traverse, we can begin the double meridian distance method by setting up Table 1.

course	Lat	Dep	DMD	DMD*Lat
AB	1,428.1	292.8	DMD_{AB}	$DMD_{AB}*1,428.1$
BC	315.4	1,019.2	DMD_{BC}	$DMD_{BC}*315.4$
CD	-881.5	-749.9	DMD_{CD}	$DMD_{CD}*(-818.5)$
DE	-927.0	515.8	DMD_{DE}	$DMD_{DE}*(-927.0)$
EA	65.0	-1,077.9	DMD_{EA}	$DMD_{EA}*65.0$
				$\Sigma(DMD*Lat)$

Table 1

$DEP_{AB}=292.8\,[ft]$

Step 1: The DMD of the first course equals the departure of the first course. (eq.2)

$$DMD_{AB}=DEP_{AB} \quad \leftarrow eq.2$$

Area #14 (cont.)

Step 2: Compute the other DMD values, which equal the DMD of the previous course, plus the departure of the previous course, plus the departure of the current course. (see eq.3, eq.4, eq.5, eq.6).

$$DMD_{AB} = 292.8\,[ft]$$

$$DMD_{AB} = 292.8\,[ft]$$

$$DMD_{BC} = DMD_{AB} + DEP_{BC} + DEP_{BC} \leftarrow eq.3$$

$$DEP_{BC} = 292.8\,[ft] \qquad DEP_{BC} = 1{,}019.2\,[ft]$$

$$DMD_{BC} = 292.8\,[ft] + 292.8\,[ft] + 1{,}019.2\,[ft]$$

$$DMD_{BC} = 1{,}604.8\,[ft]$$

There is no need to write out all DMD equations (as shown here) to solve for all DMD values. Just update Table 1 after each DMD value is calculated and use Table 1 to calculate the next DMD value.

$$DMD_{DE} = 1{,}604.8\,[ft] \qquad DEP_{EA} = -749.9\,[ft]$$

$$DMD_{CD} = DMD_{BC} + DEP_{BC} + DEP_{CD} \leftarrow eq.4$$

$$DEP_{BC} = 1{,}019.2\,[ft]$$

$$DMD_{CD} = 1{,}604.8\,[ft] + 1{,}019.2\,[ft] + (-749.9\,[ft])$$

$$DMD_{CD} = 1{,}874.1\,[ft]$$

$$DEP_{CD} = -749.9\,[ft]$$

$$DMD_{DE} = DMD_{CD} + DEP_{CD} + DEP_{DE} \leftarrow eq.5$$

$$DMD_{CD} = 1{,}874.1\,[ft] \qquad DEP_{DE} = -515.8\,[ft]$$

Surveying Practice Problems

Area #14 (cont.)

$DMD_{DE} = 1,874.1 [ft] + (-749.9 [ft]) + (-515.8 [ft])$

$DMD_{DE} = 1,640.0 [ft]$

$DMD_{DE} = 1,604.8 [ft]$ $DEP_{EA} = -1,077.9 [ft]$

$DMD_{EA} = DMD_{DE} + DEP_{DE} + DEP_{EA}$ ←*eq. 6*

$DEP_{DE} = 515.8 [ft]$

$DMD_{BC} = 1,604.8 [ft] + 1,019.2 [ft] + (-749.9 [ft])$

$DMD_{BC} = 1,874.1 [ft]$

Step 3: Multiply the DMD length for each course by the latitude of each course.

$DMD_{AB} = 292.8 [ft]$ $Latitude_{AB} = 1,428.1 [ft]$

$DMD_{AB} * Latitude_{AB} = 292.8 [ft] * 1,428.1 [ft] = 418,148 [ft^2]$

$DMD_{BC} = 1,604.8 [ft]$ $Latitude_{BC} = 315.4 [ft]$

$DMD_{BC} * Latitude_{BC} = 1,604.8 [ft] * 315.4 [ft] = 506,154 [ft^2]$

$DMD_{CD} = 1,874.1 [ft]$ $Latitude_{CD} = -881.5 [ft]$

$DMD_{CD} * Latitude_{CD} = 1,874.1 [ft] * (-881.5 [ft]) = 1,652,019 [ft^2]$

$DMD_{DE} = 1,640.0 [ft]$ $Latitude_{DE} = -927.0 [ft]$

$DMD_{DE} * Latitude_{DE} = 1,640.0 [ft] * (-927 [ft]) = -1,520,280 [ft^2]$

Area #14 (cont.)

$DMD_{EA}=1,077.9\,[ft]$ $Latitude_{EA}=65.0\,[ft]$

$$DMD_{EA}*Latitude_{EA}=1,077.9\,[ft]*65.0\,[ft]=70,064\,[ft^2]$$

Step 4: Sum the product of DMD*Lat for all courses in the traverse.

$DMD_{BC}*Lat_{BC}=506,154\,[ft^2]$

$DMD_{AB}*Lat_{AB}=418,148\,[ft^2]$ $DMD_{CD}*Lat_{CD}=-1,652,019\,[ft^2]$

$$\Sigma(DMD*Lat)=DMD_{AB}*Lat_{AB}+DMD_{BC}*Lat_{BC}+DMD_{CD}*Lat_{CD}$$
$$+DMD_{DE}*Lat_{DE}+DMD_{EA}*Lat_{EA}$$

$DMD_{DE}*Lat_{DE}=-1,520,280\,[ft^2]$ $DMD_{EA}*Lat_{EA}=70,064\,[ft^2]$

$$\Sigma(DMD*Lat)=418,148\,[ft^2]+506,154\,[ft^2]+(-1,652,019\,[ft^2])$$
$$+(-1,520,280\,[ft^2])+70,064\,[ft^2]$$

$$\Sigma(DMD*Lat)=-2,177,933\,[ft^2]$$

Table 2 shows all the calculated values for DMD and DMD*Lat.

course	Lat	Dep	DMD	DMD*Lat
CD	1,428.1	292.8	292.8	418,148
DE	315.4	1,019.2	1,604.8	506,154
EA	-881.5	-749.9	1,874.1	-1,652,019
AB	-927.0	515.8	1,640.0	-1,520,280
BC	65.0	-1,077.9	1,077.9	70,064
				-2,177,933

Table 2

Surveying Practice Problems

Area #14 (cont.)

Step 5: Plug in $\Sigma(DMD*Lat)$ into eq.1, then solve for $Area_{ABCDE}$.

$\Sigma(DMD*Lat) = -2,176,996 [ft^2]$

$$Area_{ABCDE} = \frac{|\Sigma(DMD*Lat)|}{2} \leftarrow eq.1$$

$$Area_{ABCDE} = \frac{|-2,176,996 [ft^2]|}{2}$$

Convert $Area_{ABCD}$ from units of ft^2 to acres.

$$Area_{ABCDE} = 1,088,498 [ft^2]$$

$$Area_{ABCDE} = 1,088,498 [ft^2] * \left(\frac{1 [acre]}{43,560 [ft^2]}\right)$$

$$Area_{ABCDE} = 24.99 [acre]$$

There are 43,560 square feet per acre. It is helpful to commit this conversion to memory.

Answer: $\boxed{B}$

Area #15

<u>Find:</u> Lat$_{AB}$ ←the latitude of course AB

<u>Given:</u> traverse ABCD is balanced

Area$_{ABCD}$= 6,015 [ft²] ←the area inside ABCD

course	Latitude	Departure	DMD
AB	Lat$_{AB}$	135.81	135.81
BC	Lat$_{BC}$	-12.40	259.22
CD	24.14	-116.72	130.10
DA	28.08	-6.69	6.69

all distances are in feet

A) -21.44 [ft]

B) -5.61 [ft]

C) 14.76 [ft]

D) 28.71 [ft]

....

<u>Analysis:</u>

$$\text{Area}_{ABCD}= \frac{\left| \Sigma(DMD*Lat) \right|}{2} \leftarrow eq.1$$

In this problem, we already know the area, and we are asked to solve for the latitude of course AB.

Area$_{ABCD}$=6,105 [ft²]

Solve eq.1 for $\Sigma(DMD*Lat)$

$$\Sigma(DMD*Lat)= \pm 2 * \text{Area}_{ABCD}$$

This problem appears to be a double meridian distance problem in reverse.

$$\Sigma(DMD*Lat)= \pm 2 * 6,105 \text{ [ft²]}$$

If we traverse points A, B, C and D, in order, we enclose Area ABCD in a closewise direction. Therefore, we know $\Sigma(DMD*Lat)$ is negative.

$$\Sigma(DMD*Lat)= -12,029.5 \text{ [ft]}$$

the possible solutions

A) -21.44 [ft]

B) -5.61 [ft]

C) 14.76 [ft]

D) 28.71 [ft]

At this point, it will be quickest to guess an answer for Lat$_{AB}$, and compute the resulting Area$_{ABCD}$. Solving for Lat$_{AB}$ explicitly would take too long.

Surveying Practice Problems

Area #15 (cont.)

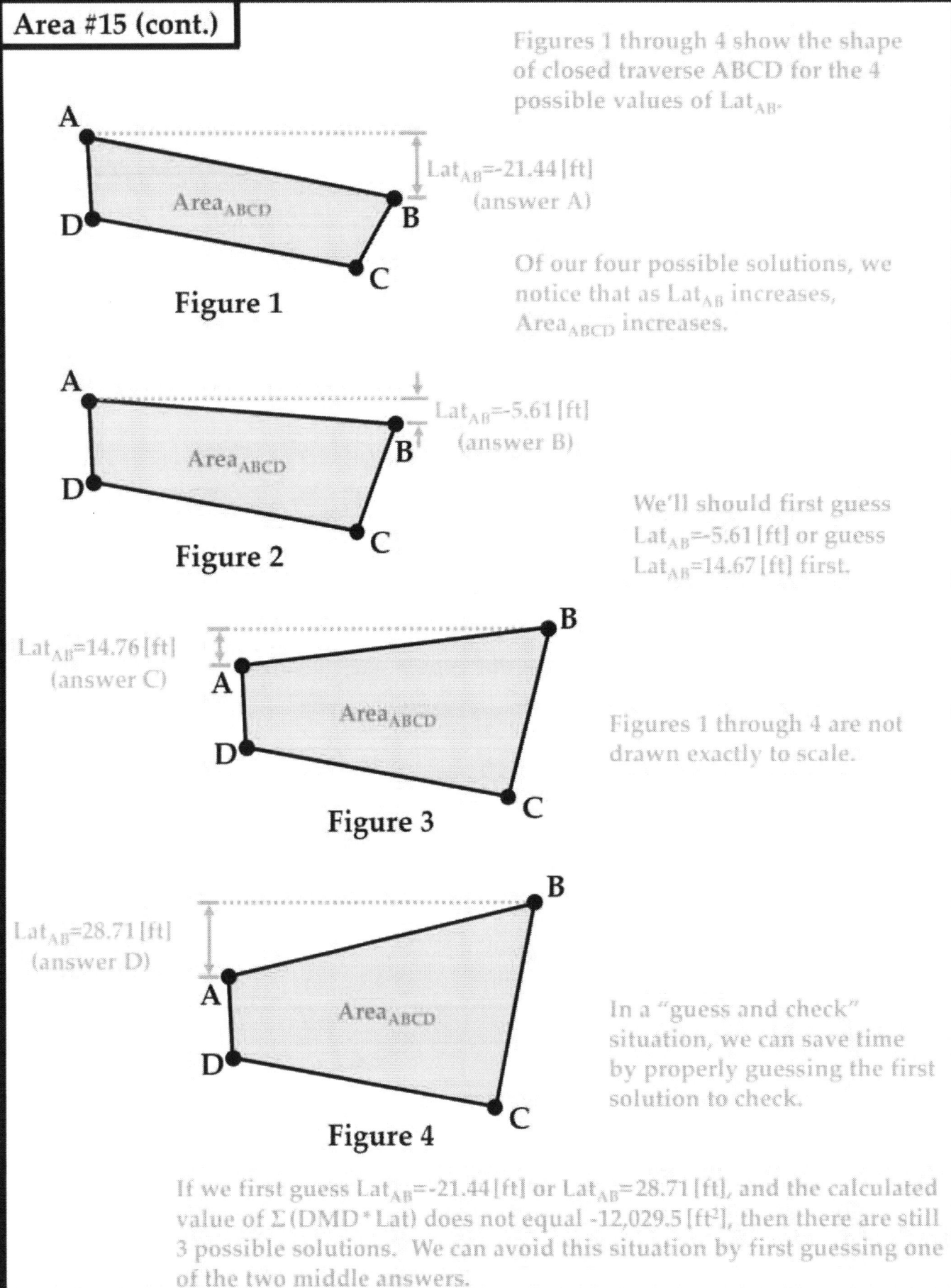

Figures 1 through 4 show the shape of closed traverse ABCD for the 4 possible values of Lat_{AB}.

$Lat_{AB}=-21.44\,[ft]$
(answer A)

Of our four possible solutions, we notice that as Lat_{AB} increases, $Area_{ABCD}$ increases.

Figure 1

$Lat_{AB}=-5.61\,[ft]$
(answer B)

We'll should first guess $Lat_{AB}=-5.61\,[ft]$ or guess $Lat_{AB}=14.67\,[ft]$ first.

Figure 2

$Lat_{AB}=14.76\,[ft]$
(answer C)

Figures 1 through 4 are not drawn exactly to scale.

Figure 3

$Lat_{AB}=28.71\,[ft]$
(answer D)

In a "guess and check" situation, we can save time by properly guessing the first solution to check.

Figure 4

If we first guess $Lat_{AB}=-21.44\,[ft]$ or $Lat_{AB}=28.71\,[ft]$, and the calculated value of $\Sigma(DMD*Lat)$ does not equal $-12{,}029.5\,[ft^2]$, then there are still 3 possible solutions. We can avoid this situation by first guessing one of the two middle answers.

Area #15 (cont.)

first guess

$$Lat_{AB}=14.67\,[ft]$$

We'll first guess and check answer C ($Lat_{AB}=14.76[ft]$).

property of a closed traverse

$$0=\sum_{i}^{N}Lat_i \leftarrow eq.2$$

Since ABCD is a closed traverse, we can compute Lat_{BC}, based Lat_{CD}, Lat_{DA}, and our assumed value for Lat_{AB}.

$$0=Lat_{AB}+Lat_{BC}+Lat_{CD}+Lat_{DA}$$

Write out eq.2, solve for Lat_{BC}, then plug in the other three latitude values and compute Lat_{BC}.

$Lat_{CD}=24.14\,[ft]$

$$Lat_{BC}=-Lat_{AB}-Lat_{CD}-Lat_{DA}$$

$Lat_{AB}=14.76\,[ft]$ $Lat_{DA}=28.08\,[ft]$

$$Lat_{BC}=-14.76\,[ft]-24.14\,[ft]-28.08\,[ft]$$

$$Lat_{BC}=-66.98\,[ft] \longleftarrow \text{based on our assumed value of } Lat_{AB}=14.76[ft]$$

Plug in the assumed values of Lat_{AB} and Lat_{BC} into Table 1.

course	Latitude	Departure	DMD	DMD*Latitude
AB	14.76	135.81	135.81	$DMD_{AB}*Latitude_{AB}$
BC	-66.98	-12.40	259.22	$DMD_{BC}*Latitude_{BC}$
CD	24.14	-116.72	130.10	$DMD_{CD}*Latitude_{CD}$
DA	28.08	-6.69	6.69	$DMD_{DA}*Latitude_{DA}$
				$\Sigma(DMD*Latitude)$

Table 1

Surveying Practice Problems

Area #15 (cont.)

Compute the DMD*Latitude for all four courses, sum all DMD*Latitude values and compare that sum to -12,029.5 [ft²].

DMD_{AB}=135.81 [ft] $Latitude_{AB}$=14.76 [ft]

$$DMD_{AB}*Latitude_{AB}=135.81[ft]*14.76[ft]=2,004.6[ft^2]$$

DMD_{BC}=259.22 [ft] $Latitude_{BC}$=-66.98 [ft]

$$DMD_{BC}*Latitude_{BC}=259.22[ft]*(-66.98[ft])=-17,362.6[ft^2]$$

DMD_{CD}=130.10 [ft] $Latitude_{CD}$=24.14 [ft]

$$DMD_{CD}*Latitude_{CD}=130.10[ft]*24.14[ft]=3,140.6[ft^2]$$

DMD_{DA}=6.69 [ft] $Latitude_{DA}$=28.08 [ft]

$$DMD_{DA}*Latitude_{DA}=6.69[ft]*28.08[ft]=187.9[ft^2]$$

$DMD_{AB}*Lat_{AB}$=2,004.6 [ft²] $DMD_{BC}*Lat_{BC}$=-17,362.6 [ft²]

$$\Sigma(DMD*Lat)=DMD_{AB}*Lat_{AB}+DMD_{BC}*Lat_{BC}$$
$$+DMD_{CD}*Lat_{CD}+DMD_{DA}*Lat_{DA}$$

$DMD_{CD}*Lat_{CD}$=3,140.6 [ft²] $DMD_{DA}*Lat_{DA}$=187.9 [ft²]

$$\Sigma(DMD*Lat)=2,004.6[ft^2]+(-17,362.6[ft^2])+3,140.6[ft^2]+187.9[ft^2]$$

$$\Sigma(DMD*Lat)=-12,029.5[ft^2]$$

Since our assumed value for Lat_{AB} results in a $\Sigma(DMD*Lat)$ value of -12,029.5 [ft²], our assumed value for Lat_{AB} of 14.76 [ft] is correct.

Answer: $\boxed{C}$

Area #16

Find: Area$_{ABCD}$ ← area inside closed traverse ABCD

Given:

Point	Northing	Easting
A	218.9	173.4
B	88.4	241.8
C	101.7	121.7
D	197.6	67.9

All northing and easting values are in units of feet

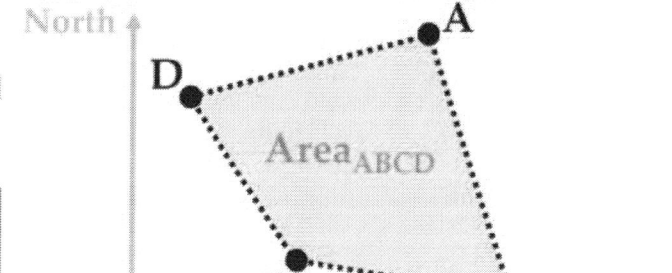

A) 12,000 [ft^2]

B) 13,000 [ft^2]

C) 24,000 [ft^2]

D) 26,000 [ft^2]

Analysis:

A) 12,000 [ft^2]
B) 13,000 [ft^2] } similar values

C) 24,000 [ft^2]
D) 26,000 [ft^2] } similar values

First, we notice answers A and B are similar, and answers C and D are similar.

We can compute an approximate area and quickly rule out 2 of the possible answers.

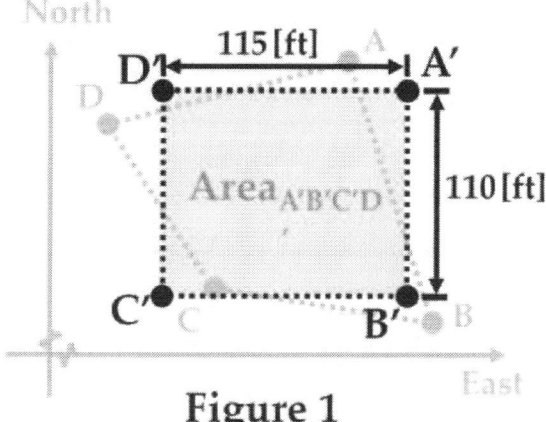

Figure 1

Figure 1 shows the outline of rectangle A'B'C'D', having an area approximately equal to Area$_{ABCD}$.

Based on the northing and easting values, we approximate rectangle A'B'C'D' has a height of 110 feet and a width of 115 feet.

$$Area_{ABCD} \approx Area_{A'B'C'D'} \leftarrow approx. 1$$

$$Area_{A'B'C'D'} = L_{D'A'} * L_{A'B'} \leftarrow eq. 1$$

$L_{D'A'} = 115[ft]$ $L_{A'B'} = 110[ft]$

Use eq.1 to compute Area$_{A'B'C'D'}$.

Surveying Practice Problems

Area #16 (cont.)

$$\text{Area}_{A'B'C'D'} = 110\,[\text{ft}] * 115\,[\text{ft}]$$

$$\text{Area}_{A'B'C'D'} = 12{,}650\,[\text{ft}^2]$$

The area of rectangle A′B′C′D′ equals 12,650 [ft²]. Therefore, Area$_{ABCD}$ is approximately 12,650 [ft²].

$$\text{Area}_{A'B'C'D'} = 12{,}650\,[\text{ft}^2]$$

$$\text{Area}_{ABCD} \approx \text{Area}_{A'B'C'D'} \leftarrow approx.\,1$$

$$\text{Area}_{ABCD} \approx 12{,}650\,[\text{ft}^2]$$

We can rule out answers C and D as possible solutions.

A) 12,000 [ft²]
B) 13,000 [ft²] $\Big\}$ **possible solutions**

~~C) 24,000 [ft²]~~
~~D) 26,000 [ft²]~~ $\Big\}$ too large

We'll compute Area$_{ABCD}$ using the double meridian distance method using Table 1.

course	Lat	Dep	DMD	DMD*Lat
DA	Lat$_{DA}$	Dep$_{DA}$	DMD$_{DA}$	DMD$_{DA}$*Lat$_{DA}$
AB	Lat$_{AB}$	Dep$_{AB}$	DMD$_{AB}$	DMD$_{AB}$*Lat$_{AB}$
BC	Lat$_{BC}$	Dep$_{BC}$	DMD$_{BC}$	DMD$_{BC}$*Lat$_{BC}$
CD	Lat$_{CD}$	Dep$_{CD}$	DMD$_{CD}$	DMD$_{CD}$*Lat$_{CD}$
				$\Sigma(\text{DMD}*\text{Lat})$

Latitude → Lat Departure → Dep Double Meridian Distance → DMD

Table 1

Begin Table 1 with course DA because point D has the smallest easting value.

Compute the latitudes of each course. Variable "N$_A$" represents the northing coordinate of point A.

$N_A = 218.9\,[\text{ft}]$ $N_D = 197.6\,[\text{ft}]$

$$\text{Lat}_{DA} = N_A - N_D = 218.9\,[\text{ft}] - 197.6\,[\text{ft}] = 21.3\,[\text{ft}]$$

Area #16 (cont.)

$N_B=88.4\,[ft]$ $N_A=218.9\,[ft]$

$$Lat_{AB}=N_B-N_A=88.4\,[ft]-218.9\,[ft]=-130.5\,[ft]$$

$N_C=101.7\,[ft]$ $N_B=88.4\,[ft]$

$$Lat_{BC}=N_C-N_B=101.7\,[ft]-88.4\,[ft]=13.3\,[ft]$$

$N_D=197.6\,[ft]$ $N_C=101.7\,[ft]$

$$Lat_{CD}=N_D-N_C=197.6\,[ft]-101.7\,[ft]=95.9\,[ft]$$

Compute the departure of each course. Variable "E_A" represents the easting coordinate of point A.

$E_A=173.4\,[ft]$ $E_D=67.9\,[ft]$

$$Dep_{DA}=E_A-E_D=173.4\,[ft]-67.9\,[ft]=105.5\,[ft]$$

$E_B=241.8\,[ft]$ $E_A=173.4\,[ft]$

$$Dep_{AB}=E_B-E_A=241.8\,[ft]-173.4\,[ft]=68.4\,[ft]$$

$E_C=121.7\,[ft]$ $E_B=241.8\,[ft]$

$$Dep_{BC}=E_C-E_B=121.7\,[ft]-241.8\,[ft]=-120.1\,[ft]$$

$E_D=67.9\,[ft]$ $E_C=121.7\,[ft]$

$$Dep_{CD}=E_D-E_C=67.9\,[ft]-121.7\,[ft]=-53.8\,[ft]$$

Table 2 shows the calculated latitudes and departure values.

Surveying Practice Problems

Area #16 (cont.)

course	Lat	Dep	DMD	DMD*Lat
DA	21.3	105.5	DMD_{DA}	$DMD_{DA}*21.3$
AB	-130.5	68.4	DMD_{AB}	$DMD_{AB}*(-130.5)$
BC	13.3	-120.1	DMD_{BC}	$DMD_{BC}*13.3$
CD	95.9	-53.8	DMD_{CD}	$DMD_{CD}*95.9$
				$\Sigma(DMD*Lat)$

Table 2

In Table 2, the units of departure and latitude are in feet.

Compute the double meridian distance (DMD) values for all four courses in the traverse using eq.2, eq.3, eq.4 and eq.5.

The DMD of the first course equals the departure of the first course.

$DEP_{DA}=105.5[ft]$

$$DMD_{DA}=DEP_{DA} \leftarrow eq.2$$

$$DMD_{DA}=105.5[ft]$$

$DMD_{DA}=105.5[ft]$ $DEP_{AB}=68.4[ft]$

$$DMD_{AB}=DMD_{DA}+DEP_{DA}+DEP_{AB} \leftarrow eq.3$$

$DEP_{DA}=105.5[ft]$

$$DMD_{AB}=105.5[ft]+105.5[ft]+68.4[ft]$$

$$DMD_{AB}=279.4[ft]$$

$DMD_{AB}=279.4[ft]$ $DEP_{BC}=-120.1[ft]$

$$DMD_{BC}=DMD_{AB}+DEP_{AB}+DEP_{BC} \leftarrow eq.4$$

$DEP_{AB}=68.4[ft]$

Area #16 (cont.)

$$DMD_{BC}=279.4[ft]+68.4[ft]+(-120.1[ft])$$

$$DMD_{BC}=227.7[ft]$$

$DEP_{DA}=-53.8[ft]$

$$DMD_{DA}=-DEP_{DA} \leftarrow eq.5$$

The DMD of the final course equals the departure of the final course, having the opposite sign.

$$DMD_{DA}=-(-53.8[ft])$$

$$DMD_{DA}=53.8[ft]$$

Compute the DMD*Lat for each course in the traverse, using eq.6, eq.7, eq.8 and eq.9.

$DMD_{DA}=105.5[ft]$ $Latitude_{DA}=21.3[ft]$

$$DMD_{DA}*Latitude_{DA}=105.5[ft]*21.3[ft]=2,247.15[ft^2]$$

$DMD_{AB}=279.4[ft]$ $Latitude_{AB}=-130.5[ft]$

$$DMD_{AB}*Latitude_{AB}=279.4[ft]*(-130.5[ft])=-36,461.7[ft^2]$$

$DMD_{BC}=227.7[ft]$ $Latitude_{BC}=13.3[ft]$

$$DMD_{BC}*Latitude_{BC}=227.7[ft]*13.3[ft]=3,028.41[ft^2]$$

$DMD_{CD}=53.8[ft]$ $Latitude_{CD}=95.9[ft]$

$$DMD_{CD}*Latitude_{CD}=53.8[ft]*95.9[ft]=5,159.42[ft^2]$$

Surveying Practice Problems

Area #16 (cont.)

Use eq.6 to sum the DMD*Lat products for all four courses.

$DMD_{DA}*Lat_{DA}=2,247.15\,[ft^2]$ $DMD_{AB}*Lat_{AB}=-36,461.7\,[ft^2]$

$$\Sigma(DMD*Lat)=DMD_{DA}*Lat_{DA}+DMD_{AB}*Lat_{AB} \quad \leftarrow eq.6$$
$$+DMD_{BC}*Lat_{BC}+DMD_{CD}*Lat_{CD}$$

$DMD_{BC}*Lat_{BC}=3,028.41\,[ft^2]$ $DMD_{CD}*Lat_{CD}=5,159.42\,[ft^2]$

$$\Sigma(DMD*Lat)=2,247.15\,[ft^2]+(-36,461.7\,[ft^2])+3,028.41\,[ft^2]+5,159.42\,[ft^2]$$

$$\Sigma(DMD*Lat)=-26,026.7\,[ft^2]$$

$\Sigma(DMD*Lat)=-26,026.7\,[ft^2]$ Use eq.7 to solve for Area_{ABCD}

$$Area_{ABCD}=\left|\Sigma(DMD*Lat)\right|\Big/2 \quad \leftarrow eq.7$$

$$Area_{ABCD}=\left|\Sigma(-26,026.7\,[ft^2])\right|\Big/2$$

$$Area_{ABCD}=13,013.4\,[ft^2]$$

Of the possible answers, $13,013.4\,[ft^2]$ is most nearly $13,000\,[ft^2]$. Answer B is correct.

Answer: $\boxed{B}$

Area #17

<u>Find:</u> Area$_{IJK}$ ← the area inside triangle IJK

<u>Given:</u>

point	Northing	Easting
I	151.8 [ft]	47.6 [ft]
J	167.9 [ft]	133.1 [ft]
K	74.1 [ft]	62.0 [ft]

the coordinates of points I, J, K

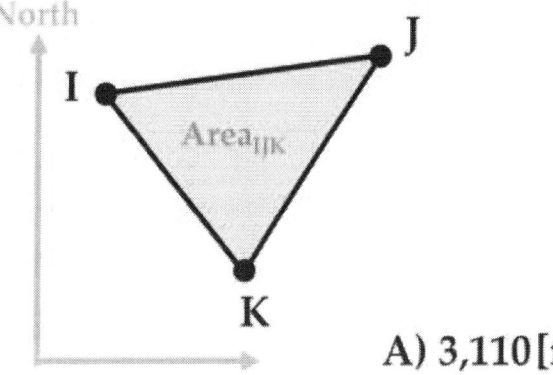

North

East

A) 3,110 [ft²]

B) 3,440 [ft²]

C) 3,770 [ft²]

D) 4,010 [ft²]

Analysis:

Use eq.1 to find the area of a polygon having N sides, when we know all northing and easting values.

first summation   second summation   absolute value bar

$$\text{Area} = \frac{\left| \sum_{n=1}^{N-1}(N_n{*}E_{n+1}-N_{n+1}{*}E_i) + \sum_{n=N}^{N}(N_n{*}E_1-N_1{*}E_n) \right|}{2} \quad \leftarrow eq.1$$

Point	Number
I	1
J	2
K	3

Table 1

For notational purposes, associate each point with a number. Point I is 1, point J is 2, and point K is 3.

Write out eq.1, for triangle IJK, then substitute the appropriate letter in the subscript.

first term   second term   third term

$$\text{Area}_{IJK} = \frac{\left| (N_I{*}E_J-N_J{*}E_I) + (N_J{*}E_K-N_K{*}E_J) + (N_K{*}E_I-N_I{*}E_K) \right|}{2} \quad \leftarrow eq.2$$

There are 3 sides in a triangle, therefore, N=3. The first summation from eq.1 results in 2 terms, in eq.2. The second summation in eq.1 (always) results in 1 term, in eq.2.

Surveying Practice Problems

Area #17 (cont.)

$N_I = 151.8$ [ft] $N_J = 167.9$ [ft]

$$\text{first term} = N_I{}^*E_J - N_J{}^*E_I \longleftarrow eq.3$$

$E_J = 133.1$ [ft] $E_I = 47.6$ [ft]

Use eq.3 to compute the first term of eq.2.

first term=151.8[ft]*133.1[ft]-167.9[ft]*47.6[ft]

first term=12,212.54[ft^2]

$N_J = 167.9$ [ft] $N_K = 74.1$ [ft]

$$\text{second term} = N_J{}^*E_K - N_K{}^*E_J \longleftarrow eq.4$$

$E_K = 62.0$ [ft] $E_J = 133.1$ [ft]

Use eq.4 to compute the second term of eq.2.

second term=167.9[ft]*62.0[ft]-74.1[ft]*133.1[ft]

second term=547.09[ft^2]

$N_K = 74.1$ [ft] $N_I = 151.8$ [ft]

$$\text{third term} = N_K{}^*E_I - N_I{}^*E_K \longleftarrow eq.5$$

$E_I = 47.6$ [ft] $E_K = 62.0$ [ft]

Use eq.5 to compute the third term of eq.2.

third term=74.1[ft]*47.6[ft]−151.8[ft]*62.0[ft]

third term=-5,884.44[ft^2]

Area #17 (cont.)

Return to eq. 2, plug in the first, second and third terms, then solve for the area of triangle IJK.

$N_J*E_K-N_K*E_J=547.09\,[\text{ft}^2]$

$N_I*E_J-N_J*E_I=12,212.54\,[\text{ft}^2]$

$N_K*E_I-N_I*E_K=-5,884.44\,[\text{ft}^2]$

$$\text{Area}_{IJK}=\frac{\left|(N_I*E_J-N_J*E_I)+(N_J*E_K-N_K*E_J)+(N_K*E_I-N_I*E_K)\right|}{2} \quad \leftarrow eq.2$$

$$\text{Area}_{IJK}=\frac{\left|12,212.54\,[\text{ft}^2]+547.09\,[\text{ft}^2]+(-5,884.44[\text{ft}^2])\right|}{2}$$

$$\text{Area}_{IJK}=3,437.60\,[\text{ft}^2]$$

The calculated area of triangle IJK is most nearly answer B.

Answer: | B |

Possible solutions:

A) 3,110 [ft²]

B) 3,440 [ft²]

C) 3,770 [ft²]

D) 4,010 [ft²]

Surveying Practice Problems

Area #18

Find: Area$_{ABCDE}$ ← the area inside pentagon ABCDE

Given:

point	Northing	Easting
A	241.76 [ft]	744.01 [ft]
B	266.05 [ft]	789.54 [ft]
C	238.11 [ft]	841.93 [ft]
D	213.07 [ft]	797.43 [ft]
E	148.62 [ft]	767.92 [ft]

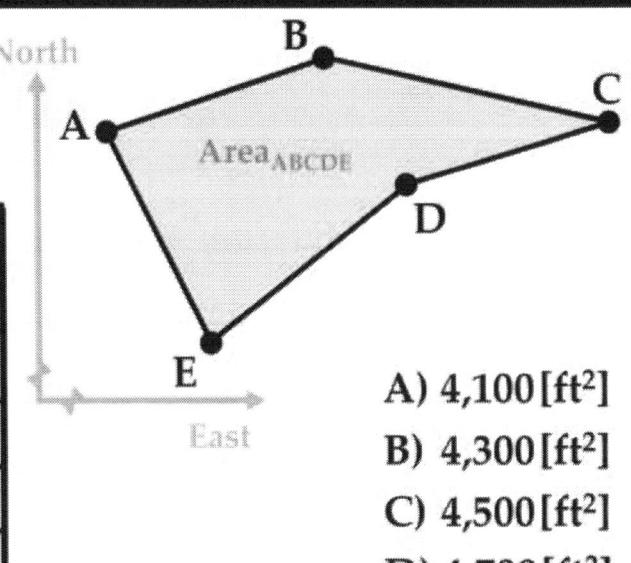

A) 4,100 [ft²]

B) 4,300 [ft²]

C) 4,500 [ft²]

D) 4,700 [ft²]

Analysis:

sum of all products ↘   sum of all products ↙

$$\text{Area} = \frac{\left| \Sigma(\searrow) - \Sigma(\nearrow) \right|}{2} \leftarrow eq.1$$

Use eq.1 to find the area of a polygon when all northing and easting values are known.

In eq.1, each diagonal arrow represents the product of one northing coordinate and one easting coordinate, see below.

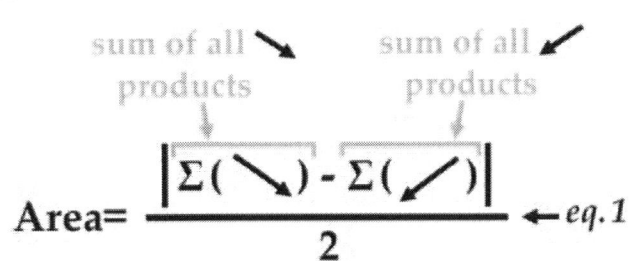

Point	Northing	Easting
A	241.76 [ft]	744.01 [ft]
B	266.05 [ft]	789.54 [ft]
C	238.11 [ft]	841.93 [ft]
D	213.07 [ft]	797.43 [ft]
E	148.62 [ft]	767.92 [ft]
A	241.76 [ft]	744.01 [ft]

Table 1

append point A beneath point E

A quick way to solve eq.1 is to:

1) Write out the northing and easting values, and append the first point (point A) to the end.

2) Draw diagonal arrows ↘ and ↙ connecting the northing of one point with the easting of the subsequent point, as shown.

3) Multiply the two coordinates connected by each arrow and plug that product into eq.2 or eq.3.

1ˢᵗ term   2ⁿᵈ term   3ʳᵈ term   4ᵗʰ term   5ᵗʰ term

$$\Sigma(\searrow) = N_A * E_B + N_B * E_C + N_C * E_D + N_D * E_E + N_E * E_A \leftarrow eq.2$$

Area #18 (cont.)

Compute the five ↘ products in eq. 2 using Table 2.

Point	Northing	Easting		
A	241.76 [ft]	744.01 [ft]		
B	266.05 [ft]	789.54 [ft]	→ 190,879 [ft²]	← 1ˢᵗ term
C	238.11 [ft]	841.93 [ft]	→ 223,995 [ft²]	← 2ⁿᵈ term
D	213.07 [ft]	797.43 [ft]	→ 189,876 [ft²]	← 3ʳᵈ term
E	148.62 [ft]	767.92 [ft]	→ 163,621 [ft²]	← 4ᵗʰ term
A	241.76 [ft]	744.01 [ft]	→ 110,575 [ft²]	← 5ᵗʰ term

Table 2

Return to eq. 2, plug in all 5 ↘ products, then compute the first summation of eq. 1.

2ⁿᵈ term = 223,995 [ft²]   4ᵗʰ term = 163,621 [ft²]

$$\Sigma(\searrow) = N_A{}^*E_B + N_B{}^*E_C + N_C{}^*E_D + N_D{}^*E_E + N_E{}^*E_A \leftarrow eq.2$$

1ˢᵗ term = 190,879 [ft²]   3ʳᵈ term = 189,876 [ft²]   5ᵗʰ term = 110,575 [ft²]

$$\Sigma(\searrow) = 190,879\,[ft^2] + 223,995\,[ft^2] + 189,876\,[ft^2]$$
$$+ 163,621\,[ft^2] + 110,575\,[ft^2]$$

$$\Sigma(\searrow) = 878,946\,[ft^2]$$

Compute the five ↙ products in eq. 2 using Table 3.

1ˢᵗ term   2ⁿᵈ term   3ʳᵈ term   4ᵗʰ term   5ᵗʰ term

$$\Sigma(\nearrow) = N_B{}^*E_A + N_C{}^*E_B + N_D{}^*E_C + N_E{}^*E_D + N_A{}^*E_E \leftarrow eq.3$$

Point	Northing	Easting		
A	241.76 [ft]	744.01 [ft]	→ 197,944 [ft²]	← 1ˢᵗ term
B	266.05 [ft]	789.54 [ft]	→ 187,997 [ft²]	← 2ⁿᵈ term
C	238.11 [ft]	841.93 [ft]	→ 179,390 [ft²]	← 3ʳᵈ term
D	213.07 [ft]	797.43 [ft]	→ 118.514 [ft²]	← 4ᵗʰ term
E	148.62 [ft]	767.92 [ft]	→ 185,652 [ft²]	← 5ᵗʰ term
A	241.76 [ft]	744.01 [ft]		

Table 3

Surveying Practice Problems

Area #18 (cont.)

Return to eq.3, plug in all 5 products, then compute the second summation of eq.1.

2nd term=187,997[ft²]   4th term=118,514[ft²]

$$\Sigma(\nearrow)=\underbrace{N_B*E_A}+\underbrace{N_C*E_B}+\underbrace{N_D*E_C}+\underbrace{N_E*E_D}+\underbrace{N_A*E_E} \leftarrow eq.3$$

1st term=197,944[ft²]   3rd term=179,390[ft²]   5th term=185,652[ft²]

$$\Sigma(\nearrow)=197,944[ft^2]+187,997[ft^2]+179,390[ft^2]$$
$$+118,514[ft^2]+185,652[ft^2]$$

$$\Sigma(\nearrow)=869,497[ft^2]$$

Return to eq.1, plug in both summations, then solve for the area of pentagon ABCDE.

$\Sigma(\searrow)=878,946[ft^2]$

$$Area_{ABCDE}=\frac{\left|\Sigma(\searrow)-\Sigma(\nearrow)\right|}{2} \leftarrow eq.1$$

$\Sigma(\nearrow)=869,497[ft^2]$

$$Area_{ABCDE}=\frac{\left|878,946[ft^2]-869,497[ft^2]\right|}{2}$$

$$Area_{ABCDE}=4,725[ft^2]$$

Each summation term includes as many products as there are points in the polygon.

Answer: $\boxed{D}$

Be sure to not forget to copy the first point's coordinates to a new row beneath the last point in the given table of coordinates before computing the products.

Angles #1

Find: A_{JKI} ← the angle formed by points J, K and I

Given:

$B_{IJ} = N 86°30'00'' E$

$B_{IK} = S 48°15'00'' E$

the bearing of line segments IJ and IK

$L_{JK} = 95.14 [ft]$ ← the length of line segments JK and IJ

$L_{IJ} = 102.88 [ft]$ ←

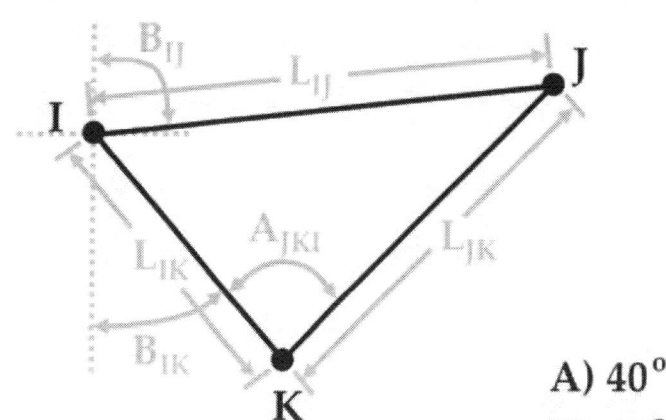

North

A) 40°

B) 45°

C) 50°

D) 55°

Analysis:

Law of Sines:

Use the law of sines to find A_{JKI}.

$$\frac{\sin A}{a} = \frac{\sin B}{b} = \frac{\sin C}{c} \leftarrow eq.1$$

$A = A_{KIJ}$

$a = L_{JK}$

$B = A_{JKI}$

$b = L_{IJ}$

In eq.1, capital letters equal the interior angles of the triangle, and lower-case letters represent the side length of the triangle, opposite the corresponding angle.

$$\frac{\sin(A_{KIJ})}{L_{JK}} = \frac{\sin(A_{JKI})}{L_{IJ}} \leftarrow eq.2$$

Plug in variables A_{KIJ}, A_{JKI}, L_{JK} and L_{IJ} into eq.1, then solve for A_{JKI}.

$$A_{JKI} = \sin^{-1}\left(\frac{\sin(A_{KIJ}) * L_{IJ}}{L_{JK}}\right) \leftarrow eq.3$$

The problem statement provides L_{IJ} and L_{JK}, we need to determine A_{KIJ}.

azimuth IJ

$$A_{KIJ} = Az_{IK} - Az_{IJ} \leftarrow eq.4$$

azimuth IK

We can find A_{KIJ} by subtracting the azimuth of line segment IJ from the azimuth of line segment IK.

Angles #1 (cont.)

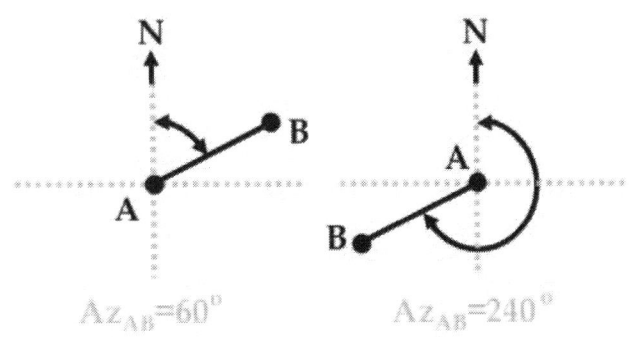

Figure 1 shows a couple azimuth measurement examples.

If an observer is standing at the first point of a line segment, and facing north, the azimuth of the line segment is the horizontal angle the observer must turn, in the clockwise direction, to face the second point of the line segment.

$$Az_{AB}=60°$$ $$Az_{AB}=240°$$

Figure 1

Unless otherwise noted, assume all azimuth values are "north-based" azimuths, as defined above.

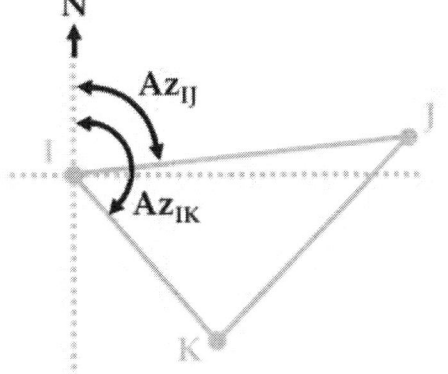

Figure 2 shows the azimuth angles of line segments IJ and IK.

Figure 2

Table 1 shows how to convert bearing angles to azimuth values, based on the quadrant of the bearing angle.

Quadrant	Azimuth
NE	Bearing
SE	180°-Bearing
SW	180°+Bearing
NW	360°-Bearing

Table 1

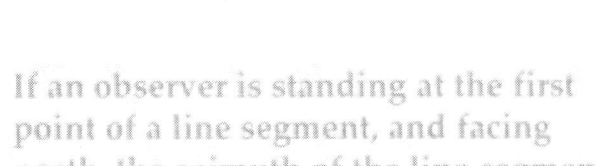

$$B_{IJ} = N\,86°30'00''\,E$$

Line IJ starts at point I and ends at point J. From point I, point J is 86.5 east of north.

Direction is important. Line segment IJ is in the NE quadrant. Line seg-ment JI heads in the SW quadrant.

Angles #1 (cont.)

$B_{IJ} = N\ 86°30'00''\ E$

$$Az_{IJ} = B_{IJ} \leftarrow eq.5$$

$$Az_{IJ} = 86°30'00''$$

Since B_{IJ} is in the NE quadrant, the azimuth angle equals the value of the bearing angle.

Use eq.5 and eq.6 to find Az_{IJ} and Az_{IK}.

$B_{IK} = S\ 48°15'00''\ E$

$$Az_{IK} = 180° - B_{IJ} \leftarrow eq.6$$

$$Az_{IK} = 180° - 48°15'00''$$

$$Az_{IK} = 131°45'00''$$

$Az_{IK} = 86°30'00''$

Plug in Az_{IJ} and Az_{IK} into eq.4, then solve for A_{KIJ}.

$$A_{KIJ} = Az_{IK} - Az_{IJ} \leftarrow eq.4$$

$Az_{IK} = 131°45'00''$

$$A_{KIJ} = 131°45'00'' - 86°30'00''$$

$$A_{KIJ} = 45°15'00''$$

Plug in the values of A_{KIJ}, L_{IJ} and L_{JK} into eq.3, and solve for A_{JKI}.

$A_{KIJ} = 45°15'00''$ $L_{IJ} = 102.88\ [ft]$

$$A_{JKI} = \sin^{-1}\left(\frac{\sin(A_{KIJ}) * L_{IJ}}{L_{JK}}\right) \leftarrow eq.3$$

$L_{JK} = 95.14\ [ft]$

Angles #1 (cont.)

$$A_{JKI} = \sin^{-1} \left(\frac{\sin(45°15'00'') * 102.88\,[\text{ft}]}{95.14\,[\text{ft}]} \right)$$

$$A_{JKI} = 50°10'16''$$

Answer: $\boxed{C}$

Angles #2

<u>Find:</u> Az_{AC} ← the azimuth of course AC

<u>Given:</u>

$B_{AB}=N\,50°E$

the bearing of course AB

$B_{BC}=S\,20°E$

the bearing of course BC

$L_{AC}=L_{BC}$

the length of side AC equals the length of side BC.

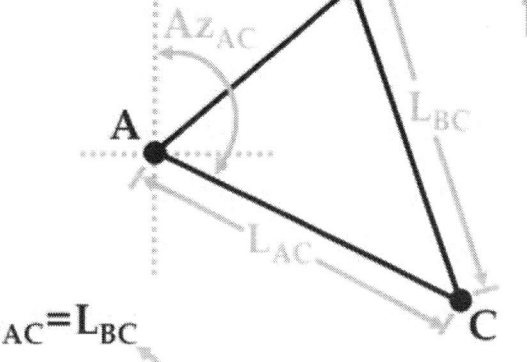

A) $110°$

B) $120°$

C) $130°$

D) $140°$

....

<u>Analysis:</u>

$$Az_{AC}=Az_{AB}+A_{CAB} \quad ←eq.1$$

Use eq.1 to calculate Az_{AC}, the azimuth of course AC.

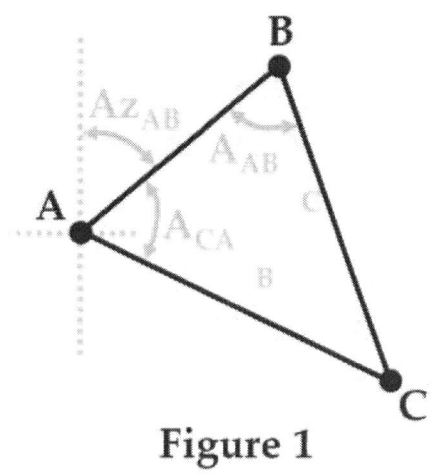

Figure 1

Figure 1 identifies the azimuth of course AB, angle CAB, and angle ABC.

$B_{AB}=N\,50°E$

$$Az_{AB}=B_{AB} \quad ←eq.2$$

Since bearing AB points in the northeast direction, Azimuth AB equals the value of bearing AB.

$$Az_{AB}=50°$$

The azimuth angle measurement does not include direction labels "N" or "E". The azimuth is measured in a clockwise direction from due north.

Surveying Practice Problems

Angles #2 (cont.)

given

$$L_{AC}=L_{BC}$$

$$A_{CAB}=A_{ABC} \leftarrow eq.3$$

Since the length of course AC equals the length of course BC, we know triangle ABC is isosceles, and angle CAB equals angle ABC.
(see Figure 1).

$A_{CAB}=A_{ABC}$

$$Az_{AC}=Az_{AB}+A_{CAB} \leftarrow eq.1$$

Substitute in angle ABC for angle CAB in eq.1.

$$Az_{AC}=Az_{AB}+A_{ABC} \leftarrow eq.4$$

$$A_{ABC}=Az_{BA}-Az_{BC} \leftarrow eq.5$$

Angle ABC equals the azimuth of course BA minus the azimuth of course BC.

$Az_{AB}=50°$

$$Az_{BA}=Az_{AB}+180° \leftarrow eq.6$$

Since course BA points in the southwest direction, azimuth BA equals azimuth AB plus 180.°

$$Az_{BA}=50°+180°$$

$$Az_{BA}=230°$$

$B_{BC}=S\,20°\,E$

$$Az_{BC}=180°-B_{BC} \leftarrow eq.7$$

Since course BC points in the south-east direction, azimuth BC equals 180° minus the value of bearing BC.

Angles #2 (cont.)

$$Az_{BC}=180°-20°$$

As before, leave out direction labels "S" and "E" when converting a bearing to an azimuth, as in eq.7.

$$Az_{BC}=160°$$

$$Az_{BA}=230° \qquad Az_{BC}=160°$$

$$A_{ABC}=Az_{BA}-Az_{BC} \leftarrow eq.5$$

Return to eq.5, substitute in Az_{BA} and Az_{BC}, then solve for A_{ABC}.

$$A_{ABC}=230°-160°$$

$$A_{ABC}=70°$$

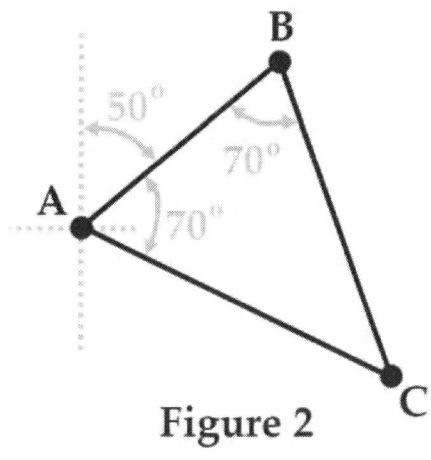

Figure 2

Figure 2 shows the calculated measurements for azimuth AB, angle CAB, and angle ABC.

$$Az_{AB}=50° \qquad A_{ABC}=70°$$

$$Az_{AC}=Az_{AB}+A_{ABC} \leftarrow eq.4$$

Return to eq.4, plug in Az_{AB} and A_{ABC}, then solve for Az_{AC}.

$$Az_{AC}=50°+70°$$

$$Az_{AC}=120° \qquad \underline{Answer:} \boxed{B}$$

Surveying Practice Problems

Angles #3

Find: A_{IJK} ←—the angle formed by points I, J and K

Given:

Course	Latitude	Departure
IJ	292.81	77.65
JK	-100.51	211.08
KI	-192.30	-288.73

the latitude and departure of each course is in units of feet.

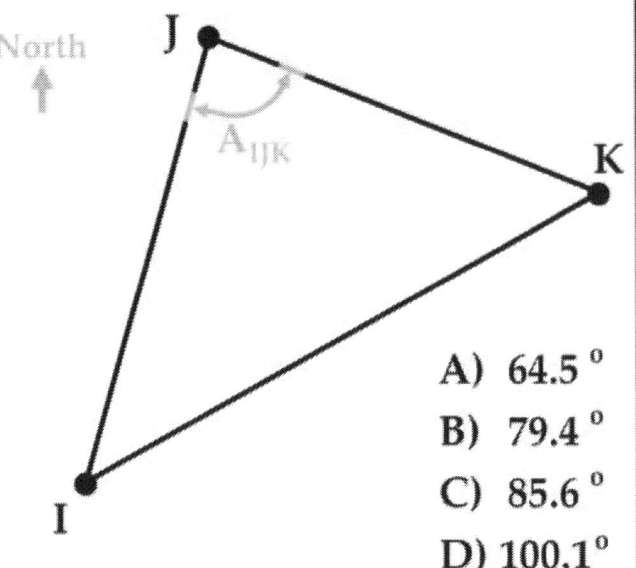

A) 64.5 °

B) 79.4 °

C) 85.6 °

D) 100.1°

Analysis:

First, we'll check to ensure the closed traverse IJK is balanced.

Lat_{JK}=-100.51 [ft]

$$\Sigma Lat=Lat_{IJ}+Lat_{JK}+Lat_{KI} \leftarrow eq.1$$

Lat_{IJ}=292.81 [ft] Lat_{IJ}=-192.30 [ft]

$$\Sigma Lat=292.81[ft]+(-100.51[ft])+(-192.30[ft])$$

A closed traverse is balanced if the sum of all latitude values and the sum of all departure values equal zero.

$$\Sigma Lat=0[ft]$$

Dep_{JK}=211.08 [ft]

Next, check the departure values.

$$\Sigma Dep=Dep_{IJ}+Dep_{JK}+Dep_{KI} \leftarrow eq.2$$

Dep_{IJ}=77.65 [ft] Dep_{IJ}=-288.73 [ft]

$$\Sigma Dep=77.65[ft]+211.08[ft])+(-288.73[ft])$$

$$\Sigma Dep=0[ft]$$

Traverse IJK is balanced.

Angles #3 (cont.)

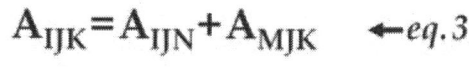

Figure 1   **Figure 2**

$$A_{IJK} = A_{IJN} + A_{MJK} \quad \leftarrow eq.3$$

Figure 1 highlights Angle IJK. Figure 2 adds point M and point N, to create right triangle IJN and right triangle MJK.

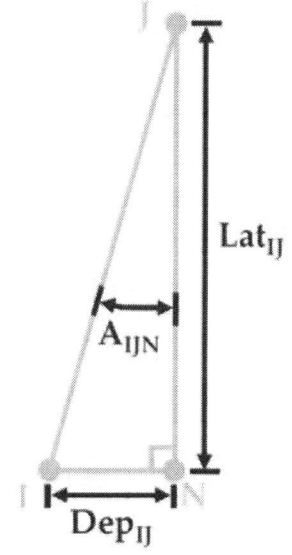

Figure 3

From Figures 1 and 2, we can solve for A_{IJK} by adding A_{IJN} and A_{MJK}, as shown in eq. 3.

Figure 3 shows right triangle IJN, and identifies A_{IJN}.

From Figure 3, we can derive eq.4. Plug in Dep_{IJ} and Lat_{IJ} into eq.4, then solve for A_{IJN}.

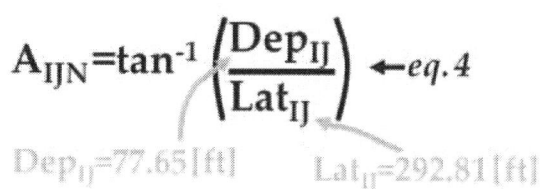

$$A_{IJN} = \tan^{-1}\left(\frac{Dep_{IJ}}{Lat_{IJ}}\right) \quad \leftarrow eq.4$$

Dep_{IJ}=77.65 [ft] Lat_{IJ}=292.81 [ft]

Angles #3 (cont.)

$$A_{IJN}=\tan^{-1}\left(\frac{77.65\,[ft]}{292.81\,[ft]}\right)$$

$$A_{IJN}=14.85°$$

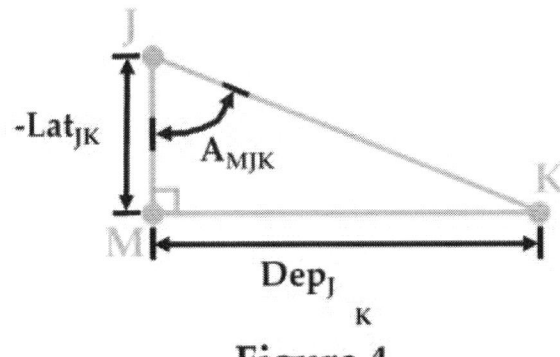

Figure 4

Figure 4 shows right triangle MJK, and identifies A_{MJK}.

From Figure 4, we can derive eq.5. Plug in Dep_{JK} and Lat_{JK} into eq.5, then solve for A_{MJK}.

$$A_{MJK}=\tan^{-1}\left(\frac{Dep_{JK}}{-Lat_{JK}}\right) \leftarrow eq.5$$

$Dep_{JK}=211.08\,[ft]$ $\qquad$ $Lat_{JK}=-100.51\,[ft]$

$$A_{MJK}=\tan^{-1}\left(\frac{211.08\,[ft]}{-(-100.51\,[ft])}\right)$$

A negative sign is added before "Lat_{JK}" in eq.5 because course JK runs in the southward direction.

$$A_{MJK}=64.54°$$

$A_{IJN}=14.85°$ $\qquad$ $A_{MJK}=64.54°$

$$A_{IJK}=A_{IJN}+A_{MJK} \leftarrow eq.3$$

Return to eq.3, plug in A_{IJN} and A_{MJK}, then solve for A_{IJK}.

$$A_{IJK}=14.85°+64.54°$$

$$A_{IJK}=79.39°$$ <u>Answer:</u> B

Angles #4

Find: Az_{YZ} ← the azimuth angle of course YZ
Given:

$B_{XW} = S\,41°25'00''\,W$

the bearing angle of course XW

$A_{WXY} = 120°00'00''$

the angle formed by points W, X and Y

$A_{XYZ} = 98°17'00''$

the angle formed by points X, Y and Z

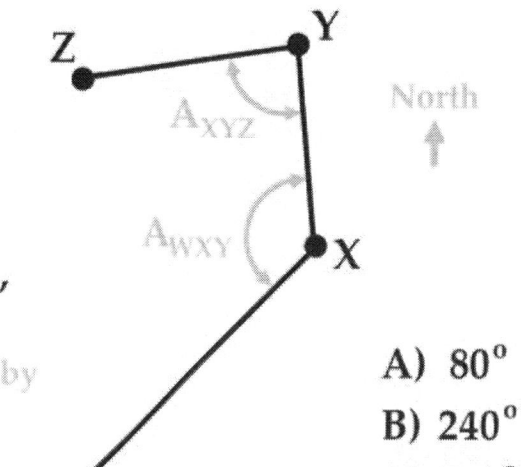

A) 80°
B) 240°
C) 250°
D) 260°

Analysis:

$$Az_{YZ} = Az_{YX} + A_{XYZ} \quad \leftarrow eq.1$$

azimuth angle of course YX

We'll use eq.1 to find the azimuth angle of course YZ.

$$0° \leq Az_{XY} < 360°$$

Note that azimuth angles range between 0° and 360°

$$Az_{YX} = Az_{XY} - 180° \quad \leftarrow eq.2$$

We can determine Az_{YX} from Az_{XY} using eq.2. Eq.2 assumes $Az_{XY} > 180°$.

$$Az_{XY} = Az_{XW} + A_{WXY} \quad \leftarrow eq.3$$

azimuth angle of course XW

Eq.3 computes Az_{XY} from Az_{XW} and A_{WXY}.

$$Az_{XW} = B_{XW} + 180° \quad \leftarrow eq.4$$

$B_{XW} = S\ 41°25'00''\ W$

Solve for Az_{XW} using B_{XW}.

Angles #4 (cont.)

$$Az_{XW} = 41°25'00'' + 180°$$

$$Az_{XW} = 221°25'00''$$

$$Az_{XW} = 221°25'00''$$

$$Az_{XY} = Az_{XW} + A_{WXY} \leftarrow eq.3$$

$$A_{WXY} = 120°00'00''$$

Return to eq.3, plug in Az_{XW} and A_{WXY}, then solve for Az_{XY}.

$$Az_{XY} = 221°25'00'' + 120°00'00''$$

$$Az_{XY} = 341°25'00''$$

$$Az_{XY} = 341°25'00''$$

$$Az_{YX} = Az_{XY} - 180° \leftarrow eq.2$$

Use eq.2 to compute Az_{YX}.

$$Az_{YX} = 341°25'00'' - 180°$$

$$Az_{YX} = 161°25'00''$$

$$A_{WXY} = 98°17'00''$$

$$Az_{YZ} = Az_{YX} + A_{XYZ} \leftarrow eq.1$$

$$Az_{YX} = 161°25'00''$$

Lastly, we'll plug in Az_{YX} and A_{XYZ} into eq.1, then compute Az_{YZ}.

$$Az_{YZ} = 161°25'00'' + 98°17'00''$$

$Az_{YZ}=259°42'00''$

Answer: $\boxed{D}$

259°42'00'' is most nearly 260°.
Select answer D.

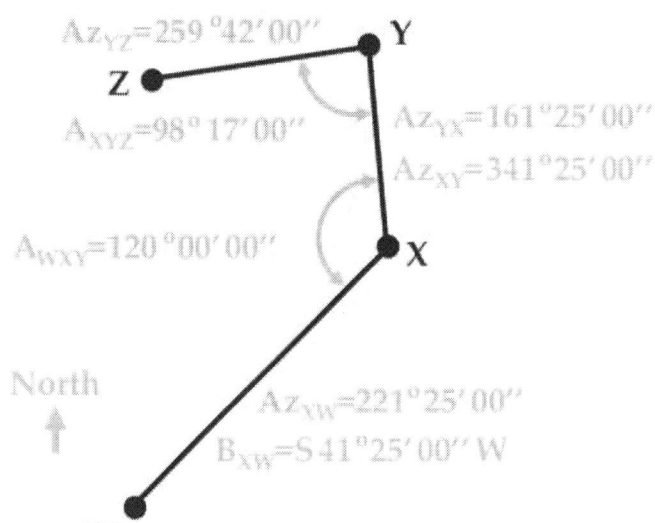

In Figure 1, we write in the known
angle measurements after they are
calculated.

Figure 1

Surveying Practice Problems

Angles #5

Find: $A_{CDE,\,bal}$ ← the interior angle CDE after closed traverse ABCDEF is balanced

Given:

$A_{FAB,meas}=48°22'15''$

$A_{ABC,meas}=103°19'27''$

$A_{BCD,meas}=157°45'08''$

$A_{CDE,meas}=98°55'07''$

$A_{DEF,meas}=88°37'18''$

$A_{EFA,meas}=222°00'45''$

the measured interior angles of traverse ABCDEF

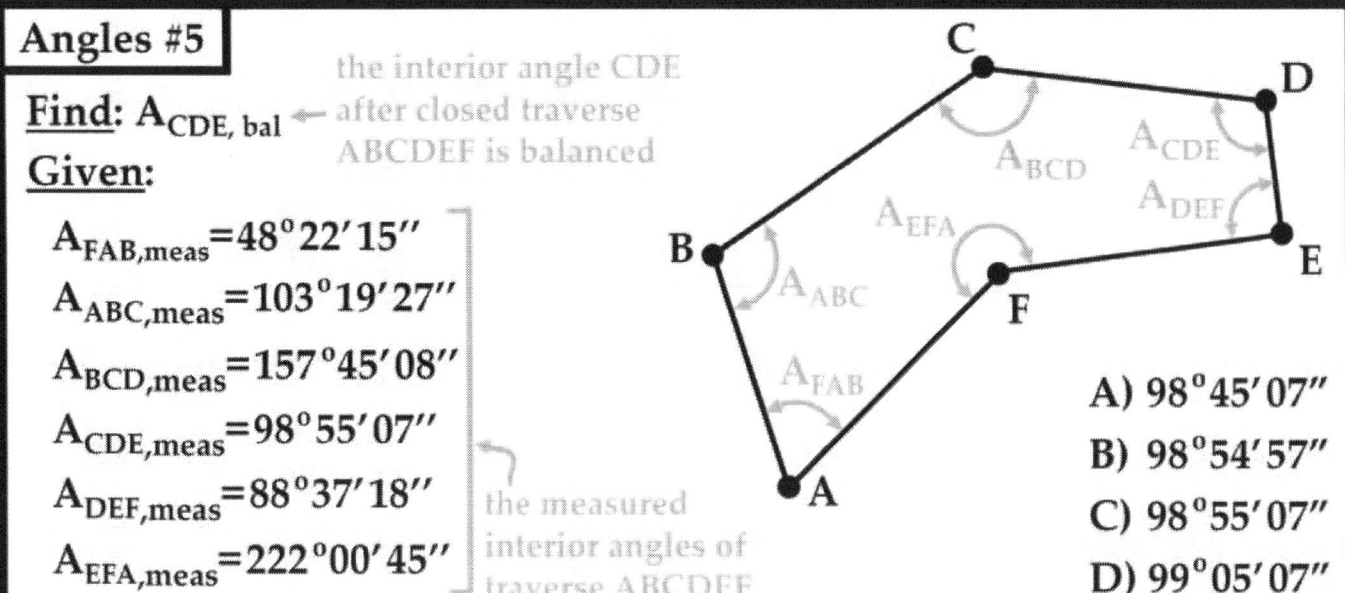

A) $98°45'07''$

B) $98°54'57''$

C) $98°55'07''$

D) $99°05'07''$

Analysis:

$$A_{CDE,bal}=A_{CDE,meas}+A_{corr} \leftarrow eq.1$$

balanced angle   measured angle   angle correction

Use eq.1 to calculate the balanced angle CDE, using the the measured angle CDE and the angle correction.

$$A_{corr}=\frac{\Sigma A_{bal}-\Sigma A_{meas}}{n} \leftarrow eq.2$$

number of sides of the traverse

The correction angle equals the sum of all interior angles of the balanced traverse minus the sum of all interior angles of the measured traverse, divided by the number of sides of the traverse, n.

$$\Sigma A_{bal}=180°*(n-2) \leftarrow eq.3$$

n=6

Use eq.3 to compute the sum of the interior angles of the balanced traverse.

$$\Sigma A_{bal}=180°*(6-2)$$

$$\Sigma A_{bal}=720°$$

Use eq.4 to compute the sum of the interior angles of the measured traverse.

$A_{FAB}=48°22'15''$ $A_{BCD}=157°45'08''$ $A_{DEF}=88°37'18''$

$$\Sigma A_{meas}=A_{FAB}+A_{ABC}+A_{BCD}+A_{CDE}+A_{DEF}+A_{EFA} \leftarrow eq.4$$

$A_{ABC}=103°19'27''$ $A_{CDE}=98°55'07''$ $A_{EFA}=222°00'45''$

Angles #5 (cont.)

$$\Sigma A_{meas} = 48°22'15'' + 103°19'27'' + 157°45'08''$$
$$+ 98°55'07'' + 88°37'18'' + 222°00'45''$$

$$\Sigma A_{meas} = 719°00'00''$$

The interior angles of traverse ABCDEF sum to exactly 1 degree less than expected.

Return to eq. 2, plug in ΣA_{bal}, ΣA_{meas}, and n, then solve for A_{corr}.

$$A_{corr} = \frac{\Sigma A_{bal} - \Sigma A_{meas}}{n} \leftarrow eq. 2$$

where $\Sigma A_{bal} = 720°00'00''$, $n = 6$, $\Sigma A_{meas} = 719°00'00''$

For ΣA_{bal}, we can also write out 720° as 720°00'00''.

$$A_{corr} = \frac{720°00'00'' - 719°00'00''}{6}$$

$$A_{corr} = 0°10'00''$$

Since 1 degree equals 60 minutes, A_{corr} divides evenly into 6 parts of 10 minutes.

$$\frac{1\,deg}{6} = \frac{60\,min}{6} = 10\,min$$

$$A_{CDE,bal} = A_{CDE,meas} + A_{corr} \leftarrow eq. 1$$

where $A_{CDE,meas} = 98°55'07''$, $A_{corr} = 0°10'00''$

Return to eq. 1, plug in $A_{CDE,meas}$ and A_{corr} then solve for $A_{CDE,bal}$.

$$A_{CDE,bal} = 98°55'07'' + 00°10'00''$$

$$A_{CDE,bal} = 99°05'07''$$

Answer: $\boxed{D}$

Surveying Practice Problems

Angles #6

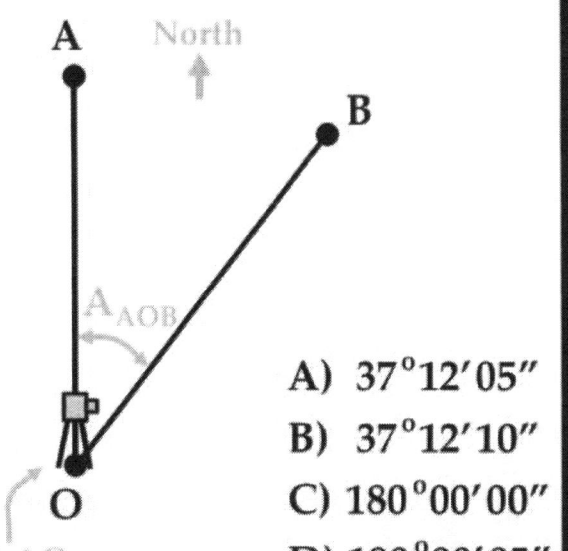

Find: A_{AOB} — the average horizontal angle measured between points A and B, from point O

Given:

Azimuth	Direct	Inverted
Az_{OA}	$0°00'00''$	$180°00'05''$
Az_{OB}	$37°12'10''$	$217°12'05''$

table of azimuth readings were taken from the total station at point O.

total station set up at point O

A) $37°12'05''$

B) $37°12'10''$

C) $180°00'00''$

D) $180°00'05''$

Analysis:

For this problem, we'll add the subscripts "D" and "I" to identify direct and inverted, respectively.

from direct measurement   from inverted measurement

$$A_{AOB} = \frac{A_{AOB,D} + A_{AOB,I}}{2} \leftarrow eq.1$$

From eq. 1, the average angle AOB is half the sum of the direct angle AOB and the inverted angle AOB.

$Az_{OB,D} = 37°12'10''$ $Az_{OA,D} = 00°00'00''$

$$A_{AOB,D} = Az_{OB,D} - Az_{OA,D} \leftarrow eq.2$$

Using eq. 2, substitute in $Az_{OB,D}$ and $Az_{OA,D}$, then solve for $A_{AOB,D}$.

$$A_{AOB,D} = 37°12'10'' - 00°00'00''$$

$$A_{AOB,D} = 37°12'10''$$

To minimize equipment error, it is not uncommon to average the direct and inverted measurements and an angle.

$Az_{OB,I} = 217°12'05''$ $Az_{OA,I} = 180°00'05''$

$$A_{AOB,I} = Az_{OB,I} - Az_{OA,I} \leftarrow eq.3$$

Using eq. 3, substitute in $Az_{OB,I}$ and $Az_{OA,I}$, then solve for $A_{AOB,I}$.

$$A_{AOB,I} = 217°12'05'' - 180°00'05''$$

$$A_{AOB,I} = 37°12'00''$$

Angles #6 (cont.)

$A_{AOB,D} = 37°12'10"$ $A_{AOB,I} = 37°12'00"$

$$A_{AOB} = \frac{A_{AOB,D} + A_{AOB,I}}{2} \leftarrow eq.1$$

Return to eq. 1, plug in the direct and inverted values of angle AOB, then solve for the average angle AOB.

$$A_{AOB} = \frac{37°12'10" + 37°12'00"}{2}$$

$$A_{AOB} = 37°12'05"$$

Answer: | A |

Answer A is correct.

Surveying Practice Problems

Angles #7

the inverted azimuth from point O, when viewing point N.

Find: $Az_{ON,I}$

Given:

$A_{MON}=203°12'35''$ — the average horizontal angle measured between points M and N, from point O

Azimuth	Direct	Inverted
Az_{OM}	$0°00'00''$	$180°00'20''$
Az_{ON}	$203°12'45''$	$Az_{OB,I}$

table of azimuth readings were taken from the total station at point O.

M

total station set up at point O

North

A_{MON}

O

N

A) $23°12'25''$

B) $23°12'35''$

C) $23°12'45''$

D) $203°12'25''$

Analysis:

$$Az_{ON,I}=A_{MON,I}+Az_{OM,I} \leftarrow eq.1$$

The inverted azimuth of course ON equals the inverted Angle MON, plus the inverted azimuth of course OM.

$$0\leq Az<360 \leftarrow ieq.1$$

azimuth angle

Since azimuth values range between $0°$ and $360°$, we may need to add or subtract $360°$ if $Az_{ON,I}$ from eq.1 falls outside this range.

from direct measurement   from inverted measurement

$$A_{MON}=\frac{A_{MON,D}+A_{MON,I}}{2} \leftarrow eq.2$$

average angle

In eq.2, the average angle MON is half the sum of the direct angle MON and the inverted angle MON.

$$A_{MON,I}=2*A_{MON}-A_{MON,D} \leftarrow eq.3$$

Solve eq.2 for the inverted angle MON.

$Az_{ON,D}=203°12'45''$

$$A_{MON,D}=Az_{ON,D}-Az_{OM,D} \leftarrow eq.4$$

Use eq.4 to solve for the direct angle MON.

$Az_{OM,D}=0°00'00''$

Angles #7 (cont.)

$A_{MON,D} = 203°12'45'' - 0°00'00''$

$A_{MON,D} = 203°12'45''$

$A_{MON,D} = 203°12'45''$

$A_{MON,I} = 2 * A_{MON} - A_{MON,D}$ ←*eq.3*

$A_{MON} = 203°12'35''$

Return to eq.3, plug in the average and direct measurements for angle MON, then solve for the inverted angle MON.

$A_{MON,I} = 2 * 203°12'35'' - 203°12'45''$

$A_{MON,I} = 203°12'25''$

$A_{MON,I} = 203°12'25''$

$Az_{ON,I} = A_{MON,I} + Az_{OM,I}$ ←*eq.1*

$Az_{OM,I} = 180°00'20''$

Next, use eq. 1 to solve for $Az_{ON,I}$, after substituting in $A_{MON,I}$ and $Az_{OM,I}$.

$Az_{ON,I} = 203°12'25'' + 180°00'20''$

$Az_{ON,I} = 383°12'45''$

out of range, needs adjustment

From ieq. 1, $0° \leq Az < 360°$, therefore we'll subtract 360° from the calculated $Az_{ON,I}$.

$Az_{ON,I} = 383°12'45'' - 360°00'00''$

$Az_{ON,I} = 23°12'45''$ <u>Answer:</u> $\boxed{C}$

Surveying Practice Problems

Angles #8

<u>Find:</u> B_{JK} ← the bearing of course JK

<u>Given:</u>

$B_{JI} = S\,23°23'40''\,E$

the bearing of course IJ

$A_{IJK} = 75°14'25''$

the angle defined by
points I, J and K

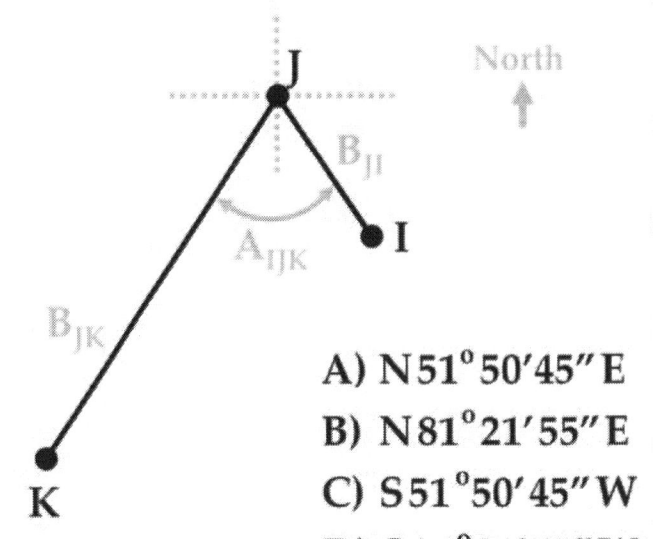

A) $N\,51°50'45''\,E$

B) $N\,81°21'55''\,E$

C) $S\,51°50'45''\,W$

D) $S\,81°21'55''\,W$

<u>Analysis:</u>

possible solutions:

northeast
quadrant
$\begin{cases} \text{A)}\ N\,51°50'45''\,E \\ \text{B)}\ N\,81°21'55''\,E \end{cases}$

southwest
quadrant
$\begin{cases} \text{C)}\ S\,51°50'45''\,W \\ \text{D)}\ S\,81°21'55''\,W \end{cases}$

We can quickly eliminate two of the four answers by determining if the the bearing of course JK is in the northeast quadrant or the southwest quadrant.

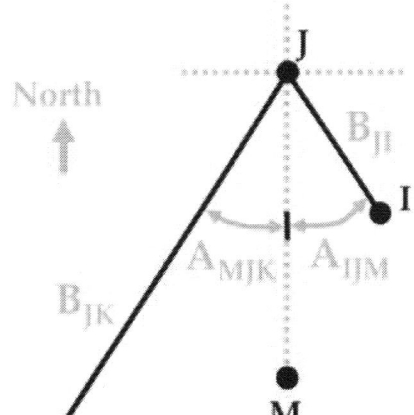

Figure 1

In Figure 1, we define a point M, directly south of point J.

From Figure 1, we suspect course JK bears in the southwest direction.

Notice how the length of each course does not affect our analysis.

If $0° < A_{MJK} < 90°$ ← *ieq.1*

then B_{JK} is in the SW quadrant

Course JK bears in the southwest direction if angle MJK is between 0° and 90°.

Angles #8 (cont.)

$B_{JI} = S\ 23°23'40''\ E$

$A_{MJK} = A_{IJK} - B_{JI} \leftarrow eq.1$

$A_{IJK} = 75°14'25''$

To add and subtract bearing measurements, we omit the directions (S and E), and only use the angle measurement.

$A_{MJK} = 75°14'25'' - 23°23'40''$

$A_{MJK} = 51°50'45''$

$A_{MJK} = 51°50'45''$

If $0° < A_{MJK} < 90°$ $\leftarrow ieq.1$

then B_{JK} is in the SW quadrant

From A_{MJK} and ieq.1, we know course JK bears in the southwest quadrant.

northeast
quadrant
$\begin{cases} \text{A) } \cancel{N\,51°50'45''\,E} \\ \text{B) } \cancel{N\,81°21'55''\,E} \end{cases}$

southwest
quadrant
$\begin{cases} \text{C) } S\,51°50'45''\,W \\ \text{D) } S\,81°21'55''\,W \end{cases}$

We can eliminate answers A and B as possible solutions.

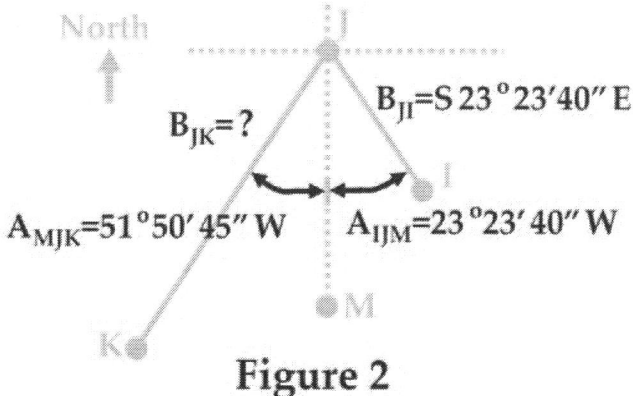

Figure 2 shows bearing JI, angle IJM and angle MJK.

$B_{JK} = ?$

$B_{JI} = S\ 23°23'40''\ E$

$A_{MJK} = 51°50'45''\ W$ $A_{IJM} = 23°23'40''\ W$

Figure 2

Since bearing angles in the southwest quadrant are measured clockwise from due south, we know B_{JK} shares the same angle value as A_{MJK}.

$B_{JK} = S\,51°50'45''\,W$

<u>Answer:</u> $\boxed{C}$

235

Surveying Practice Problems

Angles #9

Find: $B_{IJ,true}$ — the true bearing of course IJ

Given:

$B_{IJ,mag} = N 6°12'30''E$ — the magnetic bearing of course IJ

$D = 12°25'00''E$ — the magnetic declination

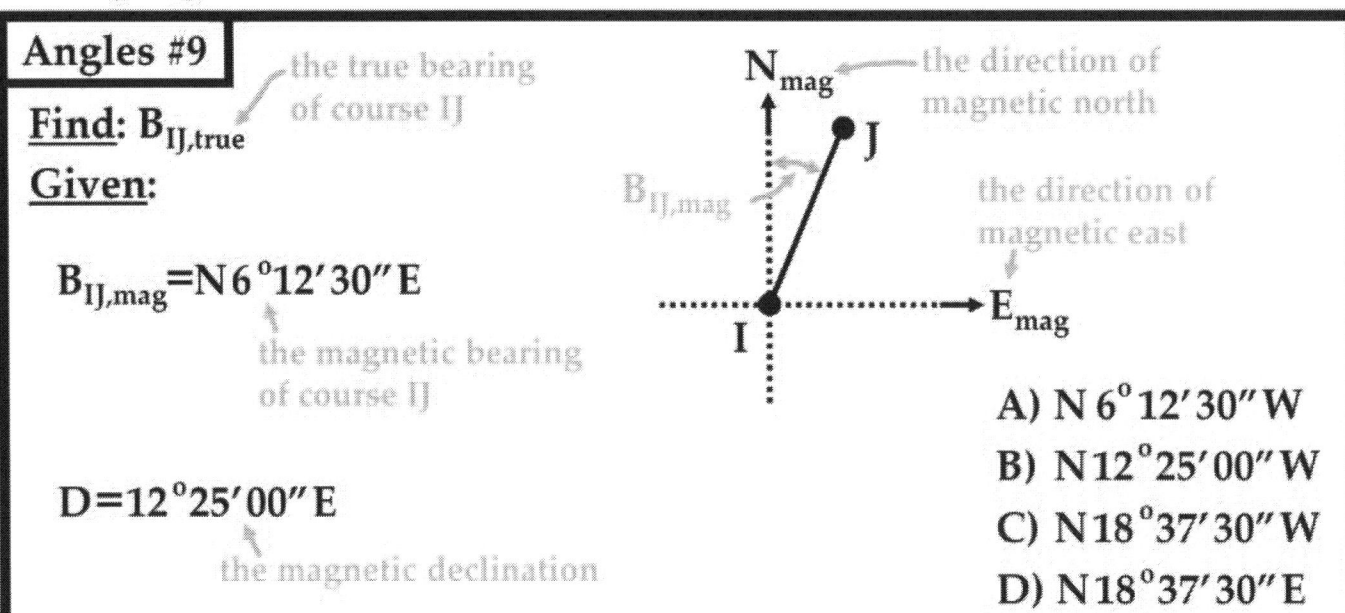

the direction of magnetic north

the direction of magnetic east

A) $N 6°12'30''W$
B) $N 12°25'00''W$
C) $N 18°37'30''W$
D) $N 18°37'30''E$

Analysis:

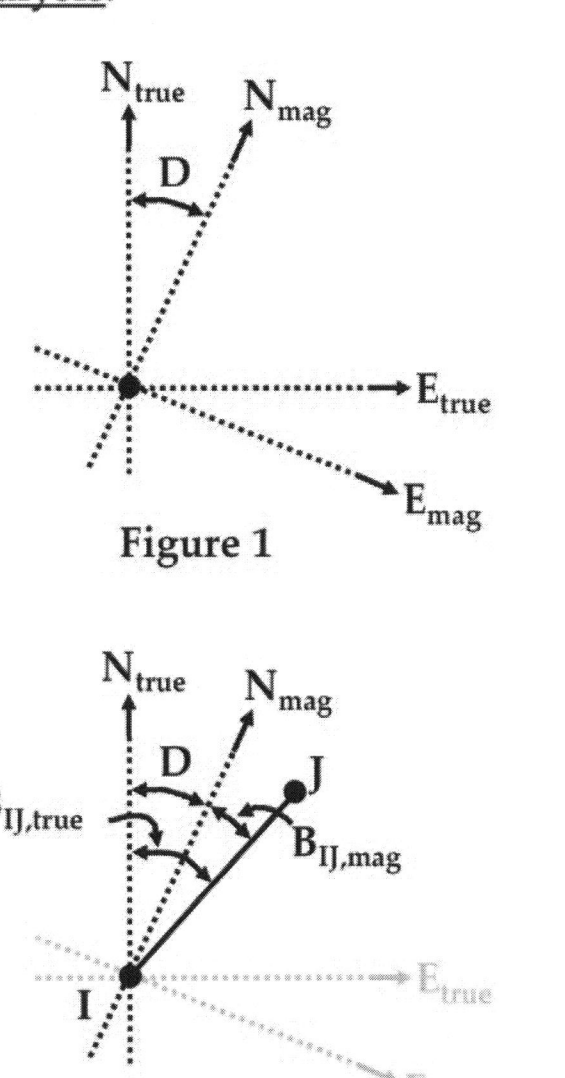

Figure 1

Figure 2

Figure 1 shows the magnetic declination, D, is the angle between true north and magnetic north.

An "East Declination" means the magnetic coordinates are rotated clockwise from the true coordinates.

"West Declination", means the magnetic coordinates are rotated counterclockwise from the true coordinates.

A declination of 12°25'00'' E means magnetic north is shifted 12°25'00'' clockwise from true north.

In Figure 2, we add course IJ. Now we can better understand the true bearing of course IJ.

The angles depicted in Figure 1 and Figure 2 are intentionally not drawn to scale.

Angles #9 (cont.)

$B_{IJ,mag} = N\,6°12'30''\,E$

$$B_{IJ,true} = B_{IJ,mag} + D \leftarrow eq.1$$

$D = 12°25'00''\,E$

$B_{IJ,true} = 6°12'30'' + 12°25'00''$

$B_{IJ,true} = 18°37'30''$

northeast
quadrant

$B_{IJ,true} = N\,18°37'30''\,E$

Answer: $\boxed{D}$

From Figure 2 we notice the true bearing of course IJ equals the magnetic bearing of course IJ, plus the east declination.

In eq.1, we assume $B_{IJ,true}$ is in the northeast quadrant. We add the angle value of the $B_{IJ,mag}$ with the angle value of the declination. If the sum of these angle values exceeds 90°, then $B_{IJ,true}$ is not in the northeast quadrant.

Since $0° < 18°37'30'' < 90°$, we know $B_{IJ,true}$ is in the northeast quadrant and we can add the 'N' and 'E' direction labels to $B_{IJ,true}$.

Surveying Practice Problems

Angles #10

Find: D ← the magnetic declination

Given:

$B_{IJ,mag} = N\,85°30'00''\,E$

the magnetic bearing of course IJ

$B_{IJ,true} = S\,87°45'00''\,E$ ← (not shown in sketch)

the true bearing of course IJ

A) $2°15'00''\,E$

B) $2°15'00''\,W$

C) $6°45'00''\,E$

D) $6°45'00''\,W$

Analysis:

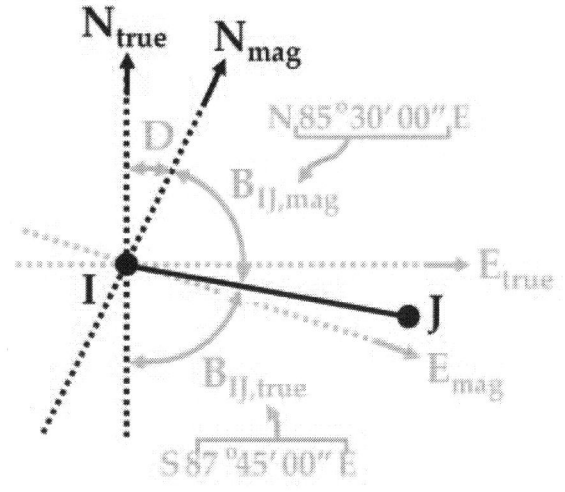

Figure 1

possible solutions →

A) $2°15'00''\,E$

~~B) $2°15'00''\,W$~~

C) $6°45'00''\,E$

~~D) $6°45'00''\,W$~~

In Figure 1, the true coordinates axes and magnetic axes are drawn out and course IJ is plotted.

From Figure 1, we notice the declination is East because the magnetic axis is rotated clockwise from the true axes.

In Figure 1, we notice the sum of the three angles ($B_{IJ,mag}$, D, and $B_{IJ,true}$) equals 180°, see eq. 1.

Knowing the declination is in the eastern direction, we can eliminate solutions B and D.

The three angles shown in Figure 1 ($B_{IJ,mag}$, D, and $B_{IJ,true}$) sum to 180°. Solve eq. 1 for the declination angle, D.

angle values

$180° = B_{IJ,mag} + D + B_{IJ,true}$ ← eq. 1

declination angle

Angles #10 (cont.)

$B_{IJ,mag} = N\,85°30'00''\,E$

$$D = 180 - B_{IJ,mag} - B_{IJ,true}$$

$B_{IJ,true} = S\,87°45'00''\,E$

Substitute in the angle values of the two bearings, then solve for the declination angle.

$$D = 180°00'00'' - 85°30'00'' - 87°45'00''$$

$$D = 6°45'00''$$

Add the "East" deflection label to the deflection angle.

$$D = 6°45'00''\,E$$

Answer: $\boxed{C}$

Surveying Practice Problems

Angles #11

Find: E_J ← the easting of point J

Given:

$A_{IJK}=127°18'25''$ ← angle created by points I, J and K

Point	Northing	Easting
I	156.70 [ft]	357.27 [ft]
J	225.91 [ft]	E_J
K	225.91 [ft]	485.19 [ft]

coordinates of points I, J and K

A) 340 [ft]
B) 410 [ft]
C) 415 [ft]
D) 420 [ft]

Analysis:

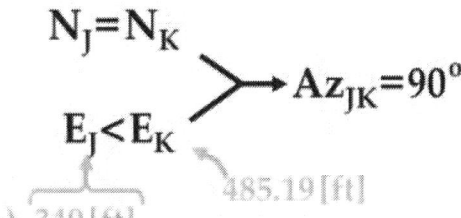

$N_J=N_K$ ⟩ → $Az_{JK}=90°$
$E_J<E_K$

485.19 [ft]

A) 340 [ft]
B) 410 [ft]
C) 415 [ft] ← possible answers
D) 420 [ft]

Since the northing of point J equals the northing of point K, and the easting of point J is less than the easting of point K, the azimuth of course JK equals 90°.

All four possible values for the easting of point J are less than the easting of point K.

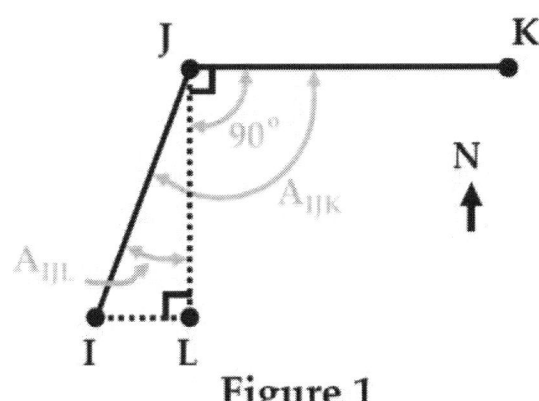

Figure 1

In Figure 1, we define point L, as a point with the same northing as point I, and the same easting as point J.

In Figure 1, points I, J and L form a right triangle.

too small → ~~A) 340 [ft]~~
B) 410 [ft]
C) 415 [ft]
D) 420 [ft]

Since $A_{IJK} > 90°$, we know $E_J > E_I$, then we can rule out 340 feet as a possible answer for E_J.

240

Angles #11 (cont.)

$A_{IJK}=127°18'25''$

$A_{IJL}=A_{IJK}-90°$ ←eq.1

We can solve for angle IJL by subtracting 90 from angle IJK.

$A_{IJL}=127°18'25'' - 90°00'00''$

$A_{IJL}=37°18'25''$

In eq. 2, we rewrite angle IJL as a function of the northing and easting values of points I and J.

$A_{IJL}=\tan^{-1}\left(\dfrac{E_J-E_I}{N_J-N_I}\right)$ ←eq.2

Solve eq. 2 for the easting of point J, then plug in the known variables and solve for E_J.

$E_I=357.27[ft]$ $N_I=156.70[ft]$

$E_J=E_I+(N_J-N_I)*\tan(A_{IJL})$

$N_J=225.91[ft]$ $A_{IJL}=37°18'25''$

$E_J=357.27[ft]+(225.91[ft]-156.70[ft])*\tan(37°18'25'')$

$E_J=410.01[ft]$

<u>Answer:</u> ☐ B

Surveying Practice Problems

Angles #12

Find: θ_C ← the interior angle at point C

Given:

$\theta_A = 96.455°$

$\theta_B = 121.809°$ — the interior angles at points A, B, D and E

$\theta_D = 198.776°$

$\theta_E = 64.016°$

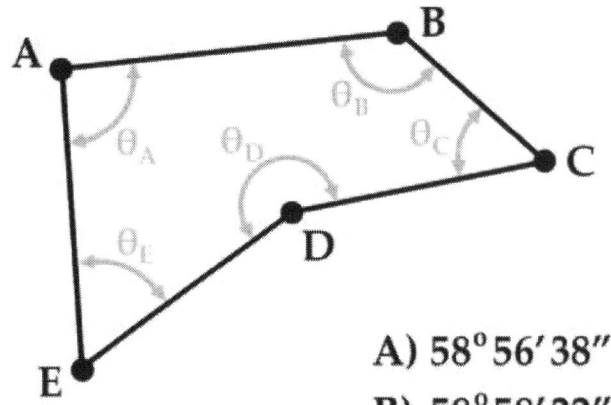

A) 58°56′38″
B) 58°58′22″
C) 59°00′14″
D) 59°01′57″

Analysis:

$$\phi = \theta_A + \theta_B + \theta_C + \theta_D + \theta_E \leftarrow eq.1$$

sum of the interior angles

In eq.1, the sum of the interior angles, ϕ, is calculated by adding each individual interior angle.

$$\theta_C = \phi - \theta_A - \theta_B - \theta_D - \theta_E \leftarrow eq.2$$

Solve eq.1 for θ_C.

$$n=5$$

$$\phi = (n-2) * 180° \leftarrow eq.3$$

Use eq.3 to compute the sum of the interior angles of an n-sided polygon.

$$\phi = (5-2) * 180°$$

A pentagon has 5 sides, therefore n=5.

$$\phi = 540°$$

Return to eq.2, plug in the values for ϕ, θ_A, θ_B, θ_D, and θ_E, then solve for θ_A.

$$\theta_A = 96.455° \qquad \theta_D = 198.776°$$

$$\theta_C = \phi - \theta_A - \theta_B - \theta_D - \theta_E \qquad \leftarrow eq.2$$

$$\phi = 540° \qquad \theta_B = 121.809° \qquad \theta_E = 64.016°$$

Angles #12 (cont.)

$\theta_C = 540° - 96.455° - 121.809° - 198.776° - 64.016°$

$$\theta_C = 58.944°$$

possible
answers →

    A) $58°56'38''$

    B) $58°58'22''$

too large → ~~C) $59°00'14''$~~

too large → ~~D) $59°01'57''$~~

unit conversion

$$\theta_C = 58° + 0.944° * \frac{60'}{1°} \quad \leftarrow eq.4$$

$$\theta_C = 58°56.64'$$

unit conversion

$$\theta_C = 58°56' + 0.64' * \frac{60''}{1'} \quad \leftarrow eq.5$$

$$\theta_C = 58°56'38.4''$$

Answer: $\boxed{A}$

Currently our value for θ_C is in "decimal degrees" (DD) notation, but the possible answers are in units "degree-minutes-seconds" (DMS) notation.

Looking at the possible answers, we can eliminate answers C and D.

We need to convert $58.944°$ to degree-minutes-seconds notation.

Multiply 0.944 degrees by 60 minutes per degree to find the number or minutes in angle θ_C.

After solving eq.4, we realize answer A is the correct answer.

We multiply 0.64 minutes by 60 seconds per minute to find the number of seconds in θ_C.

Surveying Practice Problems

Angles #13

Find: Az_{AB} ← the azimuth angle of course AB

Given:

Azimuth	Direct	Inverted
Az_{OA}	$105°55'10''$	$285°55'10''$
Az_{OB}	$116°09'25''$	$296°09'15''$

azimuth measurements from point O.

$L_{AB}=265.19\,[ft]$ ← length of course AB

$L_{OB}=358.21\,[ft]$ ← length of course OB

total station

sketch is in plan view

A) $116°09'20''$
B) $119°48'30''$
C) $130°02'40''$
D) $166°06'40''$

Analysis:

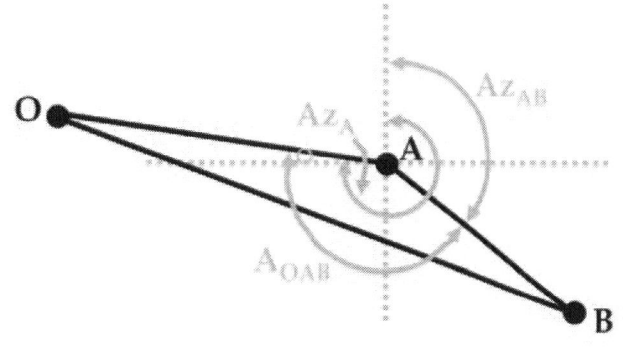

Figure 1

In this problem, ignore point C. Focus on the triangle composed of points A, B and O.

In Figure 1, angle OAB is identified. The azimuth of course AB and course AO are also identified.

Eq.1 computes the azimuth of course AB, as the azimuth of course AO minus angle OAB.

$$Az_{AB}=Az_{AO}-A_{OAB} \leftarrow eq.1$$

$$Az_{AO}=Az_{OA}+180° \leftarrow eq.2$$

The azimuth of course AO equals the azimuth of course OA plus 180°.

The azimuth of course OA equals the average azimuth measurement when spotting point A, when the total station is set up on point O.

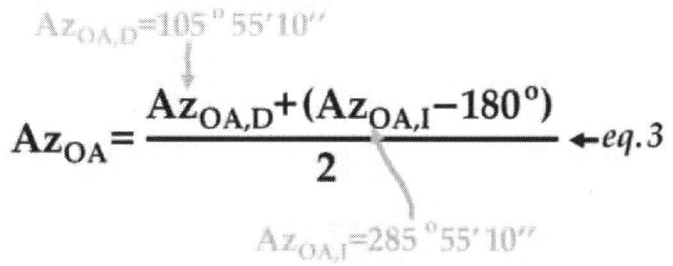

$$Az_{OA}=\frac{Az_{OA,D}+(Az_{OA,I}-180°)}{2} \leftarrow eq.3$$

$Az_{OA,D}=105°55'10''$

$Az_{OA,I}=285°55'10''$

Angles #13 (cont.)

$$Az_{OA} = \frac{105°55'10'' + (285°55'10'' - 180°)}{2}$$

$$Az_{OA} = 105°55'10''$$

Keep in mind, azimuth angles range between 0° and 360°: 0° ≤ Az < 360°

$Az_{OA} = 105°55'10''$

$$Az_{AO} = Az_{OA} + 180° \leftarrow eq.2$$

Substitute in Az_{OA} into eq. 2, then solve for Az_{AO}.

$$Az_{AO} = 105°55'10'' + 180°$$

$$Az_{AO} = 285°55'10''$$

To find angle OAB, we'll write out the law of sines (eq. 4), and solve for angle OAB (eq. 5).

Law of Sines

$$\frac{\sin(A_{OAB})}{L_{OB}} = \frac{\sin(A_{BOA})}{L_{AB}} \leftarrow eq.4$$

$$A_{OAB} = \sin^{-1}\left(\frac{\sin(A_{BOA}) * L_{OB}}{L_{AB}}\right) \leftarrow eq.5$$

Eq. 6 computes angle BOA by averaging the measured angle between points A and B, when set up on point O.

$$A_{BOA} = \left(\frac{A_{BOA,D} + A_{BOA,I}}{2}\right) \leftarrow eq.6$$

Eq. 7 and eq. 8 calculate angle BOA for direct and inverted measurements, respectively.

$Az_{OB,D} = 116°09'25''$

$$A_{BOA,D} = Az_{OB,D} - Az_{OA,D} \leftarrow eq.7$$

$Az_{OA,D} = 105°55'10''$

Angles #13 (cont.)

$$A_{BOA,D} = 116°\,09'\,25'' - 105°55'10''$$

$$A_{BOA,D} = 10°14'\,15''$$

$Az_{OB,I} = 296°09'\,15''$

$$A_{BOA,I} = Az_{OB,I} - Az_{OA,I} \leftarrow eq.\,8$$

$Az_{OA,I} = 285°55'10''$

$$A_{BOA,I} = 296°\,09'15'' - 285°55'10''$$

$$A_{BOA,I} = 10°14'\,05''$$

Return to eq. 6, plug in $A_{BOA,D}$ and $A_{BOA,I}$, then solve for A_{BOA}.

$A_{BOA,I} = 10°14'05''$

$$A_{BOA} = \left(\frac{A_{BOA,D} + A_{BOA,I}}{2} \right) \leftarrow eq.\,6$$

$A_{BOA,D} = 10°14'15''$

$$A_{BOA} = \left(\frac{10°14'15'' + 10°14'05''}{2} \right)$$

$$A_{BOA} = 10°14'\,10''$$

Return to eq. 5, plug in A_{BOA}, L_{OB}, and L_{AB}, then solve for A_{BOA}.

$A_{BOA} = 10°14'10''$ $L_{OB} = 358.21\,[ft]$

$$A_{OAB} = \sin^{-1} \left(\frac{\sin(A_{BOA}) * L_{OB}}{L_{AB}} \right) \leftarrow eq.\,5$$

$L_{AB} = 265.19\,[ft]$

Angles #13 (cont.)

$$A_{OAB}=\sin^{-1}\left(\frac{\sin(10°14'10'')*358.21[ft]}{265.19[ft]}\right)$$

$$A_{OAB}=\sin^{-1}(0.24004) \leftarrow eq.9$$

Be careful when solving for an angle using the law of sines. Sometimes the calculated angle is ambiguous. (see eq. 9)

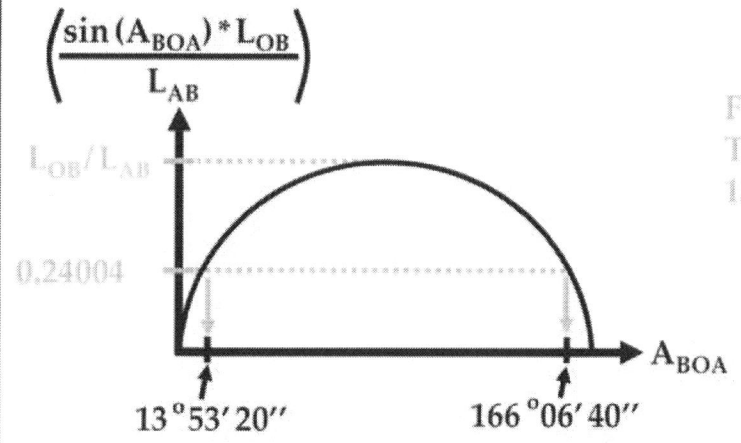

$$\left(\frac{\sin(A_{BOA})*L_{OB}}{L_{AB}}\right)$$

Figure 2 plots out the sine function. The arcsine of 0.24004 can be either 13°53'20'' or 166°06'40''.

L_{OB}/L_{AB}

0.24004

$13°53'20''$ $166°06'40''$ A_{BOA}

Figure 2

Since Figure 1 is (approximately) drawn to scale, we can tell angle OAB is much closer to 166°06'40'' than to 13°53'20''

$$A_{OAB}=166°06'40''$$

$A_{OAB}=166°06'40''$

Return to eq. 1, substitute in variables A_{OAB} and Az_{AO}, then solve for Az_{AB}.

$$Az_{AB}=Az_{AO}-A_{OAB} \leftarrow eq.1$$

$Az_{AO}=285°55'10''$

$$Az_{AB}=285°55'10''-166°06'40''$$

$$Az_{AB}=119°48'30''$$

Answer: $\boxed{B}$

Surveying Practice Problems

Angles #14

Find: A_{BAG} ← the angle formed by points B, A and G

Given:

$L_{AB}=55\,[m]$ ← the lengths of
$L_{BC}=55\,[m]$ ← line segments
$L_{CE}=85\,[m]$ ← AB, BC and CE

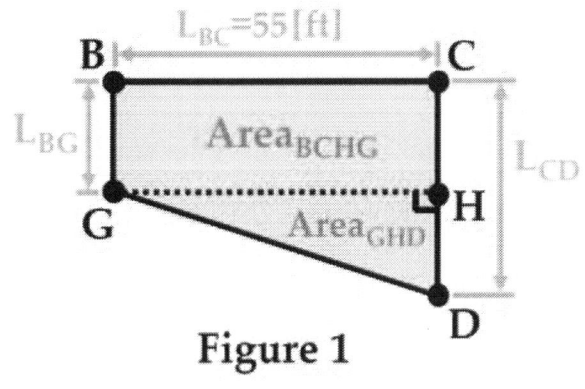

$Area_{BCDG}=Area_{GDEF}$ ← Area BCDG equals area GDEF

$N_A=N_B=N_C$ ← the northing of point A equals the northing of points B and C

A) $27°15'$

B) $28°45'$

C) $30°15'$

D) $31°45'$

Analysis:

$$A_{BAG}=\tan^{-1}\left(\frac{L_{BG}}{L_{AB}}\right) \leftarrow eq.1$$

In eq.1, we define angle BAG as the arctangent of the length of segment BG divided by the length of segment AB.

Figure 1

In Figure 1, we divide $Area_{BCDG}$ into rectangle BCHG and right triangle GHD.

Eq.2 computes the $Area_{BCDG}$ by adding $Area_{BCHG}$ and $Area_{GHD}$.

$$Area_{BCDG}= \overbrace{L_{BC}*L_{BG}}^{Area_{BCHG}} + \overbrace{0.5*L_{BC}*(L_{CD}-L_{BG})}^{Area_{GHD}} \leftarrow eq.2$$

Next, we'll determine the value of $Area_{BCDG}$ and L_{CD}, then compute L_{BG}.

$$Area_{BCEF}=Area_{BCDG}+Area_{GDEF} \leftarrow eq.3$$

Recall, the problem states: $Area_{BCDG}=Area_{GDEF}$

Angles #14 (cont.)

$L_{BC}=55\,[m]$ $L_{CE}=85\,[m]$

$$Area_{BCEF}=L_{BC}*L_{CE} \leftarrow eq.4$$

In eq.3 solve for the the area of rectangle BCEF by multiplying side lengths L_{BC} and L_{CE}.

$$Area_{BCEF}=55\,[m]*85\,[m]$$

$$Area_{BCEF}=4,675\,[m]$$

Substitute in $Area_{BCEF}$ and $Area_{BCDG}$ into eq.4, then solve for for $Area_{BCDG}$.

$Area_{BCEF}=4,675\,[m]$

$$Area_{BCEF}=Area_{BCDG}+Area_{GDEF} \leftarrow eq.3$$

$Area_{GDEF}=Area_{BCDG}$

Solve eq.3 for $Area_{BCDG}$.

$$4,675\,[m]=Area_{BCDG}+Area_{BCDG}$$

$$Area_{BCDG}=2,337.5\,[m]$$

To solve eq.2, we still need to determine the value of L_{CD}.

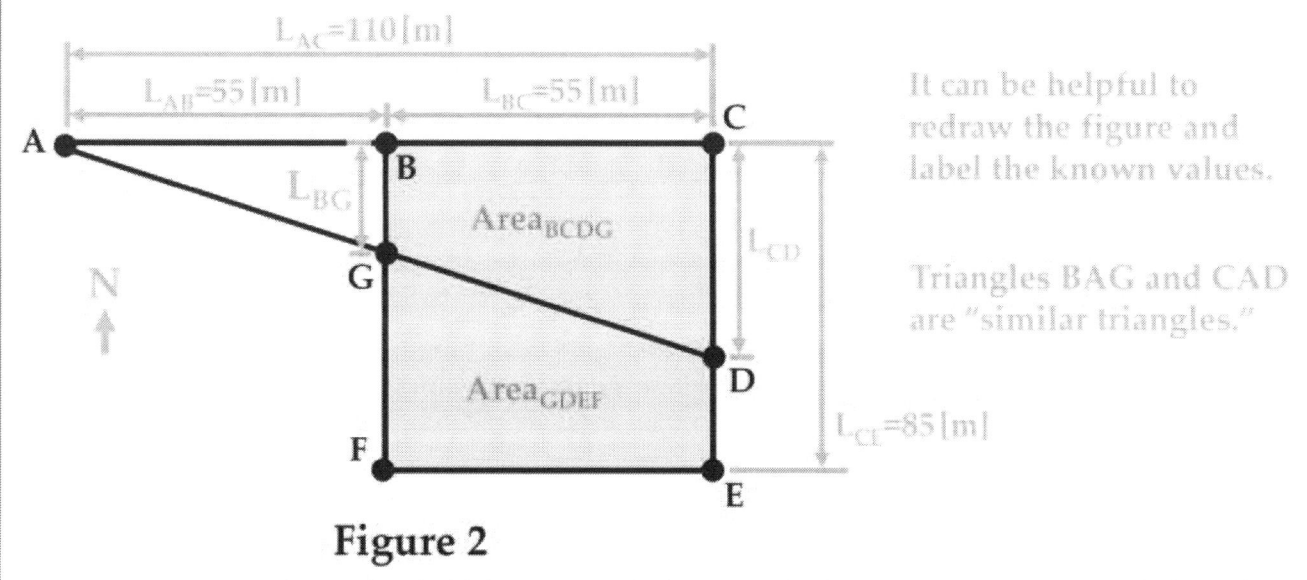

It can be helpful to redraw the figure and label the known values.

Triangles BAG and CAD are "similar triangles."

Figure 2

Surveying Practice Problems

Angles #14 (cont.)

$$\frac{L_{AB}}{L_{BG}} = \frac{L_{AC}}{L_{CD}} \leftarrow eq.5$$

From Figure 2, we notice "the length of segment AB is to the length of segment BG, as the length of segment AC is to the length of segment CD."

$L_{AC}=110\,[m]$

$$L_{CD} = \frac{L_{AC}}{L_{AB}} * L_{BG} = \frac{110\,[m]}{55\,[m]} * L_{BG}$$

$L_{AB}=55\,[m]$

Solve eq. 5 for L_{CD}, plug in the values of L_{AC} and L_{AB}, then calculate L_{CD}.

$$L_{CD} = 2 * L_{BG}$$

Return to eq. 2, plug in $Area_{BCDG}$ and L_{CD}, then solve for L_{BG}.

$Area_{BCDG}=2,337.5\,[m]$ $L_{CD}=2*L_{BG}$

$$Area_{BCDG} = L_{BC} * L_{BG} + 0.5 * L_{BC} * (L_{CD} - L_{BG}) \leftarrow eq.2$$

$L_{BC}=55\,[m]$ $L_{BC}=55\,[m]$

$$2,337.5\,[m] = 55\,[m] * L_{BG} + 0.5 * 55\,[m] * (2 * L_{BG} - L_{BG})$$

$$L_{BG} = 28.33\,[m]$$

$L_{BG}=28.33\,[m]$

$$A_{BAG} = \tan^{-1}\left(\frac{L_{BG}}{L_{AB}}\right) \leftarrow eq.1$$

Use eq.1 to find A_{BAG}.

$L_{AB}=55\,[m]$

$$A_{BAG} = 27°15'09''$$

Our calculated value for A_{BAG} is most nearly 27°15'. Answer A is correct.

Answer: $\boxed{A}$

Angles #15

<u>Find:</u> B_{KM} ← the bearing angle for course KM

<u>Given:</u>

I •

J

A_{IJK}

N
↑

$Az_{IJ}=115.774°$ ← the azimuth angle for course IJ

A_{JKM}

K •

M •

$A_{IJK}=84.338°$
↑
the angle formed by points I, J and K

$A_{JKM}=82.117°$
↑
the angle formed by points J, K and M

A) $S62.0°E$
B) $N62.0°W$
C) $S66.4°E$
D) $N66.4°W$

Analysis:

First find Az_{KM}

Then determine B_{KM}

To determine the bearing of course KM, we'll first determine the azimuth of course KM, then convert the azimuth to a bearing.

$$Az_{KM}=Az_{KJ}+A_{JKM} \quad ←eq.1$$

The azimuth of course KM equals the azimuth of course KJ, plus angle JKM.

$$Az_{KJ}=Az_{JK}-180° \quad ←eq.2$$

The azimuth of course KJ equals the azimuth of course JK, minus angle 180°. In eq.2, we assume azimuth JK is greater than 180°.

$$Az_{JK}=Az_{JI}-A_{IJK} \quad ←eq.3$$

The azimuth of course JK equals the azimuth of course JI, minus angle IJK.

$Az_{IJ}=115.774°$

$$Az_{JI}=Az_{IJ}+180° \quad ←eq.4$$

The azimuth of course JI equals the azimuth of course IJ, plus angle 180°.

$$Az_{JI}=115.774°+180°$$

Surveying Practice Problems

Angles #15 (cont.)

$$Az_{JI} = 295.774°$$

$Az_{JI} = 295.774°$

$$Az_{JK} = Az_{JI} - A_{IJK} \leftarrow eq.3$$

$A_{IJK} = 84.338°$

Substitute Az_{JI} and A_{IJK} into eq.3, then solve for Az_{JK}.

$$Az_{JK} = 295.774° - 84.338°$$

$$Az_{JK} = 211.436°$$

$Az_{JK} = 211.436°$

$$Az_{KJ} = Az_{JK} - 180° \leftarrow eq.2$$

Substitute Az_{JK} into eq.2, then solve for Az_{KJ}.

$$Az_{KJ} = 211.436° - 180°$$

Notice how the length of each course has no affect on the angle calculations.

$$Az_{KJ} = 31.436°$$

$Az_{KJ} = 31.436°$

$$Az_{KM} = Az_{KJ} + A_{JKM} \leftarrow eq.1$$

$A_{JKM} = 82.117°$

Substitute Az_{KJ} and A_{JKM} into eq.1, then solve for Az_{KM}.

$$Az_{KM} = 31.436° + 82.117°$$

$$Az_{KM} = 113.553°$$

Angles #15 (cont.)

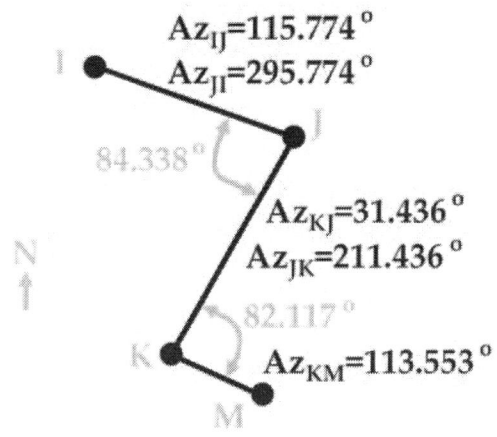

Figure 1

It can be helpful to write out the angle measurements as they are calculated, as shown in Figure 1.

Since the azimuth of course KM is between 90° and 180°, it bears in the southeast direction.

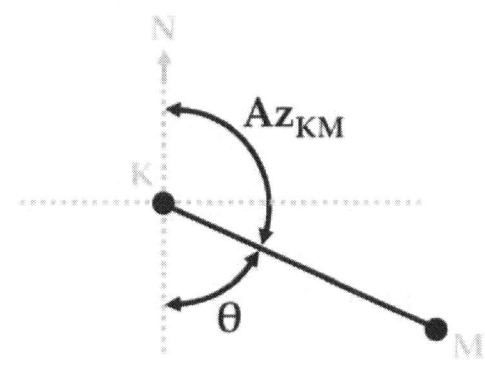

Figure 2

The bearing angle for courses heading southeast is the angle θ east of due south.

$$\theta = 180° - Az_{KM} \leftarrow eq.5$$

Eq.5 computes angle θ by subtracting the azimuth of course KM from 180°.

$$\theta = 180° - 113.553°$$

$$\theta = 66.447°$$

Course KM bears 66.447° east of due south.

$$B_{KM} = S\,66.447°\,E$$

<u>Answer:</u> C

Surveying Practice Problems

Traverse #1

Find: θ_I ← the interior angle at point I

Given:

$\theta_{I,m} = 35°15'47"$ ← the measured interior angles at points I, J and K

$\theta_{J,m} = 71°52'41"$

$\theta_{K,m} = 72°51'47"$

subscript "m"=measured

balance the closed traverse.

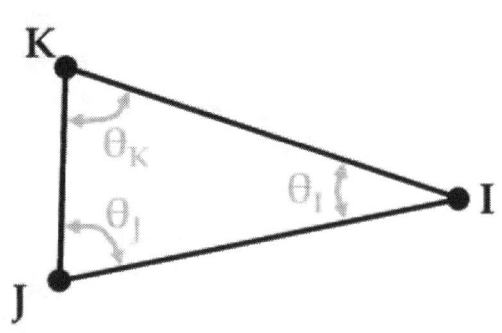

A) $35°15'32"$

B) $35°15'42"$

C) $35°15'44"$

D) $35°15'52"$

Analysis:

possible solutions

A) $35°15'32"$

B) $35°15'42"$

C) $35°15'44"$

D) $35°15'52"$

When the possible solutions are very similar. We should expect our solved solution to be very close (or exactly) one of the possible solutions.

$$\theta_I = \theta_{I,m} + \phi \leftarrow eq.1$$

correction angle

Eq.1 computes the corrected angle measurement at point I.

$$\phi = \frac{\overset{N}{\Sigma}\theta_n - \overset{N}{\Sigma}\theta_{n,m}}{n} \leftarrow eq.2$$

n=number of sides

In eq.2, $\Sigma\theta_n$ represents the sum of the interior angles of the closed traverse. N represents the number of sides of the closed traverse.

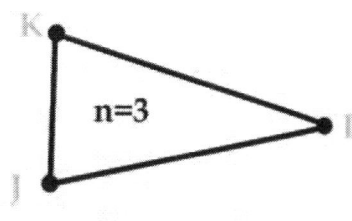

Figure 1 shows the triangular-shaped traverse has 3 sides.

Figure 1

Traverse #1 (cont.)

$$\overset{N}{\underset{}{\Sigma}}\theta_n = 180° * (n-2) \leftarrow eq.3 \qquad \overset{n=3}{\nearrow}$$

Eq. 3 computes the sum of the interior angles of a polygon with n sides, where n=3.

$$\overset{N}{\underset{}{\Sigma}}\theta_n = 180° * (3-2)$$

$$\overset{N}{\underset{}{\Sigma}}\theta_n = 180°$$

$$\theta_{J,m} = 71°52'41''$$

$$\overset{N}{\underset{}{\Sigma}}\theta_{n,m} = \theta_{I,m} + \theta_{J,m} + \theta_{K,m} \leftarrow eq.4$$

$$\theta_{I,m} = 35°15'47'' \qquad \theta_{K,m} = 72°51'47''$$

Eq. 4 computes the sum of the measured interior angles, of the traverse.

$$\overset{N}{\underset{}{\Sigma}}\theta_{n,m} = 35°15'47'' + 71°52'41'' + 72°51'47''$$

$$\overset{N}{\underset{}{\Sigma}}\theta_{n,m} = 180\ \overset{}{0}0'15''$$

There is a 15 second error in the sum of the measured angles.

$$\overset{N}{\underset{}{\Sigma}}\theta_{n,m} = 180°00'15''$$

$$\phi = \frac{\overset{N}{\underset{}{\Sigma}}\theta_n - \overset{N}{\underset{}{\Sigma}}\theta_{n,m}}{n} \leftarrow eq.2$$

$$\overset{N}{\underset{}{\Sigma}}\theta_n = 180° \qquad n=3$$

Return to eq. 2, plug in the known variables, then solve for the correction angle, ϕ.

$$\phi = \frac{180° - 180°00'15''}{3}$$

If the minutes and seconds are not included in an angle measurement, assume 0 minutes and 0 seconds.

$$\phi = -0°00'05''$$

Since the sum of the measured angles is larger than 180°, the correction angle is negative.

Surveying Practice Problems

Traverse #1 (cont.)

A) $35°15'32''$

B) $35°15'42''$

C) $35°15'44''$

D) $35°15'52''$

If the correction angle is negative, we know $\theta_I < \theta_{I,m}$. Therefore, we can rule out answer D.

$\phi = -0°00'05''$

$$\theta_I = \theta_{I,m} + \phi \quad \leftarrow eq.1$$

$\theta_{I,m} = 35°15'47''$

Substitute in the correction angle and the measured angle at point I, then solve for the corrected angle at point I.

$$\theta_I = 35°15'47'' + (-0°00'05'')$$

$$\theta_I = 35°15'42''$$

Answer: $\boxed{B}$

Traverse #2

<u>Find:</u> L_{AD} ← the distance between point A and point D, on a straight line.

<u>Given:</u>

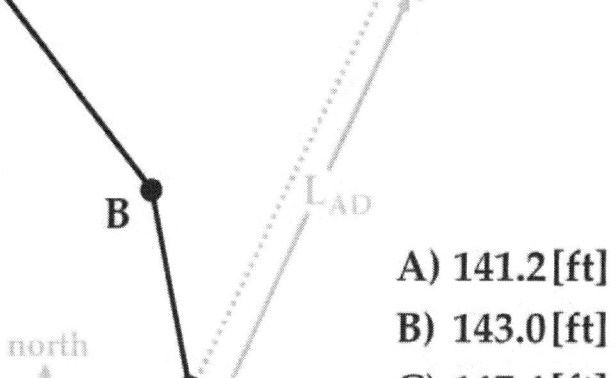

Course	Latitude	Departure
AB	57.61	-21.19
BC	98.07	-89.62
CD	-12.69	146.55

the latitude and departure of each course is in units of feet.

A) 141.2 [ft]

B) 143.0 [ft]

C) 147.4 [ft]

D) 341.4 [ft]

<u>Analysis:</u>

$$\cancel{L_{AD}=L_{AB}+L_{BC}+L_{CD}}$$

Be sure to read the problem carefully. In this problem, L_{AD} does not equal $L_{AB}+L_{BC}+L_{CD}$.

northing coordinate of point A   easting coordinate of point A

$$L_{AD}=\sqrt{(N_D-N_A)^2+(E_D-E_A)^2} \leftarrow eq.1$$

northing coordinate of point D   easting coordinate of point D

For this problem we don't need to compute the distances between each consecutive point.

Course ABCD is an "open traverse", meaning, the first and last points are at different locations.

$Lat_{AB}=57.61\,[ft]$ $Lat_{CD}=-12.69\,[ft]$

$$N_D-N_A=Lat_{AB}+Lat_{BC}+Lat_{CD} \leftarrow eq.2$$

$Lat_{BC}=98.07\,[ft]$

Eq.2 computes the distance between point A and point D in the north-south direction.

$$N_D-N_A=57.61\,[ft]+98.07\,[ft]+(-12.69\,[ft])$$

Surveying Practice Problems

Traverse #2 (cont.)

$$N_D - N_A = 142.99 \, [ft]$$

$Dep_{AB} = -21.19 \, [ft]$ $Dep_{CD} = 146.55 \, [ft]$

$$E_D - E_A = Dep_{AB} + Dep_{BC} + Dep_{CD} \quad \leftarrow eq.3$$

Eq. 3 computes the distance between point A and point D in the east-west direction.

$Dep_{BC} = -89.62 \, [ft]$

$$E_D - E_A = (-21.19 \, [ft]) + (-89.62 \, [ft]) + 146.55 \, [ft]$$

$$E_D - E_A = 35.74 \, [ft]$$

"Dep" is short for "Departure"

$E_D - E_A = 35.74 \, [ft]$

$$L_{AD} = \sqrt{(N_D - N_A)^2 + (E_D - E_A)^2} \quad \leftarrow eq.1$$

Return to eq. 1, plug in $(N_D - N_A)$ and $(E_D - E_A)$, then solve for L_{AD}.

$N_D - N_A = 142.99 \, [ft]$

$$L_{AD} = \sqrt{(142.99 \, [ft])^2 + (35.74 \, [ft])^2}$$

$$L_{AD} = 147.4 \, [ft]$$

Answer: $\boxed{C}$

In this problem we did not need to calculate the exact coordinate values of point A or point D.

Traverse #3

<u>Find:</u> EOC ←the error of closure

<u>Given:</u>

Course	Latitude	Departure
AB	457.62	-87.65
BC	-115.94	567.81
CA	-342.33	-479.84

the latitude and departure of each
course is in units of feet.

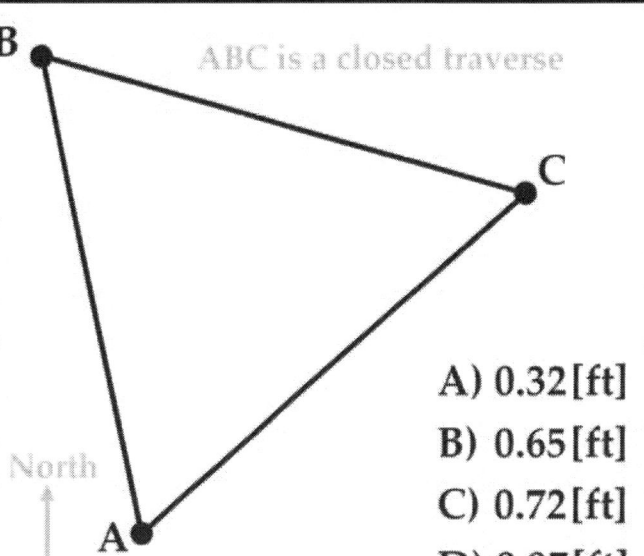

B

ABC is a closed traverse

C

North

A

East

A) 0.32 [ft]

B) 0.65 [ft]

C) 0.72 [ft]

D) 0.97 [ft]

- -

<u>Analysis:</u>

$$EOC=\sqrt{(EOC_N)^2+(EOC_E)^2} \leftarrow eq.1$$

EOC in the
north-south
direction

EOC in the
east-west
direction

For a closed traverse, the error of
closure, EOC, refers to the distance
between the first and last (measured)
coordinate points.

$$EOC_N=\Sigma(Lat) \leftarrow eq.2$$

The error of closure in the north-
south direction, EOC_N, equals the
sum of all latitude measurements.

$Lat_{AB}=457.62\,[ft]$ $Lat_{CA}=-142.33\,[ft]$

$$EOC_N=Lat_{AB}+Lat_{BC}+Lat_{CA} \leftarrow eq.3$$

$Lat_{BC}=-315.94\,[ft]$

From the given data, we can plug in
all latitude measurements into eq. 3,
and compute EOC_N.

$$EOC_N=457.62\,[ft]+(-315.94\,[ft])+(-142.33\,[ft])$$

$$EOC_N=-0.65\,[ft]$$

In a closed traverse, $EOC_N=-0.65\,[ft]$
means the traverse ends 0.65 feet south
from where it started.

Surveying Practice Problems

Traverse #3 (cont.)

$$EOC_E = \Sigma(Dep) \leftarrow eq.4$$

The error of closure in the east-west direction, EOC_E, equals the sum of all departure measurements.

$Dep_{AB} = -87.65\,[ft]$　　$Dep_{CA} = -479.84\,[ft]$

$$EOC_E = Dep_{AB} + Dep_{BC} + Dep_{CA} \leftarrow eq.5$$

$Dep_{BC} = 567.81\,[ft]$

Plug in all departure measurements into eq.5, and compute EOC_E.

$$EOC_E = (-87.65\,[ft]) + 567.81\,[ft] + (-479.84\,[ft])$$

$$EOC_E = 0.32\,[ft]$$

In a closed traverse, $EOC_E = 0.32\,[ft]$ means the traverse ends 0.32 feet east from where it started.

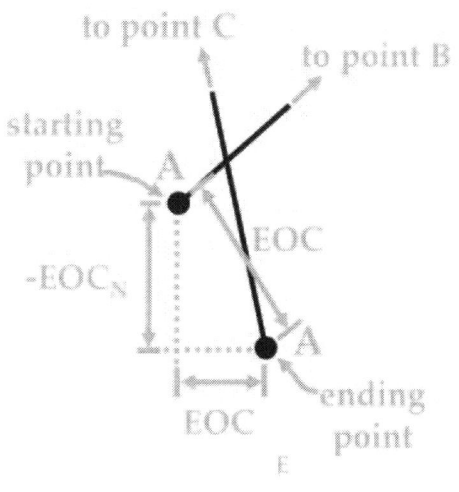

Figure 1

Figure 1 shows EOC_N, EOC_E, EOC, and the beginning and ending of the measured traverse.

Since we calculated $EOC_N = -0.65\,[ft]$, the length $-EOC_N$ in Figure 1 equals 0.65 [ft].

$EOC_N = -0.65\,[ft]$　　$EOC_E = 0.32\,[ft]$

$$EOC = \sqrt{(EOC_N)^2 + (EOC_E)^2} \leftarrow eq.1$$

Plug in EOC_N and EOC_E into eq.1, then solve for EOC.

Traverse #3 (cont.)

$$EOC=\sqrt{(\text{-}0.65\,[ft])^2+(0.32\,[ft])^2}$$

$$EOC=0.724\,[ft]$$

Since EOC_N and EOC_E are in perpendicular direction, we notice eq.1 is similar to solving for the hypotenuse of a right triangle.

Answer: $\boxed{\text{C}}$

Of the possible answers, 0.724 [ft] is most nearly 0.72 [ft]. Answer C is correct.

Surveying Practice Problems

Traverse #4

<u>Find:</u> Dep_{DA} ←the departure of course DA

<u>Given:</u> $EOC=0.54\,[ft]$ ←the error of closure for traverse ABCD

Course	Latitude	Departure
AB	191.86	395.06
BC	245.85	-17.29
CD	-378.99	-297.15
DA	-59.06	Dep_{DA}

all lengths are in feet

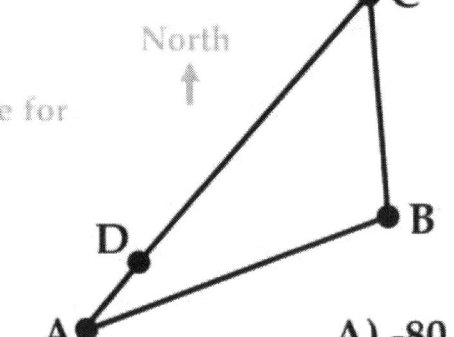

A) -80.62 [ft]

B) -80.28 [ft]

C) -80.20 [ft]

D) -80.08 [ft]

Analysis:

$$EOC_E = \Sigma(Dep) \quad \leftarrow eq.1$$

The error of closure in the east-west direction, EOC_E, equals the sum of all departure measurements.

$$EOC_E = Dep_{AB} + Dep_{BC} + Dep_{CD} + Dep_{DA} \quad \leftarrow eq.2$$

Write out eq.1 for traverse ABCD then solve for Dep_{DA}.

$$Dep_{DA} = EOC_E - Dep_{AB} - Dep_{BC} - Dep_{CD} \quad \leftarrow eq.3$$

The problem statement provides Dep_{AB}, Dep_{BC} and Dep_{CD}.

$$EOC = \sqrt{(EOC_N)^2 + (EOC_E)^2} \quad \leftarrow eq.4$$

Eq.4 computes the error of closure, based on the error of closure in northing and easting directions. Solve eq.4 for EOC_E.

$$EOC_E = \pm\sqrt{(EOC)^2 - (EOC_N)^2} \quad \leftarrow eq.5$$

$$EOC_N = \Sigma(Lat) \quad \leftarrow eq.6$$

The problem statement provides EOC. Solve for EOC_N using eq.6.

Traverse #4 (cont.)

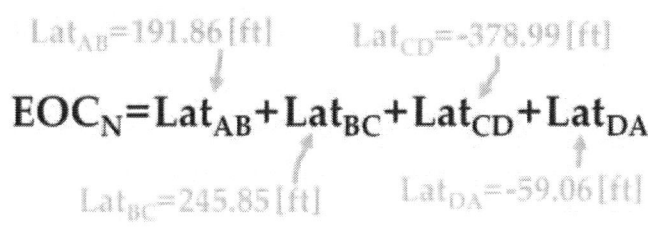

$$EOC_N = Lat_{AB} + Lat_{BC} + Lat_{CD} + Lat_{DA}$$

Write out eq.6, plug in the given latitude values, then compute EOC_N.

$$EOC_N = 191.86\,[ft] + 245.85\,[ft] + (-378.99\,[ft]) + (-59.06\,[ft])$$

$$EOC_N = -0.34\,[ft]$$

For a closed traverse, $EOC_N = -0.34\,[ft]$ means the traverse ends 0.34 feet south from where it started.

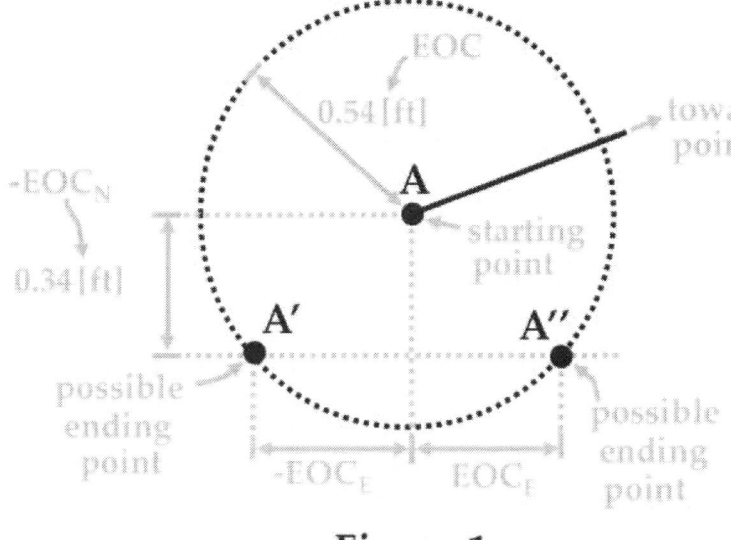

Figure 1

In Figure 1, we notice there are 2 possible ending points. Point A' (negative EOC_E) and point A" (positive EOC_E).

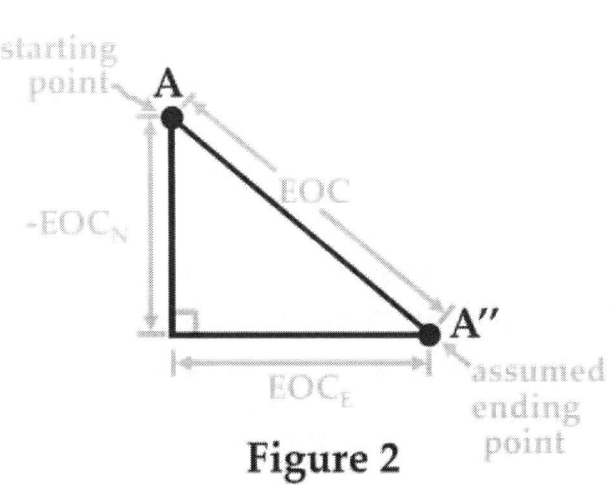

Figure 2

In Figure 2, we'll assume point A" is the ending point. Therefore EOC_E will be positive. EOC_E is calculated using right triangle trigonometry.

If point A" doesn't work, we can try point A' as the ending point.

Surveying Practice Problems

Traverse #4 (cont.)

EOC=0.54[ft]   EOC$_N$=-0.34[ft]

$$EOC_E=\pm\sqrt{(EOC)^2-(EOC_N)^2} \leftarrow eq.5$$

Plug in EOC and EOC$_N$ into eq.5, then solve for EOC$_E$.

$$EOC_E=\pm\sqrt{(0.54[ft])^2-(-0.34[ft])^2}$$

$$EOC_E=\pm0.420[ft]$$

Since we're assuming point A'' is the ending point, EOC is positive.

$$EOC_E=0.420[ft]$$

Use eq.3 to solve for Dep$_{DA}$. If Dep$_{DA}$ does not equal one of the four solutions, we'll assume point A' is the ending point.

EOC$_E$=0.42[ft]   Dep$_{BC}$=-17.29[ft]

$$Dep_{DA}=EOC_E-Dep_{AB}-Dep_{BC}-Dep_{CD} \leftarrow eq.3$$

Dep$_{AB}$=395.06[ft]   Dep$_{CD}$=-297.15[ft]

$$Dep_{DA}=0.42[ft]-395.06[ft]-(-17.29[ft])-(-297.15[ft])$$

$$Dep_{DA}=-80.20[ft]$$

Answer: C

264

Traverse #5

<u>Find:</u> ROE_{ABCD} ← the ratio of error of traverse ABCD

<u>Given:</u>

Course	Latitude	Departure
AB	98.17	-21.14
BC	19.59	117.65
CD	-53.22	-69.06
DA	-64.31	-26.87

all latitudes and departures are in feet

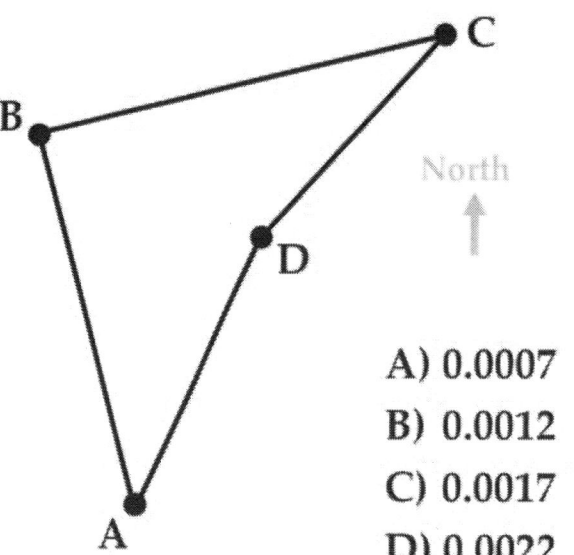

North

A) 0.0007
B) 0.0012
C) 0.0017
D) 0.0022

<u>Analysis:</u>

error of closure

$$ROE = \frac{EOC}{\Sigma L} \leftarrow eq.1$$

traverse length

The ratio of error, ROE, equals the error of closure divided by the total length of the traverse.

The ratio of error is sometimes called the "precision ratio."

$$EOC = \sqrt{(EOC_N)^2 + (EOC_E)^2} \leftarrow eq.2$$

Eq. 2 computes the error of closure (EOC), based on the error of closure in the north-south direction (EOC_N), and the error of closure in the east-west direction (EOC_E).

$$EOC_N = \Sigma(Lat) \leftarrow eq.3$$

$Lat_{AB} = 98.17\,[ft]$ $Lat_{CD} = -53.22\,[ft]$

$$EOC_N = Lat_{AB} + Lat_{BC} + Lat_{CD} + Lat_{DA} \leftarrow eq.4$$

$Lat_{BC} = 19.59\,[ft]$ $Lat_{DA} = -64.31\,[ft]$

To compute the error of closure in the north-south direction, plug in all latitude values into eq. 4, then solve for EOC_N.

$$EOC_N = 98.17\,[ft] + 19.59\,[ft] + (-53.22\,[ft]) + (-64.31\,[ft])$$

Surveying Practice Problems

Traverse #5 (cont.)

$$EOC_N = 0.23\,[ft]$$

$$EOC_E = \Sigma(Dep) \leftarrow eq.5$$

Write out eq.5, plug in the departure values, then solve for EOC_E.

$Dep_{AB} = -21.14\,[ft]$ $Dep_{CD} = -69.06\,[ft]$

$$EOC_E = Dep_{AB} + Dep_{BC} + Dep_{CD} + Dep_{DA} \leftarrow eq.6$$

$Dep_{BC} = 117.65\,[ft]$ $Dep_{DA} = -26.87\,[ft]$

$$EOC_E = (-21.14)\,[ft] + 117.65\,[ft] + (-69.06\,[ft]) + (-26.87\,[ft])$$

$$EOC_E = 0.58\,[ft]$$

With EOC_N and EOC_E, we can use eq.2 to compute EOC.

$EOC_E = 0.58\,[ft]$

$$EOC = \sqrt{(EOC_N)^2 + (EOC_E)^2} \leftarrow eq.2$$

$EOC_N = 0.23\,[ft]$

$$EOC = \sqrt{(0.23\,[ft])^2 + (0.58\,[ft])^2}$$

EOC=0.624 [ft] means the final point of the traverse is located 0.624 feet away from where it is expected to be located, due to measurement error.

$$EOC = 0.624\,[ft]$$

Before we can compute ROE (eq.1), we need to determine the total length of the traverse, by summing up the length of each course, using eq.7.

$$\Sigma L = L_{AB} + L_{BC} + L_{CD} + L_{DA} \leftarrow eq.7$$

Traverse #5 (cont.)

Compute the length of each course in the traverse using the latitude and departure values. (eq.8, eq.9, eq.10 and eq.11)

$Lat_{AB}=98.17\,[ft]$ $Dep_{AB}=-21.14\,[ft]$

$$L_{AB}=\sqrt{(Lat_{AB})^2+(Dep_{AB})^2}\leftarrow eq.8$$

$$L_{AB}=\sqrt{(97.17\,[ft])^2+(-21.14\,[ft])^2}$$

$$L_{AB}=100.42\,[ft]$$

$Lat_{BC}=19.59\,[ft]$ $Dep_{BC}=117.65\,[ft]$

$$L_{BC}=\sqrt{(Lat_{BC})^2+(Dep_{BC})^2}\leftarrow eq.9$$

$$L_{BC}=\sqrt{(19.59\,[ft])^2+(117.65\,[ft])^2}$$

$$L_{BC}=119.27\,[ft]$$

$Lat_{CD}=-53.22\,[ft]$ $Dep_{CD}=-69.06\,[ft]$

$$L_{CD}=\sqrt{(Lat_{CD})^2+(Dep_{CD})^2}\leftarrow eq.10$$

$$L_{CD}=\sqrt{(-53.22\,[ft])^2+(-69.06\,[ft])^2}$$

$$L_{CD}=87.19\,[ft]$$

$Lat_{DA}=-64.31\,[ft]$ $Dep_{DA}=-26.87\,[ft]$

$$L_{DA}=\sqrt{(Lat_{DA})^2+(Dep_{DA})^2}\leftarrow eq.11$$

Surveying Practice Problems

$$L_{CD} = \sqrt{(-64.31\,[ft])^2 + (-26.87\,[ft])^2}$$

$$L_{CD} = 69.70\,[ft]$$

Next, use eq. 7 to compute the total length of the traverse.

$L_{AB} = 100.42\,[ft]$ $L_{CD} = 87.19\,[ft]$

$$\Sigma L = L_{AB} + L_{BC} + L_{CD} + L_{DA} \leftarrow eq.7$$

$L_{BC} = 119.27\,[ft]$ $L_{DA} = 69.70\,[ft]$

$$\Sigma L = 100.42\,[ft] + 119.27\,[ft] + 87.19\,[ft] + 69.70\,[ft]$$

$$\Sigma L = 376.58\,[ft]$$

Plug in EOC and ΣL into eq. 1, then solve for ROE, the ratio of error.

$EOC = 0.624\,[ft]$

$$ROE = \frac{EOC}{\Sigma L} \leftarrow eq.1$$

$\Sigma L = 376.58\,[ft]$

It's good practice to preserve at least 3 (preferably 4) significant figures for intermediate calculations, such as, EOC = 0.624 [ft].

$$ROE = \frac{0.624\,[ft]}{376.58\,[ft]}$$

$$ROE = 0.00166$$

Answer: $\boxed{C}$

0.00166 is most nearly 0.0017. Answer C is correct.

Traverse #6

Find: Dep_{CA} ←the departure of course CA

Given: ROE=0.00124 ← the ratio of error of closed traverse ABC

Course	Latitude	Departure	Length
AB	-295.84	254.76	390.42
BC	267.41	158.91	311.06
CA	29.18	Dep_{CA}	L_{CA}

latitude, departure and length measurements in units of meters

North

A

C

B

A) -412.51 [m]

B) -412.17 [m]

C) -411.86 [m]

D) -411.54 [m]

Analysis:

Since we know ROE=0.00124, we must determine a Dep_{CA} such that the right hand side (RHS) of eq. 1 equals 0.00124.

error of closure

traverse length

$$ROE = \frac{EOC}{\Sigma L} \leftarrow eq.1$$

We'll develop equations for EOC and ΣL as a function of Dep_{CA}.

$$EOC = \sqrt{(EOC_N)^2 + (EOC_E)^2} \leftarrow eq.2$$

In eq. 2, EOC_N is the error of closure in the north-south direction, and EOC_E is the error of closure in the east-west direction.

$$EOC_N = \Sigma(Lat) \leftarrow eq.3$$

$Lat_{AB} = -295.84\ [m]$ $Lat_{CA} = 29.18\ [m]$

$$EOC_N = Lat_{AB} + Lat_{BC} + Lat_{CA}$$

$Lat_{BC} = 267.41\ [m]$

Use eq. 3 to compute EOC_N.

$$EOC_N = (-295.84\,[m]) + 267.41\,[m] + 29.18\,[m]$$

Traverse #6 (cont.)

$$EOC_N = 0.75\,[m]$$

$$EOC_E = \Sigma(Dep) \leftarrow eq.4$$

Use eq. 4 to compute EOC_E.

$Dep_{AB} = 254.76\,[m]$ $Dep_{BC} = 158.91\,[m]$

$$EOC_E = Dep_{AB} + Dep_{BC} + Dep_{CA}$$

$$EOC_E = 254.76\,[m] + 158.91\,[m] + Dep_{CA}$$

$$EOC_E = 413.67\,[m] + Dep_{CA}$$

We can write the error of closure in terms of Dep_{CA}, by plugging in EOC_N and EOC_E into eq. 2.

$EOC_E = 413.67\,[m] + Dep_{CA}$

$$EOC = \sqrt{(EOC_N)^2 + (EOC_E)^2} \leftarrow eq.2$$

$EOC_N = 0.75\,[m]$

$$EOC = \sqrt{(0.75\,[m])^2 + (413.67\,[m] + Dep_{CA})^2}$$

$$\Sigma L = L_{AB} + L_{BC} + L_{CA} \leftarrow eq.5$$

In eq. 5, the total length of traverse ABC equals the sum of the lengths of each course.

$$L_{CA} = \sqrt{(Lat_{CA})^2 + (Dep_{CA})^2} \leftarrow eq.6$$

To compute the length of course CA, plug in Lat_{CA} into eq. 6.

$Lat_{CA} = 29.18\,[m]$

Traverse #6 (cont.)

$$L_{CA}=\sqrt{(29.18\,[m])^2+(Dep_{CA})^2}$$

$$L_{CA}=\sqrt{(29.18\,[m])^2+(Dep_{CA})^2}$$

$$\Sigma L=L_{AB}+L_{BC}+L_{CA} \leftarrow eq.5$$

Plug in L_{AB}, L_{BC} and L_{CA} into eq.5.

$$L_{AB}=390.42\,[m] \qquad L_{BC}=311.06\,[m]$$

$$\Sigma L=390.42\,[m]+311.06\,[m]+\sqrt{(29.18\,[m])^2+(Dep_{CA})^2}$$

$$\Sigma L=701.48\,[m]+\sqrt{(29.18\,[m])^2+(Dep_{CA})^2}$$

Plug in ROE, EOC and ΣL into eq.1.

$$EOC=\sqrt{(0.75\,[m])^2+(413.67\,[m]+Dep_{CA})^2}$$

$$ROE=\frac{EOC}{\Sigma L} \leftarrow eq.1$$

$$ROE=0.00124$$

$$\Sigma L=701.48\,[m]+\sqrt{(29.18\,[m])^2+(Dep_{CA})^2}$$

$$0.00124=\frac{\sqrt{(0.75\,[m])^2+(413.67\,[m]+Dep_{CA})^2}}{701.48\,[m]+\sqrt{(29.18\,[m])^2+(Dep_{CA})^2}} \leftarrow eq.6$$

possible
answers
for Dep_{CA}

A) -412.51 [m]

B) -412.17 [m]

C) -411.86 [m]

D) -411.54 [m]

Rather than try to solve for Dep_{CA} explicitly, we'll pick a value for Dep_{CA}, and solve for the right hand side (RHS) of eq.6. If RHS=ROE, then we chose the correct value for Dep_{CA}.

Surveying Practice Problems

Traverse #6 (cont.)

We'll first try answer B, and plug in -412.17 [m] in for Dep_{CA}, in eq. 6., then solve for the right hand side.

$$0.00124 \overset{?}{=} \frac{\sqrt{(0.75\,[m])^2+(413.67\,[m]+Dep_{CA})^2}}{701.48\,[m]+\sqrt{(29.18\,[m])^2+(Dep_{CA})^2}} \leftarrow eq.6$$

assumed value

$Dep_{CA}=-412.17\,[m]$

$$0.00124 \overset{?}{=} \frac{\sqrt{(0.75\,[m])^2+(413.67\,[m]+(-412.17\,[m]))^2}}{701.48\,[m]+\sqrt{(29.18\,[m])^2+(-412.17\,[m])^2}}$$

$$0.00124 \neq 0.00150$$

If $Dep_{CA}=-412.17\,[m]$, the ratio of error would equal 0.00150

To reduce the RHS of eq.6, Dep_{CA} should be closer to -413.67 [m]. The only possible answer closer to -413.67 [m] than answer B, is, answer A ($Dep_{CA}=-412.51\,[m]$).

$$0.00124 \overset{?}{=} \frac{\sqrt{(0.75\,[m])^2+(413.67\,[m]+Dep_{CA})^2}}{701.48\,[m]+\sqrt{(29.18\,[m])^2+(Dep_{CA})^2}} \leftarrow eq.6$$

assumed value

$Dep_{CA}=-412.51\,[m]$

$$0.00124 \overset{?}{=} \frac{\sqrt{(0.75\,[m])^2+(413.67\,[m]+(-412.51\,[m]))^2}}{701.48\,[m]+\sqrt{(29.18\,[m])^2+(-412.51\,[m])^2}}$$

$$0.00124 = 0.00124$$

Choosing $Dep_{CA}=-412.51\,[m]$ results in a ROE of 0.00124.

Answer: | A |

Answer A is correct.

Traverse #7

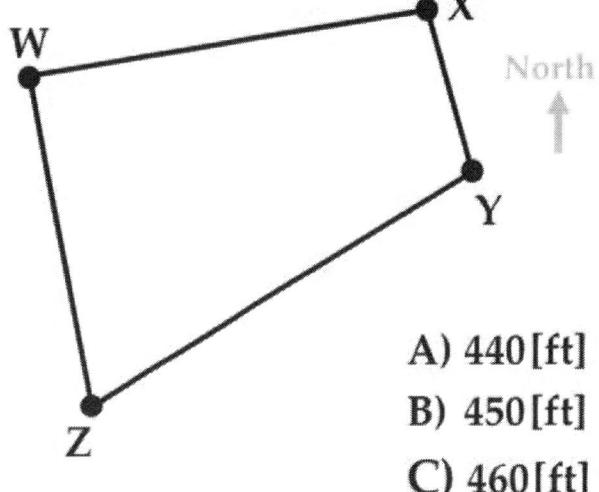

Find: L_{WXYZ} ← the length of traverse WXYZ

Given:

Course	Latitude	Departure
WX	16.49	117.90
XY	-35.18	18.55
YZ	-101.71	-121.54
ZW	120.40	-14.91

all latitudes and departures are in units of feet

A) 440 [ft]

B) 450 [ft]

C) 460 [ft]

D) 470 [ft]

- -

Analysis:

$$L_{WXYZ}=L_{WX}+L_{XY}+L_{YZ}+L_{ZW} \leftarrow eq.1$$

The distance along traverse WXYZ equals the sum of the distances of courses WX, XY, YZ and ZW.

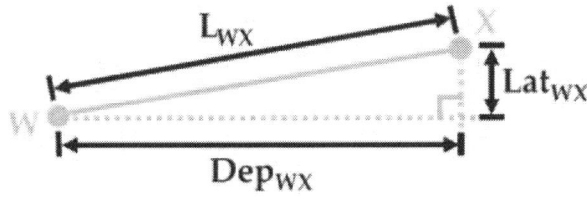

Figure 1

Figure 1 shows the lengths associated with course WX: L_{WX}, Lat_{WX} and Dep_{WX}

Plug in Lat_{WX} and Dep_{WX} into eq.2, then solve for L_{WX}.

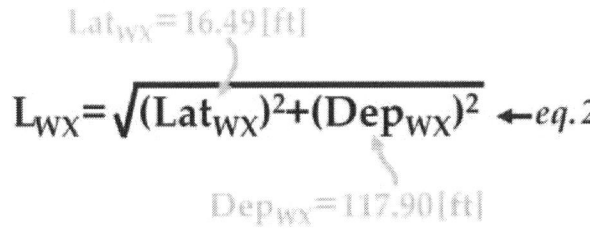

$Lat_{WX}=16.49 [ft]$

$$L_{WX}=\sqrt{(Lat_{WX})^2+(Dep_{WX})^2} \leftarrow eq.2$$

$Dep_{WX}=117.90 [ft]$

$$L_{WX}=\sqrt{(16.49 [ft])^2+(117.90 [ft])^2}$$

$$L_{WX}=119.05 [ft]$$

Traverse #7 (cont.)

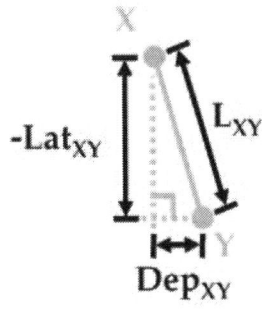

Figure 2

Figure 2 shows the lengths associated with course XY: L_{XY}, Lat_{XY} and Dep_{XY}.

In Figure 2, since Lat_{XY} is a negative value, the negative sign is added to represent a positive length.

$Lat_{XY}=-35.18\,[ft]$

$$L_{XY}=\sqrt{(Lat_{XY})^2+(Dep_{XY})^2} \leftarrow eq.3$$

$Dep_{XY}=18.55\,[ft]$

Plug in Lat_{XY} and Dep_{XY} into eq.3, then solve for L_{XY}.

$$L_{XY}=\sqrt{(-35.18\,[ft])^2+(18.55\,[ft])^2}$$

$$L_{XY}=39.77\,[ft]$$

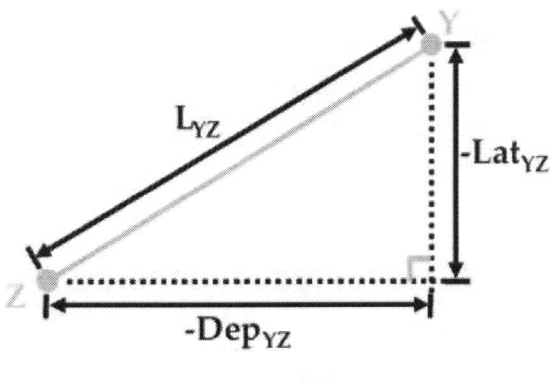

Figure 3

Figure 3 shows the lengths associated with course YZ: L_{YZ}, Lat_{YZ} and Dep_{YZ}.

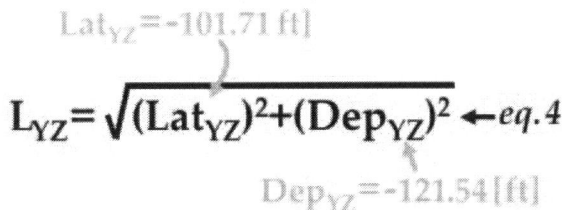

$Lat_{YZ}=-101.71\,[ft]$

$$L_{YZ}=\sqrt{(Lat_{YZ})^2+(Dep_{YZ})^2} \leftarrow eq.4$$

$Dep_{YZ}=-121.54\,[ft]$

Plug in Lat_{YZ} and Dep_{YZ} into eq.4, then solve for L_{YZ}.

Traverse #7 (cont.)

$$L_{YX}=\sqrt{(-101.71\,[ft])^2+(-121.54\,[ft])^2}$$

$$L_{YZ}=158.48\,[ft]$$

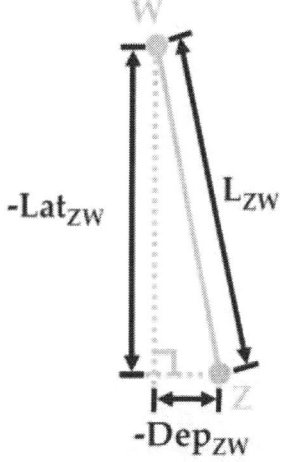

Figure 4 shows the lengths associated with course ZW: L_{ZW}, Lat_{ZW} and Dep_{ZW}.

Figure 4

This method can be used to solve for the total length of open traverses and closed traverses.

$Lat_{ZW}=120.40\,[ft]$

$$L_{XY}=\sqrt{(Lat_{ZW})^2+(Dep_{ZW})^2} \leftarrow eq.5$$

$Dep_{ZW}=-14.19\,[ft]$

Plug in Lat_{ZW} and Dep_{ZW} into eq.5, then solve for L_{ZW}.

$$L_{XY}=\sqrt{(120.40\,[ft])^2+(-14.19\,[ft])^2}$$

$$L_{XY}=121.32\,[ft]$$

$L_{WX}=119.05\,[ft]$ $L_{YZ}=158.48\,[ft]$

$$L_{WXYZ}=L_{WX}+L_{XY}+L_{YZ}+L_{ZW} \leftarrow eq.1$$

$L_{XY}=39.77\,[ft]$ $L_{ZW}=121.32\,[ft]$

Return to eq.1, plug in L_{WX}, L_{XY}, L_{YZ} and L_{ZW}, then solve for L_{WXYZ}.

$$L_{WXYZ}=119.05\,[ft]+39.77\,[ft]+158.48\,[ft]+121.32\,[ft]$$

$$L_{WXYZ}=438.62\,[ft] \qquad \underline{Answer:} \boxed{A}$$

Surveying Practice Problems

Traverse #8

Find: N_J ←the northing of point J

Given:

Point	Northing	Easting
I	29.82	65.44
J	N_J	191.40
K	43.11	307.06

measurements for northing and
easting are in unit of feet.

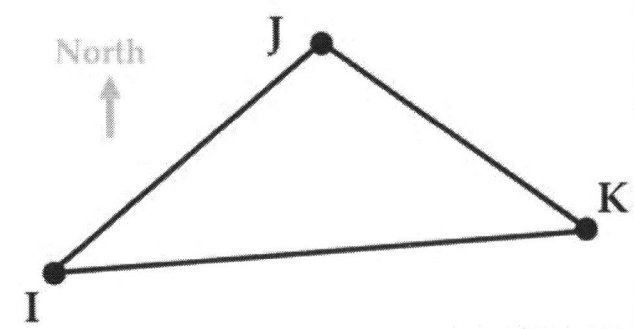

$L_{IJK}=587\,[ft]$
↑
perimeter around the
traverse IJK

A) 140 [ft]
B) 160 [ft]
C) 180 [ft]
D) 200 [ft]

Analysis:

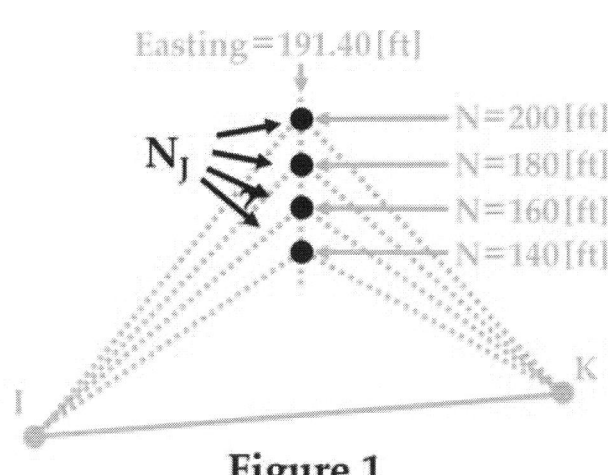

Easting=191.40 [ft]

N_J → N=200 [ft]
→ N=180 [ft]
→ N=160 [ft]
→ N=140 [ft]

I   K

Figure 1

Figure 1 shows a sketch of
traverse IJK for the four
possible values of N_J.

As the value of N_J increases,
the perimeter around
traverse IJK increases.

$$L_{IJK}=L_{IJ}+L_{JK}+L_{KI} \leftarrow eq.1$$

From the problem statement,
we know the left hand side of
eq.1 equals 587 [ft]

N_I=29.82 [ft] E_I=65.44 [ft]

Plug in N_I, N_K, E_I and E_K into eq.2,
then solve for L_{KI}.

$$L_{KI}=\sqrt{(N_I-N_K)^2+(E_I-E_K)^2} \leftarrow eq.2$$

N_K=43.11 [ft] E_K=307.06 [ft]

Traverse #8 (cont.)

$$L_{KI}=\sqrt{(29.82\,[ft]-43.11\,[ft])^2+(65.44\,[ft]-307.06\,[ft])^2}$$

$$L_{KI}=241.99\,[ft]$$

Next we want to develop an expression for variables L_{IJ} and L_{JK}, in terms of N_J.

$E_J=191.40\,[ft]$

$$L_{IJ}=\sqrt{(N_J-N_I)^2+(E_J-E_I)^2}\ \leftarrow eq.\,3$$

Use eq.3 to solve for L_{IJ}, as a function of N_J.

$N_I=29.82\,[ft]$ $E_I=65.44\,[ft]$

$$L_{IJ}=\sqrt{(N_J-29.82\,[ft])^2+(191.40\,[ft]-65.44\,[ft])^2}$$

$$L_{IJ}=\sqrt{(N_J-29.82\,[ft])^2+15,866\,[ft^2]}$$

$E_K=307.06\,[ft]$

$$L_{JK}=\sqrt{(N_K-N_J)^2+(E_K-E_J)^2}\ \leftarrow eq.\,4$$

Use eq.4 to solve for L_{JK}, as a function of N_J.

$N_K=43.11\,[ft]$ $E_J=191.40\,[ft]$

$$L_{JK}=\sqrt{(43.11\,[ft]-N_J)^2+(307.06\,[ft]-191.40\,[ft])^2}$$

$$L_{JK}=\sqrt{(43.11\,[ft]-N_J)^2+13,377\,[ft^2]}$$

Plug in the known variables into eq.1.

$L_{JK}=\sqrt{(43.11\,[ft]-N_J)^2+13,377\,[ft^2]}$

$L_{IJK}=587\,[ft]$ $L_{KI}=241.99\,[ft]$

$$L_{IJK}=L_{IJ}+L_{JK}+L_{KI}\ \leftarrow eq.\,1$$

$L_{IJ}=\sqrt{(N_J-29.82\,[ft])^2+15,866\,[ft^2]}$

Surveying Practice Problems

Traverse #8 (cont.)

$$587[\text{ft}] = \sqrt{(N_J - 29.82[\text{ft}])^2 + 15,866[\text{ft}^2]}$$
$$+ \sqrt{(43.11[\text{ft}] - N_J)^2 + 13,377[\text{ft}^2]} + 241.99[\text{ft}] \leftarrow eq.5$$

A) 140[ft]

first guess → B) 160[ft]

C) 180[ft]

D) 200[ft]

Eq. 5 contains only one unknown variable. At this point, it would be fastest to guess and check for the correct solution.

Since the right hand side (RHS) of eq. 5 increases as N_J increases, we should first guess 160[ft] or 180[ft]

guess
↓
N_J=160[ft]
↓

$$587[\text{ft}] = \sqrt{(N_J - 29.82[\text{ft}])^2 + 15,866[\text{ft}^2]}$$
$$? + \sqrt{(43.11[\text{ft}] - N_J)^2 + 13,377[\text{ft}^2]} + 241.99[\text{ft}] \leftarrow eq.5$$

N_J=160[ft] ← guess

Plug in 160[ft] in for variable N_J in eq. 5, then solve for the RHS.

?

$$587[\text{ft}] = \sqrt{(160[\text{ft}] - 29.82[\text{ft}])^2 + 15,866[\text{ft}^2]}$$
$$+ \sqrt{(43.11[\text{ft}] - 160[\text{ft}])^2 + 13,377[\text{ft}^2]}$$
$$+ 241.99[\text{ft}]$$

$$587[\text{ft}] \approx 587.59[\text{ft}]$$

For N_J=160[ft], the RHS equals 587.59[ft] which is very close to 587 [ft], closer than if we tried N_J equal to 140[ft] or 180[ft].

Answer: B

Traverse #9

Find: $N_{J,bal}$ — the northing of point J after the traverse is balanced

Given:

Point	Northing	Easting
I	20.71	16.16
J	81.54	49.11
K	150.88	7.91
L	141.29	124.57

northing and easting values in meters

← measured coordinates

balance using the compass rule

Point	Northing	Easting
I	20.71	16.16
L	140.36	125.80

↙ true coordinates

A) 80.61 [m]

B) 81.02 [m]

C) 81.30 [m]

D) 81.78 [m]

Analysis:

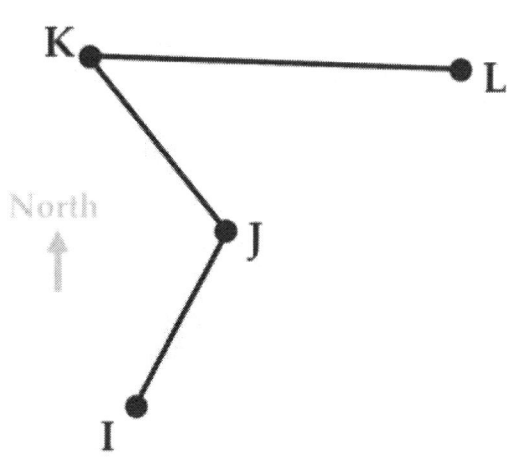

North

Figure 1

When no sketch is provided in the problem statement, it may be helpful to sketch the problem at the beginning of the analysis.

Figure 1 shows traverse IJKL.

Balancing a traverse involves adjusting the measured values to match the true (known) values of the traverse.

$$N_{J,bal} = N_{J,unbal} + c_{N_J} \leftarrow eq.1$$

correction length

Use eq.1 to convert the unbalanced northing of point J to the balanced northing of point J, by adding a correction length, c_{N_J}.

$$c_{N_J} = \underbrace{(N_{L,known} - N_{L,measured})}_{\substack{\text{error in northing} \\ \text{measurements along} \\ \text{entire traverse IJKL}}} * \underbrace{\left(\frac{L_{IJ}}{L_{IJKL}}\right)}_{\substack{\text{length} \\ \text{fraction}}} \leftarrow eq.2$$

Since, $N_{J,known} = N_{J,measured}$, then the northing of point J needs to be corrected a fraction of the distance between $N_{L,known}$ and $N_{L,measured}$.

Surveying Practice Problems

Traverse #9 (cont.)

In eq.2, the length fraction equals the distance along the traverse to the point of interest divided by the the total length of the traverse.

Write out the length fraction from eq.2.

$$c_{N_J} = (N_{L,known} - N_{L,measured}) * \left(\frac{L_{IJ}}{\underbrace{L_{IJ} + L_{JK} + L_{KL}}_{\text{length fraction}}} \right) \leftarrow eq.3$$

To solve for the length fraction, we must compute the length of all 3 individual courses.

$$N_J = 81.54[m] \quad E_J = 49.11[m]$$

$$L_{IJ} = \sqrt{(N_J - N_I)^2 + (E_J - E_I)^2} \leftarrow eq.4$$

$$N_I = 20.71[m] \quad E_I = 16.16[m]$$

Use eq.4 to solve for the length of course IJ.

$$L_{IJ} = \sqrt{(81.54[m] - 20.71[m])^2 + (49.11[m] - 16.16[m])^2}$$

$$L_{IJ} = 69.18[m]$$

$$N_K = 150.88[m] \quad E_K = 7.91[m]$$

$$L_{JK} = \sqrt{(N_K - N_J)^2 + (E_K - E_J)^2} \leftarrow eq.5$$

$$N_J = 81.54[m] \quad E_J = 49.11[m]$$

Use eq.5 to solve for the length of course JK.

$$L_{JK} = \sqrt{(150.88[m] - 81.54[m])^2 + (7.91[m] - 49.11[m])^2}$$

$$L_{JK} = 80.66[m]$$

Traverse #9 (cont.)

$N_L=141.29\,[m]$ $E_L=124.57\,[m]$

$$L_{KL}=\sqrt{(N_L-N_K)^2+(E_L-E_K)^2} \leftarrow eq.6$$

$N_K=150.88\,[m]$ $E_K=7.91\,[m]$

Use eq.6 to solve for the length of course KL.

$$L_{KL}=\sqrt{(141.29\,[m]-150.88\,[m])^2+(124.57\,[m]-7.91\,[m])^2}$$

$$L_{KL}=117.05\,[m]$$

Return to eq.3, plug in $N_{L,known}$, $N_{L,measured}$, L_{IJ}, L_{JK}, and L_{KL}, then solve for c_{N_J}.

$N_{L,known}=140.36\,[m]$ $L_{IJ}=69.18\,[m]$

$$c_{N_J}=(N_{L,known}-N_{L,measured}) * \left(\frac{L_{IJ}}{L_{IJ}+L_{JK}+L_{KL}}\right) \leftarrow eq.3$$

$N_{L,measured}=141.29\,[m]$

$L_{JK}=80.66\,[m]$ $L_{KL}=117.05\,[m]$

$$c_{N_J}=(140.36\,[m]-141.29\,[m]) * \left(\frac{69.18\,[m]}{69.18\,[m]+80.66\,[m]+117.05\,[m]}\right)$$

$$c_{N_J}=-0.24\,[m]$$

$c_{N_J}=-0.24\,[m]$ means the northing of point J should be decreased by 0.24 meters, to balance the traverse, in the north-south direction, at point J.

$N_{J,unbal}=81.54\,[m]$ $c_{N_J}=-0.24\,[m]$

$$N_{J,bal}=N_{J,unbal}+c_{N_J} \leftarrow eq.1$$

Return to eq.1, plug in the unbalanced (measured) northing for point J and the correction length, and solve for the balanced northing for point J.

$$N_{J,bal}=81.54\,[m]+(-0.24\,[m])$$

$$N_{J,bal}=81.30\,[m]$$

Answer: $\boxed{C}$

The compass rule can be used to balance open and closed traverses.

Surveying Practice Problems

Traverse #10

Find: Lat_{AB} ← the corrected latitude of course AB

Given:

North

balance traverse using transit rule

all latitude and departure measurements are in feet.

known northing and easting values

Course	Latitude	Departure
AB	78.11	-44.60
BC	88.26	31.09
CD	-14.87	104.22

Point	Northing	Easting
A	31.48	99.71
D	181.58	191.11

A) 77.35 [ft]
B) 77.50 [ft]
C) 78.72 [ft]
D) 78.87 [ft]

Analysis:

$$Lat_{AB} = Lat_{AB,meas} + c_{Lat,AB} \leftarrow eq.1$$

corrected latitude

correction distance

The corrected latitude measure of course AB equals the measured latitude of course AB, plus a correction distance.

The "measured" distance is often called the unbalanced distance.

error of closure in latitude measurements

$$c_{Lat,AB} = \frac{-EOC_{Lat}}{\sum_{i=1}^{N}|Lat_i|} * |Lat_{AB,meas}| \leftarrow eq.2$$

sum of absolute value of latitude measurements

absolute value bars

Eq.2 computes the correction to the latitude of course AB, $c_{Lat,AB}$, which is the difference between the measured latitude of course AB and the corrected latitude of course AB.

Eq.3 computes the sum of the absolute value of all latitude measurements in traverse ABCD.

$Lat_{BC} = 88.26 [ft]$

$$\sum_{i=1}^{N}|Lat_i| = |Lat_{AB}| + |Lat_{BC}| + |Lat_{CD}| \leftarrow eq.3$$

$Lat_{AB} = 78.11 [ft]$ $Lat_{CD} = -14.87 [ft]$

Plug in the three given latitude variables, then solve eq.3.

$$\sum_{i=1}^{N}|Lat_i| = |78.11 [ft]| + |88.26 [ft]| + |-14.87 [ft]|$$

Traverse #10 (cont.)

$$\sum_{i=1}^{N}\left|Lat_i\right|= 181.24\,[ft]$$

The error in closure of latitude measurements equals the sum of the measured latitude values minus the difference between northing values of the first and last point on the traverse.

$Lat_{AB}=78.11\,[ft]$ $Lat_{CD}=-14.87\,[ft]$

$$EOC_{Lat}= (Lat_{AB}+Lat_{BC}+Lat_{CD})-(N_D-N_A)\leftarrow eq.4$$

$Lat_{BC}=88.26\,[ft]$ $N_D=181.57\,[ft]$ $N_A=31.48\,[ft]$

$$EOC_{Lat}= (78.11\,[ft]+88.26\,[ft]+(-14.87\,[ft]))-(181.57\,[ft]-31.48\,[ft])$$

$$EOC_{Lat}=1.41\,[ft]$$

$EOC_{Lat}=1.41\,[ft]$ means the final measured point D is 1.41 feet further north than the true point D, as shown in Figure 1.

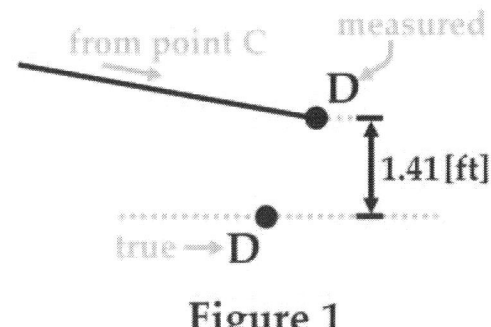

Figure 1

In Figure 1, the "true" point D is positioned somewhere along the dashed grey line, south of the "measured" point D.

Plug in the variables on the right hand side of eq. 2 and solve for the correction to the latitude of course AB.

$EOC_{Lat}=1.41\,[ft]$ $Lat_{AB,meas}=78.11\,[ft]$

$$c_{Lat,AB}=\frac{-EOC_{Lat}}{\sum\limits_{i}^{N}\left|Lat_i\right|}*\left|Lat_{AB,meas}\right|\leftarrow eq.2$$

$$\sum_{i=1}^{N}\left|Lat_i\right|=181.24\,[ft]$$

For this problem, we don't need to concern ourselves with the easting values or departures.

Surveying Practice Problems

Traverse #10 (cont.)

$$c_{Lat,AB} = \frac{-1.41\,[ft]}{181.24\,[ft]} * \left|78.11\,[ft]\right|$$

$$c_{Lat,AB} = -0.61\,[ft]$$

$$c_{Lat,AB} = -0.61\,[ft]$$

$$Lat_{AB} = Lat_{AB,meas} + c_{Lat,AB} \leftarrow eq.\,1$$

$$Lat_{AB,meas} = 78.11\,[ft]$$

Return to eq. 1, plug in the measured latitude of course AB and the latitude correction for course AB, and compute the true latitude of course AB.

$$Lat_{AB} = 78.11\,[ft] + (-0.61\,[ft])$$

$$Lat_{AB} = 77.50\,[ft]$$

Answer: $\boxed{B}$

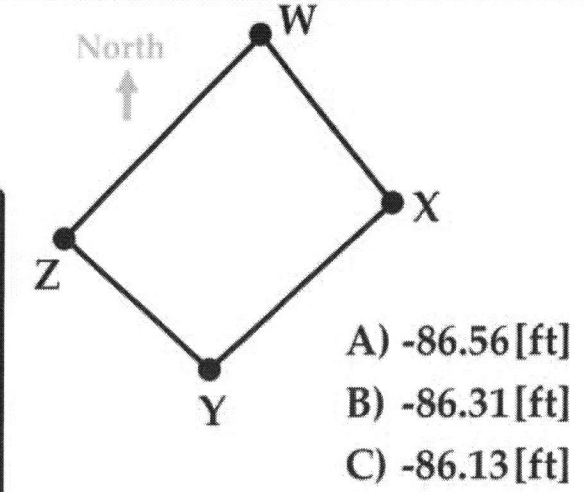

Traverse #11

<u>Find</u>: Dep_{XY} ← the corrected departure of course XY

<u>Given</u>:

Course	Latitude	Departure
WX	-112.41	67.09
XY	-102.87	-86.22
YZ	89.64	-78.11
ZW	125.07	97.59

all latitude and departure measurements are in feet.

balance the closed traverse WXYZ using the transit rule

A) -86.56 [ft]

B) -86.31 [ft]

C) -86.13 [ft]

D) **not enough information**

<u>Analysis</u>:

$$\text{Dep}_{XY}=\text{Dep}_{XY,meas}+c_{Dep,XY} \ ←eq.1$$

corrected departure

correction distance

The corrected departure of course XY equals the measured departure of course XY, plus a correction distance.

We'll use eq. 2 to calculate the correction distance for the dep-arture of course XY. (Using the transit rule to balance the closed traverse WXYZ).

error of closure in departure measurements

$$c_{Dep,XY}=\frac{-\text{EOC}_{Dep}}{\sum_{i=1}^{N}\left|\text{Dep}_i\right|}*\left|\text{Dep}_{XY,meas}\right| \ ←eq.2$$

sum of absolute value of the departure measurements

$$\text{EOC}_{Dep}=\sum_{i=1}^{N}\text{Dep}_{i,meas} \ ←eq.3$$

Use eq. 3 to solve for the error of closure in departure. For a closed traverse, the total expected departure is 0.

$\text{Dep}_{WX}=67.09\,[ft]$ $\text{Dep}_{YZ}=-78.22\,[ft]$

$$\text{EOC}_{Dep}=\text{Dep}_{WX}+\text{Dep}_{XY}+\text{Dep}_{YZ}+\text{Dep}_{ZW}$$

$\text{Dep}_{XY}=-86.22\,[ft]$ $\text{Dep}_{ZW}=97.59\,[ft]$

Plug in the measured departure values and solve for EOC_{Dep}.

Traverse #11 (cont.)

$$EOC_{Dep} = 67.09\,[ft] + (-86.22\,[ft]) + (-78.11\,[ft]) + 97.59\,[ft]$$

$$EOC_{Dep} = 0.35\,[ft]$$

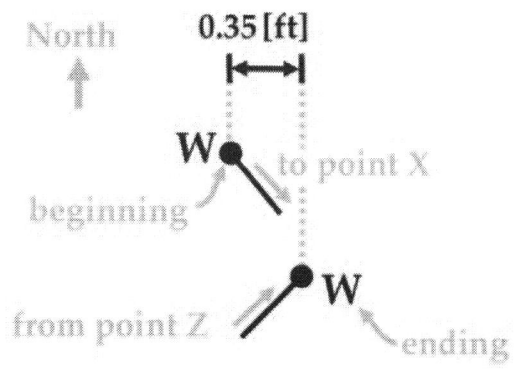

Figure 1 shows the error of closure in departure.

Figure 1

The ending point W is located on a line 0.35 feet east of the starting point W

Use eq.4 to compute the sum of absolute value of the departure measurements

$Dep_{WX} = 67.09\,[ft]$

$Dep_{YZ} = -78.11\,[ft]$

$$\sum_{i=1}^{N} |Dep_i| = |Dep_{WX}| + |Dep_{XY}| + |Dep_{YZ}| + |Dep_{ZW}| \leftarrow eq.4$$

$Dep_{XY} = -86.22\,[ft]$

$Dep_{ZW} = 97.59\,[ft]$

$$\sum_{i=1}^{N} |Dep_i| = |67.09\,[ft]| + |-86.22\,[ft]| + |-78.11\,[ft]| + |97.59\,[ft]|$$

$$\sum_{i=1}^{N} |Dep_i| = 329.01\,[ft]$$

Return to eq. 2 to compute the correction distance for the departure of course YZ.

$EOC_{Dep} = 0.35\,[ft]$

$Dep_{XY,meas} = -86.22\,[ft]$

$$c_{Dep,XY} = \frac{-EOC_{Dep}}{\sum\limits_{i=1}^{N} |Dep_i|} * |Dep_{XY,meas}| \leftarrow eq.2$$

$\sum\limits_{i=1}^{N} |Dep_i| = 329.01\,[ft]$

Plug in the known variables into eq.2, then solve for $c_{Dep,XY}$.

Traverse #11 (cont.)

$$c_{Dep,XY} = \frac{-0.35\,[ft]}{329.01\,[ft]} * \left| -86.22\,[ft] \right|$$

The correction in departure to course XY is a fraction of the error of closure in the departure.

$$c_{Dep,XY} = -0.09\,[ft]$$

$$\overset{\displaystyle c_{Dep,XY}=-0.09\,[ft]}{\textbf{Dep}_{XY} = \textbf{Dep}_{XY,meas} + \textbf{c}_{Dep,XY} \leftarrow eq.1}$$

$$Dep_{XY,meas} = -86.22\,[ft]$$

Lastly, return to eq. 1, plug in $Dep_{XY,meas}$ and $c_{Dep,XY}$, then solve for the corrected departure of course XY, Dep_{XY}.

$$Dep_{XY} = (-86.22\,[ft]) + (-0.09\,[ft])$$

$$Dep_{XY} = -86.31\,[ft]$$

Answer: $\boxed{B}$

Surveying Practice Problems

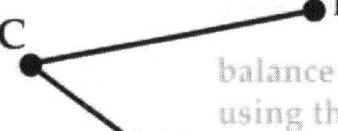

Find: E_C ←the easting of point C

Given: all latitude and departure measurements are in feet.

Course	Latitude	Departure
AB	98.71	17.16
BC	72.18	-67.28
CD	58.22	148.96

balance open traverse using the compass rule

known northing and easting values

Point	Northing	Easting
A	21.76	101.70
D	250.07	201.13

North

A) 51.25 [ft]
B) 51.41 [ft]
C) 51.75 [ft]
D) 51.91 [ft]

Analysis:

$$E_C = E_{C,meas} + c_{E_C} \quad \leftarrow eq.1$$

correction length

Use eq.1 to convert the measured easting of point C to the true easting of point C, by adding a correction length, c_{E_C}.

$$E_{A,known} = E_{A,meas} = 101.70 \,[ft] \quad \leftarrow eq.2$$

Assume Traverse ABCD begins at the known coordinates of point A.

$E_A = 101.70\,[ft] \qquad Dep_{BC} = -67.28\,[ft]$

$$E_{C,meas} = E_A + Dep_{AB} + Dep_{BC} \quad \leftarrow eq.3$$

$Dep_{AB} = 17.16\,[ft]$

We compute the measured easting at point C by adding the measured departures of course AB and course BC, to the known easting of point A.

$$E_{C,meas} = 101.70\,[ft] + 17.16\,[ft] + (-67.28\,[ft])$$

$$E_{C,meas} = 51.58\,[ft]$$

Use eq.4 to compute the required correction to the easting at point C

$$c_{E_C} = \underbrace{(E_{D,known} - E_{D,meas})}_{\text{the difference between the measured and true easting at point D}} * \underbrace{\left(\frac{L_{ABC}}{L_{ABCD}}\right)}_{\text{length fraction}} \quad \leftarrow eq.4$$

The easting of point C needs to be corrected a fraction of the dist-ance between $E_{D,known}$ and $E_{D,meas}$.

Traverse #12 (cont.)

$E_A = 101.70 [ft]$ $Dep_{BC} = -67.28 [ft]$

$$E_{D,meas} = E_A + Dep_{AB} + Dep_{BC} + Dep_{CD} \leftarrow eq.5$$

$Dep_{AB} = 17.16 [ft]$ $Dep_{CD} = 148.96 [ft]$

$$E_{D,meas} = 101.70 [ft] + 17.16 [ft] + (-67.28 [ft]) + 148.96 [ft]$$

$$E_{D,meas} = 200.54 [ft]$$

From the measured departure values, the measured easting of point D equals 200.54 feet.

$$L_{ABC} = L_{AB} + L_{BC} \leftarrow eq.6$$

$$L_{ABCD} = L_{AB} + L_{BC} + L_{CD} \leftarrow eq.7$$

The length measurements from eq. 4 are calculated using eq. 6 and eq. 7.

Compute the length of each course in traverse ABCD, using eq. 8, eq. 9 and eq. 10.

$Lat_{AB} = 98.71 [ft]$ $Dep_{AB} = 17.16 [ft]$

$$L_{AB} = \sqrt{(Lat_{AB})^2 + (Dep_{AB})^2} \leftarrow eq.8$$

$$L_{AB} = \sqrt{(98.71 [ft])^2 + (17.16 [ft])^2}$$

$$L_{AB} = 100.19 [ft]$$

$Lat_{BC} = 72.18 [ft]$ $Dep_{BC} = -67.28 [ft]$

$$L_{BC} = \sqrt{(Lat_{BC})^2 + (Dep_{BC})^2} \leftarrow eq.9$$

$$L_{BC} = \sqrt{(72.18 [ft])^2 + (-67.28 [ft])^2}$$

$$L_{BC} = 98.67 [ft]$$

Surveying Practice Problems

Traverse #12 (cont.)

Lat$_{CD}$=58.22[ft]   Dep$_{CD}$=148.96[ft]

$$L_{CD}=\sqrt{(Lat_{CD})^2+(Dep_{CD})^2} \leftarrow eq.10$$

$$L_{CD}=\sqrt{(58.22[ft])^2+(148.96[ft])^2}$$

$$L_{CD}=159.93[ft]$$

L$_{AB}$=100.19[ft]

$$L_{ABC}=L_{AB}+L_{BC} \leftarrow eq.6$$

L$_{BC}$=98.67[ft]

Return to eq.6, plug in the lengths for course AB and course BC, then solve for L$_{ABC}$.

$$L_{ABC}=100.19[ft]+98.67[ft]$$

$$L_{ABC}=198.86[ft]$$

L$_{AB}$=100.19[ft]   L$_{CD}$=159.93[ft]

$$L_{ABCD}=L_{AB}+L_{BC}+L_{CD} \leftarrow eq.7$$

L$_{BC}$=98.67[ft]

Return to eq.7, plug in the lengths for course AB, course BC, and course CD, then solve for the length of ABCD.

$$L_{ABCD}=100.19[ft]+98.67[ft]+159.93[ft]$$

$$L_{ABCD}=358.79[ft]$$

E$_{D,known}$=201.13[ft]   L$_{ABC}$=198.86[ft]

$$c_{E_C}=(E_{D,known}-E_{D,meas})*\left(\frac{L_{ABC}}{L_{ABCD}}\right) \leftarrow eq.4$$

E$_{D,meas}$=200.54[ft]   L$_{ABCD}$=358.79[ft]

Plug in the calculated values into the right hand side of eq.4, then solve for the correction to the easting at point C.

Traverse #12 (cont.)

$$c_{E_C} = (201.13[ft] - 200.54[ft]) * \left(\frac{198.86[ft]}{358.79[ft]} \right)$$

$$c_{E_C} = 0.33[ft]$$

$c_{E_C}=0.33[ft]$ means the measured easting at point C should be increased by 0.33 feet.

$$c_{E_C} = 0.33[ft]$$

$$E_C = E_{C,meas} + c_{E_C} \leftarrow eq.1$$

$$E_{C,meas} = 51.58[ft]$$

Return to eq. 1, plug in the correction distance and the measured easting of point C, then solve for the corrected easting of point C.

$$E_C = 51.58[ft] + 0.33[ft]$$

$$E_C = 51.91[ft]$$

Answer: $\boxed{D}$

Surveying Practice Problems

Photogrammetry #1

Find: $d_{AB,map}$ ← the distance between points A and B on the map

Given:

$d_{AB,earth} = 1,425 \, [ft]$

the distance between points A and B on earth

map scale = 1:3,000

the scale of the map

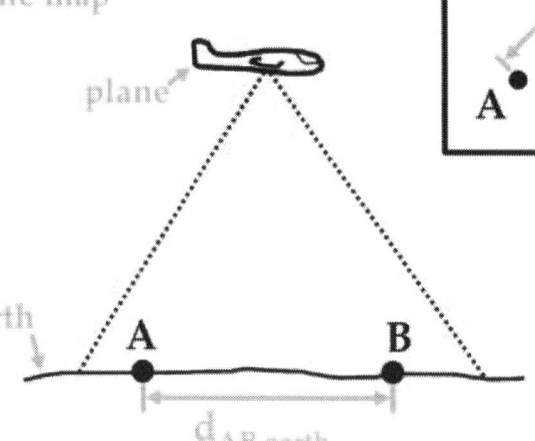

A) 0.5 [in]
B) 3.6 [in]
C) 4.2 [in]
D) 5.7 [in]

Analysis:

$$\text{map scale} = 1:3000 = \frac{1}{3,000}$$

The map scale reads "one to three thousand", which means 1 unit of length on the map corresponds to 3,000 units of length on the earth.

$d_{AB,earth} = 1,425 \, [ft]$

$$d_{AB,map} = d_{AB,earth} * \text{map scale} \leftarrow eq.1$$

$\text{map scale} = \frac{1}{3,000}$

Eq.1 shows how the distance between points A and B on the map and the distance between points A and B on earth are related by the map scale.

$$d_{AB,map} = 1,425 \, [ft] * \frac{1}{3,000}$$

For this type problem, some texts state the scale = 3,000, rather than scale = 1/3,000. Be mindful of this difference.

$$d_{AB,map} = 0.475 \, [ft] * \frac{12 \, [in]}{1 \, [ft]}$$

unit conversion

Convert feet to inches.

$$d_{AB,map} = 5.7 \, [in]$$

Answer: D

Photogrammetry #2

Find: Elev$_{plane}$ ← the elevation of the plane

Given:

$f = 6$ [in] ← the focal length of the camera

Elev$_{ground} = 1,280$ [ft]
the ground elevation

use sea level as a vertical datum

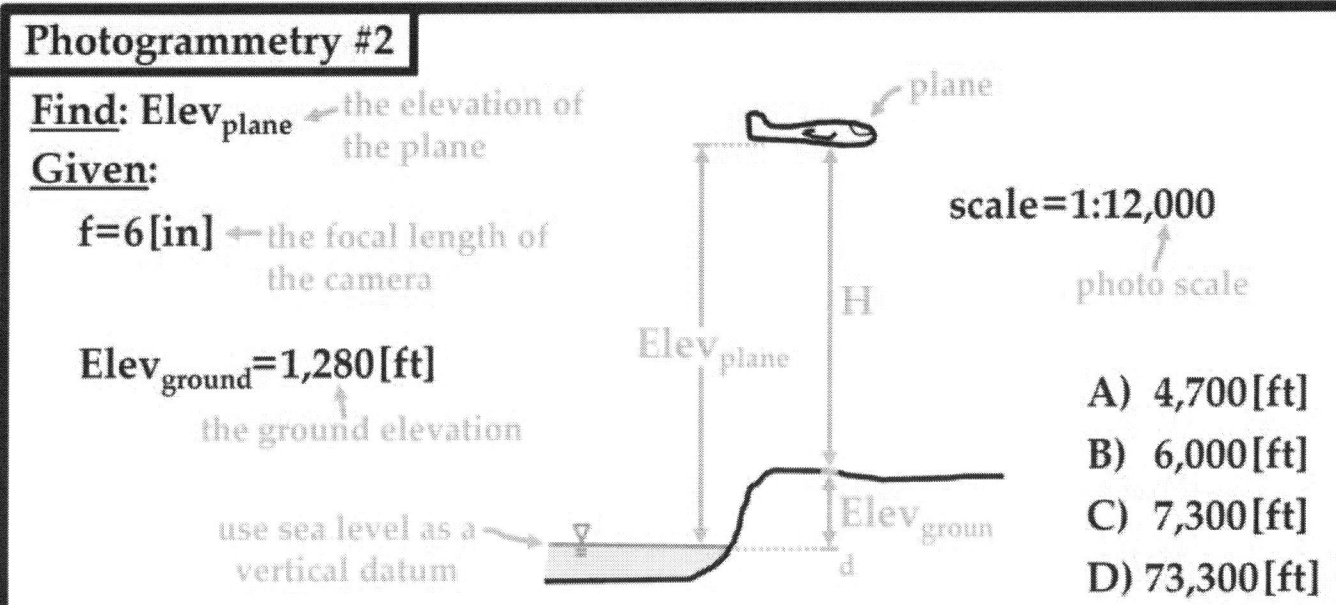

scale = 1:12,000 ← photo scale

A) 4,700 [ft]
B) 6,000 [ft]
C) 7,300 [ft]
D) 73,300 [ft]

Analysis:

$$Elev_{plane} = Elev_{ground} + H \quad \leftarrow eq.1$$

height of the plane above the ground

From the figure in the problem statement, we realize the elevation of the plane equals the ground elevation plus the height of the plane above the ground.

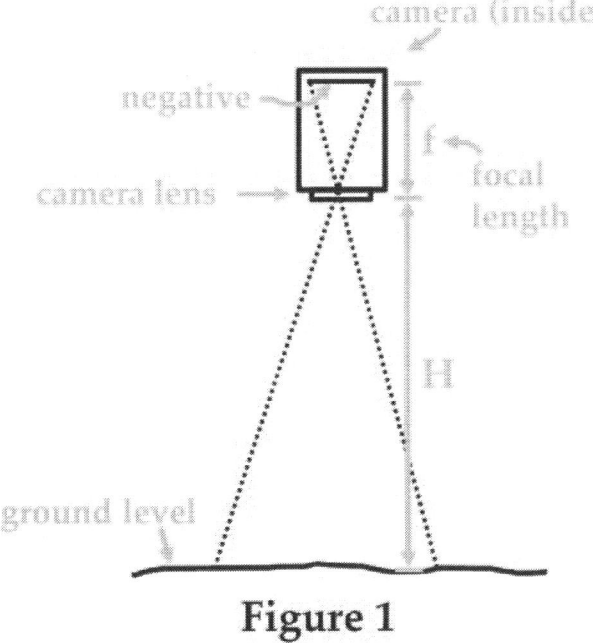

Figure 1

Figure 1 shows the focal length, f, and height of the plane above the ground, H.

The focal length is the distance between the camera lens and the negative inside the camera.

Keep in mind Figure 1 is not drawn to scale (based on the values of variables f and H)

$$scale = \frac{f}{H} \quad \leftarrow eq.2$$

Eq.2 equates the photo scale to the focal length divided by the height of the plane.

Surveying Practice Problems

Photogrammetry #2 (cont)

$f = 6\,[\text{in}]$

$$H = \frac{f}{\text{scale}} \leftarrow eq.3$$

$\text{scale} = \dfrac{1}{12{,}000}$

Solve eq.2 for the height, plug in the scale and the focal length, then solve for the height.

$$H = \frac{6\,[\text{in}]}{(1/12{,}000)}$$

The scale of $1:12{,}000$ is the same as the quotient $1/12{,}000$.

The height of the plane above the ground is 72,000 inches.

$$H = 72{,}000\,[\text{in}] * \frac{1\,[\text{ft}]}{12\,[\text{in}]}$$

unit conversion

Convert the height, H, from inches to feet by multiplying by a unit conversion.

$$H = 6{,}000\,[\text{ft}]$$

$\text{height} = 6{,}000\,[\text{ft}]$

$$\text{Elev}_{\text{plane}} = \text{Elev}_{\text{ground}} + H \leftarrow eq.1$$

$\text{Elev}_{\text{ground}} = 1{,}280\,[\text{ft}]$

Return to eq.1, plug in the ground elevation and the height of the plane above the ground, then solve for the elevation of the plane.

$$\text{Elev}_{\text{plane}} = 1{,}280\,[\text{ft}] + 6{,}000\,[\text{ft}]$$

$$\text{Elev}_{\text{plane}} = 7{,}280\,[\text{ft}]$$

Since 7,280 [ft] is most nearly 7,300 [ft], the correct answer is C.

Answer: $\boxed{\text{C}}$

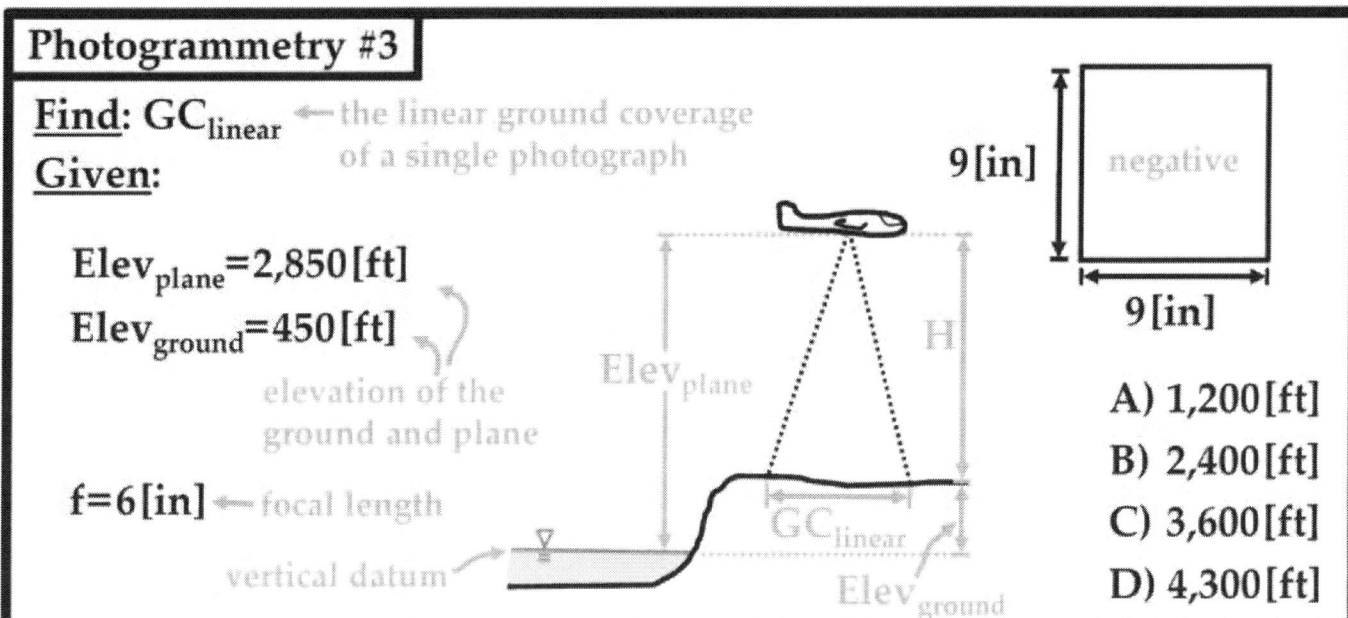

Photogrammetry #3

Find: GC_{linear} ←the linear ground coverage of a single photograph

Given:

$Elev_{plane}=2,850\,[ft]$

$Elev_{ground}=450\,[ft]$ ← elevation of the ground and plane

$f=6\,[in]$ ← focal length

vertical datum

9[in] negative

9[in]

A) 1,200[ft]
B) 2,400[ft]
C) 3,600[ft]
D) 4,300[ft]

Analysis:

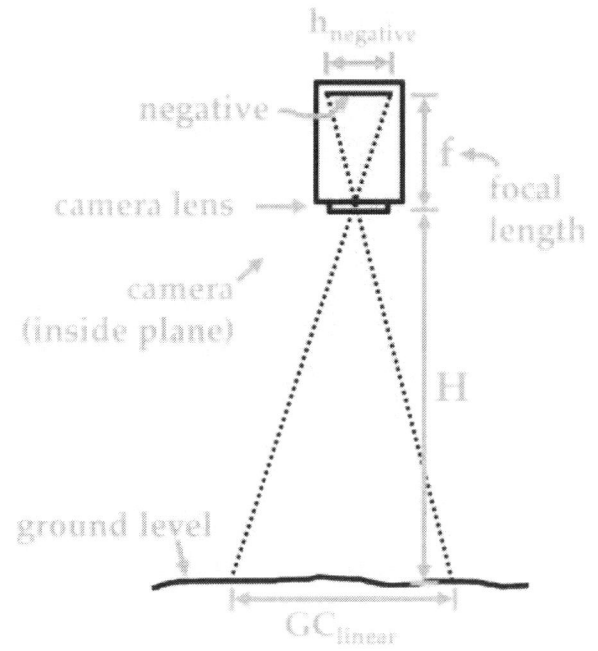

Figure 1

Figure 1 identifies the height of the negative, $h_{negative}$, and the linear ground coverage (in the direction of the flight path).

From Figure 1, we realize the height of the plane above the ground divided by the linear ground coverage is proportional to the focal length divided by the height of the negative. (see eq. 1)

$$\frac{H}{GC_{linear}} = \frac{f}{h_{negative}} \leftarrow eq.\,1$$

Solve eq.1 for the linear ground coverage term, GC_{linear}

$$GC_{linear} = \frac{H*h_{negative}}{f} \leftarrow eq.\,2$$

Surveying Practice Problems

Photogrammetry #3 (cont)

$Elev_{plane} = 2,850 [ft]$

$$H = Elev_{plane} - Elev_{ground} \leftarrow eq.3$$

$Elev_{ground} = 450 [ft]$

The height of the plane above the ground equals the elevation of the plane minus the elevation of the ground.

$$H = 2,850 [ft] - 450 [ft]$$

The ground elevation is assumed to be the average elevation of the ground.

$$H = 2,400 [ft]$$

The plane is 2,400 feet above the surface of the ground.

$H = 2,400 [ft]$ $h_{negative} = 9 [in]$

$$GC_{linear} = \frac{H * h_{negative}}{f} \leftarrow eq.2$$

$f = 6 [in]$

Return to eq.2, plug in the height of the plane, the height of the negative and the focal length, then solve for the ground coverage.

$$GC_{linear} = \frac{2,400 [ft] * 9 [in]}{6 [in]}$$

$$GC_{linear} = 3,600 [ft]$$

<u>Answer:</u> $\boxed{C}$

Photogrammetry #4

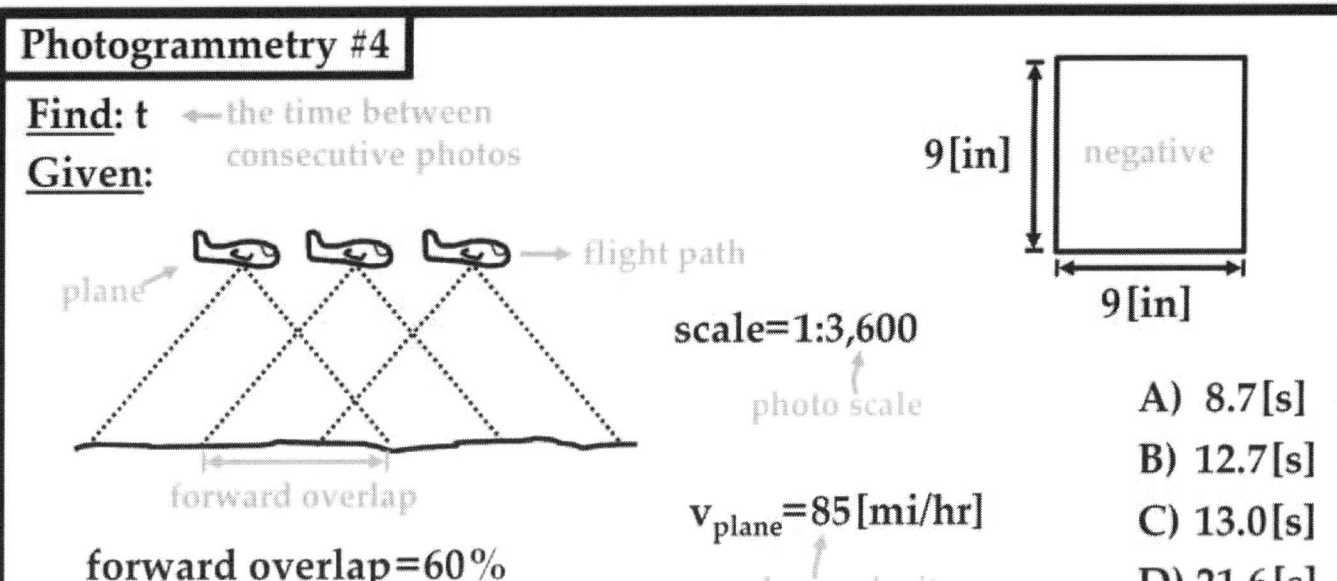

Find: t ← the time between consecutive photos

Given:

9[in] × 9[in] negative

scale=1:3,600
photo scale

v_{plane}=85[mi/hr]
plane velocity

plane → flight path

forward overlap

forward overlap=60%

A) 8.7[s]
B) 12.7[s]
C) 13.0[s]
D) 21.6[s]

Analysis:

distance = 0.40*GC_{linear}

time

$$t=\frac{distance}{velocity} \leftarrow eq.1$$

velocity = v_{plane}

Eq.1 states the time equals the distance, divided by the velocity.

For a 60% overlap, the distance between photos equals $0.4*GC_{linear}$. See Figure 1.

$$t=\frac{0.40*GC_{linear}}{v_{plane}} \leftarrow eq.2$$

We'll substitute in the variables for distance and velocity, into eq.1, to generate eq.2.

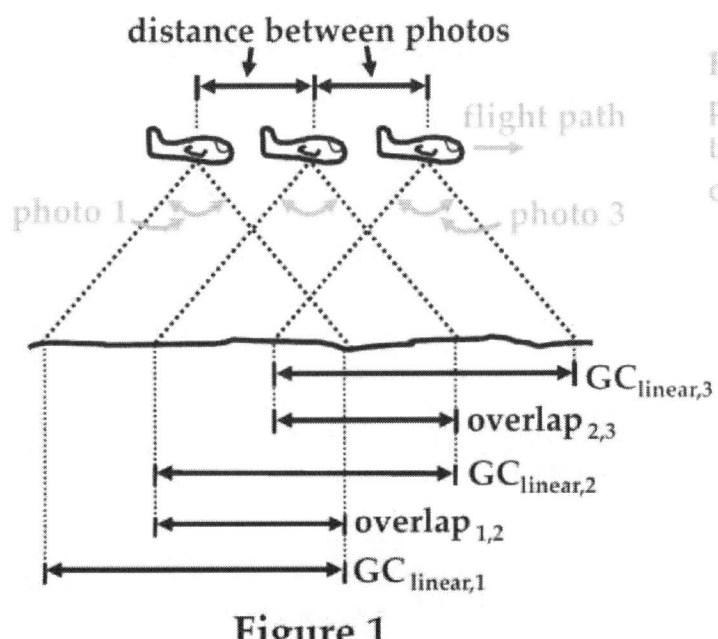

distance between photos

flight path

photo 1   photo 3

$GC_{linear,3}$
$overlap_{2,3}$
$GC_{linear,2}$
$overlap_{1,2}$
$GC_{linear,1}$

Figure 1

Figure 1 shows the location of the plane for the first 3 photos, as well as the overlapping distances between consecutive photos.

The linear ground coverage, GC_{linear} is the total linear distance on the ground, visible in a single photograph. For this problem, we're interested in the linear ground coverage in the direction of the flight path

Surveying Practice Problems

Photogrammetry #4 (cont)

Convert the plane velocity from miles per hour to feet per second.

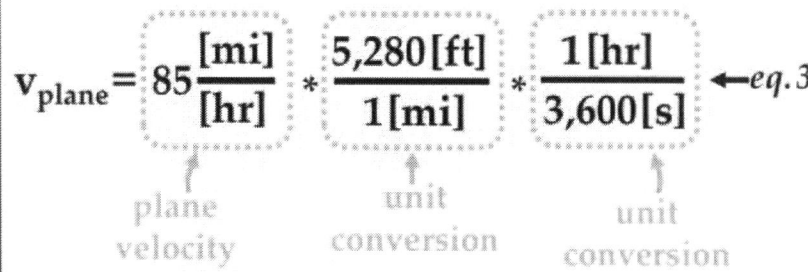

$$v_{plane} = 85 \frac{[mi]}{[hr]} * \frac{5,280\,[ft]}{1\,[mi]} * \frac{1\,[hr]}{3,600\,[s]} \leftarrow eq.3$$

plane velocity · unit conversion · unit conversion

$$v_{plane} = 124.67\,[ft/s]$$

$h_{negative} = 9\,[in]$

The linear ground coverage equals the height of the negative divided by the map scale.

$$GC_{linear} = \frac{h_{negative}}{scale} \leftarrow eq.4$$

scale = (1/3,600)

$$GC_{linear} = \frac{9\,[in]}{(1/3,600)} * \frac{1\,[ft]}{12\,[in]}$$

Convert inches to feet.

unit conversion

$$GC_{linear} = 2,700\,[ft]$$

$GC_{linear} = 2,700\,[ft]$

$$t = \frac{0.40 * GC_{linear}}{v_{plane}} \leftarrow eq.2$$

Return to eq.2, substitute in the linear ground coverage and plane velocity, then solve for the time.

$v_{plane} = 124.67\,[ft/s]$

$$t = \frac{0.40 * 2,700\,[ft]}{124.67\,[ft/s]}$$

$$t = 8.66\,[s]$$

Answer: | A |

Photogrammetry #5

Find: smallest square negative — the smallest square size negative which will show the entire GC_area

Given:

H=4,600[ft] — height of the plane above the ground

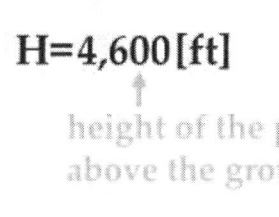

GC_{area}=360[acre] — square area of the ground in the photograph

field of view

H

square area

ground

A) 6[in]x6[in]
B) 7[in]x7[in]
C) 8[in]x8[in]
D) 9[in]x9[in]

f=8[in] — focal length

Analysis:

x[in]   negative   x[in]

Figure 1

For this problem, we'll define the variable x as the side length of the smallest square negative.

Since the area being photo-graphed is also square shaped, we will calculate the side length of that square area.

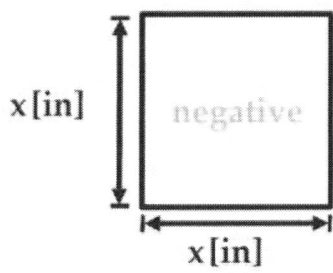

$$GC_{area}=360[acre]*\frac{43,560[ft^2]}{1[acre]} \leftarrow eq.1$$

unit conversion

Use eq.1 to convert the area from acres to square feet.

$$GC_{area}=1.568*10^7[ft^2]$$

GC_{area} is the square area on the ground being photographed.

$$GC_{linear}=\sqrt{GC_{area}} \leftarrow eq.2$$

GC_{linear} is the side length of the square area being photographed.

$$GC_{linear}=\sqrt{1.568*10^7[ft^2]}$$

Surveying Practice Problems

Photogrammetry #5 (cont)

GC_{linear}=3,960 [ft]

The length of one side of the square area being photographed must be at least 3,960 feet long.

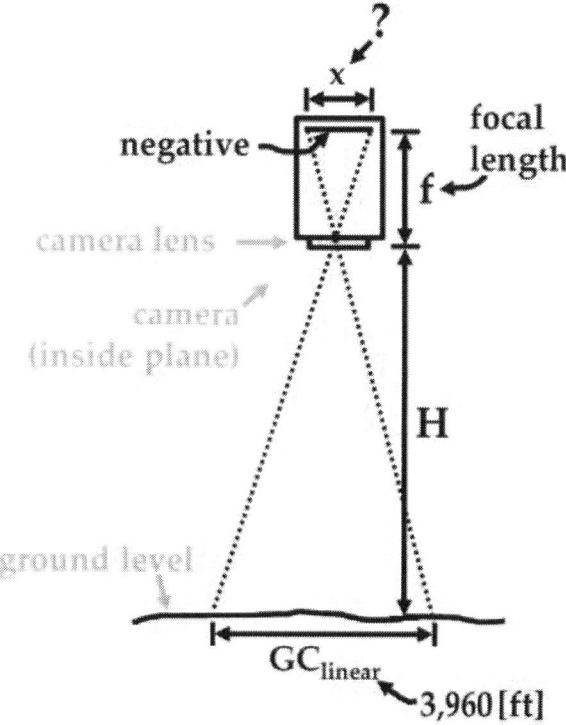

Figure 1

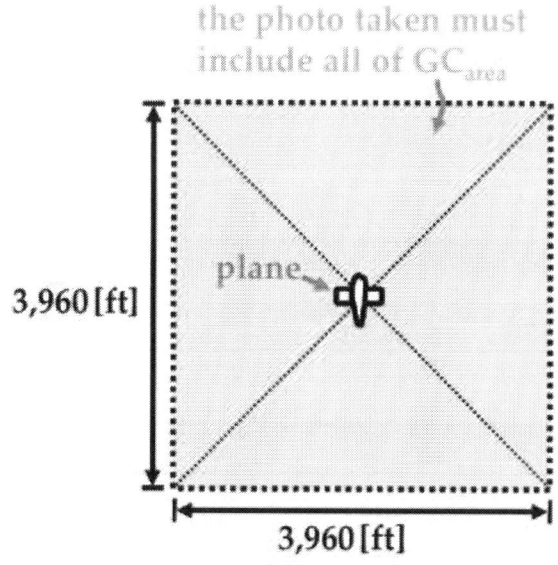

the photo taken must include all of GC_{area}

3,960 [ft]

3,960 [ft]

Figure 2

Figure 1 is a profile view showing the proportionality between the variables x, f, H and GC_{linear}.

Figure 2 is a plan view showing the plane and the dimensions of the square area, GC_{area}.

$$\frac{H}{GC_{linear}} = \frac{f}{x} \quad \leftarrow eq.3$$

Using Figure 1, we'll write out the relationship between variables x, f, H and GC_{linear} shown in eq. 3.

f=8 [in] GC_{linear}=3,960 [ft]

$$x = \frac{f * GC_{linear}}{H} \quad \leftarrow eq.4$$

H=4,600 [ft]

Solve eq. 3 for x, substitute in variables H, f, and GC_{linear} then calculate x.

Photogrammetry #5 (cont)

$$x = \frac{8[in] * 3,960[ft]}{4,600[ft]}$$

$$x = 6.89[in]$$

The minimum side length of the square negative is 6.89 inches.

Of the four choices, the minimum size negative that will show the entire 360 acres is 7 in x 7 in.

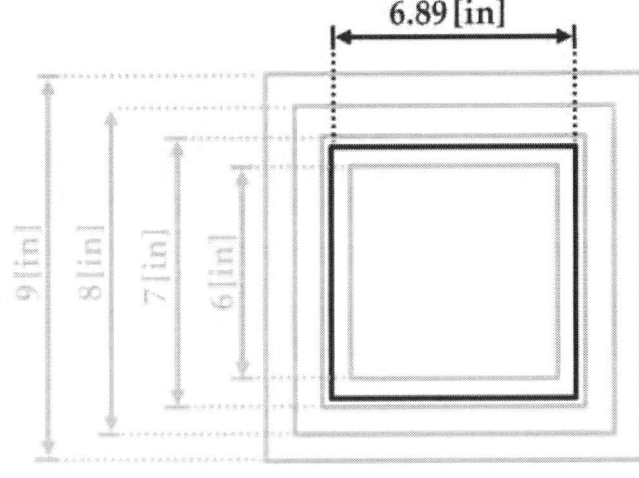

6.89 [in]

The possible solutions:

A) 6 [in] x 6 [in]

B) 7 [in] x 7 [in]

C) 8 [in] x 8 [in]

D) 9 [in] x 9 [in]

Figure 4

Since 7 [in] > 6.89 [in] the area photographed will be slightly greater than 360 [acres].

Answer B is correct.

Answer: ☐ B

Surveying Practice Problems

Photogrammetry #6

Find: f ←focal length

Given:

scale=1:2,000 ←map scale

CI=1[ft] ←contour interval

C=1,500

the C-Factor of the stereoplotter

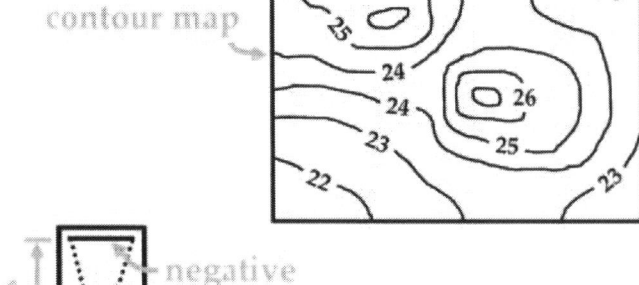

contour map

negative

camera lens

field of view

A) 6[in]
B) 8[in]
C) 9[in]
D) 12[in]

Analysis:

plane height

$$f=scale*H \;\leftarrow eq.1$$

From eq. 1, the focal length equals the scale times the height of the plane above the ground surface.

CI=1[ft]   C=1,500

$$H=CI*C \;\leftarrow eq.2$$

Eq. 2 computes the height of the plane, H, which equals, the contour index, CI, times the C factor of the stereoplotter.

$$H=1[ft]*1,500$$

$$H=1,500[ft]$$

Return to eq. 1, plug in the height of the plane and the scale, then solve for the focal length, f.

scale=1/2,000   H=1,500

$$f=scale*H$$

unit conversion

Convert the units for focal length from feet in inches.

$$f=\frac{1}{2,000}*1,500*\frac{12[in]}{1[ft]}$$

$$f=9[in]$$

Answer: $\boxed{C}$

Photogrammetry #7

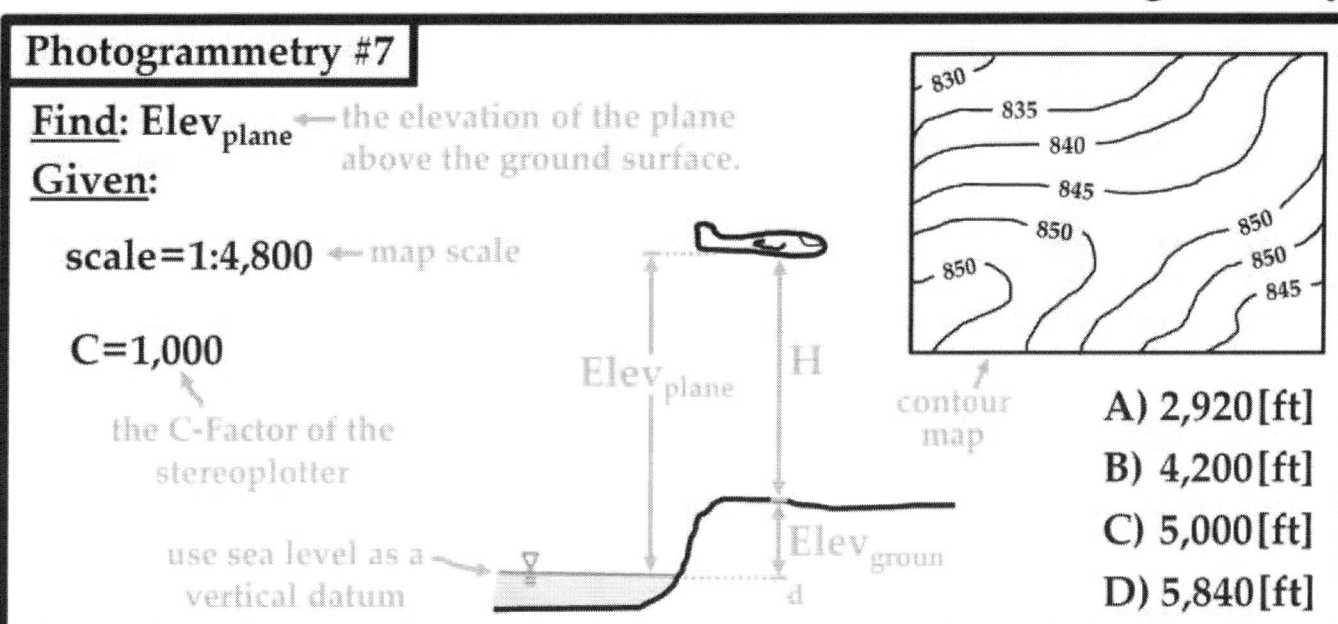

<u>Find:</u> **Elev**_{plane} ← the elevation of the plane above the ground surface.

Elev_{plane} ← the elevation of the plane above the ground surface.

<u>Given:</u>

scale=1:4,800 ← map scale

C=1,000
the C-Factor of the stereoplotter

use sea level as a vertical datum

$Elev_{plane}$ H

contour map

$Elev_{ground}$

A) 2,920 [ft]
B) 4,200 [ft]
C) 5,000 [ft]
D) 5,840 [ft]

Analysis:

$$\text{Elev}_{plane}=H+\text{Elev}_{ground} \leftarrow eq.1$$

The elevation of the plane equals the height of the plane above the ground plus the ground elevation.

$$H=CI*C \leftarrow eq.2$$

The height of the plane above the ground surface equals the contour interval times the C-factor. (eq.2)

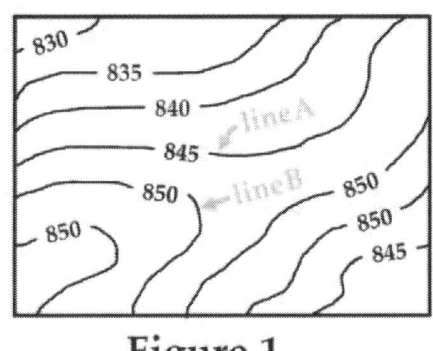

Figure 1

From the contour map in Figure 1, we can determine the contour interval, and the ground elevation.

The contour interval is the positive difference in ground elevation between adjacent contour lines, as long as those contour lines do not have the same elevation value.

$\text{Elev}_{lineA}=845\,[ft]$

$$CI = \left| \text{Elev}_{lineA} - \text{Elev}_{lineB} \right| \leftarrow eq.3$$

absolute value bars

$\text{Elev}_{lineB}=850\,[ft]$

For eq.3, we'll choose contour lines A and B, shown in Figure 1.

Eq.3 includes absolute value bars because the contour interval, CI, is always a positive value.

$$CI=\left| 845\,[ft]-850\,[ft] \right|$$

Surveying Practice Problems

Photogrammetry #7 (cont)

$$CI = 5 \, [ft]$$

The contour interval of the map is 5 feet.

$$\underset{\nearrow}{CI=5[ft]} \quad \underset{\nwarrow}{C=1,000}$$
$$H = CI * C \leftarrow eq.2$$

Return to eq. 2, plug in the contour interval and the C-Factor, then solve for the height of the plane above the ground.

$$H = 5,000 \, [ft]$$

$$Elev_{ground} = 845 \, [ft]$$

From Figure 1, we approximate the average ground elevation from the contour map to be 845[ft]

$$\underset{\searrow}{H=5,000[ft]}$$
$$Elev_{plane} = H + Elev_{ground} \leftarrow eq.1$$
$$\underset{\uparrow}{Elev_{ground}=845[ft]}$$

Return to eq. 1, plug in the plane height and ground elevation, then solve for the plane elevation.

$$Elev_{plane} = 5,000 \, [ft] + 845 \, [ft]$$

$$Elev_{plane} = 5,845 \, [ft]$$

Answer: $\boxed{D}$

Answer D is the correct answer.

Photogrammetry #8

<u>Find:</u> FL$_{min}$ ← the minimum number of flight lines to cover the entire area.

<u>Given:</u>

FO=65% ← forward overlap

SO=30% ← side overlap

scale=1:6,000 ← map scale

Area=4[mi]×10[mi]

the total area to be photographed is 10 miles long by 4 miles wide.

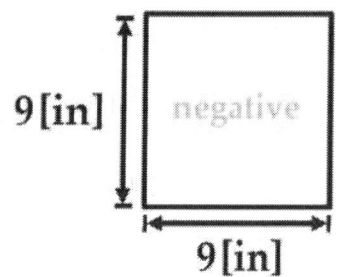

9[in]   negative

9[in]

f=6[in] ← focal length

A) 4

B) 5

C) 6

D) 7

<u>Analysis:</u>

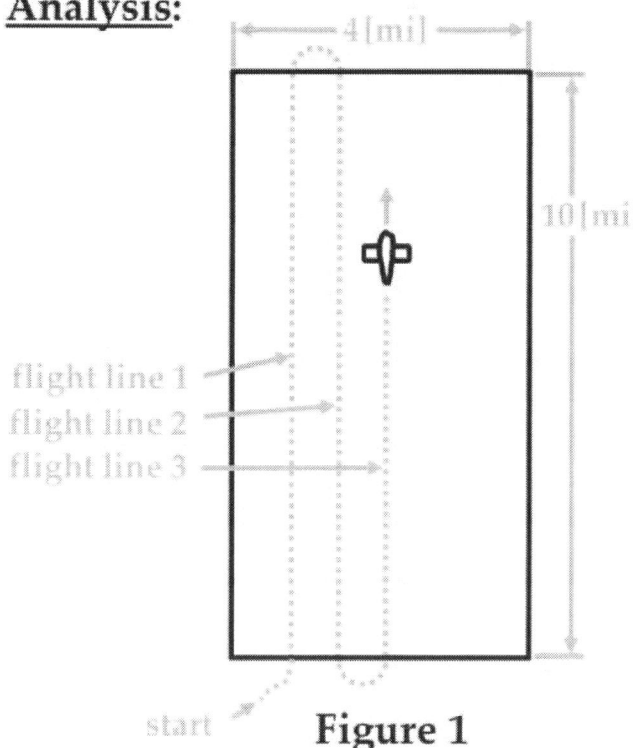

4[mi]

10[mi]

flight line 1
flight line 2
flight line 3

start

Figure 1

Figure 1 shows (in plan view) the area to be photographed is 4 miles wide by 10 miles long.

To minimize the number of flight lines, the plane should fly in the direction of the 10 mile length, as depicted in Figure 1.

The number of flight lines depends on the width of the total ground area to be photographed, the width of the ground in a single photo-graph, and the side overlap.

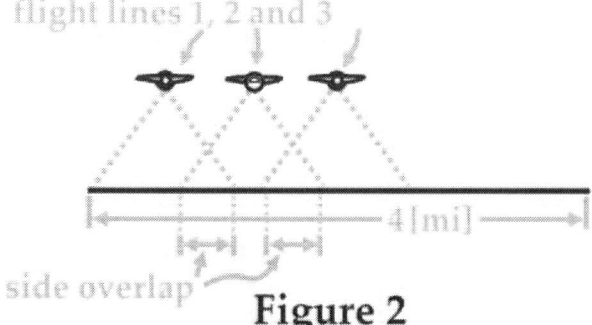

flight lines 1, 2 and 3

4[mi]

side overlap

Figure 2

Figure 2 is in profile view showing the 4 mile width of the area to be photographed, and the side overlap between adjacent flight lines.

Surveying Practice Problems

Photogrammetry #8 (cont)

$n_{width}=9\,[in]$

$$GC_{linear}=\frac{n_{width}}{scale} \leftarrow eq.1$$

$scale=1/6,000$

Using eq.1, substitute in the width of the negative and the scale, then solve for the linear ground coverage.

$$GC_{linear}=\frac{9\,[in]}{(1/6,000)} * \frac{1\,[ft]}{12\,[in]}$$

unit conversion

In eq.1, since we use the width of the negative, n_{width}, then variable GC_{linear} refers to the width of the ground covered in a single flight line

Convert inches to feet.

$$GC_{linear}=4,500\,[ft]$$

unit conversion

$$w_{total}=4\,[mi] * \frac{5,280\,[ft]}{1\,[mi]} \leftarrow eq.2$$

Convert the width of the total area from miles to feet by multiplying by 5,280 feet per mile, in eq.2.

$$w_{total}=21,120\,[ft]$$

$GC_{linear}=4,500\,[ft]$ $\quad$ $SO=0.30$

$$w_{new}=GC_{linear} * (1-SO) \leftarrow eq.3$$

Eq.3 calculates the width of the ground not already photographed in the previous flight line.

In eq.3, convert the side overlap from a percentage of 30%, to a decimal value of 0.30.

$$w_{new}=4,500\,[ft] * (1-0.30)$$

The length of w_{new} is shown in Figure 3, and does not apply to the first flight line.

$$w_{new}=3,150\,[ft]$$

Photogrammetry #8 (cont)

Figure 3 shows the first 3 flight lines, the total width (21,120[ft]), the GC_{linear} (4,500[ft]), and w_{new} (3,150[ft]).

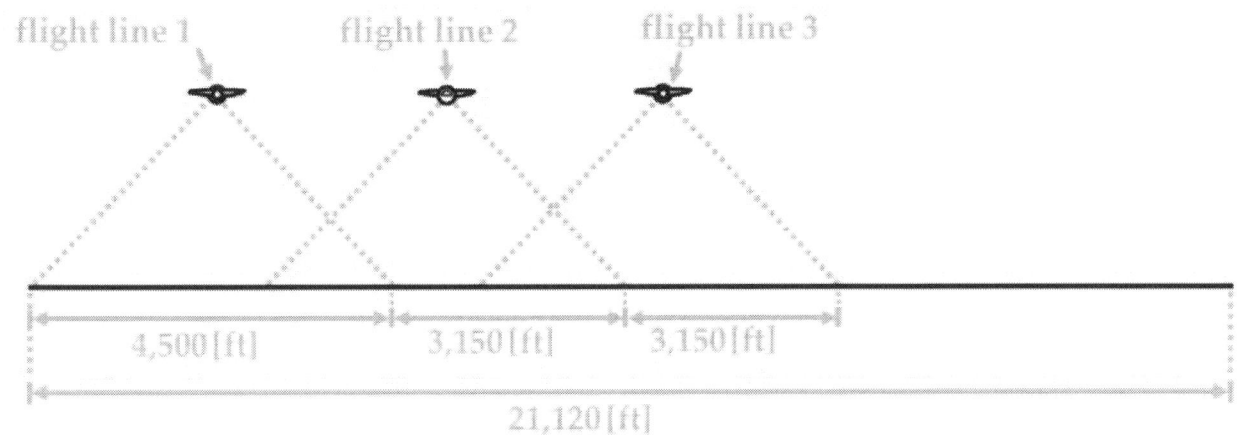

flight line 1   flight line 2   flight line 3

4,500[ft]   3,150[ft]   3,150[ft]

21,120[ft]

Figure 3

From Figure 3, we can determine a lower bound for the minimum number of flight lines, in ieq. 1.

minimum flight lines

$$GC_{linear}+w_{new}*(FL_{min}-1)\geq \text{total width} \quad \leftarrow ieq.\,1$$

Isolate FL_{min} in ieq. 1, then plug the known variables into ieq. 2, and solve for FL_{min}.

total width = 21,120[ft]

$$FL_{min}\geq \frac{\text{total width}-GC_{linear}}{w_{new}}+1 \quad \leftarrow ieq.\,2$$

$w_{new}=3,150[ft]$ $GC_{linear}=4,500[ft]$

$$FL_{min}\geq \frac{21,120[ft]-4,500[ft]}{3,150[ft]}+1$$

Round 6.28 flight paths up to 7 flight paths. Answer D is correct.

$$FL_{min}\geq 6.28$$

$$FL_{min}=7 \qquad \underline{\text{Answer:}}\;\boxed{D}$$

Surveying Practice Problems

Photogrammetry #9

Find: FO ←forward overlap between consecutive photos on the same flight line.

Given:

H=4,800 [ft] ←map scale

f=12 [in] ←focal length

air base=1,260 [ft]

the distance the plane flies between taking consecutive photos.

9 [in] negative

9 [in]

A) 60%

B) 65%

C) 70%

D) 75%

- -

Analysis:

$$FO = \frac{GC_{linear} - \text{air base}}{GC_{linear}} \leftarrow eq.1$$

Eq. 1 computes the forward overlap as a quotient of the overlapping ground coverage from two consecutive photos, divided by the ground coverage.

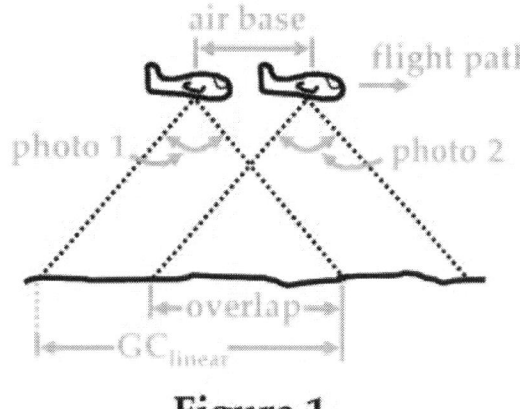

Figure 1

Figure 1 identifies the length of the air base, ground coverage, and forward overlap.

The forward overlap distance equals the linear ground cover minus the air base (the numerator of eq. 1).

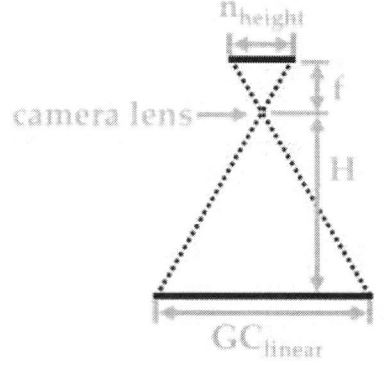

Figure 2

Figure 2 shows how the focal length and the height of the negative is proportional to the height of the plane, H, and the linear ground coverage.

Photogrammetry #9 (cont)

$$\frac{H}{GC_{linear}} = \frac{f}{n_{height}} \leftarrow eq.\,2$$

Using Figure 2, we can write out eq. 2, which defines the proportion of lengths, using the two similar triangles.

$H=4,800[ft]$ $n_{height}=9[in]$

$$GC_{linear} = \frac{H * n_{height}}{f} \leftarrow eq.\,3$$

$f=12[in]$

Solve eq. 2 for the linear ground coverage, substitute in variables H, f, and n_{height}, then calculate GC_{linear}

$$GC_{linear} = \frac{4,800[ft] * 9[in]}{12[in]}$$

$$GC_{linear} = 3,600[ft]$$

air base $=1,260[ft]$

$$FO = \frac{GC_{linear} - air\ base}{GC_{linear}} \leftarrow eq.\,1$$

$GC_{linear}=3,600[ft]$

Return to eq. 1, plug in the linear ground coverage and air base, then solve for the forward overlap.

$$FO = \frac{3,600[ft] - 1,260[ft]}{3,600[ft]}$$

$$FO = 0.65$$

We can convert the forward overlap of 0.65 to 65%, which is answer B.

Answer: B

(page intentionally left blank)

Section 3: Quick Solutions

(page intentionally left blank)

Horizontal Curves

1. A

2. C

3. D

4. B

5. A

6. B

7. A

8. C

9. D

10. D

11. C

12. C

Vertical Curves

1. B

2. B

3. B

4. A

5. D

6. C

7. A

8. A

9. D

10. B

11. B

12. C

Distance

1. C

2. A

3. B

4. D

5. A

6. C

7. B

8. D

9. A

10. D

11. D

12. A

Leveling

1. B

2. C

3. D

4. B

5. C

6. C

7. B

8. B

9. C

10. B

11. A

12. B

13. B

14. D

15. C

Area

1. A
2. B
3. B
4. D
5. C
6. D
7. B
8. B
9. A
10. B
11. D
12. B
13. A
14. B
15. C
16. B
17. B
18. D

Angles

1. C

2. B

3. B

4. D

5. D

6. A

7. C

8. C

9. D

10. C

11. B

12. A

13. B

14. A

15. C

Traverse

1. B

2. C

3. C

4. C

5. C

6. A

7. A

8. B

9. C

10. B

11. B

12. D

Photogrammetry

1. D

2. C

3. C

4. A

5. B

6. C

7. D

8. D

9. B

Notes:

Notes:

33550205R00182

Made in the USA
Lexington, KY
28 June 2014